Music and Human-Computer Interaction

Springer Series on Cultural Computing

For further volumes:
http://www.springer.com/series/10481

Simon Holland • Katie Wilkie • Paul Mulholland
Allan Seago
Editors

Music and Human-Computer Interaction

Springer

Editors
Dr. Simon Holland
Music Computing Lab
Centre for Research In Computing
The Open University
Milton Keynes, UK

Katie Wilkie
Music Computing Lab
Centre for Research In Computing
The Open University
Milton Keynes, UK

Dr. Paul Mulholland
Music Computing Lab
Centre for Research In Computing
The Open University
Milton Keynes, UK

Dr. Allan Seago
Sir John Cass Faculty of Art, Architecture
and Design
London Metropolitan University
London, UK

ISSN 2195-9056
ISBN 978-1-4471-6127-1 ISBN 978-1-4471-2990-5 (eBook)
DOI 10.1007/978-1-4471-2990-5
Springer London Heidelberg New York Dordrecht

Printed on acid-free paper

Springer is part of Springer Science+Business Media (www.springer.com)

Contents

Contributors

Anders Bouwer Intelligent Systems Lab Amsterdam (ISLA), Informatics Institute, Faculty of Science, University of Amsterdam, Amsterdam, The Netherlands

Anna Bramwell-Dicks Department of Computer Science, University of York, York, UK

Nick Bryan-Kinns Queen Mary University of London, London, UK

Ellen Campana School of Arts, Media, and Engineering, Arizona State University, Tempe, AZ, USA

Mat Dalgleish Department of Music, SSPAL, University of Wolverhampton, West Midlands, UK

Chris Dobbyn Music Computing Lab, Centre for Research in Computing, The Open University, Milton Keynes, UK

Alistair D.N. Edwards Department of Computer Science, University of York, York, UK

Robin Fencott Queen Mary University of London, London, UK

Toby Gifford Queensland Conservatorium of Music, Griffith University, Brisbane, Australia

Simon Holland Music Computing Lab, Centre for Research in Computing, The Open University, Milton Keynes, UK

Todd Ingalls School of Arts, Media, and Engineering, Arizona State University, Tempe, AZ, USA

Sergi Jordà Music Technology Group, Universitat Pompeu Fabra, Barcelona, Spain

Youngmoo E. Kim Music Entertainment Technology Laboratory, Department of Electrical and Computer Engineering, Drexel University, Philadelphia, PA, USA

Alexis Kirke Interdisciplinary Centre for Computer Music Research, School of Humanities, Music and Performing Arts, Plymouth University, Plymouth, UK

Robin Laney Music Computing Lab, Centre for Research in Computing, The Open University, Milton Keynes, UK

James McDermott Evolutionary Design and Optimization Group, Computer Science and Artificial Intelligence Laboratory, Massachusetts Institute of Technology, Cambridge, MA, USA

Alex McLean Interdisciplinary Centre for Scientific Research in Music, University of Leeds, Leeds, UK

Andrew P. McPherson Centre for Digital Music, School of Electronic Engineering and Computer Science, Queen Mary, University of London, London, UK

Eduardo Miranda Interdisciplinary Centre for Computer Music Research, School of Humanities, Music and Performing Arts, Plymouth University, Plymouth, UK

Paul Mulholland Music Computing Lab, Centre for Research in Computing, The Open University, Milton Keynes, UK

Una-May O'Reilly EvoDesignOpt Group, CSAIL, MIT, Cambridge, MA, USA

Helen Petrie Department of Computer Science, University of York, York, UK

Christopher Power Department of Computer Science, University of York, York, UK

Allan Seago Sir John Cass Faculty of Art, Architecture and Design, London Metropolitan University, London, UK

Dylan Sherry EvoDesignOpt Group, CSAIL, MIT, Cambridge, MA, USA

Dan Stowell Centre for Digital Music, Queen Mary University of London, London, UK

Ben Swift Research School of Computer Science, Australian National University, Canberra, Australia

Catherine Vuong School of Biological and Health Systems Engineering, Arizona State University, Tempe, AZ, USA

Mark Wagy Department of Computer Science and Engineering, University of Minnesota, Minneapolis, MN, USA

Isaac Wallis School of Arts, Media, and Engineering, Arizona State University, Tempe, AZ, USA

Katie Wilkie Music Computing Lab, Centre for Research in Computing, The Open University, Milton Keynes, UK

Anna Xambó Music Computing Lab, Centre for Research in Computing, The Open University, Milton Keynes, UK

Chapter 1
Music Interaction: Understanding Music and Human-Computer Interaction

Simon Holland, Katie Wilkie, Paul Mulholland, and Allan Seago

Abstract We introduce, review and analyse recent research in Music and Human-Computer Interaction (HCI), also known as Music Interaction. After a general overview of the discipline, we analyse the themes and issues raised by the other 15 chapters of this book, each of which presents recent research in this field. The bulk of this chapter is organised as an FAQ. Topics include: the scope of research in Music Interaction; the role of HCI in Music Interaction; and conversely, the role of Music Interaction in HCI. High-level themes include embodied cognition, spatial cognition, evolutionary interaction, gesture, formal language, affective interaction, and methodologies from social science. Musical activities covered include performance, composition, analysis, collaborative music making, and human and machine improvisation. Specific issues include: whether Music Interaction should be easy; what can be learned from the experience of being "in the groove", and what can be learned from the commitment of musical amateurs. Broader issues include: what Music Interaction can offer traditional instruments and musical activities; what relevance it has for domains unconnected with music; and ways in which Music Interaction can enable entirely new musical activities.

S. Holland (✉) • K. Wilkie • P. Mulholland
Music Computing Lab, Centre for Research in Computing, The Open University, Milton Keynes MK7 6AA, UK
e-mail: s.holland@open.ac.uk; k.l.wilkie@open.ac.uk; p.mulholland@open.ac.uk

A. Seago
Sir John Cass Faculty of Art, Architecture and Design, London Metropolitan University, London, UK
e-mail: a.seago@londonmet.ac.uk

S. Holland et al. (eds.), *Music and Human-Computer Interaction*, Springer Series on Cultural Computing, DOI 10.1007/978-1-4471-2990-5_1,

1.1 Introduction

This book presents state of the art research in Music and Human-Computer Interaction (also known as 'Music Interaction'). Research in Music Interaction is at an exciting and formative stage, as this book examines in detail.

The book covers a wide variety of topics including interactive music systems, digital and virtual musical instruments, theories, methodologies and technologies for Music Interaction. Innovative approaches to existing musical activities are explored, as well as tools that make new kinds of musical activity possible. The musical activities covered are similarly diverse, and include composition, performance, practice, improvisation, learning, analysis, live coding and collaborative music making, with participants ranging from laypeople and music beginners to music professionals.

Music Interaction has serious implications for music, musicians, educators, learners and those seeking deeper involvement in music. But Music Interaction is also a valuable source of challenges, new ideas and new techniques for Human-Computer Interaction (HCI) more generally, for reasons explored below.

Ball (2010) assembles a series of observations about music. There are some societies without writing and some even without visual arts, but there are none without music. Music is an evolutionary, deep-rooted, complex social activity, hypothesized by some researchers to have origins older than language (Wallin et al. 2000). Ethnographers and ethnomusicologists have documented a wide range of social functions for music in different cultures. These functions include social cohesion and group bonding, social criticism, subversion, celebration, calming, institutional stability, work co-ordination, mother-child bonding, courtship, behaviour modification and mood alteration (Wallin et al. 2000; Cross 2001).

Unlike many human activities, such as vision and language, which primarily use localised parts of the brain, music seems to involve almost all of the brain (Ball 2010). Many musical activities involve the whole body, and involve real time co-ordination with other people, while also making significant perceptual and cognitive demands (Leman 2007). Despite the rich array of human capabilities involved in music, engagement with music is often one of the very last higher mental abilities that remain for sufferers of diseases such as Alzheimer's disease (Svansdottir and Snaedal 2006).

Since prehistory, humans have worked over millennia to develop and refine interactive musical technologies ranging from bone flutes to synthesizers. We posit that from a Human-Computer Interaction perspective, such instruments may be viewed as elements in larger socio-technical systems whose components also include performers, composers, repertoires and audiences. The creators and refiners of such instruments typically take pains to create instruments capable of high degrees of expression, and which allow precision and fluency of real time control. Players of such instruments often pay painstaking attention to the effect they have on listeners' experience (even though the listener and player may be the same person). These longstanding preoccupations of musicians have striking commonalities with some of the concerns of modern day Human-Computer Interaction.

From one perspective, Music Interaction may be viewed as a sub-discipline of Human-Computer Interaction, just as Human-Computer Interaction may be viewed as a sub-discipline of Computer Science (or just as Computer Science was once viewed as a sub-discipline of Electrical Engineering). But these are not always the most useful perspectives. Music Interaction borrows countless elements from HCI, and in general is held to the same standard as HCI research. But at the same time, the practice of Music Interaction is intimately bound up with the practices of the music community. For many purposes, Music Interaction must answer to that community. When competing practices conflict, sometimes the judgements of the music community will take precedence. After all, what good is an interactive musical system if it is unsatisfactory for musical purposes?

To put it another way, because the music community has its own longstanding traditions in the rigorous treatment of interactive systems, Music Interaction has concerns that can sometimes extend beyond the consensus disciplines of HCI. Thus while Music Interaction has great commonality with present day HCI, there are subtle differences in perspective. For these and other reasons, Music Interaction has been, and remains, well placed to make distinctive contributions to HCI. Example contributions from Music Interaction to mainstream HCI include the following:

- In the early days of HCI research, much (though not all) interaction research was limited to command line interfaces. Buxton and colleagues were able to develop a new and influential body of research on gestural interaction for HCI (Buxton et al. 1979) by drawing directly on the needs, traditions and instincts of musicians (though there is also a wider story, as we outline below).
- The commercial development of the data glove, hand tracking technologies, and virtual reality systems stemmed more or less directly from Zimmerman's desire to hear himself play air guitar (Zimmerman et al. 1986; Lanier 1989).
- The Reactable project (Jordà et al. 2006), motivated directly by Music Interaction challenges, led the way in contributing several innovative and influential frameworks and tools for touch-based and tangible interaction.

It would be wrong to claim credit exclusively for Music Interaction in any of the above instances. For example, Buxton (2008) is careful to acknowledge that his pioneering music-related HCI work was informed by previous HCI research on bimanual input from Engelbart and English (1963) and Sutherland (1963). Buxton notes:

> One thing that I want to emphasize is that the real objective of the system's designers was to study human-computer interaction, not to make a music system. The key insight of Ken Pulfer, who spearheaded the music project, was that to do this effectively he needed to work with users in some rich and potent application domain. And he further realized that music was a perfect candidate. Musicians had specialized skills, were highly creative, what they did could be generalized to other professions, and perhaps most of all – unlike doctors, lawyers and other "serious" professions – they would be willing to do serious work on a flaky system at all hours of the day and night. Buxton (2008)

These tendencies of Music Interaction researchers are another reason for the continuing vigour of Music Interaction research, and its contributions to HCI.

1.1.1 *The Origins of This Book*

This book grew out of the 2011 BCS HCI refereed International Workshop on Music and Human-Computer Interaction, entitled "When Words Fail: What can Music Interaction tell us about HCI?". Following the workshop, a selection of the papers were elaborated, extended and submitted to a refereeing process for inclusion in this book. One book chapter was submitted by authors who had been unable to attend the workshop. The workshop included sessions where subgroups discussed mutually agreed research topics. One such subgroup wrote Chap. 2, "Should Music Interaction Be Easy?".

Note that the style of referencing used in this book is designed to deal with two different modes of dissemination: as a book, and as individually downloadable chapters.

1.2 Music Interaction FAQ

In the remainder of this chapter, we will give an overview of the contents of this book and of the themes and issues raised. When organising such an overview, the diverse perspectives adopted by different Music Interaction researchers tend to make any single classification system unsatisfactory. The chapters have overlapping perspectives, themes and issues, but these form interconnected networks rather than a single tree. For this reason we have structured this overview as an FAQ. This allows some answers to focus on cross cutting issues that appear in two or more chapters, and some chapters to appear in several answers, while other answers focus principally on a single chapter. Parts of the FAQ may better fit Graham's (2011) notion of Rarely Asked Questions – questions asked once or twice, but which seem interesting.

The FAQs

1.2.1 What Is Music Interaction?

Music Interaction refers to "Music and Human-Computer Interaction". Music Interaction encompasses the design, refinement, evaluation, analysis and use of interactive systems that involve computer technology for any kind of musical activity, and in particular, scientific research on any aspect of this topic. Music Interaction typically involves collaboration between researchers, interaction designers and musicians, with individuals often able to play more than one of these roles.

1.2.2 What Is a Digital Luthier?

A luthier is traditionally someone who makes or repairs stringed instruments. A digital luthier (Jordà 2005) is someone who designs and makes digital musical instruments, or who designs and makes digital augmentations to instruments. Music Interaction has a considerably wider scope than digital musical instruments alone, but digital luthiers are a respected part of the Music Interaction community.

1.2.3 What Is the Scope of Research in Music Interaction?

Music Interaction covers a wide variety of research. There are several reasons for this. Firstly, musical roles themselves are varied (e.g., digital luthier, composer, performer, analyst, soloist, accompanist, listener, amanuensis, timbre designer, improviser, learner, teacher). Secondly, many of these roles can be played by individuals or groups, and by humans or machines, or by some combination thereof. Musical materials themselves are multidimensional (e.g. they may involve melody, rhythm, harmony, timbre, gesture, language, sound, noise, and various kinds of expressivity). Diverse social contexts, genres and repertoires in music span wide ranges of human experience. Beyond the kinds of variety inherited from music itself, Music Interaction research spans diverse research areas. As noted earlier these include interactive music systems; digital musical instruments; virtual instruments; theories, frameworks, methodologies and technologies for Music Interaction; new approaches to traditional musical activities; and tools that make new kinds of musical activity possible. Interaction styles also vary widely, and may involve gesture, interface metaphor, conceptual metaphor, conceptual integration, non-speech voice control, formal language, and many other approaches. The chapters in this book populate various broadly representative points in this large multi-dimensional space.

1.2.4 Should Music Interaction Be Easy?

In 1989, at a NATO Science workshop on Interface Design in Education, Sterling Beckwith (1992), the pioneer computer music educator, reflected on music interfaces for beginners, and enquired whether ease of use was an appropriate goal for interfaces for music education. In the workshop, Beckwith drew on his personal experience with the composition teacher Nadia Boulanger, whose pedagogical strategies, he noted, often involved making musical actions harder for students, rather than easier. Such an approach may be viewed as a special case of a general technique for encouraging creativity in the arts by adding constraints (Holland 2000), or, from a psychological perspective, as adding costs to encourage greater mental evaluation before action (O'Hara and Payne 1998).

The issue of whether Music Interaction should be easy was an insightful question to raise at a time when HCI focused predominantly on usability and ease of use. Parts of this question have been explored before, for example, by Wessel and Wright (2002) in an examination of virtuosity. But in Chap. 2 ("Should Music Interaction Be Easy?") of this book, McDermott et al. (2013a) focus squarely on this issue in detail. As McDermott et al. observe, the concept of 'ease of use' sits a little uneasily with musical instruments, since:

> One does not "use" an instrument to accomplish some ultimate goal: one plays it, and often that is the only goal.

Two issues that McDermott et al. consider in particular are *engagement* and *flow* (Csikszentmihalyi 1991) for Music Interaction design. In order to remain engaging, consuming and flow-like, activities that involve musical instruments must offer continued challenges at appropriate levels of difficulty: not too difficult, and not too easy. However, as McDermott et al. argue, an activity which remains engaging in the long term often does so at the expense of being rather painful to a beginner—in other words there is a trade-off between ease of learning and long-term power and flexibility (Gentner and Nielsen 1996).

McDermott et al. argue that activities such as: instrumental performance and practice; recording, mixing and production; live-coding and turntabling; the study of theory and notation; are all activities which take place in sessions that can last for hours and must be mastered over years. Therefore the best interfaces for these tasks tend to fall towards the long-term power end of the trade-off. When the end-goal of an activity is for the sake of enjoyment of the activity itself, a suitable level of difficulty becomes acceptable and even beneficial.

McDermott et al. also consider the issue of transparency. This feeling is important to instrumentalists as artists and to skilled use of tools and systems in general. As Leman (2007) observes,

> Transparent technology should [...] give a feeling of non-mediation, a feeling that the mediation technology 'disappears' when it is used

Leman suggests that the capacity for an instrument (in the hands of an experienced player) to disappear from consciousness transforms it into

> a conduit for expression rather than an object in its own right

The issue of the distinction between embodied cognition and symbolic mental processing is considered. Embodied cognition is a view of perception in which perception and action are inextricably linked (Wilson 2002). Leman (2007) argues that musical experience involves embodied cognition, rather than symbolic mental processing.

Finally Chap. 2 ("Should Music Interaction Be Easy?") conducts a detailed examination of various different dimensions of difficulty that can apply in Music Interaction – concluding that some are avoidable and others unavoidable.

1.2.5 How Can Music Interaction Benefit Traditional Musical Instruments and Their Players?

In Chap. 7 ("Piano Technique as a Case Study in Expressive Gestural Interaction") of this book, McPherson and Kim (2013) explore how perspectives drawn from Music Interaction can be used to cast light on the nature of expressive expert performance on traditional keyboard instruments. They further use the resulting analysis to pioneer new and subtler means of expression. McPherson and Kim take as a starting point the objective measurement of the results of striking a traditional piano key. The striking velocity is shown, for most practical purposes, to be the sole determinant of the sound produced by a given note. This is contrasted with the subjective experience of expert players who carefully control diverse aspects of the gestures they make, in order to influence specific expressive outcomes.

Drawing on empirical studies by Goebl et al. (2004) and Suzuki (2007), McPherson and Kim confirm that the differences in objectively measured note production produced by diverse carefully executed variants in aspects of gesture are negligible. However, they argue that there is strong evidence that, for expert performers, the overall sequence of gestures constitute a key part of how the performer is able to conceive, remember and integrate an expressive performance. McPherson and Kim go on to identify specific dimensions of key motions that are important for expert performers, and use principal components analysis to establish a meaningful correlation between these dimensions of movement and expressive intent. This work has several useful outcomes. Firstly, it aids our understanding of the nature of expert expressive keyboard performance. Secondly, it exemplifies one way in which embodied cognition can illuminate music cognition and Music Interaction (see also Sect. 1.2.9 in this chapter). Thirdly, it provides a solid foundation for pioneering more subtle means of expression in innovative keyboard instruments.

1.2.6 How Can Music Interaction Be Applied to Interaction in Non-musical Domains?

There is a large research literature on sonification and auditory user interfaces – loosely speaking, user interfaces that employ non-speech audio to communicate information – though this is a broader field than that might imply. A good place to start exploring such research is the annual proceedings of ICAD, the International Conference for Auditory Display, for example Bearman and Brown (2012). Music Interaction research has some overlaps with sonification, for example where musical tones are used to communicate information in the background (Brewster et al. 1993). However, Music Interaction research has other kinds of application in domains that are not themselves musical – for example Affective Music Interaction, as outlined below. Chapter 4 ("Affective Musical Interaction: Influencing Users' Behaviour and Experiences with Music", Bramwell-Dicks et al. 2013) and Chap. 10 ("Pulsed Melodic Processing – The Use of Melodies in Affective Computations for Increased Processing Transparency", Kirke and Miranda 2013) in this book explore two illuminating possibilities for applying Music Interaction to non-musical purposes.

1.2.6.1 How Can Music Be Used to Alter Users' Behaviour and Experience in Non-musical Applications?

In user interfaces for non-musical domains, when music or audio is part of interaction design, the purpose is generally to communicate information, sometimes redundantly, or to take advantage of background human auditory pattern recognition (Bearman and Brown 2012; Brewster et al. 1993) or to help focus attention when needed.

In Chap. 4 ("Affective Musical Interaction: Influencing Users' Behaviour and Experiences with Music") of this book, Bramwell-Dicks et al. (2013) examine the use of music in interaction design for a different purpose – namely to alter users' behaviour and experience – i.e. for persuasive and affective purposes. Chapter 4 ("Affective Musical Interaction: Influencing Users' Behaviour and Experiences with Music") discusses how the use of music to affect mood and behaviour in real world contexts has been the subject of a great deal of research, for example in supermarkets, religious ceremonies, cinema, medical procedures, casinos, sports performance, and telephone hold systems. In such contexts, consistent measurable changes in behaviour and experience caused by music have been identified. There has been less research on the application of such techniques to computer-mediated systems – where the technique is known as 'Affective Musical Interaction' – but there have been some studies in computer-related areas such as computer gaming, virtual learning environments and online gambling (Bramwell-Dicks et al. 2013). This chapter presents a case study examining an affective musical extension designed for general computing. The case study focuses in particular on modifying users' behaviour when using email clients.

1.2.6.2 How Can Computation Be Organised to Communicate Emotion Musically?

In Chap. 10 ("Pulsed Melodic Processing – The Use of Melodies in Affective Computations for Increased Processing Transparency") of this book, Kirke and Miranda (2013) propose an imaginative reorganisation of the fundamentals of computing, dubbed "Affective Computation". The aim is to give all executing processes properties such that users may aurally monitor them in terms of emotional states. The proposal starts from the smallest elements of computation (bits, bytes and logic gates – for example as implemented in virtual machines) and continues up to higher levels of computational organisation such as communication protocols and collaborating agents. Models of computation generally prioritise efficiency and power, but Kirke and Miranda propose partially trading off efficiency in return for better emotional understandability by users, in the following sense. Taking the Valence/Arousal model of emotion as a starting point (Kirke and Miranda 2009), this chapter reviews existing research about musical ways of communicating emotions, and considers how this might be applied to data streams. A proposal is made for encoding data streams using both pulse rates and pitch choice in a manner appropriate for general computation, but which can also encode emotional states. Music Logic gates are then specified which can simultaneously process data and, as an inherent side effect, modulate representations of emotional states. The chapter then presents three case studies: a simulation of collaborating military robots; an analyser of emotion in texts; and a stock market analyser. Through the case studies, the case is made that such a framework could not only carry out computations effectively, but also communicate useful information about the state of computations. Amongst other benefits, this could provide diagnostic information to users automatically, for example in the case of hardware malfunction.

1.2.7 *What Lessons Does the Experience of 'Being in the Groove' Offer for Music Interaction?*

In Chap. 5 ("Chasing a Feeling: Experience in Computer Supported Jamming"), Swift (2013) analyses improvisational group music making, or jamming, and considers what implications can be drawn for Music Interaction design and HCI more generally. Swift argues that musicians who are jamming are generally not motivated by money, nor audience, or by reputation (see also Sects. 1.2.10 and 1.2.15 in this chapter). Rather, what is sought is the feeling of "being in the groove". This term can have several meanings, some of which have been explored by ethnomusicologists such as Doffman (2009), and by musicologists such as Hughes (2003). The notion of being in the groove that Swift examines has strong links with the ideas of flow (Csikszentmihalyi 1991) and group flow, as studied in musical and other improvisational contexts by Sawyer and DeZutter (2009). Swift notes:

> The jamming musician must both play and listen, act and react; balancing the desire to be fresh and original with the economies of falling back on familiar patterns and the need to fit musically with the other musicians

Swift presents a longitudinal study of musicians learning to improvise and interact via a novel iPhone-based environment called *Viscotheque*, and proposes a range of approaches to explore the nature of jamming more deeply. Swift argues that as general computing continues to impinge on creative, open-ended task domains, analysis of activities such as jamming will increasingly offer lessons to HCI more widely.

1.2.8 *What Issues Face Agents for Real-Time Collaborative Improvisation?*

In Chap. 16 ("Appropriate and Complementary Rhythmic Improvisation in an Interactive Music System"), Gifford (2013) examines in detail the issues faced in the design of real time improvisatory agents that play in ensembles, typically alongside human improvisers. Real time improvisatory agents must generate improvised material that is musically appropriate and that fits in with the rest of the ensemble. If they do not contribute anything new, their contribution risks being boring. This mirrors the more general need in music for a balance between predictability and novelty, to avoid the twin dangers of boredom or incoherence (Holland 2000). Gifford traces related analyses back to Aristotle's theory of mimesis (350 BCE), Meyer's tension-release theory of expectation and ambiguity (1956), Narmour's expectation theory of melody (1990) and Temperley's cognitive approach to musical structure (2001). The issue of ambiguity in this context as noted by Meyer and others has interesting links with Gaver et al.'s (2003) analysis of ambiguity as a resource for HCI designers.

In order to explore the need for improvisatory agents both to fit in with others and to generate appropriate novelty, Gifford presents a system that balances both imitative and inference-based techniques. Imitative techniques are an example of what Rowe (1993) calls transformative systems, and the inference-based techniques are an example of Rowe's category of generative systems. Gifford notes that from a Music Interaction point of view, a key characteristic of the inference-based component of such systems is that they must be "humanly tweakable". Other important issues in agent improvisation include: criteria for switching between imitative and intelligent action; criteria for deciding which kinds of imitative actions to initiate and when; and criteria for deciding how much latitude to allow in imitation.

1.2.9 What Can the Study of Embodied Cognition Offer to Music Interaction?

Embodiment in cognitive science is associated with the view that many kinds of knowledge, cognition and experience are intrinsically bound up with gesture, perception and motor action, rather than with symbolic processing (Leman 2007). The view that musical knowledge, cognition and experience are embodied has long been a theme (both explicitly and implicitly) in music-related research disciplines, for example in ethnomusicology (Baily 1985; Blacking 1977); in music psychology (Clarke 1993; Todd 1989); and in computer music (Desain and Honing 1996; Waiswisz 1985) More recently, Zbikowski (1997a, b), Leman (2007) and others have offered evidence that many musical activities are carried out through mechanisms of embodied cognition, rather than symbolic mental processing.

Embodiment has also become highly influential in HCI, as part of the so-called third wave of HCI (Harrison et al. 2007), and in connection with physicality and tangible interaction (Hornecker 2011). An influential early account of the implications of embodiment for interaction design can be found in Dourish's seminal work (2001) on Embodied Interaction.

Dourish argued that the shift towards embodied perspectives in HCI was driven by "the gradual expansion of the range of human skills and abilities that can be incorporated into interaction with computers". Subsequent research in embodiment explored diverse views: Anderson (2003) surveyed three contrasting approaches grounded in three different traditions (namely, Artificial intelligence, Linguistics, and Dourish's philosophically grounded approach); Rohrer (2007) enumerated 12 different dimensions of embodiment in cognitive science ranging from neurophysiology and conceptual metaphor to phenomenology; Klemmer et al. (2006) itemized five thematic implications for interaction design as follows: *thinking through doing, performance, visibility, risk, and thickness of practice.* As regards the last of these thematic implications, notions of 'communities of practice' have particular relevance to Music Interaction. Klemmer et al. (2006) explored the roles that well designed interfaces can play in learning by doing, and learning in communities of practice. There are many ways in which embodied perspectives can be put to good use in Music Interaction. In broad terms, embodiment encourages a focus on gesture and perception and on physical and tangible interaction styles – for examples see: Chap. 7 ("Piano Technique as a Case Study in Expressive Gestural Interaction", McPherson and Kim 2013); Chap. 6 ("The Haptic Bracelets: Learning Multi-Limb Rhythm Skills from Haptic Stimuli While Reading", Bouwer et al. 2013a); and Chap. 12 ("Song Walker Harmony Space: Embodied Interaction Design for Complex Musical Skills", Bouwer et al. 2013b).

However, there are other, less obvious ways of exploiting embodied cognition in Music Interaction. In Chap. 15 ("Towards a Participatory Approach for Interaction Design Based on Conceptual Metaphor Theory: A Case Study from Music Interaction"), Wilkie et al. (2013) suggest a way in which universal low-level sensorimotor patterns can be exploited to simplify Music Interaction of more or less any kind, whether overtly physical or not.

1.2.9.1 How Can Embodied Cognition Be Applied Systematically to Music Interaction?

In Chap. 15 ("Towards a Participatory Approach for Interaction Design Based on Conceptual Metaphor Theory: A Case Study from Music Interaction"), Wilkie et al. (2013) focus on a specific detailed theory of embodied cognition, the theory of conceptual metaphor (Lakoff and Núñez 2000; Johnson 2005; Rohrer 2005, 2007) and its application to Music Interaction design. Note that this approach is distinct from the older and better-known approach of user interface metaphor (Preece et al. 1994) which utilizes familiar aspects of the domain in order to assist users in making inferences about the behavior and operation of interactive systems.

By contrast, the theory of conceptual metaphor draws on linguistic and other evidence to argue that all human cognition is grounded in universal low-level sensory motor patterns called image schemas (Lakoff and Núñez 2000; Johnson 2005; Rohrer 2005, 2007). Many image schemas have associated special purpose inference mechanisms. For example, the CONTAINER image schema is associated with reasoning about containment relationships.

Conceptual metaphor theory details how image schemas, and their associated inference mechanisms can be mapped onto other concepts to create new cognitive mechanisms, which can then be composed to deal with any kind of cognitive activity. For example, the CONTAINER image schema is mapped onto abstract concepts to allow reasoning about abstract forms of containment, such as categories.

In order to apply this approach to embodiment to Music Interaction design, Wilkie et al. review previous work in applying conceptual metaphor theory to user interface design and to music theory. Previous work has suggested that interface design approaches based on conceptual metaphor can make interaction more intuitive and more rapid to use (Hurtienne and Blessing 2007) and can be used to identify points of design tension and missed opportunities in interface design

(Wilkie et al. 2010). Wilkie et al. propose a method by which an approach using conceptual metaphors can be used guide the design of new musical interfaces in collaboration with musicians. This approach is of wide generality, and could be applied in principle to any kind of Music Interaction.

1.2.10 How Does Collaborative Digital Music Interaction Contrast with Collaboration in HCI?

One of the distinctive challenges of Music Interaction research is to explore ways in which technology can help people to make music together. Such approaches can be diverse. For example, the Reactable (Jordà et al. 2006), and earlier systems such as Audiopad (Patten et al. 2002) created new approaches to collaborative musical systems based on touch surfaces. By contrast, NINJAM (Mills 2010) offers quasi-real time musical collaboration over the Internet by sharing synchronised compressed audio from distributed participants. NINJAM sidesteps uncontrollable variations in network latency by delaying all contributions by precisely one measure. In a further, contrasting approach, Song Walker Harmony Space (Holland et al. 2011) makes use of asymmetrical collaborative whole body interaction. The word 'asymmetrical' here indicates a departure from the traditional collaborative approach to performing tonal harmonic sequences. Traditionally, each participant contributes a voice or instrumental part. By contrast, in this particular asymmetrical approach, different participants are responsible for different layers of abstract musical structure e.g. harmonic path, modulation and inversion (see Chap. 12 ("Song Walker Harmony Space: Embodied Interaction Design for Complex Musical Skills") of this book, Bouwer et al. 2013b). Further, by rotating their roles, participants can discover how such harmonic abstractions interact. Because enacting each role involves physical movements of the whole body, awareness of others' actions and intentions is promoted. By this and other means, this design makes use of embodiment and enaction to provide concrete experience of abstract musical structures (see also Sect. 1.2.9 of this chapter and Stoffregen et al. 2006).

Diverse approaches to collaborative music making, such as the three approaches outlined above, reflect the diversity of approaches in Music Interaction. Two chapters that explore distinctive aspects of collaborative digital Music Interaction in detail are outlined below.

1.2.10.1 How Does Research in Collaborative Forms of Music Interaction Relate to CSCW?

In Chap. 11 ("Computer Musicking: HCI, CSCW and Collaborative Digital Musical Interaction") of this book, Fencott and Bryan-Kinns' (2013) work on collaborative Music Interaction draws on the discipline of Computer Supported Cooperative Work

(CSCW). This is a specialized area of HCI that focuses on the nature of group work and the design of systems to support collaboration. CSCW emphasizes social context and borrows from related disciplines such as ethnography and distributed cognition.

Fencott and Bryan-Kinns note that many systems for collaborative musical interaction require specialised hardware. The resultant inaccessibility tends to inhibit widespread take-up of otherwise useful systems. This leads Fencott and Bryan-Kinns to focus on commonplace tools such as laptops as vehicles for musical collaboration, and on the development of collaborative software to match. Traditional philosophies and theories of music emphasize the role of concrete musical artifacts such as scores and recordings. By contrast, Chap. 11 ("Computer Musicking: HCI, CSCW and Collaborative Digital Musical Interaction") makes use of Small's (1998) argument that in collaborative contexts, instances of creative behaviour, and perceptions, or responses to them, are a more useful focus (see also Sect. 1.2.7 in this chapter). In order to help frame distinctions between CSCW in general, and Computer Supported Musical Collaboration in particular, Chap. 11 ("Computer Musicking: HCI, CSCW and Collaborative Digital Musical Interaction") draws on Small's (1998) notion of 'Musicking'. This viewpoint sees many kinds of musical engagement as social rituals through which participants explore their identity and relation to others. Other useful perspectives include Flow (Csikszentmihalyi 1991) and Group Flow (Sawyer and DeZutter 2009). Fencott and Bryan-Kinns have created custom-designed collaborative software for their empirical work to explore how different software interface designs affect characteristics such as: group behavior; emergent roles; and subjective preferences. Key issues include privacy, how audio presentation affects collaboration, how authorship mechanisms alter behavior, and how roles are negotiated.

1.2.10.2 How Can Social Science Methodologies Be Adapted to Study Collaborative Music Interaction?

In Chap. 14 ("Video Analysis for Evaluating Music Interaction: Musical Tabletops"), Xambó et al. (2013) focus on shareable musical tabletops, and examine how video analysis can be used for various purposes: to improve interaction design; to better understand musical group interactions; and to explore the roles that coordination, communication and musical engagement play in group creativity and successful performance. Various approaches, concepts and distinctions that are useful in evaluating new musical instruments are considered. These approaches include:

- task-based evaluation (Wanderley and Orio 2002);
- open task approaches (Bryan-Kinns and Hamilton 2009);
- musical metaphors for interface design (Bau et al. 2008);
- measures of degrees of expressiveness and quality of user experience (Bau et al. 2008; Kiefer et al. 2008; Stowell et al. 2008);

- usability versus usefulness (Coughlan and Johnson 2006), and
- measures of collaboration such as mutual engagement (Bryan-Kinns and Hamilton 2009).

Xambó et al. note that analytic and methodological techniques for exploring collaborative Music Interaction typically draw on the tradition of video-based studies of interaction in social sciences (Jordan and Henderson 1995; Heath et al. 2010). This chapter explores how these methodologies and approaches such as grounded theory (Glaser and Strauss 1967; Lazar et al. 2009) can be better adapted for the needs of exploring collaborative Music Interaction.

1.2.11 What Is the Role of Evolutionary Interaction in Music?

Evolutionary computing encompasses a range of loosely biologically inspired search techniques with general applications in computer science. These techniques tend to have in common the following: an initial population of candidate solutions to some problem; a fitness function to select the better solutions (for some executable notion of "better"); and techniques (sometimes, but not always, mutation and recombination) that can use the survivors to create new promising candidate solutions. Evolutionary computing is typically highly iterative, or highly parallel, or both, and is generally suited to large search spaces. Evolutionary computing techniques have been widely applied in music computing, particularly for composition (Biles 1994; Collins 2008; MacCallum et al. 2012) and less often for sound synthesis (McDermott et al. 2007; Seago et al. 2010). Music often involves large multidimensional search spaces, and in that respect is well suited to evolutionary computation. However, for many musical purposes, some human intervention is needed to guide search in these spaces, which gives rise to crucial issues in Music Interaction. Two chapters in this book examine contrasting perspectives on these Music Interaction issues.

In their examination of evolutionary interaction in music in Chap. 13 ("Evolutionary and Generative Music Informs Music HCI—And *Vice Versa*"), McDermott et al. (2013b) note that much research in interactive evolutionary computing in music has focused on music representation. This has had the great merit of allowing evolutionary search to be carried out on high-level musical structures rather than relying on laborious note-level search. But McDermott et al. note that far less attention has been paid to applying insights from HCI to the conduct of the search. Two of the principal Music Interaction issues identified in Chap. 13 ("Evolutionary and Generative Music Informs Music HCI—And *Vice Versa*", McDermott et al. 2013b) are as follows. Firstly, for many musical purposes, the selection or 'fitness' decisions involve aesthetic judgements that are hard to formalise. Consequently human interaction is typically required for each round of the evolutionary process. But crucially, human decisions are much slower than machine decisions – a problem known as the fitness evaluation bottleneck (Biles 1994). Therefore, as

Chap. 13 ("Evolutionary and Generative Music Informs Music HCI—And *Vice Versa*", McDermott et al. 2013b) points out, interactive evolutionary computation of all kinds is typically restricted to small populations and few generations. Even then, without careful interaction design, "users become bored, fatigued, and annoyed over long evolutionary runs" (Takagi 2001). The second principal Music Interaction issue that McDermott et al. identify is that, typically, the fitness evaluation interaction paradigm does not allow much flexibility and creative use. There is a risk that users simply end up working on an assembly line composed of repetitive choices. Chapter 13 ("Evolutionary and Generative Music Informs Music HCI—And *Vice Versa*", McDermott et al. 2013b) explores in depth, with case studies, strategies by which the application of approaches from Music Interaction might address this situation.

By contrast with the focus in Chap. 13 ("Evolutionary and Generative Music Informs Music HCI—And *Vice Versa*", McDermott et al. 2013b) on applying evolutionary interaction to composition, in Chap. 9 ("A New Interaction Strategy for Musical Timbre Design"), Seago (2013) considers musical timbre design. Musical timbre is complex and multidimensional, and there is a 'semantic gap' between the language we use to describe timbres, and the means available to create timbres (Seago et al. 2004). In other words, most musicians find it hard, using existing synthesis methods, to generate an arbitrary imagined sound, or to create a sound with given properties specified in natural language. This does not generally reflect a limitation of the expressivity of synthesis methods, but is rather a Music Interaction problem. After reviewing various potential approaches, Seago explores how an evolutionary interaction approach can be applied to the timbre design problem. The broad idea is that a user selects among candidate timbres, which are used to seed new candidates iteratively until the desired timbre is found.

Various kinds of timbre spaces are examined, and criteria necessary for timbre spaces to support such an approach are established. Seago then describes the search procedure employed to generate fresh candidates in a case study timbre design system. The fundamental interaction design behind this approach is amenable to a variety of tactically different design instantiations. A representative set of variant designs are compared empirically.

1.2.12 What Music Interaction Issues Are Raised by Rhythm?

Music, unlike, say, painting or architecture, is organized in time. Rhythm plays a central role in the temporal organization of music. Rhythm also plays a key role in organising the attentional resources of the listener (Thaut 2005). In the case of visual input, fragments of visual information gathered from discontinuous saccades (i.e. fast eye movements) are unconsciously assembled into a subjectively smooth visual field. Similarly, when we listen to music and other rhythmic sounds, our subjective experience of a continuously available stream of sound is assembled without conscious intervention from fragments of information gathered during bursts of aural attention whose contours depend on the periodicity of the sound.

This process helps to husband the limited cognitive resources available for live processing of auditory data.

Early theoretical treatments of rhythm musicology stressed organising principles such as poetic feet (Yeston 1976) and emphasised a priori integer ratio treatments of meter and polyrhythm (Lerdahl and Jackendoff 1983). However, more recent theories (Large 2008) describe phenomena such as meter as emergent features of the way our brains perceive and process periodic events, using biological mechanisms of neural entrainment (Angelis et al. 2013). Due to the temporal nature of rhythm and its relationship to entrainment and attentional resources, embodied and enactive approaches (Dourish 2001; Stoffregen et al. 2006) to Music Interaction that engage with active physical movement rather than symbolic representation alone can be particularly appropriate.

Chapter 6 ("The Haptic Bracelets: Learning Multi-Limb Rhythm Skills from Haptic Stimuli While Reading" Bouwer et al. 2013a) explores an example of such an approach, through a Music Interaction system for rhythm called the Haptic Bracelets. The Haptic Bracelets are designed to help people learn multi-limbed rhythms, that is, rhythms that involve multiple simultaneous streams. Multi-limbed rhythm skills are particularly important for drummers, but are also relevant to other musicians, for example particularly piano and keyboard players. Dalcroze and others (Holland et al. 2010) suggest that the physical enaction of rhythm plays an important role in the full development not only of performance skills, but also of skills in composition and analysis. Beyond music, there are claims that these skills may contribute to general well-being, for example in improving mobility (Brown 2002) and alertness, and helping to prevent falls for older people (Juntunen 2004; Kressig et al. 2005). The development of skills of this nature may also be relevant in rehabilitation, for example from strokes or injury (Huang et al. 2010). In Chap. 3 ("Amateur Musicians, Long-Term Engagement, and HCI"), Wallis et al. (2013) explore some of the possibilities for rhythm games in connection with Parkinson's disease.

Chapter 6 ("The Haptic Bracelets: Learning Multi-Limb Rhythm Skills from Haptic Stimuli While Reading") investigates in particular how well the Haptic Bracelets can help wearers to learn multi-limbed rhythms in the background while they focus their attention on other tasks such as reading comprehension.

1.2.13 How Much HCI Is Used in Music Interaction?

Up until recently, many designers of new musical instruments (though this is only one part of Music Interaction research) have paid less attention to HCI research than might be expected when designing and evaluating new musical instruments. This is reflected in the history of two relevant scientific conferences. The ACM SIGCHI Conference on Human Factors in Computing Systems (CHI) is the principal scientific conference for Human Computer Interaction. The 'New Instruments for Musical Expression' conference (NIME) is the premier conference focused on scientific research into new musical instruments and new means of musical expression. Historically, NIME began life as a workshop at CHI in 2001. However, the nascent NIME community very quickly opted instead to form an independent conference. Xambó et al. (2013), in Chap. 14 ("Video Analysis for Evaluating Music Interaction: Musical Tabletops") of this book, note that as NIME developed:

> an analysis of the NIME conference proceedings (Stowell et al. 2008) shows that since the beginning of the conference in 2001 (Poupyrev et al. 2001), few of the papers have applied HCI methods thoroughly to evaluate new music instruments.

There may be good reasons for this. Sengers (2006), in the wider context of design, queried the extent to which it is beneficial for interaction design to become 'scientific' and made a "plea for a recognition of creative design's unique epistemological status". Linson (2011) makes a related point in the context of digital musical instrument design. However, Xambó et al. go on to observe

> … the benefits of adapting HCI evaluation to these novel interfaces for music may benefit both the designers who can improve the interface design, and the musicians who can discover or expand on the possibilities of the evaluated tool …

In Chap. 8 ("Live Music-Making: A Rich Open Task Requires a Rich Open Interface"), Stowell and McLean (2013) observe:

> Wanderley and Ori (2002) made a useful contribution to the field by applying experimental HCI techniques to music-related tasks. While useful, their approach was derived from the "second wave" task-oriented approach to HCI, using simplified tasks to evaluate musical interfaces, using analogies to Fitts' Law to support evaluation through simple quantifiable tests. This approach leads to some achievements, but has notable limitations. In particular, the experimental setups are so highly reduced as to be unmusical, leading to concerns about the validity of the test. Further, such approaches do not provide for creative interactions between human and machine.

Still, in recent years, HCI has greatly broadened its perspectives, methods and techniques. The growth of the third wave of HCI, which draws on influences such as ethnography, embodied cognition, phenomenology and others has led HCI to embrace a range of perspectives, including the value of ambiguity (Gaver et al. 2003), values related to play and games, and the importance of experiential characteristics (Dourish 2001; Harrison et al. 2007). A steady stream of new applications and adaptions of mainstream HCI ideas to Music Interaction can be seen in the literature. To take just a few examples: Borchers (1999) applied HCI patterns to the design of interactive music systems; Wanderley and Ori (2002) advocated the systematic borrowing of tools from HCI for musical expression; Hsu and Sosnick (2009) considered approaches borrowed from HCI for evaluating interactive music systems; O'Modhrain (2011) proposed a framework for the evaluation of Digital Musical Instruments; Wilkie et al. (2010) applied new ideas from embodied interaction theory to Music Interaction; and there have been two recent special issues of Computer Music Journal on HCI (CMJ 34:4 Winter 2010, and CMJ 35:1 Spring 2011). See Sect. 1.2.10.2 of this chapter for further examples.

In general, there are currently many rich opportunities for the continued mutual exchange of ideas between Music Interaction and HCI. Stowell and McLean (2013) observe in Chap. 8 ("Live Music-Making: A Rich Open Task Requires a Rich Open Interface"):

> Music-making HCI evaluation is still very much an unfinished business: there is plenty of scope for development of methodologies and methods.

They continue:

> Much development of new musical interfaces happens without an explicit connection to HCI research, and without systematic evaluation. Of course this can be a good thing, but it can often lead to systems being built which have a rhetoric of generality yet are used for only one performer or one situation. With a systematic approach to HCI-type issues one can learn from previous experience and move towards designs that incorporate digital technologies with broader application – e.g. enabling people who are not themselves digital tool designers.

1.2.14 *What Role Does Spatial Cognition Play in Music Interaction?*

As observed in other FAQ answers, one of the most important developments in HCI has been "the gradual expansion of the range of human skills and abilities that can be incorporated into interaction with computers" (Dourish 2001). Spatial cognition, a powerful aspect of embodied cognition, is one area that has considerable scope for such application in Music Interaction.

Applications of spatial cognition in Music Interaction can arise whenever an appropriate spatial mapping onto some musical domain can be identified or constructed. The key requirement is that the mapping should enable spatial cognition to be re-appropriated to carry out rapidly and intuitively some set of useful musical operations or inferences. For example, the guitar fret board and piano keyboard are two elegant instrument designs that exploit mappings of this kind. Applications are not limited to instrument design, as Chap. 12 ("Song Walker Harmony Space: Embodied Interaction Design for Complex Musical Skills", Bouwer et al. 2013b) demonstrates. Other examples include Prechtl et al. (2012), Holland and Elsom-Cook (1990) and Milne et al. (2011a, b). There are strong overlaps between spatial cognition, gesture and embodiment, as explored in Chap. 6 ("The Haptic Bracelets: Learning Multi-Limb Rhythm Skills from Haptic Stimuli While Reading", Bouwer et al. 2013a), Chap. 7 ("Piano Technique as a Case Study in Expressive Gestural Interaction", McPherson and Kim 2013) and Chap. 15 ("Towards a Participatory Approach for Interaction Design Based on Conceptual Metaphor Theory: A Case Study from Music Interaction", Wilkie et al. 2013). See also Sects. 1.2.5, 1.2.9, and 1.2.16 in this chapter.

Chapter 12 ("Song Walker Harmony Space: Embodied Interaction Design for Complex Musical Skills", Bouwer et al. 2013b) explores Harmony Space, a multi-user interactive music system (Holland et al. 2011). Harmony Space employs spatial mapping to allow universal human spatial skills such as identification of direction, containment, intersection, movement and similar skills to be re-appropriated to deal with complex musical tasks. The system enables beginners to carry out harmonic tasks in composition, performance, and analysis relatively easily, and can give novices and experts insights into how musical harmony works. Tonal harmony is a demanding area of music theory, and harmonic concepts can be difficult to learn, particularly for those who do not play an instrument. Even for experienced instrumentalists, a firm grasp of abstract harmonic concepts can be hard to acquire.

Harmony Space uses a spatial mapping derived from Balzano's group theoretic characterization of tonal harmony (Holland 1989). Harmony Space extends this mapping by a process known as conceptual integration (Fauconnier and Turner 2002) to allow various higher level harmonic abstractions to be visualised and manipulated using extensions of a single principled spatial mapping. Harmony Space forms an interesting contrast with systems such as Milne and Prechtl's Hex Player and Hex (Milne et al. 2011a; Prechtl et al. 2012), which uses a two-dimensional mapping of pitches to promote melodic playability. By contrast, Harmony Space uses a three-dimensional mapping of pitch, and a two-dimensional mapping of pitch class, to promote harmonic insight, visualization of harmonic abstractions, and explicit control of harmonic relationships.

Different versions of Harmony Space have been designed to allow players to engage with the underlying spatial representation in different ways. Variant interaction designs include the desktop version (Holland 1992), a tactile version (Bird et al. 2008) and a whole body interaction version with camera tracking and floor projection (Holland et al. 2009). Chapter 12 ("Song Walker Harmony Space: Embodied Interaction Design for Complex Musical Skills", Bouwer et al. 2013b) examines Song Walker Harmony Space, a multi-user version driven by whole body interaction (Holland et al. 2011) that involves dance mats, hand controllers and a large projection screen. This version encourages the engagement of spatial intuitions by having players physically enact harmonic movements and operations.

Chapter 12 ("Song Walker Harmony Space: Embodied Interaction Design for Complex Musical Skills", Bouwer et al. 2013b) presents preliminary results from a study of the Song Walker system. It examines a study in which beginners and expert musicians were able to use Song Walker carry out a range of collaborative tasks including analysis, performance, improvisation, and composition.

1.2.15 What Lessons for Music Interaction and HCI Can Be Learned from Amateur Instrumentalists?

In Chap. 3 ("Amateur Musicians, Long-Term Engagement, and HCI"), Wallis et al. (2013) examine the case of musical amateurs who practice musical instruments, sometimes over years. Amateurs may spend thousands of hours forming a deep relationship with one or more musical instruments. Generally there will be no monetary incentive or social pressure to practice; there may be no social activity at all involved; issues of reputation may not be involved; recorded outputs may be trivial, irrelevant or non-existent. Such patterns of activity and motivation are unremarkable from the point of view of Music Interaction, but have not been a central concern in mainstream HCI. The relative neglect of this pattern of behaviour in HCI should not be overstated; as Wallis et al. notes, there are HCI strategies for designing interfaces variously for purposes of: fun (Blythe et al. 2003); games (Malone 1984) and enjoyable, positive user experiences (Hassenzahl and Tractinsky 2006). However, none of these quite encompass the distinctive activities and motivations of amateur musicians.

In order to gain better theoretical tools for investigating long term amateur engagement with musical instruments, Wallis et al. use self determination theory (Ryan and Deci 2000) to analyse such engagement in terms of three intrinsic motives: mastery, autonomy and purpose. Wallis et al. point out that self determination theory (SDT) differs from other theories of motivation such as Reiss's (2004), Tinto's (1975), and Maslow's (1970), in appearing better suited to account for the behaviour of amateur instrumentalists. Wallis et al. argue that all three intrinsic motives from SDT apply particularly well to engagement with musical instruments. Chapter 3 ("Amateur Musicians, Long-Term Engagement, and HCI"), Wallis et al. (2013) goes on to analyse musical instruments to look for design characteristics that might encourage these motivations in players. Wallis et al. find seven such abstract design characteristics: incrementality, complexity, immediacy, ownership, operational freedom, demonstrability and co-operation. These design characteristics emerge specifically from analysing amateur musicians, but they are interesting to compare with work by Green and others from mainstream HCI theory on the 'Cognitive Dimensions of devices and notations' (Blackwell et al. 2001). Both may be viewed as lists of high-level design properties that can be applied to analyse interaction problems, but whereas the Cognitive Dimension approach focuses on usability, Wallis et al.'s approach focuses on engagement.

Chapter 3 ("Amateur Musicians, Long-Term Engagement, and HCI"), Wallis et al. (2013) presents a case study using a rehabilitative rhythm game for Parkinson's patients. This chapter explores how the seven design characteristics might be used as heuristic design tools to help give interaction designs outside of music some of the properties of strong engagement found in the relationship of committed amateur musicians with their instruments.

1.2.16 How Can Formal Language and Gesture Be Integrated in Music Interaction?

In Chap. 8 ("Live Music-Making: A Rich Open Task Requires a Rich Open Interface"), Stowell and McLean (2013) argue that music-making is both rich and open-ended. This has implications for how Music Interaction should work. 'Rich' refers here both to the many varieties of social and emotional outcomes that arise from engagement with music, and the multidimensional and highly combinatorial nature of the materials that musicians can exchange in performance and composition. 'Open' refers to the unbounded nature of the space of acceptable musical innovations, including compositions, performances, and genres. Stowell and McLean argue that real flexibility and power in computer-mediated systems comes from the ability of processes to *modify themselves*, and that this can be controlled effectively only with the full power of formal languages.

At the same time, there are presently limitations to the effectiveness of formal languages as means of controlling live musical performances. To look at this from another perspective, gestures are intrinsic to the way many musicians engage with music, as explored in detail in Chap. 7 ("Piano Technique as a Case Study in Expressive Gestural Interaction") by McPherson and Kim (2013).

A separate but related problem is that many composers and improvisers have idiosyncratic conceptualisations of the musical materials they work with. Often, the way that one musician embeds musical materials into a formal language may not be congenial to another musician, or even to the same musician at a different time. Consequently, some researchers have developed techniques such as Aspect Oriented Music Representation (AOMR) (Hill et al. 2007) to allow dynamic changes to the way musical materials are embedded in formal languages, and changes of formal languages, while preserving musical relationships.

Combining the notions of formal language and gesture, while emphasising the need to balance flexibility, immediacy and power, Stowell and McLean argue that we need to find a new kind of Music Interaction, based on "open interfaces". Such interfaces would be able to respond not only to the fluidity of gesture, and to allow visual thinking where appropriate but would also allow the precision and power of formal language. This chapter explores these ideas in the context of live coding, the practice of making improvised music in public by writing and modifying code in real time, for example using music programming systems such as Super Collider. This chapter also considers programming languages that use two-dimensional constructions to allow visual and linguistic capabilities to support each other, and discusses a prototype music programming language designed to advance this idea.

1.3 Conclusion

As the above FAQs outline, this book explores the diversity and energy of recent work in Music Interaction, and demonstrates some of the opportunities for further research. As argued in the present chapter, the book also demonstrates some of the ways in which Music Interaction can act as a source of fresh perspectives and approaches for Human-Computer Interaction more generally.

Acknowledgements Thanks to Rose Johnson, Grégory Leplâtre, co-organisers of the 2011 BCS HCI International Workshop on Music and Human-Computer Interaction and to all workshop participants. Thanks to Paul Marshall, Andy Milne and Martin Clayton for reading parts of this chapter. Thanks to Helen Desmond and Ben Bishop of Springer for patient support.

References

Anderson, M. L. (2003). Embodied cognition: A field guide, artificial intelligence, *149*(1), 91–130, ISSN 0004-3702.

Angelis, V., Holland, S., Clayton, M., & Upton, P. J. (2013). *Journal of New Music Research, 42*, 1.

Aristotle (350 BCE). *The Poetics* (trans: Butcher, S.H.). Cambridge, MA: MIT Classics Archive. http://classics.mit.edu/Aristotle/poetics.html. Accessed 21 Jan 2013.

Baily, J. (1985). Music structure and human movement. In P. Howell, I. Cross, & R. West (Eds.), *Musical structure and cognition*. London: Academic.

Ball, P. (2010). *The music instinct: How music works and why we can't do without it*. London: Bodley Head.

Bau, O., Tanaka, A., & Mackay, W. E. (2008). The A20: Musical metaphors for interface design. In *Proceedings of NIME 2008* (pp. 91–96). http://www.nime.org/archive/, http://www.nime.org/proceedings/2008/nime2008_091.pdf. Accessed 21 Jan 2013.

Bearman, N., & Brown, E. (2012). Who's sonifying data and how are they doing it? A comparison of ICAD and other venues since 2009. In *Proceedings of the 18th international conference on auditory display* (pp. 231–232). Atlanta: Georgia Institute of Technology.

Beckwith, S. (1992). Hunting musical knowledge in darkest medialand. In A. Edwards & S. Holland (Eds.), *Multimedia interface design in education*. Hiedelberg: Springer.

Biles (1994). GenJam: A genetic algorithm for generating jazz solos. In *Proceedings of the 1994 international computer music conference*. San Francisco: ICMA (The International Computer Music Association).

Bird, J., Holland, S., Marshall, P., Rogers, Y., & Clark, A. (2008). Feel the force: Using tactile technologies to investigate the extended mind. In *Proceedings of Devices that Alter Perception workshop (DAP 08), as part of Ubicomp 2008*, Seoul, Korea (pp. 1–4).

Blacking, J. (Ed.). (1977). *The anthropology of the body*. London: Academic.

Blackwell, A. F., Britton, C., Cox, A., Green, T. R. G., Gurr, C., Kadoda, G., Kutar, M. S., Loomes, M., Nehaniv, C. L., Petre, M., Roast, C., Roe, C., Wong, A., & Young, R. M. (2001). *Cognitive dimensions of notations: Design tools for cognitive technology. Cognitive technology: Instruments of mind* (pp. 325–341). Berlin/New York: Springer

Blythe, M., Overbeeke, K., Monk, A., & Wright, P. (2003). *Funology: From usability to enjoyment*. New York: Springer.

Borchers, J. (1999, August 22–26). Designing interactive music systems: A pattern approach. In *Proceeding of Human-Computer Interaction: Ergonomics and User Interfaces, Proceedings of HCI International '99 (the 8th International Conference on Human-Computer Interaction)*, Munich, Germany (Vol. 1).

Bouwer, A., Holland, S., & Dalgleish, M. (2013a). The haptic bracelets: Learning multi-limb rhythm skills from haptic stimuli while reading. In S. Holland, K. Wilkie, P. Mulholland, & A. Seago (Eds.), *Music and human computer interaction* (pp. 101–122). London: Springer.

Bouwer, A., Holland, S., & Dalgleish, M. (2013b). Song Walker harmony space: Embodied interaction design for complex musical skills. In S. Holland, K. Wilkie, P. Mulholland, & A. Seago (Eds.), *Music and human computer interaction* (pp. 207–222). London: Springer.

Bramwell-Dicks, A., Petrie, H., Edwards, A. D. N., & Power, C. (2013). Affective musical interaction: Influencing users' behaviour and experiences with music. In S. Holland, K. Wilkie, P. Mulholland, & A. Seago (Eds.), *Music and human computer interaction* (pp. 67–84). London: Springer.

Brewster, S. A., Wright, P. C., & Edwards, A. D. N. (1993). An evaluation of earcons for use in auditory human-computer interfaces. In *Proceedings of the INTERACT '93 and CHI '93 conference on human factors in computing systems* (CHI '93) (pp. 222–227). New York: ACM.

Brown, M. (2002). Conductive education and the use of rhythmical intention for people with Parkinson's disease. In I. Kozma & E. Balogh (Eds.), *Conductive education occasional papers* (Vol. 8, pp. 75–80). Budapest: International Peto Institute.

Bryan-Kinns, N., & Hamilton, F. (2009). Identifying mutual engagement. *Behaviour & Information Technology, 31*(2), 101–125, 201 pp.

Buxton, W. (2008). My vision isn't my vision: Making a career out of getting back to where I started. In T. Erickson & D. McDonald (Eds.), *HCI remixed: Reflections on works that have influenced the HCI community* (pp. 7–12). Cambridge, MA: MIT Press.

Buxton, W., Sniderman, R., Reeves, W., Patel, S., & Baecker, R. (1979). The evolution of the SSSP score editing tools. *Computer Music Journal, 3*(4), 14–25+60.

Clarke, E. F. (1993). Generativity, mimesis and the human body in music performance. *Contemporary Music Review, 9*, 1–2.

Collins, N. (2008). The analysis of generative music programs. *Organised Sound, 13*(3), 237–248.

Coughlan, T., & Johnson, P. (2006). Interaction in creative tasks: Ideation, representation and evaluation in composition. In R. Grinter, T. Rodden, P. Aoki, Ed Cutrell, R. Jeffries, and G. Olson (Eds.), *Proceedings of the SIGCHI Conference on Human Factors in Computing Systems (CHI '06)* (pp. 531–540). New York: ACM.

Cross, I. (2001). Music, mind and evolution. *Psychology of Music, 29*(1), 95–102.

Csikszentmihalyi, M. (1991). *Flow: The psychology of optimal experience*. New York: Harper Collins.

Desain, P., & Honing, H. (1996). Modeling continuous aspects of music performance: Vibrato and Portamento. In B. Pennycook & E. Costa-Giomi (Eds.), *Proceedings of the international music perception and cognition conference*, Montreal: McGill University.

Doffman, M. (2009). Making it groove! Entrainment, participation and discrepancy in the 'conversation' of a Jazz Trio. *Language & History, 52*(1), 130–147.

Dourish, P. (2001). *Where the action is: The foundations of embodied interaction*. Cambridge: MIT Press.

Engelbart, D., & English, W. (1968). A research centre for augmenting human intellect. In *Proceedings of the fall joint computer conference* (pp. 395–410). San Francisco. http://sloan.stanford.edu/mousesite/Archive/ResearchCenter1968/ResearchCenter1968.html. Accessed 21 Jan 2013.

Fauconnier, G., & Turner, M. (2002). *How we think: Conceptual blending and the mind's hidden complexities*. New York: Basic Books.

Fencott, R., & Bryan-Kinns, N. (2013). Computer musicking: HCI, CSCW and collaborative digital musical interaction. In S. Holland, K. Wilkie, P. Mulholland, & A. Seago (Eds.), *Music and human computer interaction* (pp. 189–206). London: Springer.

Gaver, W. W., Beaver, J., & Benford, S. (2003). Ambiguity as a resource for design. In *Proceedings of the SIGCHI conference on human factors in computing systems* (CHI '03) (pp. 233–240). New York: ACM Press.

Gentner, D., & Nielsen, J. (1996). The Anti-Mac interface. *Communications of the ACM, 39*(8), 70–82.

Gifford, T. (2013). Appropriate and complementary rhythmic improvisation in an interactive music system. In S. Holland, K. Wilkie, P. Mulholland, & A. Seago (Eds.), *Music and human computer interaction* (pp. 271–286). London: Springer.

Glaser, B. G., & Strauss, A. L. (1967). *Discovery of grounded theory: Strategies for qualitative research*. Chicago: AldineTransaction.

Goebl, W., Bresin, R., & Galembo, A. (2004). Once again: The perception of piano touch and tone. Can touch audibly change piano sound independently of intensity? In *Proceedings of the International Symposium on Musical Acoustics*. Nara, Japan.

Graham, P. (2011) *Rarely asked questions*. http://paulgraham.com/raq.html. Accessed 8 Oct 2011.

Harrison, S., Tatar, D., & Sengers, P. (2007). The three paradigms of HCI. In *Proceedings of Alt. Chi. session at the SIGCHI conference on human factors in computing systems*. San Jose, California, USA.

Hassenzahl, M., & Tractinsky, N. (2006). User experience—a research agenda. *Behavior & Information Technology, 25*(2), 91–97.

Heath, C., Hindmarsh, J., & Luff, P. (2010). *Video in qualitative research*. London: Sage.

Hill, P., Holland, S., & Laney, R. (2007). An introduction to aspect-oriented music representation. *Computer Music Journal, 31*(4), 45–56.

Holland, S. (1989). *Artificial intelligence, education and music: The use of artificial intelligence to encourage and facilitate music composition by novices*. PhD thesis, IET, Open University, UK, pp. 28–62.

Holland, S., & Elsom-Cook, M. (1990). Architecture of a knowledge-based tutor. In M. Elsom-Cook (Ed.), *Guided discovery tutoring*. London: Paul Chapman Publishing Ltd.

Holland, S. (1992). Interface design for empowerment: A case study from music. In S. Holland & A. Edwards (Eds.), *Multimedia interface design in education*. Hiedelberg: Springer.

Holland, S. (2000). Artificial intelligence in music education: A critical review. In E. Miranda (Ed.), *Readings in music and artificial intelligence, contemporary music studies* (Vol. 20, pp. 239–274). Amsterdam: Harwood Academic Publishers.

Holland, S., Marshall, P., Bird, J., Dalton, S. N., Morris, R., Pantidi, N., Rogers, Y., & Clark, A. (2009). Running up Blueberry Hill: Prototyping whole body interaction in harmony space. In *Proceedings of the third conference on tangible and embodied interaction* (pp. 92–98). New York: ACM.

Holland, S., Bouwer, A., Dalgleish, M., & Hurtig, T. (2010). Feeling the beat where it counts: Fostering multi-limb rhythm skills with the Haptic Drum Kit. In *Proceedings of the TEI 2010*, Boston, Cambridge, MA.

Holland, S., Wilkie, K., Bouwer, A., Dalgleish, M., & Mulholland, P. (2011). Whole body interaction in abstract domains. In D. England (Ed.), *Whole body interaction*. London: Springer.

Hornecker, E. (2011). The role of physicality in tangible and embodied interactions. *Interactions, 18*(2), 19–23.

Hsu, W., & Sosnick, M. (2009). Evaluating interactive music systems: An HCI approach. In *Proceedings of New Interfaces for Musical Expression (NIME)* 2009. New York: NIME.

Huang, K., Starner, T., Do, E., Weiberg, G., Kohlsdorf, D., Ahlrichs, C., & Leibrandt, R. (2010). Mobile music touch: Mobile tactile stimulation for passive learning. In *Proceedings of the 28th international conference on human factors in computing systems (CHI '10)* (pp. 791–800). New York: ACM.

Hughes, T. S. (2003). *Groove and flow: Six analytical essays on the music of Stevie Wonder*. PhD thesis, University of Washington, Seattle.

Hurtienne, J., & Blessing, L. (2007). Design for intuitive use – testing image schema theory for user interface design. In *Proceedings of the 16th international conference on engineering design*, Paris, France (pp. 1–12).

Johnson, M. (2005). The philosophical significance of image schemas. In B. Hampe & J. Grady (Eds.), *From perception to meaning: Image schemas in cognitive linguistics* (pp. 15–33). Berlin/New York: Mouton de Gruyter.

Jordà, S. (2005). Digital Lutherie. *Universitat Pompeu Fabra*. PhD Thesis.

Jordà, S., Kaltenbrunner, M., Geiger, G., & Alonso, M. (2006). The reacTable: A tangible tabletop musical instrument and collaborative workbench. In *ACM SIGGRAPH 2006 Sketches* (SIGGRAPH '06). New York: ACM.

Jordan, B., & Henderson, A. (1995). Interaction analysis: Foundations and practice. *The Journal of the Learning Sciences, 4*(1), 39–103.

Juntunen, M. L. (2004). *Embodiment in Dalcroze Eurhythmics*. PhD thesis, University of Oulu, Finland.

Kiefer, C., Collins, N., Fitzpatrick, G. (2008). HCI methodology for evaluating musical controllers. A case study. In *Proceedings of the international conference on New Interfaces for Musical Expression (NIME'08)* (pp. 87–90). University of Sussex.

Kirke, A., & Miranda, E. (2009). A survey of computer systems for expressive music performance. *ACM Surveys, 42*(1), 1–41.

Kirke, A., & Miranda, E. (2013). Pulsed melodic processing – The use of melodies in affective computations for increased processing transparency. In S. Holland, K. Wilkie, P. Mulholland, & A. Seago (Eds.), *Music and human computer interaction* (pp. 171–188). London: Springer.

Klemmer, S. R., Hartmann, B., & Takayama, L. (2006). How bodies matter: Five themes for interaction design. In *Proceedings of the 6th conference on Designing Interactive Systems (DIS '06)* (pp. 140–149). New York: ACM.

Kressig, R. W., Allali, G., & Beauchet, O. (2005). Long-term practice of Jaques-Dalcroze eurhythmics prevents age-related increase of gait variability under a dual task. *Letter to Journal of the American Geriatrics Society, 53*(4), 728–729.

Lakoff, G., & Núñez, R. E. (2000). *Where mathematics comes from*. New York: Basic Books.

Lanier, J. (1989). *Personal communication with Simon Holland and other attendees at 1989*. Nato advanced reasearch workshop on multimedia interface design in education, Lucca, Italy.

Large, E. W. (2008). Resonating to musical rhythm: Theory and experiment. In S. Grondin (Ed.), *The psychology of time* (pp. 189–231). Bingley: Emerald.

Lazar, J., Feng, J. H., & Hochheiser, H. (2009). *Research methods in human-computer interaction*. Chichester: Wiley.

Leman, M. (2007). *Embodied music cognition and mediation technology*. Cambridge, MA: MIT Press.

Lerdahl, F., & Jackendoff, R. (1983). *A generative theory of tonal music*. Cambridge: MIT Press.

Linson, A. (2011). Unnecessary constraints: A challenge to some assumptions of digital musical instrument design. In *International computer music conference 2011*. Huddersfield: University of Huddersfield.

MacCallum, R. M., Mauch, M., Burt, A., Leroi, A. M. (2012). Evolution of music by public choice. In R. E. Lenski (Ed.), *Proceedings of the National Academy of Sciences of the United States of America, 109*(30), 12081–12086. doi:10.1073/pnas.1203182109.

Malone, T. (1984). Heuristics for designing enjoyable user interfaces: Lessons from computer games. In J. C. Thomas & M. L. Schneider (Eds.), *Human factors in computer systems*. Norwood: Ablex.

Maslow, A. (1970). *Motivation and personality*. New York: Harper and Rowe.

McDermott, J., Griffith, N. J. L., & O'Neill, M. (2007). Evolutionary GUIs for sound synthesis. In M. Giacobini (Ed.), *Applications of evolutionary computing* (Vol. 4448, pp. 547–556). Heidelberg: Springer.

McDermott, J., Gifford, T., Bouwer, A., & Wagy, M. (2013a). Should music interaction be easy? In S. Holland, K. Wilkie, P. Mulholland, & A. Seago (Eds.), *Music and human computer interaction* (pp. 29–48). London: Springer.

McDermott, J., Sherry, D., & O'Reilly, U. (2013b). Evolutionary and generative music informs music HCI—and vice versa. In S. Holland, K. Wilkie, P. Mulholland, & A. Seago (Eds.), *Music and human computer interaction* (pp. 223–240). London: Springer.

McPherson, A. P., & Kim, Y. E. (2013). Piano technique as a case study in expressive gestural interaction. In S. Holland, K. Wilkie, P. Mulholland, & A. Seago (Eds.), *Music and human-computer interaction* (pp. 123–138). London: Springer.

Meyer, L. (1956). *Emotion and meaning in music*. Chicago: Chicago University Press.

Mills, R. (2010). Dislocated sound: A survey of improvisation in networked audio platforms. In *Proceedings of the NIME 2010*. http://www.nime.org/proceedings/2010/nime2010_186.pdf. Accessed 14 Jan 2012.

Milne, A. J., Xambó, A., Laney, R., Sharp, D. B., Prechtl, A., & Holland, S. (2011, May 30–June 1). Hex Player—A virtual musical controller. In *The International Conference on New Interfaces for Musical Expression 2011* (NIME '11) (pp. 244–247). Oslo, Norway.

Milne, A. J., Carlé, M., Sethares, W. A., Noll, T., & Holland, S. (2011b). Scratching the scale Labyrinth. In C. Agon, M. Andreatta, G. Assayag, E. Amiot, J. Bresson, & J. Mandereau (Eds.), *Proceedings of mathematics and computation in music*. LNCS Vol 6726 ISBN 978-3-642-21589-6, 180–195

Narmour, E. (1990). *The analysis and cognition of basic musical structures*. Chicago: University of Chicago Press.

O'Modhrain, S. (2011). A framework for the evaluation of digital musical instruments. *Computer Music Journal, 35*(1), 28–42.

O'Hara, K. P., & Payne, S. J. (1998). The effects of operator implementation cost on planfulness of problem solving and learning. *Cognitive Psychology, 35*(1), 34–70.

Patten, J., Recht, B., & Ishii, H. (2002). Audiopad: A tag-based interface for musical performance. In *Proceedings of the 2002 conference on New interfaces for musical expression (NIME '02).* University of Singapore (pp. 1–6).

Poupyrev, I., Lyons, M. J., Fels, S., & Blaine, T. (Bean). (2001). New interfaces for musical expression. In *CHI '01 extended abstracts on human factors in computing systems (CHI EA '01)* (pp. 491–492). New York: ACM.

Prechtl, A., Milne, A., Holland, S., Laney, R., & Sharp, D. (2012, Spring) A MIDI sequencer that widens access to the compositional possibilities of novel tunings. *Computer Music Journal, 16*(1), 42–54.

Preece, J., Rogers, Y., Sharp, H., Benyon, D., Holland, S., & Carey, T. (1994). Cooperative design. In *Human-computer interaction* (pp. 375–379). England: Addison-Wesley.

Reiss, S. (2004). Multifaceted nature of intrinsic motivation: The theory of 16 basic desires. *Review of General Psychology, 8*(3), 179–193.

Rohrer, T. (2005). Image schemata in the brain. In B. Hampe & J. Grady (Eds.), *From perception to meaning: Image schemata in cognitive linguistics*. Berlin: Walter de Gruyter.

Rohrer, T. (2007). The body in space: Dimensions of embodiment. In T. Ziemke, J. Zlatev, R. Frank, & R. Dirven (Eds.), *Body, language, and mind: Embodiment* (pp. 339–378). Berlin: Walter de Gruyter.

Rowe, R. (1993). *Interactive music systems*. Cambridge, MA: MIT Press.

Ryan, R., & Deci, E. (2000). Self-determination theory and the facilitation of intrinsic motivation, social development, and well-being. *American Psychologist, 55*(1), 68–78.

Sawyer, R. K., & DeZutter, S. (2009). Distributed creativity: How collective creations emerge from collaboration. *Psychology of Aesthetics, Creativity, and the Arts, 3*(2), 81–92.

Seago, A. (2013). A new interaction strategy for musical timbre design. In S. Holland, K. Wilkie, P. Mulholland, & A. Seago (Eds.), *Music and human computer interaction* (pp. 153–170). London: Springer.

Seago, A., Holland, S., & Mulholland, P. (2004). A critical analysis of synthesizer user interfaces for timbre, people and computers – XVIII proceedings of human computer interaction 2004 Sept 2004 (pp. 105–106). London: Springer.

Seago, A., Holland, S., & Mulholland, P. (2010). A novel user interface for musical timbre design. Audio Engineering Society AES, In *Proceedings of 128th convention* (pp. 22–25). London.

Sengers, P. (2006). Must design become *scientific*? Paper presented at workshop on exploring design as a research activity, as part of Sixth Conference on Designing Interactive Systems. (DIS'06), University Park, PA.

Small, C. (1998). *Musicking: The meanings of performing and listening*. Hanover: Wesleyan University Press.

Stoffregen, T. A., Bardy, B. G., & Mantel, B. (2006). Affordances in the design of enactive systems. *Virtual Reality, 10*(1), 4–10.

Stowell, D., & McLean, A. (2013). Live music-making: A rich open task requires a rich open interface. In S. Holland, K. Wilkie, P. Mulholland, & A. Seago (Eds.), *Music and human computer interaction* (pp. 139–152). London: Springer. http://www.nime.org/archive/, http://www.nime.org/proceedings/2008/nime2008_081.pdf. Accessed 21 Jan 2013.

Stowell, D., Plumbley, M. D., & Bryan-Kinns, N. (2008). Discourse analysis evaluation method for expressive musical interfaces. In *Proceedings of the NIME'08* (pp. 81–8). http://www.nime.org/archive/, http://www.nime.org/proceedings/2008/nime2008_081.pdf. Accessed 21 Jan 2013.

Sutherland, I. E. (1963). *Sketchpad: A man-machine graphical communication system*. PhD thesis, Massachusetts Institute of Technology (Published in 2003 as Technical Report No. 574). Cambridge: University of Cambridge. http://www.cl.cam.ac.uk/techreports/UCAM-CL-TR-574.pdf. Accessed 5 Jan 2013.

Suzuki, H. (2007). Spectrum analysis and tone quality evaluation of piano sounds with hard and soft touches. *Acoustical Science and Technology, 28*(1), 1–6.

Svansdottir, H. B., & Snaedal, J. (2006). Music therapy in moderate and severe dementia of Alzheimer's type: A case–control study. *International Psychogeriatrics, 18*(4), 613–621.
Swift, B. (2013). Chasing a feeling: Experience in computer supported jamming. In S. Holland, K. Wilkie, P. Mulholland, & A. Seago (Eds.), *Music and human computer interaction* (pp. 85–100). London: Springer.
Takagi, H. (2001). Interactive evolutionary computation: Fusion of the capabilities of EC optimization and human evaluation. *Proceedings of the IEEE, 89*(9), 1275–1296.
Temperley, D. (2001). *The cognition of basic musical structures*. Cambridge, MA: MIT Press.
Thaut, M. H. (2005). *Rhythm music and the brain: Scientific foundations and clinical applications*. New York: Routledge.
Tinto, V. (1975). Dropout from higher education: A theoretical synthesis of recent research. *The Review of Higher Education, 45*(1), 89–125.
Todd, N. (1989). A computational model of rubato. *Contemporary Music Review, 3*, 1.
Waiswisz, M. (1985). The hands, a set of remote MIDI-controllers. In *Proceedings of the 1985 international computer music conference* (pp. 313–318). San Francisco: International Computer Music Association.
Wallin, N. L., Merker, B., & Brown, S. (Eds.). (2000). *The origins of music*. Cambridge: MIT Press.
Wallis, I., Ingalls, T., Campana, E., & Vuong, C. (2013). Amateur musicians, long-term engagement, and HCI. In S. Holland, K. Wilkie, P. Mulholland, & A. Seago (Eds.), *Music and human computer interaction* (pp. 49–66). London: Springer.
Wanderley, M. M., & Orio, N. (2002). Evaluation of input devices for musical expression: Borrowing tools from HCI. *Computer Music Journal, 26*(3), 62–76.
Wessel, D. L., & Wright, M. (2002). Problems and prospects for intimate musical control of computers. *Computer Music Journal, 26*(3), 11–22.
Wilkie, K., Holland, S., & Mulholland, P. (2010). What can the language of musicians tell us about music interaction design? *Computer Music Journal, 34*(4), 34–48.
Wilkie, K., Holland, S., & Mulholland, P. (2013). Towards a participatory approach for interaction design based on conceptual metaphor theory: A case study from music interaction. In S. Holland, K. Wilkie, P. Mulholland, & A. Seago (Eds.), *Music and human computer interaction* (pp. 259–270). London: Springer.
Wilson, W. (2002). Six views of embodied cognition. *Psychonomic Bulletin and Review, 9*(4), 625–636.
Xambó, A., Laney, R., Dobbyn, C., & Jordà, S. (2013). Video analysis for evaluating music interaction: Musical tabletops. In S. Holland, K. Wilkie, P. Mulholland, & A. Seago (Eds.), *Music and human computer interaction* (pp. 241–258). London: Springer.
Zbikowski, L. M. (1997a). Conceptual models and cross-domain mapping: New perspective on 446 theories of music and hierarchy. *Journal of Music Theory, 41*(2), 193–225.
Zbikowski, L. M. (1997b). Des Herzraums Abschied: Mark Johnson's theory of embodied 448 knowledge and music theory. *Theory and Practice, 22–23*, 1–16.
Zimmerman, T. G., Lanier, J., Blanchard, C., Bryson, S., & Harvill, Y. (1986). A hand gesture interface device. In J. M. Carroll & P. P. Tanner (Eds.), *Proceedings of the SIGCH conference on human factors in computing systems* (*CHI '87*) (pp. 189–192). New York: ACM.

Chapter 2
Should Music Interaction Be Easy?

James McDermott, Toby Gifford, Anders Bouwer, and Mark Wagy

Abstract A fundamental assumption in the fields of human-computer interaction and usability studies is that interfaces should be designed for ease of use, with a few exceptions such as the trade-off with long-term power. In this chapter it is argued that in music interaction the situation is far more complex, with social, technical, artistic, and psychological reasons why difficulty is in some cases a good thing, and in other cases a necessary evil. Different aspects of static and time-varying difficulty in music interaction are categorised. Some specific areas in which difficulty seems to be inextricably linked to positive aspects of music interaction are described. This is followed by discussion of some areas in which difficulty is undesirable and, perhaps, avoidable. Examples are drawn from music interaction research in general and from other chapters of this book in particular.

J. McDermott (✉)
Evolutionary Design and Optimization Group, Computer Science and Artificial Intelligence Laboratory, Massachusetts Institute of Technology, Cambridge, MA 02139, USA
e-mail: jmmcd@csail.mit.edu

T. Gifford
Queensland Conservatorium of Music, Griffith University, Brisbane, Australia
e-mail: t.gifford@griffith.edu.au

A. Bouwer
Intelligent Systems Lab Amsterdam (ISLA), Informatics Institute, Faculty of Science, University of Amsterdam, Amsterdam, The Netherlands
e-mail: andersbouwer@uva.nl

M. Wagy
Department of Computer Science and Engineering, University of Minnesota, Minneapolis, MN 55455, USA
e-mail: wagyx001@umn.edu

S. Holland et al. (eds.), *Music and Human-Computer Interaction*, Springer Series on Cultural Computing, DOI 10.1007/978-1-4471-2990-5_2,

2.1 Introduction

In interaction studies, there is a fundamental assumption that all else being equal, systems should be as easy as possible to use. This focus is evident in the literature. Nielsen's (2003) list of five components of usability (learnability, efficiency, memorability, errors, and satisfaction) uses the terms "easy" and "easily" three times in five short sentences. It is good to remember both halves of the phrase attributed to Einstein (though apparently only a paraphrase): *everything should be as simple as possible, but no simpler*. There are cases where other goals must take priority at the expense of ease of use, and music interaction (the interactions between humans and tools in the domain of music) seems to be one of them. So what makes music interaction different?

We can begin with language. The term "user", prevalent in the language of interaction studies, is a bad fit in music. It contains an implicit assumption that the computer is viewed as an inanimate object, in which the relationship of the computer to the user is that of a tool (Karlstrom 2007). Music systems occupy a spectrum of autonomy including what Rowe (2001) calls the "instrument paradigm" and the "player paradigm". In the *player* paradigm the computer is viewed as an agent, and the human is better described as an interactor than a "user". Even in the *instrument* paradigm the term "user" strikes some discord. One does not "use" an instrument to accomplish some ultimate goal: one plays it, and often that is the only goal. As Tanaka (2000) says, an instrument is not a utilitarian tool, which only needs to be easy to use in a specific context and whose development need only be characterised by ever greater efficiency. Instead, "What might be considered imperfections or limitations from the perspective of tool design often contribute to a 'personality' of a musical instrument" (Tanaka 2000). Indeed, efficiency is less important than *engagement*, a term which brings to mind the concept of *flow* (Csikszentmihalyi 1991; for more see Sect. 2.3).

Engaging, consuming, flow-like activities such as music are characterised by being at an appropriate level of difficulty: not too difficult, and not too easy. Often an activity which remains engaging in the long term does so at the expense of being rather painful to a beginner—in other words there is an important trade-off between ease of learning and long-term power and flexibility (Gentner and Nielsen 1996). Instrumental performance and practice, recording, mixing and production, live-coding and turntabling, the study of theory and notation—all of these are activities which take place in sessions that can last for hours and are mastered over years. Therefore the best interfaces for these tasks tend to fall towards the long-term power end of the trade-off.

One of the most characteristic aspects of music interaction is the extent to which skilled musicians become one with their instruments. Leman (2008) identifies the importance of this *transparency*: "Transparent technology should [. . .] give a feeling of non-mediation, a feeling that the mediation technology 'disappears' when it is used" (Leman 2008: 2). This feeling is important to instrumentalists as artists and to skilled use of tools and systems in general.

Hand-in-hand with transparency goes the crucial concept of *embodied cognition*. Embodied cognition is a view of perception in which perception and action are inextricably linked (Wilson 2002). Leman (2008) argues that musical experience involves embodied cognition, rather than symbolic mental processing, even in the case of passive listening. On the other hand, Hunt and Hermann (2011) emphasise the divergence of experience between the player, inside the control loop, and the listener outside it.

Paine (2009) proposes that "the issue of embodied knowledge is vital in both the learning and teaching of musical performance skills and the relationship the musician has to their instrument". He suggests that the capacity for an instrument (in the hands of an experienced player) to disappear from consciousness transforms it into "a conduit for expression rather than an object in its own right". A musical tool which encourages *internalisation* of its concepts (van Nimwegen et al. 2004) seems essential for fluid, real-time use.

Armstrong (2006) suggests that the "prevailing guiding metaphors of [...] HCI are at odds with the embodied/enactive approach". Within interaction design, two subfields that do embrace the embodied perspective are haptics (Gillespie and O'Modrain 2011) and tangible interfaces (Hornecker 2011), both of which have frequently been used in music interaction design (Jordà et al. 2007).

Another distinction between music interaction and more general interaction studies is made explicit by Stowell and McLean (2013) in this volume: they say that applying typical experimental HCI techniques to musical tasks is in some ways useful, but "the experimental setups are so highly reduced as to be unmusical, leading to concerns about the validity of the test. Further, such approaches do not provide for creative interactions between human and machine." Music interaction, it seems, must be studied in its native environment. More broadly, the language of experience design is perhaps more appropriate than that of usability for discussing music interaction. Experience design privileges consideration of the holistic experience of the interaction, which by nature is longitudinal, and must incorporate temporal changes in the human due to the interaction—see Sect. 2.3.

In order to do productive research in music interaction, it is necessary to correctly specify our goals. In many cases they do coincide with the typical goals of interaction studies, including the elimination of unnecessary difficulty. In others it is better to identify the aspects where ease of use should not be made a priority. In this chapter, then, we consider where and why music interaction should be difficult. Our goal is not a set of definitive findings but a framing of the questions and distinctions. Our scope includes all types of creative music interaction, including instrumental performance, virtual instruments and effects, laptop performance, turntabling and similar, notation and sequencing tasks, and production.

The remainder of this chapter is laid out as follows. In Sect. 2.2, a simple framework of multiple types of difficulty is set out. The learning curve model of time-varying difficulty, crucial to understanding long-term activities typical of music interaction, is described in Sect. 2.3. In Sect. 2.4, the sometimes counter-intuitive *advantages* of difficulty in music interaction are categorised. Section 2.5

describes aspects of music interaction where difficulty is genuinely undesirable and unnecessary, corresponding to areas where HCI and interaction design have the opportunity to contribute. Section 2.6 concludes.

2.2 Dimensions of Difficulty

Difficulty is not a one-dimensional variable. Various real and virtual instruments, software interfaces, and music hardware all exhibit their own characteristic types of difficulty, with different interfaces making some things easier and some things more difficult. Sometimes, there is a trade-off between these factors. In this section some *dimensions of difficulty* are categorised.

2.2.1 Physical Difficulty

Most computer software requires of users a minimal set of physical abilities: typing, pointing and clicking with the mouse, and looking at the screen. The same is true of music software in general, and studio hardware adds little to this set. However musical instruments can require a lot more. Pianists require at least an octave span in each hand. Stringed instruments require finger strength and, in early stages, some endurance of pain in the fingertips. Wind instruments can require great physical effort to produce the required air pressure, while holding a long note also requires physical effort and practise. The intense physical demands of rock drumming have been demonstrated by Smith et al. (2008). Long-term practice of instruments can lead to muscle and nerve injuries. In contrast, non-contact instruments such as the theremin and Sound Spheres (Hughes et al. 2011) make minimal physical demands.

Physical inconvenience can also be relevant, ranging from immobile equipment such as studios and church organs, to highly inconvenient equipment such as the double bass, down to pocket-size smartphone instruments and even to "disappearing" equipment (Kock and Bouwer 2011).

2.2.2 Difficulty of Dexterity and Coordination

All instruments require some dexterity and coordination. Many require the fingers, the hands, or the limbs to do different things at the same time. Often, there is a disassociation between the choice of notes and the control of timing and expressiveness. Some instruments require additional tools to be used as extensions of the body (or instrument), such as drum sticks or the bow for string instruments.

On string instruments such as guitar and electric bass, the presence of frets supports playing in tune, which is much harder to learn on a fretless instrument, such as violin or double bass. However, fretted instruments do not allow for the same flexibility in intonation and expressiveness (e.g., vibrato) as fretless instruments. In the case of guitar, this lack has been addressed by the use of additional devices such as the bottleneck slide and the tremolo bar (allowing vibrato to go down as well as up).

An analogous distinction can be made in wind instruments, where the trombone has one telescopic slide, instead of valves to control pitch. Circular breathing, required for some wind instruments, seems to present both a physical and a coordination problem.

Mixing on studio hardware requires coordination in terms of handling various controls in a timely manner, but many of these actions can nowadays be recorded and coordinated automatically by computer controlled systems. Interactive music software seldom requires much dexterity or coordination.

2.2.3 *Difficulty Between Imagination and Realisation*

A chief difficulty in the tasks of mixing and mastering of recordings is that of *identifying* the required changes, for example noticing an undesirable compression effect or an improvement that could be made to an equalisation setting. When the required change has been identified, making that change is often trivial. Although the main requirement is an internal "auditory imagination", a good interface can help, for example by making A/B comparison convenient or by showing a spectrogram visualisation.

2.2.4 *Nonlinearities, Discontinuities and Interactions in Control*

The tin whistle's scale is linear: within an octave, each higher note just requires the removal of the next finger. In contrast, the recorder's scale has nonlinearities in which previously-removed fingers must be replaced for later notes. There is also a discontinuity in both, and in many wind instruments, when overblowing is required to produce higher octaves. Extreme examples of nonlinearity include the *rackett*, a Renaissance double-reed instrument with unusually complex fingering, and the button accordion, which features a two-dimensional layout of controls for each hand, and in some cases can be *bisonoric* ("push" and "pull" notes are distinct).

Nonlinearities and discontinuities are also common in synthesizer parameters. Interactions between parameters also cause problems (Seago 2013, in this volume). Much research into timbre control is aimed at reducing unnecessary nonlinearities, discontinuities, and interactions (e.g. Hughes et al. 2011).

2.2.5 Polyphony, Multiple Streams and Multiple Paths

It would be problematic to state that polyphonic instruments are more difficult than monophonic ones, since a fair comparison would require aspects other than polyphony to be equalised between the instruments, a condition that can rarely be achieved in practise. However it seems fair to state that playing a monophonic melody on a polyphonic instrument is easier than playing multiple lines simultaneously. Playing a pseudo-polyphonic piece such as a Bach Partita on a "mostly monophonic" instrument like the violin requires the performer not only to handle the multiple streams of music but to differentiate between them through dynamics and articulation. Live computer performers, turntablists, and studio mixers often have to handle multiple streams of music simultaneously, again imposing a larger cognitive burden (see Stowell and McLean 2013, in this volume). Some instruments and equipment allows any given action to be performed in multiple different ways, the simplest example being the choice of guitar string for a given pitch. This flexibility can be both an advantage and a disadvantage.

2.2.6 Difficulty of Repertoire

The violin and viola are very similar instruments, but because of the greater number of compositions written for violin, and the generally higher demands imposed on playing skills, the violin can be said to be more difficult in terms of repertoire.

2.2.7 Tuning Systems and Graphical Layout

In the case of traditional instruments, the tuning system embedded in the instrument's design and graphical layout determines to an important degree how players conceptualize the interaction with their instrument.

On a piano, the notes in the scale of C are easily recognizable and playable as they correspond to the white keys on the instrument. Transposing a piece to another key makes the black keys necessary, and therefore changes the spatial pattern of keys to be played and the pattern of finger movements required. On a guitar, on the other hand, it is often possible to transpose a tune to another key by moving all the notes up or down the neck. Determining whether there are any flat or sharp notes being played is much easier on a piano than on a guitar, however. These are examples of how the graphical layout of notes on a musical instrument offers "representational guidance" (Suthers 2001) by facilitating the expression and inspection of certain kinds of information rather than other kinds.

Several string instruments (e.g., violin, cello, mandolin) have four strings tuned in fifths (e.g., G, D, A, E, from low to high, on the violin). This allows a player to reach a large range of notes to be played in a single position. On the double bass (and bass guitar), the four strings are tuned in fourths (E, A, D, G) instead. The greater dimensions of the bass do not allow the same range of notes to be played in one position as smaller instruments, so this difference in tuning is practical, but it also makes it difficult to transfer experience in playing one instrument to another. On a guitar, all of the six strings (E, A, D, G, B, E) are tuned in fourths, except one (the B-string). This is again practical especially for chord shapes, but makes scales which cross the G and B strings inconsistent. To make matters even more complicated conceptually, some musicians tune their instrument in alternative ways to make a particular tune easier to play, or to better accommodate their playing style (e.g., slide guitarists often tune in open tunings, such as D, G, D, G, B, D, to allow playing chord shapes directly with the slide).

In summary, considerations of physical playability can conflict with that of conceptual systematicity. Physics also constrains the set of possible tuning systems, especially in wind instruments. The variety of musical instruments and tuning systems in use today is a result of cultural history, showing that people are quite flexible in the relationships they recognise between musical qualities and physical ones.

2.2.8 *Conceptual Difficulty*

As explained in Sect. 2.2.7, the design of a music interaction system may support some conceptual activities and prevent or limit others. When we turn to other music interaction systems, other forms of conceptual difficulty arise. Sequencer programs often contain a wealth of functionality and options which may be difficult to find or remember. Mathematically-oriented synthesizer algorithms lead to large numbers of numerical control parameters which do not correspond to most users' musical intuitions. Programming languages used in livecoding are another example of conceptual difficulty (see Stowell and McLean 2013, this volume).

2.3 Learning Curves: Difficulty Over Time

As previously outlined, all musical instruments, equipment, and software present the user with various types of difficulty in varying degrees. Such difficulties are not static, but dynamic. Time-varying aspects of difficulty are discussed in this section.

A natural model originating in the psychology literature is the "learning curve" (Bills 1934; Ritter and Schooler 2002). The learning curve is a task or activity's characteristic pattern of difficulty versus time. Steep growth in the curve indicates slow progress. Note that difficulty does not always increase with time.

Several aspects of difficulty in music interaction can be described in terms of learning curves. For example, Wallis et al. (2013) in this volume discuss the idea of "maximum potential complexity", saying: "there is such potential complexity in music that no individual can be said to fully master any instrument". For non-trivial instruments, the learning curve remains non-zero indefinitely. Virtuosi push the limits of whatever instrument they choose. There is always room to grow, and if an instrument seems relatively easy in some respect, it encourages a more difficult repertoire.

The learning curve is useful in describing the difficulties experienced by musical beginners. Instruments such as piano with which musical sounds can be produced immediately, by default, have less of a "learning hump" (i.e. high values for difficulty at the very start of the curve) than instruments such as woodwind in which early attempts can produce distinctly non-musical sounds. Fretted instruments avoid one of the major early learning humps associated with free-pitch instruments such as the violin. Polyphony is another early learning hump avoided by some instruments. In contrast, "instruments such as diatonic harmonica are not hard to take up initially, but have large challenge jumps corresponding with times when advanced techniques such as note-bending must be learned" (Wallis et al. 2013, this volume). Hence it is essential to model these difficulties as time-varying.

It seems natural to think of the "ideal" learning curve as being initially low with gradual increase in difficulty over time. Such a curve would have the advantages of not discouraging beginners, rewarding effort, and remaining non-trivial indefinitely. A key concept is that of *flow* (Nakamura and Csikszentmihalyi 2002). Being *in flow* means "the subjective experience of engaging just-manageable challenges by tackling a series of goals, continuously processing feedback about progress, and adjusting action based on this feedback." In these circumstances, people sometimes experience enjoyment of the activity for its own sake; loss of self-consciousness; focussed concentration; and a sense of control. It is regarded as a highly positive experience, both in terms of enjoyment and in terms of effective learning or productivity. Both too-easy and too-difficult tasks can break flow, so the ideal learning curve again exhibits a gradual increase in difficulty.

Van Nimwegen et al. (2004) distinguish between *internalised* and *externalised* learning. They show that systems which require the user to internalise knowledge (as opposed to relying on external cues) present greater initial difficulty, but are more robust to disruption. Internalised knowledge leads to greater independence, "better knowledge", and long-term retention. It seems essential to fluid, real-time use of any system.

Teachers, instructors, or mentors often play a role in stimulating development and motivation by selecting material that is just within reach. As described by Hedegaard (2005), Vygotsky's concept of the zone of proximal development has been influential in informing instructional planning. This refers to the difference between the tasks that a learner is capable of with and without expert guidance (Hedegaard 2005).

2.4 Where Music Interaction Must Be Difficult

In many cases, what difficulty exists in music interaction is not easily eliminated because it is inextricably linked with some property seen as desirable. Some such properties are set out in this section.

2.4.1 Open-Endedness and Long-Term Engagement

For many musicians, composing music or playing an instrument is an end in itself, not a means to an end (Swift 2013, in this volume). An appropriate degree of difficulty seems to be inextricably linked to the motivation for such *autotelic* activities (Wallis et al. 2013, in this volume; Nakamura and Csikszentmihalyi 2002). Satisfaction in musical activities derives partly from accomplishing goals of appropriate difficulty. There is a great contrast with the tools and interfaces typically studied in usability research, where the aim is usually to "get the job done" as quickly and efficiently as possible. When the end-goal of an activity is for the sake of enjoyment of the activity itself, a suitable level of difficulty becomes acceptable and even beneficial.

A second component of the motivation for autotelic activities, in general, is the potential for *long-term engagement.* A skill which can be mastered in the short term may be of interest as a means to an end, but less so for its own sake. Long-term engagement with a skill such as composition or performance is possible because they are unlimited both in the possibilities and the challenge they can offer. Most musical instruments have large and varied repertoires, and with the possible exception of a few trivial instruments, no player can be said to have ever fully mastered an instrument.

It is interesting to think about cases in which music interaction *is* limited. Popular video games like Guitar Hero and Rock Band (Harmonix Music Systems 2005, 2007) offer a good case study. Such games are very popular, and anecdotal evidence suggests that they can kindle an interest in music and musical performance in non-musicians. They seem to promote long-term engagement to a surprising degree. Research suggests that playing these games "feels like" making music "because the affective experience of making music is so bound up with embodied performance", which includes elements of theatrical play and social interaction (Miller 2009). However, a real disadvantage is that these games seem to be dead ends. The "guitar" controller is not intended for independent musical control, since its controls depend on game context. There is a discontinuity between the game controllers and true guitars. In contrast, drumming games usually feature a true MIDI drum kit as the controller, albeit a cut-down one. Real drumming skills transfer directly to such a kit and vice versa. Therefore there is the potential for a beginner in such a game to experience unlimited growth by switching seamlessly to a real drum kit when the game is outgrown.

It is easy to imagine that such a process might become a fundamental part of a musician's self-narrative and self-image. One's self-narrative as an instrumentalist includes experiences such as early memories of an instrument, first skilled performance witnessed, first ownership, and so on. One's self-image is an important aspect of autotelic activities, including components such as one's sense of autonomy, of dedication, and of authenticity. An instrumentalist is not only a player of music, but also a fan who has witnessed virtuosic performances, and may regard favourite players as role models. As such, there is little possibility of "blaming the tools": instead there is a strong positive example to help the beginner to work through an initially steep learning curve. One's relationship with the instrument might be strengthened by a feeling of having been together "through thick and thin": again, difficulty contributes to long-term engagement. In contrast to typical HCI, errors in performance can even lead to new interpretations and goals, for example in instrumental improvisation.

A final point in this connection is that our aesthetic senses seem tuned to detect and enjoy *open-endedness*. A sense of mystery has been shown to appeal broadly to all humans, in both real landscapes and landscape art (Thornhill 2003). It is the idea that one can see far enough ahead to know that there is more beyond. The appeal of these features has been explained in evolutionary terms. We are naturally curious creatures. "Mystery is the promise of more useful information, and the mental inference of mystery draws us into the scenario for more information gathering" (Thornhill 2003). It has thus been seen as a fundamental root of our visual, and possibly also *cross-domain* aesthetics (Ruso et al. 2003). Open-ended activities including musical composition and the learning of instruments may trigger this evolutionary sense of enjoyable mystery in the same way.

2.4.2 Expressivity, Creativity and Flexibility

Ease of learning in interfaces tends to go along with being locked-down, inflexible, inexpressive, or non-amenable to creative, unexpected use. It trades off against the long-term power of the interface, as described in Sect. 2.1.

A common technique in HCI is to hide rarely-used controls in menus or configuration panels (Nielsen 2006). Contrast this with the interface of a typical mixing desk. Such an interface is clearly not optimized for the beginner's ease of use. It requires an assumption that studio engineers are willing to take time to learn the interface well. It is motivated partly by the consideration that a mixing desk must be used in real-time. Menus are useful for organizing and hiding controls, but take time to navigate. For intense, real-time tasks, there is a benefit to having every single control and indicator immediately available to the eye and hand. In this, mixing desks may have something more in common with airplane cockpits than with office software.

Beginners sometimes find western music notation a gratuitous obstacle. Since the beginner starts by mentally translating every note from the staff to a note-name and thence to a physical action, it seems natural to do away with the staff and simply use note-names (C E G C') or solfège (do mi so do') as notation. However musical notation has been optimized for a different scenario. It makes patterns and motifs in the music visually obvious, so that an experienced musician can read and play a semi-familiar piece live. This requires a type of gestalt comprehension of perhaps multiple bars at a glance that could not come from text.

The trade-off is again evident in sequencer software. Programs such as *GarageBand* (Apple 2011), a simplified sequencer, are appealing and relatively easy to use for beginners. Seasoned users might find that it lacks options or that some tasks are relatively cumbersome or slow. In contrast, a "tracker-style" sequencer interface such as *Jeskola Buzz* (Tammelin 1999) is intimidating to beginners, but seen as irreplaceable by its more experienced fans. Advanced users who prefer such interfaces tend to take advantage of the relatively high-capacity keyboard input channel, as opposed to the low-capacity mouse channel.

The type of creativity which drives some saxophone players (for example) to use malformed notes, squeaks and wheezes as part of their music cannot be predicted or allowed for. Think of the artist who sets out to produce a painting but ends up with a sculpture. Hofstadter (1979) uses the phrase "jumping out of the system" for such creativity. If a system is rigid, then patching it to allow a particular, anticipated jump might only make it more rigid for other, unanticipated ones.

2.4.3 Demonstrating Virtuosity

In musical performance, demonstrating virtuosity may be central to the intended experience (Wagner 1830). Virtuosity cannot exist without difficulty. Virtuosity must also be identifiable as such by the audience. Wallis et al. (2013) in this volume argue that demonstrations of skill are an important motivating factor for people to learn and play musical instruments. Levitin (2006) suggests that musical ability, like any craft, carries a level of prestige associated with the commitment of time and energy required to attain mastery.

In order to attain mastery over an instrument, it is helpful if the design of the instrument remains relatively stable. Massey points out that "constant design changes make truly skilled use impossible" (2003). This sets up an interesting contrast between traditional acoustic instruments, and digital music interfaces. Where an instrument such as a violin has a rich cultural history of continued use and exploration, software interfaces such as a Pure Data patch may be created for a single performance. Whilst there is certainly skill associated with creating a Pure Data patch, this skill may not be evident to the audience.

The issue of demonstrating virtuosity is of particular concern in a digitally mediated context, such as laptop performance, where the disconnect between physical gestures and sonic results obscures the skill of the performer, resulting in a loss of perceived performativity (Stuart 2003) and authenticity (Paine 2009). Collins comments: "Unfortunately, much of the complexity of these real-time systems [generative, etc.] is lost on a potential audience, excepting those few connoisseurs who sneak round the back to check the laptop screen. An artist using powerful software like SuperCollider or Pure Data cannot be readily distinguished from someone checking their e-mail whilst DJing with iTunes" (Collins 2003: 1). Artists in such cases may feel unappreciated, and the audience short-changed.

In live-coding (Stowell and McLean 2013, this volume) program code will often be projected for an audience to see. While the audience may not understand the code *per se,* live coders argue that the audience can nevertheless recognise virtuosity in this manner (TOPLAP 2011). Other methods of informing and indirectly educating the audience may also have a role to play.

2.4.4 Communicating Effort and Emotion

As remarked above, the complexity and skill of a laptop performance is often invisible to the audience. A related problem concerns physical effort. Audiences have been trained to associate physical effort in performances with emotional intensity and commitment to the music. Physical effort intensifies the experience of the audience. This is true even in the refined setting of the symphony orchestra, where the audience sit quietly but the players and the conductor may work up a real sweat. Indeed a more general association between physical effort and commitment is the inevitable consequence of an evolutionary environment in which important tasks were physical and social actors required the ability to judge each others' contribution to a shared task, and the relative difficulty of different tasks. In the case of musical performance, the specific problem is that although virtual instruments and laptops have removed the need for the player to input significant energy to produce an intense performance, the audience's desire for commitment and authenticity on the part of the performer remains. Thus even a painful struggle on the part of the performer is not entirely negative: "One has to suffer a bit while playing" (Krefeld and Waisvisz 1990). The audience may also require cues from the performers to help recognise, for example, a particularly intense or emotional section of the music. "[T]he physical effort you make is what is perceived by listeners as the cause and manifestation of the musical tension of the work" (Krefeld and Waisvisz 1990). It is awkward or impossible to communicate such intensity via a laptop instrument which requires only typing, or a smartphone application whose control surface is just a few square inches, or a virtual instrument which requires no physical contact whatsoever.

2.5 Where Music Interaction Could Be Easier

Despite the arguments put forward above, there remain aspects of music interaction which do not benefit from difficulty. These are areas where interaction studies have made contributions to music interaction, or have the opportunity to do so.

2.5.1 *Transient and Frivolous Music*

Many musical activities are primarily intended to be transient and/or frivolous. Good examples include Guitar Hero and Rock Band (Harmonix Music Systems 2005, 2007) and similar games, and (according to musical tastes) "air guitar" and "air conducting". In the latter there is no aim of demonstrating virtuosity or performing, simply the enjoyment of pretending to play along. Some instruments seem particularly associated with frivolous playing, e.g. the ukulele is seen as easy to pick up and play while doing something else, such as watching television. Many virtual instruments, smartphone instruments (e.g. Smule 2008) and generative methods (e.g. Earslap 2011) may also be described as close to being toys. This is no criticism, merely recognition that in such cases, the aim is to allow the user some type of expressivity without difficulty. In the ideal case, the user will get something good, but something different, no matter what he or she does. A simple technique is to map all gestures to diatonic scales, to avoid many obviously wrong notes. "Bloom" (Eno and Chilvers 2009) not only constrains the user's inputs to a diatonic scale, but it allows the user to do nothing at all and still obtain interesting music. On the other hand, it prevents fine-grained control of the music.

2.5.2 *Peripheral and Technical Tasks*

Many musical tasks can be regarded as being of a technical nature, or as inessential to the artistic process. Removing the burden of these tasks would help musicians to concentrate on the essentials. As a rather trivial example, tuning up is not a core task, but it presents a minor difficulty to some players. Electric guitars with software-based modification of tuning (Line 6 *Variax* guitar, introduced in 2003), and automatic mechanical tuning systems (AxCent Tuning Systems 2013 and Gibson's *robot guitar*, introduced in 2007) are already available.

Many musicians do not want to spend time creating new timbres. For them, FM or granular synthesis parameters, for example, with their technical names and many nonlinearities, discontinuities and interactions, are an obstacle and a distraction from the core goal. In these cases it is useful to provide a good set of presets. There is also motivation for easy-to-use, simplified interfaces based on ideas like iterative search (see Seago 2013, this volume; McDermott et al. 2007).

Many musicians avoid mixing and mastering of their recordings. The vast majority of professionals out-source these tasks. Among amateurs, a shortcut like the mythical "soundgoodizer" would be very popular. Only a few musicians acquire the expertise to use production as an expressive tool. The types of tools best suited to these two groups differ in obvious ways. Similar remarks apply to live sound engineering and to some sequencers and hard-disk recorders.

2.5.3 Learning Humps and Layered Affordance

One obvious disadvantage of difficulty is its toll on beginners: they struggle, suffer from wrong notes and inflict them on those in their vicinity, and sometimes give up. Among fourth-grade students, the perceived difficulty of an instrument is the main factor in deciding not to play it (Delzell and Leppla 1992). Musical pedagogy is concerned with ways of helping beginners past these "learning humps". A music curriculum for young children (NCCA 2011) suggests using simplified scales such as the pentatonic (p. 100), simplified notation such as "stick notation" for rhythms (p. 93), and "stepping-stone" instruments such as the recorder (p. 106).

The same is true in research into new music interfaces. A good example is the "Haptic Bracelets" (Bouwer et al. 2013a, this volume). A haptic learning system helps to make building-block skills easier to acquire, reducing an initial learning hump. Later "the training wheels come off", and the user's ultimate goal is to reach an unaided mastery. The violin training system of Johnson et al. (2011) helps players learn good bowing technique initially, using real-time feedback, and importantly provides a constant guard against regression to bad technique. In the field of harmony, regarded as difficult due to its many abstract concepts and rules, employing embodied cognition to make the subject matter more concrete and engaging seems promising, as in "Song Walker Harmony Space" (Bouwer et al. 2013b, this volume).

Such examples demonstrate that in some areas the right interfaces and systems can help beginners without detracting from the positive aspects of difficulty. Perhaps further examples are possible. Imagine a "beginners' violin" which restricted notes to a well-tuned pentatonic scale for the first year, allowing the beginner to learn basic skills like stance and bowing in a relatively painless way. This restriction could be lifted gradually, to allow a full diatonic and then chromatic scale, and eventually also the in-between pitches needed for vibrato and slurs. Such an instrument would grow with the player. Crucially, such an instrument would not represent a dead-end, since with the lifting of restrictions the player would have unlimited room for growth. The learning curve for such an instrument would be far less intimidating than that for a standard violin. A partial implementation might require little more on the technical side than an electric violin, "auto-tune" software, and headphones.

There are two possibilities for controlling the gradual increase in difficulty which would be needed for such a hypothetical instrument or interface. In some cases the player could choose when to lift the restrictions and increase difficulty. This is *layered affordance*. An alternative is to have the system use heuristic learning methods to judge when the player or user is ready for a more complex, difficult, or open interface. This intriguing possibility might be termed *adaptive affordance*. Compare the ideas of "progressive" and "staged disclosure" (Jones 1989; Nielsen 2006).

Some existing systems use variations on this idea. A good example is the *Continuator*, or musical flow machine, of Pachet (2003). It is intended to produce "flow" experiences in the user by adapting the complexity of its musical interactions to the user's skill. Another example is the *Jambot* (Gifford 2013, this volume), which provides real-time rhythmic accompaniment to a human musician, and aims to produce a level of rhythmic complexity that is complementary to the rhythmic complexity of the human performer. Computer game designers also understand that to keep players engaged the game must be easy to start, and increase in difficulty as the player becomes more skilled. Computer games, including music-oriented ones such as Guitar Hero and Rock Band (Harmonix Music Systems 2005, 2007), implement this behaviour through the use of "levels" of difficulty. The level is self monitoring, in that mastery of a given level is the trigger for the next level of difficulty.

2.5.4 *Instruction and Meta-Cognition*

Musical training is a field where one-on-one instruction and apprenticeship is very common, and often seen as important for musical growth. Intelligent tutoring systems and intelligent learning environments allow, to some degree, computer-based personalized instruction, which offers potential for applications in music, including score-reading, improvisation and composition tasks (Brandao et al. 1999; Holland 2000). Cook (1998) has emphasized the importance of dialogue in open-ended creative domains such as music, and studied interactions between music teachers and students related to motivation, creativity and critical thinking. His framework for knowledge mentoring can help recognize opportunities for instructional planning to stimulate meta-cognitive activities. Another important factor in acquiring musical skills, besides the amount of practice, is the method of practice. In studies comparing musicians of varying skill level, advanced musicians have been found to use more complex, more abstract, and more flexible practising strategies than less skilled musicians (Gruson 1988). Combining work in this area with learning environments could lead to technology that supports musicians in improving their practising strategies.

2.6 Conclusions

It is fascinating to analyse music interaction using the methods of HCI and interaction design. It tells us something about music interaction, but perhaps also something about the methods of study. The following *gedankenexperiment* makes the point well: "If our field [interaction design] had existed at the time that these musical instruments [accordions and others] were evolving, would we have told them [their designers] to toss the design in the trashcan as TOO COMPLEX for any users to master?" (Boese 2006). It illustrates an important distinction. The fields of HCI and interaction design are *not wrong* in their assumptions and findings that users sometimes find interfaces frustrating, and that productivity can be improved through good design. However the very vocabulary being used here—users, frustration, and productivity—seems ill-suited to describe music interaction. Users are musicians. Productivity can't be measured. Frustration is part of a musician's growth. A musician who learns and plays for love of music is in a very different mind-set from that of a software user, impatient to carry out a task.

Within the broader domain of music interaction, this chapter has been focussed on *difficulty*. A simple taxonomy of dimensions of difficulty and the learning-curve model have been described. Various aspects of music interaction have been set out in which difficulty is counter-intuitively positive, or linked to positive features. In these cases, it is clear that typical interaction studies techniques should not be applied blindly with the aim of banishing difficulty. The "user-friendly" interfaces likely to result might turn out to be uninteresting to musicians.

Some aspects of music interaction have also been described in which difficulty is, on the other hand, negative and unnecessary. In these cases there are opportunities for interaction studies to be applied and to make clear improvements to existing systems. One can speculate that musical instruments, and in particular their capacity for long-term engagement, flexibility and expressivity could serve as a model for new musical systems: making new musical interfaces with these qualities is a challenge and an opportunity.

In all cases, it seems to be essential to recognise music as a distinct set of activities with distinctive goals and mindsets. Music interaction must be studied in its native environment. The contributions to this book, many already mentioned in this chapter, approach music interaction using HCI and interaction design methods, but informed by experience and insight into music and musicians.

Acknowledgments Thanks are due to the organisers of the 2011 British Computer Society HCI conference workshop "When Words Fail: What can Music Interaction tell us about HCI?", and to all participants in the workshop break-out group on the topic of difficulty in music interaction: Rose Johnson, Isaac Wallis, Alex McLean, Peter Quinn, Andrew McPherson, Mat Dalgleish, JMcD, and AB. JMcD is funded by an IRCSET/Marie Curie Inspire Fellowship.

References

Apple. (2011). GarageBand. http://www.apple.com/ilife/garageband. Accessed 12 Sept 2011.

Armstrong, N. (2006). *An enactive approach to digital musical instrument design*. PhD thesis, Princeton University, Princeton.

AxCent Tuning Systems. (2013). http://www.axcenttuning.com. Accessed 21 Jan 2013.

Bills, A. G. (1934). *The curve of learning*. New York: Longmans, Green and Co.

Boese, C. (2006). Usability of accordions. Interaction design association web forum. http://www.ixda.org/node/18728. Accessed 11 Sept 2011.

Bouwer, A., Holland, S., & Dalgleish, M. (2013a). The Haptic Bracelets: Learning multi-limb rhythm skills from haptic stimuli while reading. In S. Holland, K. Wilkie, P. Mulholland, & A. Seago (Eds.), *Music and human-computer interaction* (pp. 101–122). London: Springer. ISBN 978-1-4471-2989-9.

Bouwer, A., Holland, S., & Dalgleish, M. (2013b). Song walker harmony space: Embodied interaction design for complex musical skills. In S. Holland, K. Wilkie, P. Mulholland, & A. Seago (Eds.), *Music and human-computer interaction* (pp. 207–221). London: Springer. ISBN 978-1-4471-2989-9.

Bozkurt, B. (2011). Otomata. http://www.earslap.com/projectslab/otomata. Accessed 20 Nov 2011.

Brandao, M., Wiggins, G., & Pain, H. (1999). Computers in music education. In *Proceedings of the AISB'99 symposium on musical creativity* (pp. 82–88).

Collins, N. (2003). Generative music and laptop performance. *Contemporary Music Review, 22*(4), 67–79.

Cook, J. (1998). Mentoring, metacognition and music: Interaction analyses and implications for intelligent learning environments. *International Journal of Artificial Intelligence in Education, 9*, 45–87.

Csikszentmihalyi, M. (1991). *Flow: The psychology of optimal experience*. New York: Harper Collins.

Delzell, J. K., & Leppla, D. A. (1992). Gender association of musical instruments and preferences of fourth-grade students for selected instruments. *Journal of Research in Music Education, 40*(2), 93–103. doi:10.2307/3345559.

Eno, B., & Chilvers, P. (2009). Bloom. http://www.generativemusic.com/bloom.html. Accessed 20 Nov 2011.

Gentner, D., & Nielsen, J. (1996). The Anti-Mac interface. *Communications of the ACM, 39*(8), 70–82. http://www.useit.com/papers/anti-mac.html. Accessed 9 Sept 2011.

Gifford, T. (2013). Appropriate and complementary rhythmic improvisation in an interactive music system. In S. Holland, K. Wilkie, P. Mulholland, & A. Seago (Eds.), *Music and human-computer interaction* (pp. 271–286). London: Springer. ISBN 978-1-4471-2989-9.

Gillespie, R., & O'Modrain, S. (2011). Embodied cognition as a motivating perspective for haptic interaction design: A position paper. In *World haptics conference*. Istanbul: IEEE.

Gruson, L. M. (1988). Rehearsal skill and musical competence: Does practice make perfect? In J. A. Sloboda (Ed.), *Generative processes in music: The psychology of performance, improvisation, and composition* (pp. 91–112). New York: Oxford University Press.

Harmonix Music Systems. (2005). *Guitar Hero*. Sunnyvale: Red Octane.

Harmonix Music Systems. (2007). *Rock Band*. Redwood City: Electronic Arts.

Hedegaard, M. (2005). The zone of proximal development as basis for instruction. In H. Daniels (Ed.), *An introduction to Vygotsky* (pp. 227–252). New York: Routledge.

Hofstadter, D. R. (1979). *Gödel, Escher, Bach: An eternal golden braid*. New York: Penguin Books.

Holland, S. (2000). Artificial intelligence in music education: A critical review. In E. Miranda (Ed.), *Readings in music and artificial intelligence, contemporary music studies* (Vol. 20, pp. 239–274). Amsterdam: Harwood Academic Publishers.

Hornecker, E. (2011). The role of physicality in tangible and embodied interactions. *Interactions, 18*(2), 19–23.

Hughes, C., Wermelinger, M., & Holland, S. (2011). Sound spheres: The heuristic design and evaluation of a non-contact finger-tracking virtual musical instrument. In *Proceedings of the 8th sound and music computing conference*, Padova, Italy. http://oro.open.ac.uk/28709/. Accessed 8 Mar 2012.

Hunt, A., & Hermann, T. (2011). Interactive sonification. In T. Hermann, A. Hunt, & J. G. Neuhoff (Eds.), *The sonification handbook*. Berlin: Logos Verlag.

Johnson, R., Van der Linden, J., & Rogers. Y. (2011). Prototyping for the wild: Reflections on the design of MuSense, a lightweight wearable practice aid for the violin. BCS HCI workshop "When words fail: What can music interaction tell us about HCI?" 4 July 2011. Northumbria University, Newcastle upon Tyne. http://mcl.open.ac.uk/Workshop. Accessed 8 Mar 2012.

Jones, M. K. (1989). *Human-computer interaction: A design guide*. Englewood Cliffs: Educational Technology.

Jordà, S., Geiger, G., Alonso, M., & Kaltenbrunner, M. (2007). The reacTable: Exploring the synergy between live music performance and tabletop tangible interfaces. In *Proceedings of the international conference* Tangible and Embedded Interaction (TEI07).

Karlstrom, P. (2007). *Existential phenomenology and design—Why "ready-to-hand" is not enough*. Unpublished, available: http://petter.blogs.dsv.su.se/files/2011/02/Existential_phenomenolgy-and-HCI.pdf. Accessed 9 Sept 2011.

Kock, S.V., & Bouwer, A. (2011). *Towards wearable support for nomadic musicians*. Paper presented at workshop "When words fail: What can music interaction tell us about HCI?" at the British conference on human-computer interaction, 4 July 2011, Newcastle, UK.

Krefeld, V., & Waisvisz, M. (1990). The hand in the web: An interview with Michel Waisvisz. *Computer Music Journal, 14*(2), 28–33.

Leman, M. (2008). *Embodied music cognition and mediation technology*. Cambridge: The MIT Press.

Levitin, D. (2006). *This is your brain on music: The science of a human obsession*. East Rutherford: Penguin Putnam.

Massey, A. (2003). Music and the arts: usability in fact and as metaphor. http://www.usabilityprofessionals.org/usability_resources/conference/2003/massey_music_arts.html. Accessed 12Sept 2011.

McDermott, J., Griffith, N. J. L., & O'Neill, M. (2007). Evolutionary GUIs for sound synthesis. In *Applications of evolutionary computing*. Berlin/Heidelberg: Springer.

Miller, K. (2009). Schizophonic performance: Guitar Hero, Rock Band, and Virtual Virtuosity. *Journal of the Society for American Music, 3*(4), 395–429. doi:10.1017/S1752196309990666.

Nakamura, J., & Csikszentmihalyi, M. (2002). The concept of flow. In C. R. Snyder (Ed.), *Handbook of positive psychology* (pp. 89–105). New York: Oxford University Press.

National Council for Curriculum and Assessment (Ireland). (2011). Arts education: Music. http://www.curriculumonline.ie/en/Primary_School_Curriculum/Arts_Education/Music/Arts_Education_Music_arts.html. Accessed 12 Sept 2011.

Nielsen, J. (2003). Usability 101: Introduction to usability. http://www.useit.com/alertbox/20030825.html. Accessed 9 Sept 2011.

Nielsen, J. (2006). Progressive disclosure. http://www.useit.com/alertbox/progressive-disclosure.html. Accessed 9 Sept 2011.

Pachet, F. (2003). The continuator: Musical interaction with style. *Journal of New Music Research, 32*(3), 333–341.

Paine, G. (2009). Gesture and morphology in laptop music performance. In R. Dean (Ed.), *The Oxford handbook of computer music* (pp. 214–232). New York: Oxford University Press.

Ritter, F. E., & Schooler, L. J. (2002). The learning curve. In: *International encyclopedia of the social and behavioral sciences* (pp. 8602–8605). Amsterdam: Pergamon. http://www.iesbs.com/

Rowe, R. (2001). Machine musicianship. Cambridge, Massachusetts: MIT Press.

Ruso, B., Renninger, L. A., & Atzwanger, K. (2003). Human habitat preferences: A generative territory for evolutionary aesthetics research. In E. Voland & K. Grammer (Eds.), *Evolutionary aesthetics* (pp. 279–294). Heidelberg/Berlin/NewYork: Springer.

Seago, A. (2013). A new interaction strategy for musical timbre design. In S. Holland, K. Wilkie, P. Mulholland, & A. Seago (Eds.), *Music and human-computer interaction* (pp. 153–170). London: Springer. ISBN 978-1-4471-2989-9.

Smith, M., Burke, C., Draper, S., & Potter, C. (2008). The energy cost of rock drumming: a case study. European College of Sport Science (ECSS) 13th annual Congress, July 2008, Estoril, Portugal.

Smule. (2008). iPhone Ocarina. http://ocarina.smule.com/. Accessed 20 Nov 2011.

Stowell, D., & McLean, A. (2013). Live music-making: A rich open task requires a rich open interface. In S. Holland, K. Wilkie, P. Mulholland, & A. Seago (Eds.), *Music and human-computer interaction* (pp. 139–152). London: Springer. ISBN 978-1-4471-2989-9.

Stuart, C. (2003). The object of performance: Aural performativity in contemporary laptop music. *Contemporary Music Review, 22*(4), 59–65.

Suthers, D. D. (2001). Towards a systematic study of representational guidance for collaborative learning discourse. *Journal of Universal Computer Science, 7*(3).

Swift, B. (2013). Chasing a feeling: Experience in computer supported jamming. In S. Holland, K. Wilkie, P. Mulholland, & A. Seago (Eds.), *Music and human-computer interaction* (pp. 85–100). London: Springer. ISBN 978-1-4471-2989-9.

Tammelin, O, (1999). Jeskola Buzz. http://jeskola.net/buzz. Accessed 12 Sept 2011.

Tanaka, A. (2000). Musical performance practice on sensor-based instruments. In *Trends in gestural control of music*. Centre Pompidou: IRCAM.

Thornhill, R. (2003). Darwinian aesthetics informs traditional aesthetics. In E. Voland & K. Grammer (Eds.), *Evolutionary aesthetics* (pp. 9–35). Berlin: Springer.

TOPLAP. (2011). http://www.toplap.org/index.php/ManifestoDraft. Accessed 12 Sept 2011.

Van Nimwegen, C., van Oostendorp, H., & Schijf, H. J. M. (2004). Externalization vs. Internalization: The influence on problem solving performance. In *Proceedings of the IEEE International Conference on Advanced Learning Technologies (ICALT'04)*. Piscataway: IEEE.

Wagner, R. (1830). *The virtuoso and the artist* (trans. Ellis, W.). http://users.belgacom.net/wagnerlibrary/prose/wagvirtu.htm. Accessed 9 Sept 2011.

Wallis, I., Ingalls, T., Campana, E., & Vuong, C. (2013). Amateur musicians, long-term engagement, and HCI. In S. Holland, K. Wilkie, P. Mulholland, & A. Seago (Eds.), *Music and human-computer interaction* (pp. 49–66). London: Springer. ISBN 978-1-4471-2989-9.

Wilson, W. (2002). Six views of embodied cognition. *Psychonomic Bulletin and Review, 9*(4), 625–636.

Chapter 3
Amateur Musicians, Long-Term Engagement, and HCI

Isaac Wallis, Todd Ingalls, Ellen Campana, and Catherine Vuong

Abstract Musical instruments have a property of long-term engagement: people frequently become so engaged with them that they practice and play them for years, despite receiving no compensation other than enjoyment. We examine this phenomenon by analysing how the intrinsic motives mastery, autonomy, and purpose are built into the design of musical instruments; because, according to the self-determination theory of motivation, these three motives impact whether an activity might be found enjoyable. This analysis resulted in the identification of seven abstract qualities, inherent to the activity of music making or to the design of musical instruments, which contribute to the three intrinsic motives. These seven qualities can be treated as heuristics for the design of human-computer interfaces that have long-term engagement. These heuristics can be used throughout the design process, from the preliminary stage of idea generation to the evaluation stage of finished prototypes. Interfaces with instrument-like long-term engagement would be useful in many applications, both inside and outside the realm of music: they seem particularly suited for applications based on the attainment of long-term goals, which can be found in fields such as physical fitness, rehabilitation, education, and many others. In this chapter, we discuss an interface prototype we created and its pending evaluation. This interface, a rehabilitative rhythm game, serves as a case study showing how the heuristics might be used during the design process.

I. Wallis (✉) • T. Ingalls • E. Campana
School of Arts, Media, and Engineering, Arizona State University, Tempe, AZ 85287, USA
e-mail: iwallis@asu.edu; testcase@asu.edu; ecampana@asu.edu

C. Vuong
School of Biological and Health Systems Engineering, Arizona State University, Tempe, AZ, USA
e-mail: catherine.vuong@asu.edu

S. Holland et al. (eds.), *Music and Human-Computer Interaction*, Springer Series on Cultural Computing, DOI 10.1007/978-1-4471-2990-5_3,

3.1 Introduction

Musical instruments draw a high level of engagement from musicians. Amateur musicians, in particular, exhibit a great deal of engagement with regard to practicing instruments. They are not paid for practicing, but many do so on a near-daily basis over the course of years. They are often self-taught, picking up knowledge and techniques from peers and Internet research. For them, practicing is a form of entertainment on par with television. The ability of musical instruments to draw this level of engagement from hobbyist musicians stands in contrast to many human-computer interfaces: as any interface developer can attest, it is challenging to create an interface which does not quickly grow tiresome to users.

Most literature from the intersection of music and HCI focuses on the development of new interfaces for making music. Some of this literature focuses on the application of HCI principles to instrument design (e.g. Wanderley 2002; Wessel and Wright 2001). Of that, some is authored by expert musicians, and seems focused on interfaces for other expert musicians (e.g. Trueman and Cook 2001). Here, we take a different approach: instead of using concepts from HCI to improve musical instrument design, we look for qualities of musical instruments that inspire long-term engagement as seen in amateur musicians. Then we generalise these qualities for application in the development of HCI.

If any qualities of instruments exist which inspire long-term engagement, and can apply to HCI, it follows that these qualities should be considered possible design elements when trying to make engaging interfaces. Using psychological literature as inspiration, we looked at the design of instruments and the activity of music performance in order to identify any qualities that satisfy these constraints. The seven qualities we identified are discussed in this chapter. These qualities can be thought of simultaneously as potential qualities of devices or interfaces (such as instruments), potential qualities of activities (such as music performance), and as design goals or heuristics when creating interfaces for long-term engagement.

3.2 The Motivation to Play Instruments

One theory explaining the behaviours of hobbyist musicians is the self-determination theory (SDT) of motivation (Ryan and Deci 2000). In SDT, behaviour results from intrinsic or extrinsic motives. Extrinsic motives are related to factors out of the individual's direct control, such as rewards or punishments (e.g. grades, remuneration). Intrinsic motives come from within the individual, and have more to do with the sense of enjoyment. People that are intrinsically motivated to perform an activity, do so without regard for extrinsic incentives. In empirical validations of SDT, it was found that intrinsically motivated participants tend to perform better and persist longer in a given activity than extrinsically motivated participants. It was also found that incentivising an activity with rewards or punishments serves to decrease the level of intrinsic motivation of activity participants. This highlights an important difference between SDT and other relevant theories of motivation such as Reiss's multifaceted theory of motivation (2004), Tinto's theories of student persistence (1975), or Maslow's hierarchy of needs (1970). These theories hold all motives to be similar in kind and additive; therefore an individual's motivation to do an activity is determined by adding up the impacts of a variety of physiological needs, outside incentives, sociocultural factors, and intrinsic motives. However, because of the way intrinsic and extrinsic motivation levels interact with one another, this paradigm does not hold in SDT. Overall motivation to do an activity can be less than the sum of intrinsic and extrinsic motivation for that activity.

Amateur musicians, and other hobbyists, do not receive or require extrinsic incentives in order to remain engaged with their activity. For this reason, SDT seems to be a very useful theory of motivation for study about long-term engagement as it regards music—it is also frequently cited in music education literature (e.g. Austin et al. 2006; Hallam 2002). SDT defines three intrinsic motives: mastery, autonomy, and purpose.[1] People tend to enjoy activities containing these intrinsic motives; for example, all hobbies seem to have at least one of them. Instrument playing has all three intrinsic motives, and the field of HCI can be informed by the way music and instruments facilitate these motives.

Although many non-musical activities have the property of long-term engagement, instrument playing is especially relevant to HCI, because there are some conceptual similarities between instruments and human-computer interfaces. Just as HCI is designed to simplify and enable a variety of complex tasks, instruments exist to simplify and enable the act of music generation. If defined broadly enough, the category of interfaces includes musical instruments, and one might say musicians use instruments to "interface" with sound, audiences, and each other. In addition to these conceptual similarities, there are aspects of instrument playing which could be incorporated into the field of HCI to great benefit, such as the following:

- Instrument practice is a way for musicians to gradually attain their long-term goals of musical expertise. Some interfaces are similarly based on the achievement of long-term goals.
- Instrumentalists practice in order to attain skill so they can perform complex music more easily. This is a useful paradigm in HCI when difficulty cannot be avoided: **practice-oriented HCI** can facilitate the attainment of skill thereby allowing users to manage higher levels of difficulty.
- Instrument learning results in nuanced and masterful bodily movement in instrumentalists. Tangible, gestural, or motion-based interfaces can also benefit from nuanced and masterful movement.

The following sections describe the relationship between instruments and the intrinsic motives in more detail. We treat the intrinsic motives as qualities of activities, interfaces, or interface designs; all of these can be characterised according to the degree they facilitate the intrinsic motives, and this allowed the use of analytical reasoning to examine why each intrinsic motive might exist in instruments.

[1]Per Ryan and Deci, the intrinsic motives are labelled competence, autonomy, and relatedness. We adopt nomenclature used by Pink (2009).

Table 3.1 Summarises design heuristics proposed in this chapter, and describes their impact on long-term engagement

Motive	Heuristic	Description	Impact
Mastery	Incrementality	Whether progression in difficulty from beginner to expert is gradual	Maximises flow state in users; impacts persistence within activity
	Complexity	Potential complexity of interaction; ceiling of expertise	Impacts longevity of long-term engagement
	Immediacy	Whether obstacles to participating in the activity are low	Impacts number of people initiating and persisting in the activity
Autonomy	Ownership	Whether users have options, configurability, or ways to express or invest themselves	Imparts sense that the interface is best suited for user
	Operational Freedom	Whether interaction seems driven by user or interface	Lack of free operation leads to boredom
Purpose	Demonstrability	Whether user can demo expertise to other	Incentivises mastery and draws new users
	Cooperation	Whether users can work together	Fosters community of sharing and motivating

Through this process, we inferred the existence of seven qualities contributing to the intrinsic motives in instruments. These qualities are conceptual and abstract, but each satisfies the conditions discussed in the introduction to this chapter: First, they each increase long-term engagement by contributing to the existence of mastery, autonomy, or purpose. Second, although they describe aspects of instruments or the act of playing instruments, they easily transfer to the field of HCI. Some users will always exhibit more engagement than others, but interfaces with these qualities should prompt more engagement in users over a long term. The qualities are discussed in the following subsections and summarised in Table 3.1.

3.2.1 Mastery

People are motivated by mastery if they feel they are good at, or capable of becoming good at, something difficult. In looking at instruments for conceptual qualities contributing to mastery, we found three that are applicable in HCI development: **incrementality** of increases in challenge; maximum potential **complexity** of interaction; and **immediacy**, meaning a lack of obstacles or delays in practicing the activity. These qualities are discussed in the following subsections.

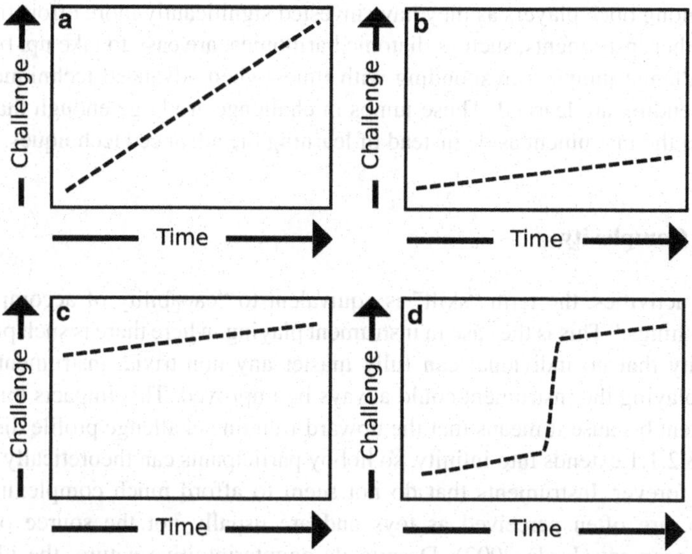

Fig. 3.1 Incrementality profiles. (**a**) Ideal profile for long-term engagement. (**b**) Users may grow bored in the short term. (**c**) Users may be overwhelmed at the outset. (**d**) Users may be engaged at first, but overwhelmed at the challenge jump

3.2.1.1 Incrementality

Incrementality describes the gradualness of the learning curve in an activity. The motive of mastery is due in part to the pursuit of flow (Csikszentmihalyi 1990). Flow is an enjoyable mental state attainable through performing activities that are complex but not overwhelming. Extrapolating from this, it follows that the challenge involved in any long-term activity inducing flow will likely conform to a specific profile over time: it will start small for beginners, then increase gradually as skill is attained (Fig. 3.1). If challenge increases too quickly, participants may become overwhelmed and quit, and if it increases too slowly, participants may become bored and lose interest. The way this challenge profile is manifested varies from activity to activity. Video games, for example, manage challenge through levels and scoring. Instrumentalists, on the other hand, manage their own challenge levels: there is such a diversity of music available to learn that musicians at all skill levels typically have an abundance of appropriately difficult music.

There are differences in incrementality between instruments, and these differences illustrate relationships between incrementality, the size of a user base, and the dedication of a user base. For example, it takes practice to play one's first notes on an oboe. There are fewer players of this type of instrument than instruments that are easy to play notes on, such as piano. However, dedication is probably higher among oboe players as they have invested significantly more effort from the outset. Other instruments, such as diatonic harmonica, are easy to take up, but have large challenge jumps corresponding with times when advanced techniques such as note bending are learned. These jumps in challenge are large enough that some people set the instrument aside instead of learning the advanced techniques.

3.2.1.2 Complexity

In many activities, the term "skill" is equivalent to "capability of accomplishing complex things." This is the case in instrument playing, where there is such potential complexity that no individual can fully master any non-trivial instrument; some facet of playing the instrument could always be improved. This impacts long-term engagement because it means that the upward-trending challenge profile discussed in Sect. 3.2.1.1 extends into infinity, so hobby participants can theoretically remain engaged forever. Instruments that do not seem to afford much complexity, such as kazoo, are often perceived as toys and are usually not the source of long-term engagement (Jordà 2002). Despite its counterintuitive nature, the idea that interactive complexity is a positive design trait is not new to the field of HCI: for example, Norman (2010) provides an exhaustive argument in favour of design complexity.

The quality of complexity is related to other heuristic qualities discussed in this chapter: it can be thought of as the ceiling or end-point of the incrementality profile, and it is also a frequent by-product in systems containing high levels of ownership and operational freedom (these qualities are discussed in Sect. 3.2.2). Interaction complexity should not be forced on beginning users, and designers should avoid extraneous or confusing interface elements, but the potential for complex interactions should exist for users with sufficient skill levels. Systems should not, for example, demand endless repetition from users, nor present overly repetitive feedback. Once users encounter perceived limits to a system's interactive complexity, their engagement may drop. Consider video gaming: once players have defeated a game, they will probably play it less frequently.

3.2.1.3 Immediacy

Some instruments are practiced as a daily hobby, in part, simply because they are easy to practice in this way. These instruments can be left on a stand in a convenient location, so picking them up and playing a few notes takes little effort. This is an example of immediacy. Activities with immediacy have minimal obstacles, where obstacles can come in logistic, temporal, or economic forms. Anything that serves to delay the practice of an activity constitutes a reduction in immediacy.

Differences in immediacy exist between instruments, and these differences illustrate a relationship between immediacy and instrument popularity. Traditional harps have less immediacy than harmonicas because they are not portable and much more expensive. Traditional organs have less immediacy than guitars because guitars are fairly ubiquitous while organs are rare and fixed to specific sites. Software instruments have less immediacy than flutes because of the delay involved in starting up the computer and launching the software.

Since immediacy impacts the likelihood of someone taking up an activity and persisting within it, interface designers should note that a relationship will exist between immediacy and the size of the user base. Therefore, if other things are equal, one way of promoting an interface's success is ensuring it has the quality of immediacy. In many cases, this will entail careful selection of the HCI delivery vehicle, as this will impact many factors relating to immediacy, such as: latency and start-up times, ease of setup and use, portability or ubiquitousness, and how expensive an interface is to obtain. For example, immediacy is a common factor between many recent successful interfaces delivered via the iPhone, Nintendo Wii, or Macbook.

3.2.2 Autonomy

People are motivated by autonomy if they feel they freely choose to do an activity, and do it in their own way. Lack of autonomy seems to restrict motivation greatly even when there is a high degree of mastery and purpose. An everyday example of this lies in the many employees who dislike their jobs despite high levels of skill and teamwork involved. Incentivising activities that might otherwise be intrinsically motivating with reward or punishment is counterproductive, in terms of engagement, as this reduces feelings of autonomy (Ryan and Deci 2000). In looking at instruments for conceptual qualities contributing to autonomy, we found two that are applicable in interface design: **ownership** of activity, and **operational freedom** within the activity. These qualities are discussed in the following subsections.

3.2.2.1 Ownership

In musical instruments, mastery and autonomy are related. The diversity of music affords its incrementality and complexity, and also affords a completely individualised path of learning for instrumentalists. Ergo, each musician can consider their playing style to be unique, best suited for them, and therefore "owned" by them. Renowned masters of music provide case studies on stylistic ownership: for example, Franz Liszt and Art Tatum are both considered absolute masters of the piano, yet their styles and techniques were highly dissimilar. The sense of ownership is one factor allowing musicians to consider their music to be a form of self-expression. Since playing styles are developed with great effort over the course of long periods of time, ownership in instrumental performance also represents investment that may deter musicians from quitting.

One way to transfer the concept of ownership to HCI design is to integrate options and end-user configurability into the interface. Another way, used frequently in video games, consists of rewarding accomplishment of interface goals with access to new customisations, interactions, or advanced features. A less obvious tactic for transferring the concept of ownership to HCI, advocated by Sengers and Gaver (2005), is intentionally making interaction or feedback very abstract, so users must construct the meaning of the interface for themselves.

3.2.2.2 Operational Freedom

Musicians perceive few restrictions on their freedom to play an instrument in their own way, because they can draw from a large number of playing styles or techniques whenever they wish. When numerous ways to interact with an interface exist which can be applied at will, that interface can be said to have operational freedom. Interfaces containing operational freedom will tend to also have potential interactive complexity. Some users may not use their operational freedom to do very complex things, but potential complexity exists nonetheless, because users are capable of combining or sequencing interactions in innovative ways to create complex outcomes. When operational freedom is very limited users may lose engagement rapidly.

Sometimes in HCI, specific user interactions are desired, either because of the application or because of other factors such as constraints in the sensing technology. For example, movement rehabilitation systems often need to encourage beneficial movement habits while discouraging poor movement habits (e.g. Wallis et al. 2007). Designing for operational freedom can be challenging in these circumstances, but musical instruments provide an applicable model. As noted by Jordà (2002), instruments have affordances, and these affordances lead to stylistic similarities among the players of any given instrument. Expert musicians are sometimes capable of going beyond the natural affordances of an instrument, but in most cases playing techniques will converge to the most efficient and ergonomic possible. Transferring this concept to HCI development, when specific user interactions are needed, designers can integrate affordances into their interfaces so users will gravitate to desired interactions without perceiving restricted operational freedom. This insight is not new to the field of HCI: many theorists have expounded on the topic of designing affordances (e.g. Gaver 1991; Norman 2002).

3.2.3 *Purpose*

According to SDT, the motive of purpose is evoked by activities containing a social element or an element of relatedness with other people. Purpose seems to be important when people are deciding to take on new hobbies, or choosing between otherwise similar hobbies. For instance, there are few differences between guitar and ukulele in terms of mastery and autonomy, but ukulele players are much less common. Social factors may cause some of this difference in popularity.

In hobbies outside the realm of music, purpose varies widely: some hobbies are competitive, some hobbies are based on communities of like-minded people, some hobbies afford quality time with family, and so forth. In looking at instrumental music performance for conceptual qualities contributing to purpose, we found two that seem applicable in interface design: **demonstrability** of skill, and **cooperation** among users. These two qualities seem well suited for helping a hobby proliferate quickly through a populace. They are discussed in the following subsections.

3.2.3.1 Demonstrability

People often learn instruments in order to attain skill and play for others. They may initially choose to take up an instrument because they have heard impressively performed music on that instrument (Manturzewska 1990). Demonstrability is related to mastery, because it is the payoff for attaining expertise in an activity. Demonstrability is also related to autonomy: music is thought of as a form of self-expression precisely due to its autonomous qualities. If interfaces are designed such that users produce something that can be displayed, performed, or shared in some way, this will encourage users to attain greater levels of skill, and these users may impress and attract more new users.

3.2.3.2 Cooperation

Music making can be done in solo or ensemble settings. The option to play in ensembles contributes to the motive of purpose, as musicians are often motivated to practice by the prospect of jam sessions, drum circles, duets, and so forth. These represent social opportunities, allowing players to spend time with peers and make new friends. As noted by Swift in this volume (2013), musicians often describe a shared feeling of euphoria, immersion, and engagement when playing or improvising music well together. Cooperation also allows musicians to teach one another, inspire one another, and motivate one another. If interfaces are designed to be used in group settings, and efforts are made to increase community among users (for example, through online forums and wikis) this will help increase overall engagement within the user base. It will also help attract new users and speed the attainment of skill in the user community as a non-competitive environment of knowledge sharing and group discovery develops. According to Tinto's theories of student persistence (1997), social integration will also reduce an individual's likelihood of quitting.

3.3 Application to HCI Development

Since the seven qualities discussed in Sect. 3.2 contribute to the intrinsic motivation of instrument playing, we propose to use them as a set of heuristics for designing interfaces that are intrinsically motivating. The resulting heuristic design framework is summarised in Table 3.1. Whenever HCI developers design systems that could benefit from long-term engagement, these heuristics can be used as catalysts for thought. Developers should ask themselves questions like: "Is this system demonstrable?" or "Would different sensing technology make this system more immediate?" The qualities underlying these heuristics are not the only ones possibly inspiring long-term engagement: for example, many engaging hobbies are more competitive than cooperative. The popularity of the instrument-playing hobby indicates, however, that this set of qualities is compelling.

The heuristics can be considered at any stage of design; this includes preliminary idea generation and analysis of finished prototypes. The most utility might be drawn from the heuristic framework if it is applied at the very outset of the design process, when the designer has done nothing except identify a human-centred problem to be addressed with an interface (where the problem could benefit from long-term engagement in users). This will help avoid premising the interface on some application or type of interaction that is not conducive to long-term engagement. Designers using these strategies will tend to create interfaces that have creative elements, game-like elements, or elements of knowledge or skill building. Not coincidentally, one or more of these elements are found in essentially all hobbies. However, if for some reason the interface cannot contain any of these elements, this framework may prove to be of little assistance.

When using the heuristics to inform the preliminary idea of an interface, it may be useful for designers to address the human-centred problem from the perspective of creating engaging activities, rather than engaging interfaces. In other words, the interface being developed should be thought of as a portal or facilitator to an engaging activity. This is helpful in part because there are numerous existing hobbies and activities that people find engaging over long time periods. These can be mined for ideas: if a compelling activity already exists that can be facilitated with interfaces (e.g. word puzzles), designers may be able to create a slightly modified interface for that activity which also addresses the human-centred problem (e.g. an interface using word puzzles to help users learn foreign languages).

Some HCI theories are focused on strategies for designing interfaces that deliver fun, enjoyable, positive user experiences (e.g. Blythe et al. 2003; Hassenzahl and Tractinsky 2006; Malone 1984). The ideas in this chapter represent one possible approach for accomplishing this; in fact, they are readily applicable to the design of interfaces in which there is no human-centred problem being addressed beyond that of entertainment or self-expression. However, numerous human-centred problems exist in more utilitarian realms such as education, fitness, or rehabilitation, which could benefit greatly from interfaces facilitating long-term engagement. Interfaces addressing these problems must be engaging, because unless users adopt and use these interfaces frequently over a long period of time, these systems will not succeed in their human-centred goals.

If interfaces have long-term engagement, users will freely opt to use them, and the interfaces will draw these users repeatedly back over time. This suggests that the ideas in this paper might be used in the design of practice-oriented HCI: interfaces helping users practice and perform tasks that are unavoidably difficult. For example, in some applications, complex and rapid-paced interactions are required from users. These situations are like music in that practice is required. Interfaces can be designed to facilitate that practice and make it enjoyable. Similarly, sometimes large-scale complex deliverables are needed from users. Clearly, engaging interfaces might help users stay on task; but perhaps less obviously, practice-oriented interfaces might also help users attain skill at producing the deliverables more quickly and easily. An analogy illustrating this lies in the difference between composers and improvisers of music. Whereas a composer might painstakingly score musical events over the course of hours or days, a practiced improviser might create music of the same complexity with little effort, taking only the requisite time to produce the notes on the instrument.

Practice-oriented HCI may prove to be an important concept as new tangible, gestural, and motion analysis-based interfaces emerge in the marketplace. Such interfaces often afford a greater degree of nuance and technical skill than traditional keyboard-and-mouse interfaces, but nuance and technical skill are attained with practice. If people practiced these interfaces in the way amateur musicians practice instruments, they might eventually be capable of efficient, nuanced, and technically skilled interface control. This also suggests that interfaces could be designed for the sole purpose of getting users to focus more awareness on their own bodily movements. Movement awareness is beneficial in itself—ergonomic movement techniques such as the Alexander Technique are built around it (Jones 1997).

3.3.1 HCI Evaluation for Long-Term Engagement

Although there is no single optimal method for evaluating various interfaces for long-term engagement, long-term engagement user studies will tend to have certain commonalities. For instance, participant recruitment should be based solely on interest, and continuing participation should also be based on interest. Payments, incentives, or rewards for participation should be avoided. These will distort the data because long-term engagement is related to intrinsic motivation, which is depressed and eclipsed by extrinsic incentives. Therefore, one potential challenge when evaluating interfaces for long-term engagement is attracting study participants.

Most evaluations of long-term engagement will require accurate tracking of the time each participant spends on the interface. The sum total of the time spent can then be compared to the amount of time available to participants. This results in a frequency-of-use ratio loosely correlating with engagement levels.

This frequency-of-use ratio is an indirect metric (engagement cannot be quantified directly) and may be considered misleading in cases where participants are actually engaged with some activity coinciding with interface usage. For example, collage artists may frequently use photo-editing software, but this does not prove engagement with the interface: if the software did not exist the artists would work with scissors. In many cases, however, the reason long-term engagement is desired is because it maximises frequency-of-use, in which case this caveat may not apply.

Interface designers may wish to evaluate interfaces with regard to the seven heuristics. Such evaluations could prove very informative. Using quantitative evaluation techniques to measure the heuristics would be difficult and fraught with problems, however. First, the qualities the heuristics are based on are abstract constructs and cannot be measured directly, so any metrics used will be indirect metrics and may have misleading properties. Second, each quality is highly variable in its manifestation within an interface: for example, operational freedom means something different in video games, where users freely control animated characters, than it does in virtual musical instruments, where users freely control sounds. It would be challenging to construct a measurement of operational freedom equally applicable in both types of interfaces. Quantitative evaluations of the heuristics may be most useful when comparing heuristic levels between different versions of singular interfaces; it is more likely the versions will manifest the qualities in comparable ways.

Although the heuristic qualities cannot be easily evaluated with quantitative methods, they can be evaluated using standard qualitative methods. Heuristic evaluation is typically done through having a small sample of users rate the interface according to each heuristic, making note of any issues found that result in poor ratings. This should lead to the discovery of any major design problems, as these will be noted by all users, and also result in the identification of a number of areas of possible improvement discovered by smaller subsets of users (Nielsen and Molich 1990). In addition to the standard heuristic evaluation, surveys or interviews can be performed in order to glean heuristic-specific information, using both broad-scope questions (e.g. "What do or don't you like about this system?") and heuristic-specific questions (e.g. "Do you find this system too easy or hard? Do you find it gives you enough freedom?"). Observation of user interaction with the interface will also prove informative: if it is observed that participants have gained the ability to improvise and be creative with a complex interface, for example, this could indicate a degree of familiarity that comes with engagement and frequent practice.

Efforts should be made to gather the impressions of participants and researchers at every stage of system usage. Participants at the beginning and end stages of engaging with the system will provide especially important insights. Understanding the quality of complexity in an interface, for example, may require data from participants who are beginning to lose interest. This points to an obvious challenge when evaluating interfaces for long-term engagement: the length of time required. Engagement with a well-designed interface could conceivably last a lifetime, but full understanding of interface deficiencies or possible improvements requires data from a sample of users who became engaged with, and subsequently lost interest in, the interface. The ideal evaluation would not end until all participants quit using the interface of their own volition, but that could take a prohibitively long period of time.

3.3.2 Case Study: A Rehabilitative Game for Parkinson's Patients

This section describes a case study that is currently underway. At this stage, the heuristics have been used to design an interface, and a prototype exists, but evaluation of long-term engagement is pending. This section is meant only to provide an example of heuristic usage in the design process.

Research shows early-stage Parkinson's disease patients can slow deterioration in some symptoms by performing wide-amplitude movement exercises as part of their physical therapy. There are a variety of exercises for this purpose, but the wide-amplitude nature of the movements is the key common factor (Farley and Koshland 2005). Physical therapists may guide patients through these exercises in one-on-one sessions or in groups. With the latter, the therapist leads the group from the front of the room in an arrangement similar to that seen in aerobics classes. Unfortunately, some Parkinson's patients may not find the exercises engaging, due to their repetitious nature. Or, with the group classes, patients may feel self-conscious when performing movement exercises in front of others.

If an interface were developed requiring users to perform wide-amplitude movements in order to do an engaging activity, this could benefit many Parkinson's patients. In looking at relevant existing activities, rhythm games seem suited to this human-centred problem. Existing rhythm games have similarities with aerobics classes: *Wii Step*,[2] for example, is modelled directly on step-aerobics. Recent studies suggest that movement-based video games may be an effective means of engaging and rehabilitating patients of all ages (Sugarman et al. 2009; Clark and Kraemer 2009). Therefore, in this case study we created a rhythm game early-stage Parkinson's patients might use, designed to encourage wide-amplitude arm movements.

3.3.2.1 Standard Rhythm Games

Rhythm games, as exemplified by popular video games such as *Wii Step*, *Guitar Hero* (Harmonix 2005), and *Dance Dance Revolution* (Konami 1998), challenge players to closely synchronise with a complex sequence of actions. This sequence of actions is given by the game, and action timing is usually related to a background song in some way. For this reason, it is useful to think of each sequence-song

[2] *Wii Step* is in Nintendo's *Wii Fit* (2008) suite of games.

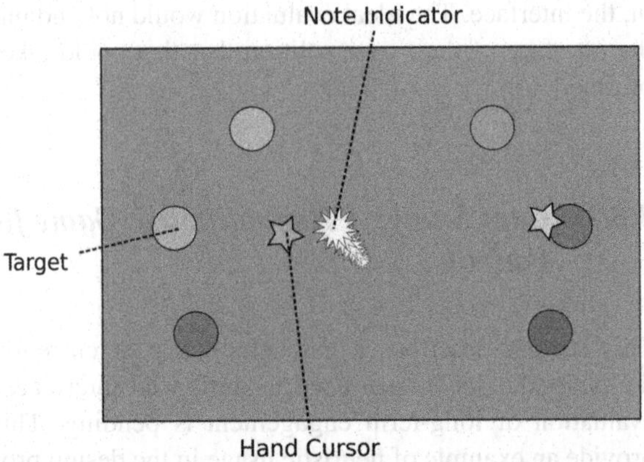

Fig. 3.2 This is a diagram of visual layout in the case study rehabilitative game

combination as a game session, or a song-game. Most rhythm games contain large libraries of song-games. Existing rhythm games are fairly well designed in terms of the heuristics related to mastery. They have incrementality, because their song-game libraries are large and diverse enough that players at all levels will find song-games of an appropriate difficulty. They also have a measure of immediacy, as they are relatively low-cost and easy to set up. They are somewhat limited in potential complexity: once the most difficult song-games can be defeated with ease, players are unlikely to continue being engaged.

The case study system uses a visual interface layout similar to that seen in Fig. 3.2. This interface contains three interactive elements: (1) *Hand Cursors* are visual indicators, the locations of which are driven by motion tracking on the player's hands—we use Microsoft's Kinect sensor to perform this hand tracking. (2) *Targets* are areas of the virtual space that the player must touch in accordance with the game's sequence of actions. Each target is attached to a musical pitch. (3) *Note Indicators* make up the sequence of actions; these radiate out from the centre toward individual targets. Whenever a note indicator reaches a target, a hand cursor must simultaneously touch that target. If this happens, the target's musical tone, which is a melodic tone designed to accompany the background track, will play. If not, a less pleasant "flubbed" sound will occur.

3.3.2.2 Applying the Heuristic Framework: A Creative Mode

The object of rhythm games, synchronising with song-game action sequences, is not conducive to the motive of autonomy. Therefore, in order to increase long-term engagement, a creative mode is added to this system. This creative mode allows players to create their own song-games. In the creative mode, there are no note indicators telling players where and when to reach for targets, and targets play melodic tones whenever touched by the hand cursors (instead of when touched simultaneously by hand cursors and note indicators). This effectively turns the interface into a virtual musical instrument. A background track still plays, but is chosen by the player and uploaded from among the player's own audio files. To create a song-game, players improvise along with their selected background track using the interface. The notes they play are saved as an action sequence into a centralised location. Then others can play that action sequence as a song-game: generated note indicators will direct users to play the saved improvisation.

This creative mode simultaneously solves many problems. It adds ownership because it lets players select their own background tracks. It adds free operation through letting players improvise. It adds demonstrability through the production of new song-games that are sharable (this is also a rehabilitative feature allowing physical therapists to create song-games attuned to their patients). It even adds complexity, because it results in an ever-expanding song-game library. Cooperation is the only heuristic quality not explicitly improved by the creative mode; however, that could be improved through the creation of online forums, wikis, and videos pertaining to the game. It could be improved further if a two-person creative mode were implemented, affording musical concepts like call-and-response.

3.3.2.3 Evaluating the Rhythm Game for Long-Term Engagement

This evaluation of the case study interface is pending. The system will be installed, as if it were an arcade game, in a public area of a university building where classes are held. This ensures that a significant number of possible users will frequently pass by due to their class schedules. Anyone who wishes may register for a login and password, after which they may play the rhythm game for free as much as they like. Users need not provide their real names upon registration; however, we will request their email addresses so that we can resupply forgotten passwords and follow up with players once they have lost interest with the game. The study will run for 3 months. This time period is based in part upon the length of a university semester, as the majority of our participants will be students with classes scheduled near the evaluation installation.

The login accounts will be used to track how often people return to play the game, and to calculate frequency-of-use over the population of account-holders. Between song-games, survey questions will appear. These questions will be designed to: (1) ascertain levels of player engagement; (2) obtain overall player impressions on the game's design, (3) gain an understanding of the interface with regard to the heuristics, and (4) determine the extent to which individual users have been engaged by musical performance or video games in the past, so we can control for that.

Since this game is partially intended to serve as proof-of-concept for the theories in this chapter, blocks of users will have different levels of access to game features. For example, some users will not have access to easy song-games, and others will not have access to difficult ones; this should give us a better understanding of incrementality in our interface. Some users will have no access to the creative mode; this should allow us to better understand the impact of those qualities enhanced by the creative mode. Like many theoretical frameworks based in psychology, the ideas presented in this chapter may never be proven in any definitive sense. However, if the heuristics are shown to result in a more engaging interface design in our case, this suggests they may be used to increase long-term engagement in other interfaces.

3.4 Conclusion

In this chapter, we began the process of creating a theory of design for interfaces containing the quality of long-term engagement. According to the self-determination theory of motivation, engaging activities are intrinsically motivated by the qualities of mastery, autonomy, and purpose. We examined why these motives are elicited in amateur musicians, extrapolating seven properties of instruments and music contributing to the three intrinsic motives. These seven properties—incrementality, complexity, immediacy, ownership, operational freedom, demonstrability, and cooperation—are transferrable to the field of HCI as heuristics for the design of interfaces which are engaging over longer time periods. These heuristics can be used in every stage of interface design, from generation of ideas through evaluation of finished prototypes.

An example system was designed, as a case study, using these heuristics. This system is a rehabilitative rhythm game, differing from other rhythm games in the addition of a creative mode enhancing the heuristic qualities related to autonomy and purpose. This system has been prototyped, and an evaluation of this system with regard to long-term engagement is among our next steps. This evaluation will help validate and refine elements of the heuristic framework.

In summary, we believe that if the intrinsic motives of mastery, autonomy, and purpose are explicitly designed into HCI, long-term engagement will be increased. Instruments provide these motives through the seven qualities discussed in this chapter. Therefore, integrating these qualities into interfaces is one way to make them more engaging over the long term. Interfaces with long-term engagement would be useful in various applications, including applications based on long-term goals, applications benefitting from practiced users, and applications for enjoyment and self-expression. Lastly, the ideas in this chapter can be used to maximise the impact and success of any human-computer interface, because engaging interfaces are likely to become popular interfaces.

Acknowledgments The material in this chapter is partially supported by the National Science Foundation CISE Infrastructure grant under Grant No. 0403428 and IGERT Grant No. 0504647. Thanks to Kristi Rogers for her helpful comments.

References

Austin, J., Renwick, J., & McPherson, G. (2006). Developing motivation. In G. McPherson (Ed.), *The child as musician*. New York: Oxford University Press.

Blythe, M., Overbeeke, K., Monk, A., & Wright, P. (2003). *Funology: From usability to enjoyment*. New York: Springer.

Clark, R., & Kraemer, T. (2009). Clinical use of Nintendo Wii bowling simulation to decrease fall risk in an elderly resident of a nursing home: A case report. *Journal of Geriatric Physical Therapy, 32*(4), 174–180.

Csikszentmihalyi, M. (1990). *Flow: The psychology of optimal experience*. New York: Harper and Row.

Farley, B., & Koshland, G. (2005). Training big to move faster: The application of the speed–amplitude relation as a rehabilitation strategy for people with Parkinson's disease. *Experimental Brain Research, 167*, 462–467.

Gaver. (1991). Technology affordances. In *Proceedings of the CHI '91*. New Orleans, USA, April 27–May 02.

Hallam, S. (2002). Musical motivation: Towards a model synthesising the research. *Music Education Research, 4*(2), 225–244.

Harmonix (2005). Guitar hero. http://www.guitarhero.com. Accessed 22 May 2011.

Hassenzahl, M., & Tractinsky, N. (2006). User experience—a research agenda. *Behavior and Information Technology, 25*(2), 91–97.

Jones, F. (1997). *Freedom to change: Development and science of the Alexander technique*. London: Mouritz.

Jordà, S. (2002). FMOL: Toward user-friendly, sophisticated new musical instruments. *Computer Music Journal, 26*(3), 23–39.

Konami. (1998). Dance dance revolution. http://www.konami.com/ddr. Accessed 22 May 2011.

Malone, T. (1984). Heuristics for designing enjoyable user interfaces: Lessons from computer games. In J. C. Thomas & M. L. Schneider (Eds.), *Human factors in computer systems*. Norwood: Ablex.

Manturzewska, M. (1990). A biographical study of the life-span development of professional musicians. *Psychology of Music, 18*, 112–139.

Maslow, A. (1970). *Motivation and personality*. New York: Harper and Rowe.

Nielsen, J., & Molich, R. (1990). Heuristic evaluation of user interfaces. In *Proceedings of the CHI '90*, Seattle, USA, April 1–5.

Nintendo, E. A. D. (2008). Wii fit. http://wiifit.com. Accessed 15 Nov 2011.

Norman, D. (2002). *The design of everyday things*. New York: Basic Books.

Norman, D. (2010). *Living with complexity*. Cambridge, MA: MIT Press.

Pink, D. (2009). *Drive: The surprising truth about what motivates us*. New York: Riverhead Books.

Reiss, S. (2004). Multifaceted nature of intrinsic motivation: The theory of 16 basic desires. *Review of General Psychology, 8*(3), 179–193.

Ryan, R., & Deci, E. (2000). Self-determination theory and the facilitation of intrinsic motivation, social development, and well-being. *The American Psychologist, 55*(1), 68–78.

Sengers, P., & Gaver, B. (2005). Designing for interpretation. HCI Int, Las Vegas, USA, July 22–27.

Sugarman, H., Weisel-Eichler, A., Burstin, A., & Brown, R. (2009). Use of the Wii Fit system for the treatment of balance problems in the elderly: A feasibility study. Virtual rehabilitation international conference, Haifa, Israel, June 29–July 2.

Swift, B. (2013). Chasing a feeling: Experience in computer-supported jamming. In S. Holland, K. Wilkie, P. Mulholland, & A. Seago (Eds.), *Music and human-computer interaction* (pp. 85–100). London: Springer. ISBN 978-1-4471-2989-9.

Tinto, V. (1975). Dropout from higher education: A theoretical synthesis of recent research. *The Review of Higher Education, 45*(1), 89–125.

Tinto, V. (1997). Classrooms as communities: Exploring the educational character of student persistence. *Journal of Higher Education, 68*(6), 599–623.

Trueman, D., & Cook, P. (2001). BoSSA: The deconstructed violin reconstructed. *Journal of New Music Research, 29*, 2.

Wallis, I., Ingalls, T., Rikakis, T., Olsen, L., Chen, Y., Xu, W., & Sundaram, H. (2007). Real-time sonification of movement for an immersive stroke rehabilitation environment. In *Proceedings of the international conference audit display*, Montréal, Canada, June 26–29.

Wanderley, M. (2002). Evaluation of input devices for musical expression: Borrowing tools from HCI. *Computer Music Journal, 26*, 3.

Wessel, D., & Wright, M. (2001). Problems and prospects for intimate musical control of computers. In *Proceedings of the CHI workshop new interfaces music expression*, Seattle, USA, April 1–2.

Chapter 4
Affective Musical Interaction: Influencing Users' Behaviour and Experiences with Music

Anna Bramwell-Dicks, Helen Petrie, Alistair D.N. Edwards, and Christopher Power

Abstract In Human-Computer Interaction (HCI) use of the auditory channel normally involves communicating information to users in the form of short, auditory messages. Given the recent trend of HCI research towards incorporating experiential objectives, we propose that the auditory channel could also be exploited for affective intent. In particular, music could be integrated within interactive technologies as a vehicle to influence users' behaviour and their experiences. This chapter describes some of the research conducted from other fields that already embrace the affective characteristic of music within their context. The limited amount of research exploiting music affectively in an HCI environment is discussed; including a review of our previous work involving Ambient Music Email (AME), an affective musical extension for email clients. By reflecting on how other subjects investigate the affective nature of music, this chapter aims to show that the HCI field is falling behind and inspire further work in this area. In fact, there are a wide variety of potential motivations for working with affective musical interaction, with a vast realm of potential research avenues, some of which are proposed here.

4.1 Introduction

At the highest level of abstraction, the principal objective for using sounds in interactive technologies is usually to communicate information to users in the form of auditory messages. The specific incentives for using auditory messages can vary widely, but some examples include:

A. Bramwell-Dicks (✉) • H. Petrie • A.D.N. Edwards • C. Power
Department of Computer Science, University of York, York YO10 5GH, UK
e-mail: afbd500@york.ac.uk; helen.petrie@york.ac.uk; alistair.edwards@york.ac.uk; christopher.power@york.ac.uk

S. Holland et al. (eds.), *Music and Human-Computer Interaction*, Springer Series on Cultural Computing, DOI 10.1007/978-1-4471-2990-5_4,

- improving usability by providing users with auditory feedback to indicate a successfully completed interaction. For example, in mobile phone interfaces sounds can inform users that they have clicked on an icon (Brewster 2002).
- presenting data in an auditory format to aid domain-specific understanding and interpretation. For example, with seismic data (Quinn and Meeker 2001) or algorithms (Brown and Hershberger 1992).
- alerting users to the occurrence of a particular event. For example, alarms on medical devices (Sanderson 2006).
- making graphical interfaces (Edwards 1989) and data (Mansur et al. 1985) accessible to people with visual disabilities.

Although the scope of information portrayed audibly to users varies, the clear objective is to communicate information. We suggest that additional objectives can be realized by exploiting the auditory mode in different ways. There is the potential for sounds to be incorporated into interfaces in order to affect how people act when using a particular technology (i.e. the user's behaviour) as well as affecting their experiences, including felt emotions and mood. To affect users through the auditory mode, a type of audio source that has been somewhat overlooked in human-computer interaction (HCI) can be used, that of music.

This chapter describes how other fields already exploit music for its affective qualities, with both behavioural and experiential motivations. In addition, the limited amount of research in the HCI area relating to affective musical interactions is discussed, including our previous work involving the Ambient Music Email (AME) extension to email clients. Inspired by the work from other fields, a research proposal for investigating affective musical interaction is presented. In particular, considering what aspects of user experience and behaviour might be affected with music, how we can measure the impact of music on users and which musical parameters can be manipulated.

4.2 Audio Interaction

Communicating information to users has been a predominant feature of HCI research since the field's inception. Early interfaces conveyed information to users in the form of on-screen text alongside information that could be gathered audibly, for example, disc write sounds (Brewster 2003). The invention of the Graphical User Interface (GUI) permitted alternative methods to communicate information to the user visually, for example by using icons and colour. Relatively recent improvements in sound card capabilities have enabled much more detailed and precise information to be communicated audibly. This section describes how non-speech audio sounds and music have, historically, been used to communicate messages to users.

4.2.1 Non-speech Audio Interaction

Typically, auditory HCI research has concentrated on using three types of sounds; speech, sound effects e.g. Auditory Icons (Gaver 1986), and pitched tones e.g. Earcons (Blattner et al. 1989). With the latter non-speech audio types, the sounds have associated meanings that the user must decipher to understand the message that is being portrayed.

To communicate information quickly, non-speech audio sounds are often short in length. Although sometimes these sounds form part of an audio family or style, they can be quite disconnected, as they are typically distinct, separate entities. The original Earcon design proposal states that the motives employed must be kept short so that they do not resemble musical tunes which, when played repeatedly throughout the day, might irritate users (Blattner et al. 1989). Generally, the potential to annoy users with auditory interfaces has been the major aesthetic consideration taken by researchers. Typically, the intensity levels (or volume) of the sounds incorporated in audio interfaces is chosen with care, as the primary cause of irritation among users is thought to be sounds that are too loud (Brewster 1998).

Assigning meaning to individual or small groups of sounds is a compartmentalized, reductionist approach. The focus is on the messages communicated by the individual constituent sounds, rather than by the broader soundscape. With the exception of Blattner et al.'s (1989) concern about repeating Earcons, it is the annoyance caused by individual sounds rather than the impact of the wider soundscape that is usually considered.

4.2.2 Music Interaction

As auditory HCI research has evolved into using music as an additional form of non-speech audio the concentration on message communication has continued, although a more holistic approach is adopted. Music has been employed in interfaces to help users identify programming bugs (Vickers and Alty 2002), understand algorithms (Alty et al. 1997) and navigate unfamiliar locations (Jones et al. 2008). These examples of the use of music in an HCI context retain the primary objective of communicating auditory messages to users via the auditory channel. However, there are a few examples of HCI-related research exploiting the affectivity of music, described in Sect. 4.4 of this chapter.

Beyond a technological context, music is becoming ubiquitous in modern society, but not solely as a means of communication. People spend a large proportion of their time listening to music, whether this is focused, attentive listening (e.g. listening to an album to relax or going to a concert), accompanied listening where music is purposefully chosen to accompany an activity (e.g. choosing to listen to music on an mp3 player while exercising) or incidental listening (e.g. hearing background music in shops). Actively listening to music, or incidentally hearing music, rarely has the purpose of communicating a message; music is played for enjoyment or to provide a particular atmosphere. Given that people tend to listen to music for reasons other than receiving information, should auditory HCI research give more attention to alternative motivations when including music within interactive technologies?

4.3 Music as an Affective Medium

There is a growing body of evidence, from a wide variety of research fields, supporting the assertion that music has properties that can affect people, some of which is described here. Empirical research investigating the impact of music on consumers has been conducted in shops, supermarkets and restaurants, with a particular focus on music's influence on peoples' spending behaviour, with the ultimate aim of improving profitability. Additionally, empirical work has been performed in gyms where the objective was to investigate how music can improve sporting performance. In an education context, music has also been shown to impact on students' performance. Furthermore, a branch of Music Psychology is specifically dedicated to research examining the relationship between music and emotion; investigating whether music can change how someone feels or whether people are simply able to perceive emotions expressed by a piece of music (see Juslin and Sloboda 2010).

It should be noted however, that the research areas that incorporate investigating the effects of music in their remit are not limited to those described in this chapter. For example, music is integrated into films and television programs purely for its experiential characteristics. Whilst the justification for music inclusion in this context is often based purely on the belief that music enhances the screen watching experience, there have also been some examples of empirical investigations towards understanding how music impacts on film plots (e.g. see Bullerjahn and Güldenring 1994).

4.3.1 Shopping

An objective of marketing researchers is to identify different tactics for increasing a company's profitability. In a shopping context, this includes discovering which "*atmospherics*" (Kotler 1973) encourage consumers to spend more money. Marketing researchers have been investigating the affect that music has on purchasing behaviour since the 1980s; it is no coincidence that shoppers nowadays often browse and make purchases with a background musical accompaniment.

Music has been shown to impact on shoppers' behaviour in a variety of ways. The tempo of the background musical accompaniment has a significant effect on the speed that consumers walk around a supermarket and the amount of money that they spend (Milliman 1982). In this study, Milliman found that slow tempo music makes people walk significantly slower around the supermarket. These consumers spent significantly more time and more money than those shopping with a fast tempo musical accompaniment. Does this result extend to an HCI context? Would the tempo of background music affect the speed that people browse when online shopping and thus, the amount of money that they spend?

The genre of background music has also been shown to affect the amount of money that people spend (Areni and Kim 1993) in a wine store. The real life purchasing behaviour of shoppers over a 2-month period was compared in two conditions, with background Classical or Top-Forty music. The results showed that a Classical music accompaniment caused the shoppers to spend significantly more money as they purchased more expensive products, though the volume of sales was comparable across both musical genres. Does this result extend to online shopping? For example, when purchasing furniture are people more likely to buy the expensive items if their browsing activity is accompanied by Classical music?

Another wine-purchasing study investigated how the nationality of the music being played in the wine aisle of a supermarket affected the type of wine that was purchased (North et al. 1999). Shoppers bought significantly more French wine when the music in the wine aisle was French and significantly more German wine when the accompanying music was German. This study was performed in a UK supermarket so was not confounded due to the country of investigation. Of further interest is the fact that the shoppers did not believe their wine purchases were influenced by the music they heard, though they did often accept that the French music made them think of France and vice versa. The authors state that *"the finding is consistent with the notion that music can prime related knowledge and the selection of certain products if they fit with that knowledge"* (North et al. 1999).

In an HCI environment, this result could suggest that if a particular online retailer wanted to encourage sales of, for example, a particular film then playing the theme tune, even if it was not an overtly familiar theme tune, may prime the customers into purchasing that film. It is worth noting that the methods adopted by these studies involved collating data from genuine shoppers that were spending their own money when purchasing real products from physical shops. As such, these studies have very strong ecological validity.

4.3.2 Restaurant Dining

Researchers have also investigated the influence of music on diners in restaurants. Music preference is a key indicator of how long people will remain in a restaurant although the tempo of the music was not found to have any effect (Caldwell and Hibbert 2002), contrasting with a study by Milliman (1986) where music tempo was shown to impact on the speed of dining. There is no technological equivalent of dining in a restaurant, although ordering food can be conducted online. Nevertheless, the dining context has presented yet more studies that consider tempo as a key element of music that can change behaviour as well as demonstrating that preference affects how long someone engages in a particular activity. This latter result may extend to HCI. If someone is performing a tedious task involving interactive technologies, accompanying this activity with music that they enjoy may subconsciously encourage them to continue the task for longer.

4.3.3 Gambling

As in shops, music is an integral element of the real world gambling experience. An observational study in amusement arcades showed that perceptions of the clientele's musical preferences determined the type of music played in amusement arcades (Griffiths and Parke 2005). In areas of the arcade that were frequented predominantly by older, female players Easy Listening music was played. While in the areas and at times when the clientele was chiefly young men the background music was in a Rock or Dance style. Finally, the area of the arcade that catered for teenagers mainly played Pop and Dance music in the afternoons. This study was observational rather than empirical, but demonstrated that music is customary in the real world gambling environment. Despite the pervasiveness of music within casinos and amusement arcades there has been limited empirical attention focused on the affect of music on the clientele. Again, it appears that music forms an integral element of the gambling experience due to the belief that music increases profitability, rather than based on solid, scientific evidence.

4.3.4 Sport

Music can also have a positive impact on athletic performance. Researchers have played music to athletes both prior to (Bishop et al. 2007) and during (Waterhouse et al. 2010; Simpson and Karageorghis 2006; Edworthy and Waring 2006) sporting activities. These studies are both qualitative and quantitative in approach, but tend to focus on measuring changes in behaviour rather than experience (although Edworthy and Waring's (2006) study does take subjective measures of Affect as well). It is unclear in the pre-performance studies if the athlete is engaged in another activity whilst listening or if they are focusing solely on the music. However, in the duration studies the music accompanies a specific sporting activity, whether this is cycling (Waterhouse et al. 2010), sprinting 400 m (Simpson and Karageorghis 2006) or walking/running on a treadmill (Edworthy and Waring 2006). As such, the music definitely acts as an accompaniment to another activity. There is evidence to suggest that sporting performance may be improved because the accompanying music acts as a distractor from discomfort (Waterhouse et al. 2010; Edworthy and Waring 2006). It is arguable that the focus of the athlete's attention is quite strongly on the music and not the activity. Again, this leads us to consider whether a users' sense of discomfort can be negated using music.

4.3.5 Education

Education is another key area where there has been much research focusing on the impact of music on students. A study by Thompson et al. (2011) focused on the affect of music tempo and intensity on reading comprehension. This study found that fast tempo, high intensity background instrumental music had a significant negative effect on reading comprehension, while slow tempo music had no significant effect in either high or low intensity conditions.

4.3.6 Music Psychology

Music psychologists have researched if and how music can elicit an emotional response in listeners for some time. There is some disagreement within the field as to whether listeners can perceive emotions from music (the cognitivist view) or if music can actually change listeners' felt emotions (the emotivist view) (Krumhansl 1997). Given the differing music emotion theories it is important to distinguish between felt emotions and perceived emotions when discussing emotion and music. Our research takes the latter, emotivist viewpoint, which is supported by a growing body of empirical evidence (Livingstone et al. 2007). Extending this viewpoint to HCI, we ask if music can be included in interfaces to positively enhance users' felt emotions, especially in stressful or boring situations?

The traditional approach of music psychologists when studying how music affects emotions in listeners is to conduct a laboratory-based study where music is played to participants and emotional reactions measured. The measurement techniques employed in these laboratory studies range from subjective measures such as self-reporting scales (e.g. Gfeller et al. 1991; Lychner 1998) to objective psychophysiological measurement techniques (Hodges 2010) including neuroimaging scans (Gosselin et al. 2006), heart rate and facial activity (Lundqvist et al. 2009).

Conducting experiments in a laboratory is a typical, valid psychological approach to a research question. Nonetheless, this does not really represent the true nature of most interactions that people have with music. Some music psychologists have extended their approach by considering how situational factors influence musically affected felt emotions. Someone's reaction will normally differ depending on the situation they find themselves in. For example, the experience when listening to music in a concert is very different to the experience of hearing the same song played over a shop's PA system (Sloboda and Juslin 2010). The discrepancy in experience is due to hearing music in an ordinary, everyday environment in comparison to hearing it on a special occasion (Sloboda 2010).

One method of overcoming the limitation of the focused listening approach adopted in laboratory experiments is to employ the Experience Sampling Method (ESM) (Larson and Csikszentmihalyi 1983). Sloboda and O'Neill (2001) and Sloboda (2010) used the ESM to investigate how people listened to music in their everyday lives. The participants in this study carried an electronic pager with them during waking hours for a week. At random intervals, once in every 2-h period, they received a page instructing them to answer questions about their current experience as soon as possible. Music was experienced in 44% of episodes but only 2% of those music experiences involved participants actively listening to music as opposed to the participants hearing music while undertaking another activity. This result reveals that focused attention on music is atypical of most listening situations. Instead, it is far more common for musical experiences to include passive hearing of music in the background with selective attention when needed.

When considering the best methods for evaluating interfaces with an affective musical component, laboratory-based experiments using subjective and objective psychophysiological measures should be considered, particularly with early-stage experiments. Later on, other appropriate methods can be adopted, including diary-studies and surveys, particularly when identifying areas that may benefit from affective musical interactions. Depending on the type of interface developed, the ESM may also be an appropriate method.

4.4 Music as an Affective Medium in HCI

The previous section described research from wide-ranging subject areas regarding the exploitation of music's affectivity. While the major focus for using music in HCI has been on communication, there are a few instances where an affective objective has been adopted. This section provides details relating to some of the previous work that has been conducted involving affective musical interactions, within the HCI setting.

4.4.1 Computer Gaming

One domain where we might expect auditory interaction's research focus to extend away from message communication is computer gaming. This is an area that is purely experiential; computer games designers already exploit music, sound effects and speech to create the optimum game playing experience.

Researchers have begun considering the impact that music has on gamers' levels of immersion. A study by Sanders and Cairns (2010) identified that music preference i.e. whether the gamer enjoyed the music or not, significantly impacted on gamers' immersion levels. The aim of the original study was to use music as a means of manipulating immersion in an investigation of the relationship between immersion and time perception. However, the authors found that the initial choice of music was not liked by the participants and therefore had a negative affect on immersion, to the extent that in the non-music condition the participants actually became more immersed. Repetition of their experiment with a different choice of music, that the participants enjoyed, had a positive affect on immersion.

Another computer gaming study took an objective measurement approach when investigating the physiological stress response due to built-in game music (Hébert et al. 2005). In this experiment, the participants played a first person shooter game (Quake III Arena, ID Software, 1999) in either the silence condition (no music or sound effects) or the music condition (built-in "pop-techno style" music only, with no sound effects). Saliva samples were taken at intervals after playing the game. Analysis of the samples revealed that the that cortisol levels, an indicator of stress, were significantly higher in the music group 15 min after completion of game playing *"when cortisol levels are assumed to reflect the stress induced by the game"* (Hébert et al. 2005).

Further research in a computer gaming context has investigated the affect that personal music preference has on driving game performance and enjoyment (Cassidy and MacDonald 2010). In situations were the participants self-selected the accompanying music for the driving game they enjoyed the experience more, whilst performance and experience diminished when the experimenter selected the music. This demonstrates that music preference is a key experiential factor, and when trying to positively influence users' experiences, options for preference should be incorporated within the interface.

Given that computer gaming is a purely experiential activity and music is an integral element of the majority of computer games, the scarcity of research regarding the impact of music on computer gamers is somewhat unexpected. Although the field is emerging, it appears that music is incorporated in computer games on artistic merit and the anecdotal notion that music improves game-playing experience, rather than as a result of scientific verification of a hypothesis.

4.4.2 Typing Speed and Accuracy

One of the only examples of research investigating how music affects users' behaviour in an HCI environment dates back to 1931. The impact of Jazz and Dirge music on a person's typing speed and accuracy was evaluated alongside a control condition with no musical accompaniment (Jensen 1931). This study found that the speed of typing was significantly slower in the Dirge music condition. Further, while the numbers of errors in the Dirge and Silence conditions were comparable, Jazz music had a demonstrable impact on typing accuracy. The authors warn that this leaves *"no doubt as to the seriousness of the influence of jazz music on typing, so far as errors are concerned"* (Jensen 1931).

Nowadays, the relationship that people have with music is ubiquitous; music forms an ever-present part of daily life, considerably more so than it did in the 1930s. Given our familiarity with completing tasks while listening to music, including typing, would these results still stand today? Jensen does not pose any explanations for the discrepancy between the effects of Jazz and Dirge music on typing accuracy. However, we speculate that there are two possible explanations. Firstly, that it may have been due to the tempo of the Jazz music, which presumably will have had a faster tempo than the Dirge music. Secondly, it is likely that the Jazz music contained syncopated rhythms that may account for the increase in error rate. At present, these explanations are just supposition, but it would certainly be interesting to investigate this further in a modern setting, to see if the result still stands today.

4.4.3 Online Gambling

The influence of music on online gambling behaviour has recently been the focus of a couple of empirical studies. The effect of background music tempo on gambling behaviour when playing online roulette has been investigated in two studies (Dixon et al. 2007; Spenwyn et al. 2010). The risk of the bet (i.e. the amount of money spent) and the speed at which bets were placed were recorded for no music, slow music and fast tempo music (Dixon et al. 2007). The definitions of slow and fast tempo come from Milliman's (1982) supermarket study (where slow tempo is less than 72 beats per minute (bpm) and fast tempo is greater than 94 bpm). The results showed that the music's tempo had no affect on risk-taking behaviour. Although, the speed at which people placed bets was significantly higher in the fast tempo condition. A similar study by Spenwyn et al. (2010) concluded similar results. Here the authors speculated that the relationship between tempo and speed of bets is due to the increased arousal felt by participants in the fast tempo music condition. The authors also propose that online gambling websites should have an option to turn off musical accompaniment as players are more likely to become addicted with fast tempo musical accompaniment as the time for contemplation between bets is reduced (Spenwyn et al. 2010). Nevertheless, they also acknowledge that some websites or casinos may wish to profiteer by ensuring that the tempo of any music playing is fast, thus encouraging faster betting with less time for someone to consider the consequences of placing a bet.

Given the limited empirical attention given to the impact of music on gambling behaviour in real world casinos and arcades it is interesting that the virtual world equivalent has received considerably more empirical attention. This contrasts with the shopping situation where there has been much research in a physical context with little, if any, in the corresponding online environment. Perhaps this is due to the perception that as online gambling is an entertainment activity background music is more acceptable. The results from the online gambling research show that even in a laboratory-based gambling context music has a substantial impact on the players' behaviour. The participants in these studies did not place bets with their own money, therefore conceding no risk, neither could they win any real money from the gambling activity. Although the ecological validity of studies conducted in this manner is reduced, significant outcomes can still be achieved, verifying the acceptability of the method.

4.4.4 Virtual Learning Environments

In an Education context, Immersive Virtual Worlds have been investigated to verify if they are an appropriate medium for learning (Richards et al. 2008). Here, researchers considered how music from computer game soundtracks affects learning, specifically remembering facts. This research found that, for one particular musical stimulus, the number of accurately memorised facts was significantly higher. The authors suggest that this piece of music may have been more congruent with the material being taught, hence the improvement in fact recall with this particular background music (Richards et al. 2008).

4.4.5 Email Management

One of the first pieces of empirical research investigating how music can affect someone's emotional experiences, rather than behaviour, was performed by the authors of this chapter (Bramwell-Dicks 2010; Bramwell-Dicks et al. 2011). A Wizard-of-Oz prototype for an Ambient Music Email (AME) extension to email clients was developed. The AME prototype played continuous background Ambient music and when new emails arrived in a monitored email account, a musical notification phrase (a chromatic scale) played over the top. The objective for the AME was to positively influence user's felt emotions by exploiting the affective properties of music.

The emotion altering potential of the AME was evaluated in a laboratory setting. Participants audibly monitored an email account whilst performing an occupying task. The email account was monitored under two conditions (i) using the AME prototype and (ii) using a standard email monitoring application. At pseudo-random intervals the email account received a new email prompting the participants to complete an online survey to assess their felt emotions.

The results showed that music did have a significant impact on how the participant's felt emotions changed over time. In both conditions there was a drop-off in the positive felt emotions during the experiment, possibly as they became bored. However, the size of this drop-off was significantly smaller in the music condition than the non-music condition. In other words, the AME kept the participants' positive felt emotions higher over the duration of the experiment. This was a positive result that adds weight to the argument that musical interfaces can be used to positively influence felt emotions. Contrastingly, the AME's impact on the participants' negative felt emotions had somewhat surprising results. Over time, in both conditions, the negative emotions increased; this is not surprising given the element of boredom in their task. In the AME condition, however, the size of increase in negative emotions was larger than in the non-music condition. Therefore, the AME increased negative felt emotions over time, which was an unexpected result, especially given the improvement in positive felt emotions.

A few explanations for this increase in negativity were offered (Bramwell-Dicks 2010). Further listening to the Ambient music used within the AME revealed that it contained repeated instances of discords that did not resolve. A discord is *"a chord which is restless, jarring to the ear, requiring to be resolved in a particular way if its presence is to be justified by the ear"* (Kennedy and Kennedy 2007). In the theoretical framework of underlying mechanisms that evoke emotions in music listeners, Juslin and Västfjäll (2008) include *"expectancy violations"* as a contributing factor. As such, the music's characteristic of repeated instances of unresolving dissonance may be a causal factor that increased the strength of negative emotions felt by the participants. Though, this explanation requires further investigation before it can be verified.

Additionally, there were some methodological issues that may have added stress to the participants. The musical notification phrase that alerted the participants to the presence of an unread email in the account may have been too difficult for the participants to identify. A preliminary experiment was conducted to help choose the most appropriate notification phrase i.e. one that was easy to identify whilst also combining pleasantly with the background music. Participants in the preliminary study listened to the background Ambient music whilst performing the same occupying task used in the later AME study. The participants had to tell the experimenter whenever they heard a musical notification phrase over the top of the background music. This process was repeated for a number of potential notification phrases. The method employed in this preliminary study was very similar to that used in the AME study with one key difference – the time between instances of the notification phrase being played in the AME study varied between 1 and 7 min, while in the preliminary experiment there was only 15 s between notifications. Therefore, in the AME study the participants spent 20 min in each condition, but this was reduced to less than 2 min in the preliminary study, for each of the potential notification phrases.

The results from the preliminary study showed that all of the potential notification phrases were easy to identify, and the most pleasant ones were those that had not been pitch-shifted (or transposed). As such, it was felt that the chromatic scale notification phrase should be easy for participants to identify when audibly monitoring an email account. However, the experimenter observed that some of the AME study participants actually found it relatively hard to identify the musical notification phrase. It appeared that the participants had to split their attention between the occupying task and actively listening out for the notification phrase, rather than focusing their attention on the occupying task and passively hearing the notification phrase. The extra cognitive load required in splitting attention between the occupying task and active listening may have added some stress to the participants, thus affecting their negative emotions. In the preliminary experiment the participants were not engaged in the occupying task for sufficiently long periods of time between notifications to become engrossed in the task. In direct comparison, in the non-music condition of the AME study it was very straightforward for participants to identify the audible notification phrase, as there were no other sounds in the room at the time. Therefore, they were able to focus their full cognitive attention on the occupying task without a need to split their attention.

As a result, any future research using a musical interface that requires the user to distinguish features of the music to interpret the information being communicated will need preliminary studies that are carefully designed in such a way that they closely mirror the precise environment of the later experiments. In this example, should the preliminary study have been longer, with the time between instances of the notification expanded to match that employed in the AME study, the participants may have had to split their attention to identify the notification phrase and would therefore have reported it as slightly harder to identify. This is an important lesson for verifying the appropriateness of the sound design in any music interface that integrates alerts alongside background music.

4.5 Research Proposition

The aims for our research involving musically affective interactions are to identify if and how music can be included in interface designs to positively affect user experience and behaviour in a broad range of areas. The research will focus on the following questions. When music is integrated within an interactive technology:

- how are the users' experiences and behaviour affected?
- what features of the music affects users' experiences and behaviour?
- what features of the users' engagement with the music affects the users' experiences or behaviour?

The first challenge is to refine these broad statements by identifying what elements of experience and behaviour we hope to affect with music (i.e. the dependent variables) and what musical features are to be manipulated (i.e. the independent variables).

4.5.1 Dependent Variables

There are a vast number of dependent variables that might be appropriate to research in this context. For example, does music affect accuracy when completing repetitive, boring tasks such as data entry? Can musical interfaces make stressful situations become more pleasant? Or can musical interfaces make mundane tasks more enjoyable? Generally speaking, behavioural characteristics can be measured objectively using quantitative methods, such as comparing time taken to complete tasks. While experience variables can either be measured subjectively by asking how the participant feels or objectively by taking measures of physiological responses e.g. heart rate.

4.5.2 Independent Variables

The independent variable may simply be two conditions, music versus non-music. Alternatively, the independent variables may focus attention on particular parameters of the music. There are numerous elements of music that can be altered as independent variables. These elements include tempo, pitch range, key, modality, dynamics, and rhythmic properties e.g. syncopation and whether the piece is lyrical or instrumental. Additionally, stylistic elements such as genre and instrumentation could be manipulated. Otherwise, properties of the listener's engagement with the music can also be manipulated. For example, do they like or dislike the music? Is it familiar? Is the style of music one that they regularly listen to?

4.6 Potential Research Avenues

Music has the ability to affect how people behave and, arguably, how they feel. As such, there is clear potential for integrating music within technological interfaces to positively affect users' experiences and behaviour. However, there is clearly also the potential for music to be incorporated in such a way that it causes negative experiences or has an exploitative impact on behaviour, particular with regard to consumers. At present, the idea of music integration for affective interaction may seem novel with no potential for mass adoption. Nevertheless, we argue that if music can be incorporated so that it improves behaviour and experiences then there is the potential for affective musical interfaces to become a typical feature of technology.

For example, maintaining and monitoring email accounts has become a vastly stressful experience for many people due to the wealth of emails sent and received on a daily basis (Shiels 2010). If the interface can positively affect the feelings of stressed email users by incorporating affective elements, including music, then there is the potential for the interface to be widely adopted. Additionally, if typing behaviour is more accurate and faster with a particular musical accompaniment then perhaps there is an argument that secretaries should be listening to an affective musical soundtrack when undertaking their dictation.

The online gambling research discussed previously demonstrates that even with no monetary risk or gain for the participants the influence of music on their behaviour was significant. Therefore, it seems fairly surprising that the marketing research regarding tempo and music genre has not been repeated in an online shopping context. Perhaps this is due to the concern that music does not align with an online shopping setting and could potentially annoy users. Nevertheless, given the prevalence for music in physical shops, it is a perhaps surprising that online shops do not incorporate music within their virtual shopping experience to endorse their branding and to affect purchasing behaviour online.

Research investigating the impact of music on peoples' behaviour and experiences will always be constrained to a particular domain, some of which, at face value, may seem more appropriate than others. However, if it is shown that music can have a positive affect on people in one domain, it can be argued that music may also have the potential to positively affect people in other, seemingly less appropriate contexts. For example, the AME project incorporated music into an interface that runs constantly in the background; monitoring email is not normally someone's primary attentive focus. In this case, positive emotions were enhanced, demonstrating that music can have a positive emotional impact on users in their primary attentive task as well as monitoring email, though future experiments will need to verify this.

The HCI field has been slow to incorporate music within interfaces, particularly with the aim of positively affecting users. However, as exhibited by this chapter, many other areas have already investigated the affective impact that music has on people. These fields regularly exploit this affective characteristic of music to positively influence behaviour and experiences. This chapter has, hopefully, demonstrated that there is great potential for future research in the area of affective musical interaction within an HCI context.

Acknowledgments Anna Bramwell-Dicks is supported by a UK Engineering and Physical Sciences Research Council Doctoral Training Account studentship.

References

Alty, J. L., Rigas, D., & Vickers, P. (1997). Using music as a communication medium. In *CHI '97 extended abstracts on human factors in computing systems: Looking to the future* (pp. 30–31) Atlanta, Georgia: ACM, 1120234. doi:10.1145/1120212.1120234

Areni, C. S., & Kim, D. (1993). The influence of background music on shopping behavior: Classical versus Top-Forty music in a wine store. *Advances in Consumer Research, 20*(1), 336–340.

Bishop, D. T., Karageorghis, C. I., & Georgios, L. (2007). A grounded theory of young tennis players' use of music to manipulate emotional state. *Journal of Sport & Exercise Psychology, 29*, 584–607.

Blattner, M. M., Sumikawa, D. A., & Greenberg, R. M. (1989). Earcons and icons: Their structure and common design principles. *Human Computer Interaction, 4*(1), 11–44. doi:10.1207/s15327051hci0401_1.

Bramwell-Dicks, A. (2010). *Towards AME: Exploring the use of ambient music within an email interface*. Dissertation, University of York, York.

Bramwell-Dicks, A., Petrie, H., Edwards, A. D. N., & Power, C. (2011). Affecting user behaviour and experience with music: A research agenda. BCS HCI workshop "When words fail: What can music interaction tell us about HCI?" 8 May 2011. Northumbria University, Newcastle Upon Tyne. http://mcl.open.ac.uk/Workshop. Accessed 8 Mar 2012.

Brewster, S. A. (1998). *Sonically-enhanced drag and drop*. Paper presented at the international conference on auditory display, Glasgow, 1–4 Nov.

Brewster, S. A. (2002). Overcoming the lack of screen space on mobile computers. *Personal and Ubiquitous Computing, 6*(3), 188–205. doi:10.1007/s007790200019.

Brewster, S. A. (2003). Non-speech auditory output. In J. A. Jacko & A. Sears (Eds.), *The human computer interaction handbook: Fundamentals, evolving technologies and emerging applications* (pp. 220–240). London: Lawrence Erlbaum Associates Inc.

Brown, M. H., & Hershberger, J. (1992). Color and sound in algorithm animation. *Computer, 25*(12), 52–63. doi:10.1109/2.179117.

Bullerjahn, C., & Güldenring, M. (1994). An empirical investigation of effects of film music using qualitative content analysis. *Psychomusicology, 13*, 99–118.

Caldwell, C., & Hibbert, S. A. (2002). The influence of music tempo and musical preference on restaurant patrons' behavior. *Psychology and Marketing, 19*(11), 895–917. doi:10.1002/mar.10043.

Cassidy, G. G., & MacDonald, R. A. R. (2010). The effects of music on time perception and performance of a driving game. *Scandinavian Journal of Psychology, 51*(6), 455–464. doi:10.1111/j.1467-9450.2010.00830.x.

Dixon, L., Trigg, R., & Griffiths, M. (2007). An empirical investigation of music and gambling behaviour. *International Gambling Studies, 7*(3), 315–326. doi:10.1080/14459790701601471.

Edwards, A. D. N. (1989). Soundtrack: An auditory interface for blind users. *Human Computer Interaction, 4*(1), 45–66. doi:10.1207/s15327051hci0401_2.

Edworthy, J., & Waring, H. (2006). The effects of music tempo and loudness level on treadmill exercise. *Ergonomics, 49*(15), 1597–1610. doi:10.1080/00140130600899104.

Gaver, W. W. (1986). Auditory icons: Using sound in computer interfaces. *Human Computer Interaction, 2*(2), 167–177. doi:10.1207/s15327051hci0202_3.

Gfeller, K., Asmus, E., & Eckert, M. (1991). An investigation of emotional response to music and text. *Psychology of Music, 19*(2), 128–141. doi:10.1177/0305735691192004.

Gosselin, N., Samson, S., Adolphs, R., Noulhiane, M., Roy, M., Hasboun, D., Baulac, M., & Peretz, I. (2006). Emotional responses to unpleasant music correlates with damage to the parahippocampal cortex. *Brain, 129*(10), 2585–2592. doi:10.1093/brain/awl240.

Griffiths, M., & Parke, J. (2005). The psychology of music in gambling environments: An observational research note. *Journal of Gambling Issues, 13*. doi:10.4309/jgi.2005.13.8.

Hébert, S., Béland, R., Dionne-Fournelle, O., Crête, M., & Lupien, S. J. (2005). Physiological stress response to video-game playing: The contribution of built-in music. *Life Sciences, 76*(20), 2371–2380. doi:10.1016/j.lfs.2004.11.011.

Hodges, D. A. (2010). Psychophysiological measures. In P. N. Juslin & J. A. Sloboda (Eds.), *Handbook of music and emotion: Theory, research, applications* (pp. 279–311). Oxford: Oxford University Press.

Jensen, M. B. (1931). The influence of jazz and dirge music upon speed and accuracy of typing. *Journal of Educational Psychology, 22*(6), 458–462. doi:10.1037/h0074752.

Jones, M., Jones, S., Bradley, G., Warren, N., Bainbridge, D., & Holmes, G. (2008). ONTRACK: Dynamically adapting music playback to support navigation. *Personal and Ubiquitous Computing, 12*(7), 513–525. doi:10.1007/s00779-007-0155-2.

Juslin, P. N., & Sloboda, J. A. (2010). *Handbook of music and emotion: Theory, research, applications*. Oxford: Oxford University Press.

Juslin, P. N., & Västfjäll, D. (2008). Emotional responses to music: The need to consider underlying mechanisms. *The Behavioral and Brain Sciences, 31*(5), 559–575. doi:10.1017/S0140525X08005293.

Kennedy, M., & Kennedy, J. (2007). *"discord". The concise oxford dictionary of music*. Oxford: Oxford University Press.

Kotler, P. (1973). Atmospherics as a marketing tool. *Journal of Retailing, 49*(4), 48.

Krumhansl, C. L. (1997). An exploratory study of musical emotions and psychophysiology. *Canadian Journal of Experimental Psychology, 51*(4), 336–353. doi:10.1037/1196-1961.51.4.336.

Larson, R., & Csikszentmihalyi, M. (1983). The experience sampling method. *New Directions for Methodology of Social & Behavioral Science, 15*, 41–56.

Livingstone, S. R., Mühlberger, R., Brown, A. R., & Loch, A. (2007). Controlling musical emotionality: An affective computational architecture for influencing musical emotions. *Digital Creativity, 18*(1), 43–53. doi:10.1080/14626260701253606.

Lundqvist, L.-O., Carlsson, F., Hilmersson, P., & Juslin, P. N. (2009). Emotional responses to music: Experience, expression, and physiology. *Psychology of Music, 37*(1), 61–90. doi:10.1177/0305735607086048.

Lychner, J. A. (1998). An empirical study concerning terminology relating to aesthetic response to music. *Journal of Research in Music Education, 46*(2), 303–319. doi:10.2307/3345630.

Mansur, D. L., Blattner, M. M., & Joy, K. I. (1985). Sound graphs: A numerical data analysis method for the blind. *Journal of Medical Systems, 9*(3), 163–174. doi:10.1007/bf00996201.

Milliman, R. E. (1982). Using background music to affect the behavior of supermarket shoppers. *The Journal of Marketing, 46*(3), 86–91. doi:10.2307/1251706.

Milliman, R. E. (1986). The influence of background music on the behavior of restaurant patrons. *Journal of Consumer Research, 13*(2), 286–289. doi:10.1086/209068.

North, A. C., Hargreaves, D. J., & McKendrick, J. (1999). The influence of in-store music on wine selections. *Journal of Applied Psychology, 84*(2), 271–276. doi:10.1037/0021-9010.84.2.271.

Quinn, M., & Meeker L. D. (2001). *Research set to music: The climate symphony and other sonifications of ice core, radar, DNA, seismic and solar wind data.* Paper presented at the international conference on auditory display, Espoo, Finland, 29 July–1 August.

Richards, D., Fassbender, E., Bilgin, A., & Thompson, W. F. (2008). An investigation of the role of background music in IVWs for learning. *Research in Learning Technology, 16*(3), 231–244. doi:10.1080/09687760802526715.

Sanders, T., & Cairns, P. (2010). *Time perception, immersion and music in videogames.* Paper presented at BCS HCI, University of Abertay, Dundee, 6–10 Sept.

Sanderson, P. (2006). The multimodal world of medical monitoring displays. *Applied Ergonomics, 37*(4), 501–512. doi:10.1016/j.apergo.2006.04.022.

Shiels, M. (2010). Google's priority inbox aims to conquer e-mail overload BBC. http://www.bbc.co.uk/news/technology-11133576. Accessed 8 Mar 2011.

Simpson, S. D., & Karageorghis, C. I. (2006). The effects of synchronous music on 400-m sprint performance. *Journal of Sports Sciences, 24*(10), 1095–1102. doi:10.1080/02640410500432789.

Sloboda, J. A. (2010). Music in everyday life: The role of emotions. In P. N. Juslin & J. A. Sloboda (Eds.), *Handbook of human emotion: Theory, research, applications* (pp. 493–514). Oxford: Oxford University Press.

Sloboda, J. A., & Juslin, P. N. (2010). At the interface between the inner and outer world: Psychological perspectives. In P. N. Juslin & J. A. Sloboda (Eds.), *Handbook of music and Emotion: Theory, research, applications* (pp. 73–97). Oxford: Oxford University Press.

Sloboda, J. A., & O'Neill, S. A. (2001). Emotions in everyday listening to music. In P. N. Juslin & J. A. Sloboda (Eds.), *Music and emotion: Theory and research* (pp. 415–429). Oxford: Oxford University Press.

Spenwyn, J., Barrett, D., & Griffiths, M. (2010). The role of light and music in gambling behaviour: An empirical pilot study. *International Journal of Mental Health and Addiction, 8*(1), 107–118. doi:10.1007/s11469-009-9226-0.

Thompson, W. F., Schellenberg, E. G., & Letnic, A. K. (2011). Fast and loud background music disrupts reading comprehension. *Psychology of Music.* doi:10.1177/0305735611400173.

Vickers, P., & Alty, J. L. (2002). When bugs sing. *Interacting with Computers, 14*(6), 793–819. doi:10.1016/S0953-5438(02)00026-7.

Waterhouse, J., Hudson, P., & Edwards, B. (2010). Effects of music tempo upon submaximal cycling performance. *Scandinavian Journal of Medicine & Science in Sports, 20*(4), 662–669. doi:10.1111/j.1600-0838.2009.00948.x.

Chapter 5
Chasing a Feeling: *Experience* in Computer Supported Jamming

Ben Swift

Abstract Improvisational group music-making, informally known as 'jamming', has its own cultures and conventions of musical interaction. One characteristic of this interaction is the primacy of the *experience* over the musical artefact—in some sense the sound created is not as important as the feeling of being 'in the groove'. As computing devices infiltrate creative, open-ended task domains, what can Human-Computer Interaction (HCI) learn from jamming? How do we design systems where the goal is not an artefact but a felt experience? This chapter examines these issues in light of an experiment involving 'Viscotheque', a novel group music-making environment based on the iPhone.

5.1 Introduction

This volume offers a glimpse into the diverse ways in which music making practices are being influenced by computational support. Augmented traditional instruments (McPherson and Kim 2013, this volume) artificial musical intelligence (Gifford 2013, this volume), live coding (Stowell and McLean 2013, this volume)—each of these musical contexts has specific cultures and challenges. Some of these musical contexts existed in some form prior to the advent of their enabling technologies, others did not.

Creative, open-ended task domains are a hallmark of 'third wave' HCI (Fallman 2011), and music interaction is a natural fit for this growing body of theory. Improvisational group music-making is one such musical practice which presents new challenges to the interaction designer. In this chapter, we consider the practice of improvisational group music-making and its relationship to HCI.

B. Swift (✉)
Research School of Computer Science, Australian National University, Canberra, Australia
e-mail: ben.swift@anu.edu.au

S. Holland et al. (eds.), *Music and Human-Computer Interaction*, Springer Series on Cultural Computing, DOI 10.1007/978-1-4471-2990-5_5,

In this chapter we shall use the term ‘jamming’ to refer to the practice of improvisational group music-making. In particular, we refer to music-making contexts where a primary motivator for participation is the feeling of the activity itself. The primary motivation is not financial remuneration, the adulation of an audience, or the preservation of a recorded artefact for posterity. This definition is open to criticism; the term jamming may be used to describe musical contexts which do not satisfy all of these criteria. Also, reducing the motivations of a jamming musician to a single factor is impossible; the expert jazz musician may still do what she does simply for the thrill of it, even when she is paid for her gigs and there is an audience to applaud her. It is, however, necessary to define terms for the sake of clarity, and this is the definition we shall use in this chapter.

As well as a discussion of the nature of jamming and its implications for HCI, we present a case study of computer supported jamming. Drawing on the author’s own training and experience as a jazz guitarist, we have designed the Viscotheque digital musical instrument (DMI). Viscotheque is an iPhone-based mobile musical instrument and associated infrastructure designed with jamming in mind. We conducted a longitudinal study of the system involving musicians familiar with the practice of jamming. We present some observations from this study in Sect. 5.4, as well as some implications for the design and evaluation of interactive systems for improvisational music making in Sect. 5.5.

5.1.1 Improvisational Interaction

The degree of improvisation inherent in a group activity can be seen to lie along a continuum. Some activities are largely pre-scripted, others contain both scripted and unscripted elements, still others are completely unscripted. Group activities which fall at the more improvisational end of this spectrum can be difficult to make sense of to the uninitiated. When roles are fluid and ill defined; when outcomes are not pre-determined but negotiated on the fly—how do improvising groups do what they do?

The canonical example of an improvising group in music is the jazz ensemble (MacDonald and Wilson 2006). From a simple trio all the way up to a big band ensemble, improvisation is an integral part of what it is to play jazz (Berliner 1994). Of course, improvisation is not unique to jazz; it is a feature of many other musical styles and traditions, and many non-musical activities as well, such as improvisational theatre troupes (Sawyer and DeZutter 2009). Scholarly work on improvisational music-making has largely been concerned with jazz, although rock-influenced ‘jam bands’ such as The Grateful Dead have been considered as well (Tuedio 2006).

A great deal of skill and training is required to participate in improvisational group music-making at a high level. Each musical utterance must be made in response to the current musical context, including the contributions of all the other musicians. The jamming musician must both play and listen, act and react; balancing the desire to be fresh and original with the economies of falling back on familiar patterns and the need to fit musically with the other musicians. Managing these tensions means that improvisational groups are inherently fluid; the actions and roles of the group members are not pre-ordained, but negotiated and re-negotiated on-the-fly. While each member of the group brings their own experiences and sensibilities to the activity, the creative output of the group is not the singular vision of any of the individuals, or even the sum of their individual contributions: "in collaborative improvisation, a creative product emerges that could not even in theory be created by an individual" (Sawyer 2007).

5.1.2 *The Feeling of Jamming Together*

Musicians have their own vocabulary for talking about what they do when they jam together. This vocabulary can help us to understand the process of jamming as experienced by its practitioners. In Ingrid Monson's interviews with professional jazz musicians, the metaphor of dialogue or conversation was used to describe the act of improvising together (Monson 1996). High points in their music-making were described as 'saying something', expressing something meaningful through their playing. This is a helpful metaphor: conversation connotes a sharing of ideas, a call-and-response paradigm, the potential for intimacy and shared vocabulary. 'Grooving' is another term used by musicians to describe the feeling of playing together (Doffman 2009). This term has subtly different meanings depending on usage. It can refer to a specific beat or rhythmic pattern, or the practice of playing early on certain beats and late on others. It is also used by musicians to refer to peak moments in a performance. In this latter sense, grooving is not simply a cognitive state, it has an affective and embodied dimension—it is *felt* (Ashley 2009).

Jamming groups do not always reach these lofty peaks. One day a group might really be in the groove, the next day they may be flat. When it works, though, the experience of jamming together can provide a sense of satisfaction and connection with others that few other activities can (Mazzola 2008). The sensation of being 'in the groove', while difficult to describe in words, represents a real shared experience prized by musicians across many different musical traditions (Lamont 2009).

The theoretical lens of flow theory (Csikszentmihalyi 1991) is often used to examine 'peak experience' in jamming, and indeed instrumental music-making in general (Wallis et al. 2013, this volume). Although Csikszentmihalyi was originally concerned with flow experiences in individuals, Sawyer (himself a jazz pianist) has described flow in improvisational groups, including as jazz ensembles (Sawyer 2006). Flow describes the state in which an individual's skill level is commensurate to the difficulty of the complex task being performed. The intrinsic pleasure of finding flow in an activity provides an explanation for why some activities are inherently pleasurable and satisfying, even when they provide no discernible reward (outside of this satisfaction). Flow is a theory of *intrinsic motivation*, as distinct from the extrinsic rewards which often motivate participation in a given activity.

Ultimately, it is immensely satisfying to be a part of a jamming group in this state of flow, and the feeling is contagious (Bakker 2005). Given our definition of jamming from Sect. 5.1, we suggest that this experience of 'peak jamming' is the ultimate goal of the jamming group; it is what keeps the musicians coming back to jam sessions. We are not claiming that this is the case for any particular jamming group, people and motivations are too complicated to make these kind of normative claims. If it is true, however, that there *exist* music-making groups and subcultures for which the felt experience is paramount, we must be mindful of this as we seek to design interactive digital artefacts to support this jamming.

5.2 The Smartphone as a DMI for Jamming

Modern 'smartphones', with their capacitive multi-touch screens and array of other sensors (Essl and Rohs 2009), are affording groups of musicians new avenues of creative engagement. Smartphones are but one material form-factor being utilised for DMI design (see Paine (2010) for a taxonomy of DMI design approaches), but their affordability and availability provide obvious advantages over custom hardware. In this, musicians are finding new ways to jam together, and to share in that familiar collaborative, improvisational experience (Tanaka 2006). The instruments may be different to the jazz band, but at some level the goal—to experience that feeling of flow—is the same.

Fallman (2011) is careful to point out that technology does not necessarily make things 'better', and HCI practitioner must be careful when wading into the domain of ethics. An optimistic reading of this trend may consider it a 'democratisation' (Tanaka 2010) of music-making. The experience of jamming is being brought within the reach of anyone with an appropriate phone in their pocket. The nature of a phone as a constant companion also opens up the possibility of spontaneous jam sessions, turning idle moments and new acquaintances into opportunities to jam. A more pessimistic interpretation of this trend may lament the dumbing down of a complex, skilful activity, and perhaps a loss of the nuance and ceremony surrounding jamming. The truth probably lies somewhere between these two poles, but it is important to remember that this next chapter of ubiquitous digital musical interaction has not yet been played out.

5.2.1 Analysis and Evaluation

Designers of DMIs are aware of the need to build tools which afford expressivity and that sense of 'saying something' (Dobrian and Koppelman 2006). However, determining both the nature and degree of success in this endeavour is a difficult task (O'Modhrain 2011). Evaluation techniques from more traditional HCI have been adapted for musical interaction contexts, such as setting basic musical tasks

(Wanderley and Orio 2002) which are comparatively easy to assess. Jamming, however, is not amenable to this type of reductionism. Indeed, 'mistakes' such as wrong notes are often sites of inspiration, perturbing the musical status quo and having an overall positive effect on the trajectory of a musical performance (McDermott et al. 2013, this volume).

For tasks which involve the production of an artefact, such as a document or other representation of knowledge, the success of the activity or interface can be measured by the quality of the artefact produced. Jamming, however, is not primarily concerned with the production of an artefact, and indeed there may not be any persistent tangible result of a jam session.

This is not a problem *per se*, but it does present challenges. How do we make design decisions without a meaningful metric for comparison? How do we reconcile our desire to have a nuanced view of the human, felt experience so central to these systems with our longing as data-driven scientists to crunch numbers, generate metrics, and compare p-values?

In jamming, HCI is confronted by a teleological difference between creative, improvisational tasks (such as jamming) and more 'prosaic' ones (Springett 2009). In a word processor, the ultimate goal of the user is the production of a high-quality document. The contribution of HCI theory is to make this task as pleasant an experience as possible. In an improvisational computer-music environment, the goal of the participant is to have an experience: of flow, connection, groove. The musical output of the system is merely a means to that end. In these two different contexts the role of the *created artefact* and the *experience of making it* are reversed. In what ways can the tools of HCI theory still be useful, and where do they fall down?

The recent emphasis on user experience (UX) provides some opportunities for designers of DMIs for jamming. In UX parlance, jamming falls into the category of 'an experience' (Forlizzi and Battarbee 2004)—it has a well defined beginning and end. Subjective reports, such as questionnaires and semi-structured interviews, are a common way of building a picture of the experience of participants with technology.

Bardzell and Bardzell (2008) suggest an approach based on criticism, rather than evaluation. Drawing on twentieth century critical theory, their proposed interaction criticism prescribes "interpretive analysis that explicates relationships among elements of an interface and the meanings, affects, moods, and intuitions they produce in the people that interact with them". Interaction criticism proposes four loci of analysis: the designer, artefact, user, and social context. These elements are all deeply interconnected, the aim of this approach is not to claim any independence between them. Rather, they provide a much needed common basis and vocabulary for examining interactive digital environments for complex activities like jamming.

The concept of criticism, rather than evaluation, also provides an explicit scope for expert judgements. As Bardzell notes, expert judgements happen all the time in design, whether implicitly or explicitly. This has always been true for the design of musical instruments, which tend to evolve (and stabilise) within their cultures and communities of use. The violin is not the result of a rigorous series of controlled experiments to determine the optimal size and shape for the violin body. Musicians and craftsmen made expert judgements at many points in the design process, based on their experience and observation of the instrument as a tool for music making. We must not be afraid to take the same methodological stance in the design of DMIs.

5.3 Jamming in Viscotheque: A Case Study

So, to summarise the key points so far:

1. Jamming is a complex activity, involving the interaction of many entangled processes and musical contributions.
2. Jamming is about chasing a felt experience—when it works, it feels *amazing*.
3. We need to keep this experiential and subjective focus as we design and evaluate computer supported jamming with DMIs.

The Viscotheque is an iPhone application designed with these considerations in mind. The design process has been motivated by the question: 'what does it feel like to jam together using a new, smartphone based instrument? ' In the remaining part of this chapter we share some observations from a field trial of the instrument.

5.3.1 Designing the Viscotheque Application: Mapping and Feedback

In any DMI, the key design decisions to be made are related to the mapping of the input manipulations (finger touches, device orientation, etc.) to the feedback (sonic, visual and tactile) provided to the musician (Miranda and Wanderley 2006). The Viscotheque instrument is necessarily constrained to use the iPhone touch screen and sensors. This affords certain modes of physical interaction and precludes others. However, constraint is a natural part of any instrumental design, and even extreme constraints have been shown to allow for a divergence of creative practices in the hands of skilled musicians (Gurevich et al. 2010).

The Viscotheque is best described as a multi-touch sample triggering and manipulation tool. The iPhone's screen is partitioned into four different zones, each of which triggers a different audio loop. Each loop is a short (4–8 s) audio clip of a single instrument (guitar, piano, drums or percussion) playing a simple pattern. The patterns are each one bar long, so that looping them results in a continuous stream of music with a constant pulse. The four different samples are not matched to each other—they have different tempos, accents and key signatures. This is by design, so that any coherence between the loops will be as a result of the effortful interaction between the jamming musicians.

Touching the screen with one finger triggers the sample associated with that zone, and the sample continues to play on a loop while at least one finger remains touching

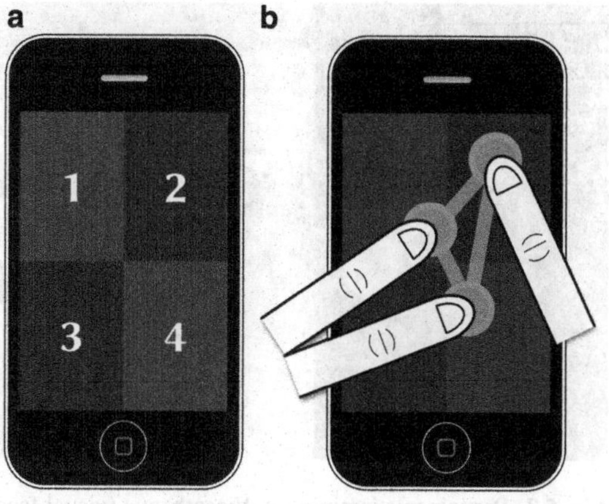

Fig. 5.1 Viscotheque app interface. The four zones are shown in (**a**). Upon touching the screen, the dots provide feedback as to the position of the fingers—the screenshot presented here (**b**) shows three fingers incident on the screen

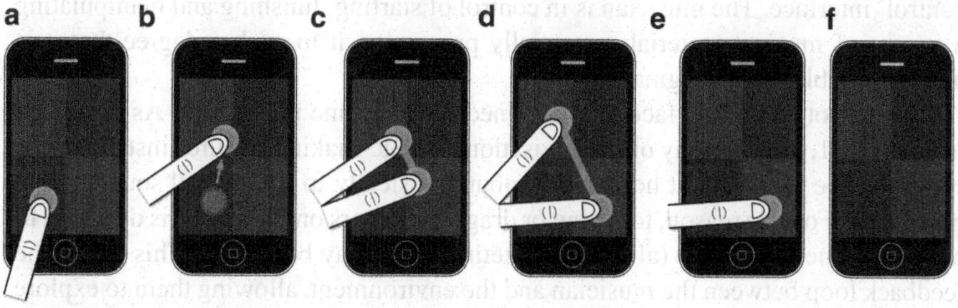

Fig. 5.2 An example of sample playback and manipulation on the Viscotheque interface. (**a**) Single touch down starts loop playback. (**b**) Dragging the touch on-screen adjusts lowpass filter cutoff. (**c**) Second touch, no immediate change to sound. (**d**) Loop continues to play, 'stretch' gesture applies slowdown effect. (**e**) Second touch removed, loop continues to play (at slower speed). (**f**) Finger removed, loop playback stops immediately

the screen. Adding a second or third touch mutates the original loop rather than triggering a second loop in parallel. When the last finger is removed from the screen, the sound stops immediately.

Dragging a finger around on the screen or adding more fingers changes the processing applied to the sound. Up to three different fingers can be used at once (see Fig. 5.1), and the effect the finger position(s) has on the sound depends on the number of fingers on the screen. When just one finger is dragged across the screen, a low-pass filter is applied. When two fingers, the volume and the playback speed are modulated; when three fingers, a pitch-shifting effect is applied.

This interface allows for complex multi touch gestures, potentially involving several fingers, which affords the musician a large sonic range in which to create and respond in a jam (see Fig. 5.2). With regard to the mobile music interaction design patterns proposed by Flores et al. (2010), the Viscotheque is primarily a 'process

Fig. 5.3 Participants jamming in Viscotheque (visual feedback display shown on *left*)

control' interface. The musician is in control of starting, finishing and manipulating a stream of musical material, potentially processing it to such a degree that it is unrecognisable as the original sample.

The Viscotheque interface was designed for real-time interaction. As discussed in Sect. 5.1.1, the interplay of improvisational music-making requires instantaneous choices to be made about how to contribute musically to the overall sound at any given time. For this reason, touching or dragging fingers on the screen is designed to have an immediate effect (although sometimes this may be subtle). This closes the feedback loop between the musician and the environment, allowing them to explore the extent of their sonic agency. The mappings are designed to be intuitive, using conceptual metaphors wherever possible, such as 'up' and 'down' in relation to pitch and volume (Wilkie et al. 2010).

Each musician controls their own sonic output, one musician cannot affect another's sound. Each musician's sound is mixed together and played through the same set of speakers, the musicians do not have an individual 'foldback' speaker to monitor their own contributions in isolation. The musicians must take care to listen to one another, and not to simply make the loudest noise possible and drown one another out.

To aid the musicians in orienting themselves, particularly as they are learning and exploring the instrument, visual feedback is provided to all participants on a large screen. The screen provides an indication of the gestural state (that is, the finger positions) of all the musicians at the current moment in time (see Fig. 5.3). Each participant's fingers are colour coded to match the colours on their own device screens.

5.3.2 Architecture

The Viscotheque environment in totality consists of any number of iPhones (or indeed any iOS device) running the Viscotheque application, plus a central laptop (the Viscotheque server) which hosts the audio sampling engine and generates the real-time visual feedback. The Viscotheque server is implemented in the Impromptu audiovisual programming environment (Sorensen and Gardner 2010).

Each iPhone sends Open Sound Control (OSC) messages over the wi-fi local network to the server. Upon receiving these control messages, the appropriate processing is applied to the sound, and all the musician's sounds are played back through a PA system. Although the mobile devices cannot be used without the server, we shall often refer to the iPhone running the Viscotheque application as the 'instrument'. A central server architecture was used to allow for more complex audio processing and to facilitate logging of the interaction data for later analysis.

The Viscotheque is designed for co-located musicians, all participants jam together in the same room. While there is no technical reason to impose this restriction, peak moments in jamming are shared experiences, and non-verbal and embodied modes of communication are an important part of this activity.

A previous iteration of the Viscotheque system is described in more detail in Swift et al. (2010).

5.3.3 Experimental Approach

We conducted a series of experiments to study the nature of jamming in Viscotheque. Twelve participants (recruited from the university's music school) were divided into four groups of three. The primary instrument played varied between the musicians, and was one of either guitar, piano, or voice. Each musician's training was in the western classical tradition.

Each group, having no initial experience with the Viscotheque DMI, attended four jam sessions over a 4 week period. The groups were kept consistent over the 4 week period to allow the musicians to build a musical rapport. We observed the musicians as they explored the possibilities of the interface and began to develop their own styles and techniques as both individuals and coherent groups (Fig. 5.4).

These jam sessions were recorded in detailed system logs and also with a video camera which recorded the entire session (a still from one of the sessions is shown in Fig. 5.3). After the jam, the participants took part in a semi-structured focus group interview to discuss the experience, as per Stewart et al. (2006).

One key decision regarding the experimental design was to leave the sessions as open-ended as possible. The participants were not given any training in using the interface, although they could ask questions about the system in the interviews. No instructions were given to the groups about what they were trying to achieve, although as musicians familiar with 'jamming' they brought with them their own expectations of what to do in an improvisational setting.

The goal of the experiment was to see what patterns and cultures of use would emerge as the groups learned to jam together in Viscotheque. While the semi-controlled 'laboratory' setting opens the work up to criticisms of sterility and inauthenticity, there are significant advantages to being able to log every finger

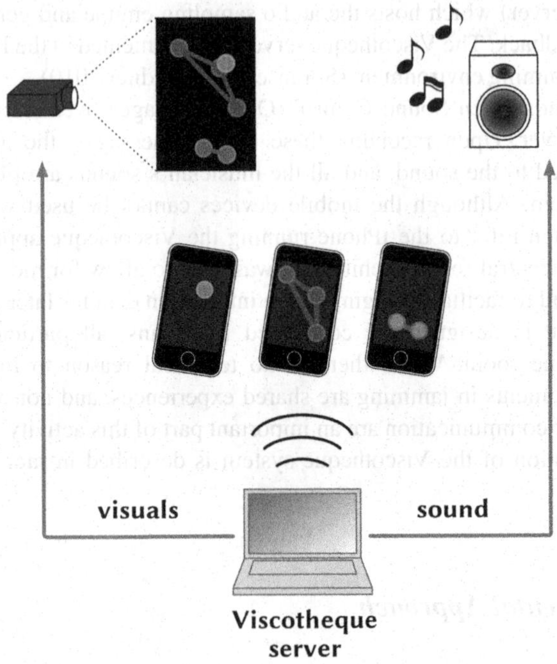

Fig. 5.4 Viscotheque system architecture. The musicians, represented by the iOS devices, are co-located and presented with real-time sonic and visual feedback

trace and capture every facial expression. More than this, though, the goal was to see how the participants described the experience, and to see if the groups experienced moments of deep satisfaction and euphoria associated with the best parts of improvisational music-making. How did the best bits happen, and what did they *feel* like?

5.4 Results

The video recordings of the sessions show encouraging signs of immersion and engagement between the participants. At various points heads were bobbing, shared smiles were visible, eyes were closed—all good (although potentially misleading) indicators of the depth of musical connection and engagement between participants.

The sonic interaction did not always conform to what would conventionally be defined as music. As they familiarised themselves with the sonic possibilities of the interface, the musicians at times created some dissonant and chaotic soundscapes. However, there were moments which were much more sonically coherent, at least to the western ear. The participants, in the interviews, described a conscious effort to 'match' or 'fit' with the musical contributions of the others.

In the designer's view, the interaction between the participants was largely chaotic, with each participant attempting to find a sound they liked, or which was in some way compelling. A sound may have been compelling for a number of reasons, such as novelty, an interesting timbre, a catchy rhythm or melody, or some other factor. Once one of the participants discovered such a sound, there would be a concerted effort from the other participants to fit with this sound, and to produce a sound which was sonically coherent in the current context. Sometimes the participants were able to achieve this, and sometimes they were not able to before the original compelling sound—the catalyst—disappeared, perhaps because of boredom or a lack of skill. When these moments of coherence did occur, they sometimes persisted for a short time (up to 60 s), as the musicians made subtle variations to their sounds in an attempt to develop the groove further. Then, after this time, these moments of coherence would disappear, either gradually dissolving or catastrophically breaking down.

The group interviews provide the participants with a chance to reflect and discuss the experience directly after it occurs. Reflecting on one of their sessions, group 3 described a deep satisfaction and enjoyment reminiscent of that discussed in Sect. 5.1.2. Participants are labelled P1–P12, interviewer is denoted by INT.

P7 *And then, and then you just, like, kindof recoup, and go back, and something—like there's points where there's something where it just all works, and for a second you just get that 'holy crap, let's just bottle this right now'*

P8 *(laughing) Yeah*

P9 *Yeah*

P7 *Grab it, and just seize onto it, and figure out what exactly it is, because this is awesome*

Similarly, in group 2

P4 *For me, it's similar to other experiences I've had with other musicians, it's that moment of 'that's really cool', and yeah… it only really comes from playing music with other people, but it's like (clicks fingers) just a feeling where you go 'wow, that's clicking and that's awesome'. Yeah.*

INT *Do you think it can…*

P4 *It's something where you're working together, everyone's contributing to this really cool sound, yeah.*

INT *Yeah, sure.*

P5 *It was a lot more fun this week. Last week was more of a puzzle, trying to work it out, but this week it was a lot more free.*

Again, in group 3

P7 *Yeah, I think what I enjoyed from it was the points when something would… you could just feel that little *click*, and it would just, you just kindof went 'bang! ' – fell into this position, and it was like – 'ok, this is it, we're here, we've got it'…*

P8 *yeah*

P7 *. . . and then it would just be, like,* P8 *would start doing this, just a little tap or something like that, and then it would work . . .*

P9 *yeah*

P7 *. . . and then* P9 *would just bring up something like that, and I would just, kindof, be messing with this thing, and it would all just accidentally fall into place.*

P8 *(emphatically) Yeah, I wasn't even *trying* to make it work, it would just work . . .*

P7 *. . . and it was just experimenting, yeah. And then when it worked, or when we found something that we all linked, it was, like—'bang!', it was just, like, you know . . . a lion pouncing on a zebra, or something.*

ALL *(laughter)*

P9 *. . . just flick the switch, it was like, 'bang', it worked.*

The groups described moments of frustration as well. Sometimes this frustration was directed towards the interface, sometimes towards their inability to make the sound that they felt the musical context called for, and sometimes the group's unwillingness or inability to listen to each other and try and play together.

While a few short excerpts with minimal context taken from 8 h of group interviews cannot convey the whole picture, it is clear that at times the participants are describing a felt experience akin to that of being in the groove. This was an exploratory field trial—the lack of a control group makes it difficult to be specific about the causality of these experiences. Indeed, this is one of the most difficult problems in DMI research, particularly in a jamming context. These results are presented here to give a concrete example of the issues discussed in Sect. 5.2.

5.5 Chasing a Feeling

The design approach taken by Viscotheque was motivated by an analysis of (and first hand experience with) the problem domain of jamming. In musical HCI, as indeed in all forms of HCI, this is a vital first step. In particular, the improvisational nature of jamming and skill required for fluency impose different instrumental constraints to those in more structured forms of music-making.

Four weeks is a very short time over which to examine the evolving practices of jamming in with a new instrument, even for musicians trained in the skills and conventions of jamming. Indeed, we hope to conduct longer studies in the future, and with more diverse users, including non-musicians. However, we are encouraged at the descriptions of the peak moments experienced by the musicians in this short time. This feedback, as well as the insights taken from the observations of the jamming groups in action, will be used to further shape and refine the Viscotheque interface.

The problem of chasing a feeling manifests itself in two ways in the design of DMIs for jamming. Firstly, as discussed in Sect. 5.1.2, the ultimate goal of the jamming group is a feeling; an experience. Yet experience can be so fickle;

so subject to forces beyond our control, and certainly beyond the control of the interaction designer. Our moment to moment experience is influenced by the complex web of relationships and influences that enfold us at every moment and in every aspect of our lives.

The second manifestation of this problem is in evaluating the success of our DMIs. In this sense we are not the musicians chasing a feeling ourselves, we are the designers and HCI practitioners trying to pin down the moments and antecedents of a specific feeling in others. This is an increasingly common problem in HCI more broadly (see Sect. 5.2.1), perhaps musical HCI can lead the way? Going forward, there are four approaches which seem promising:

- **Expert judgements**: can we have experts assess the participant's activity and assign a score based on their knowledge of the task domain? This is the approach taken by Bryan-Kinns and Hamilton (2009). A mature discipline of Interaction Criticism (Bardzell and Bardzell 2008) could provide a foundation for these expert judgements.
- **Qualitative data analysis**: this includes qualitative analysis of interviews, such as the Discourse Analysis method presented in Stowell et al. (2008) and the Grounded Theory approach of Glaser and Strauss (1967).
- **Unsupervised learning**: should we restrict ourselves to statistical techniques which require no class labels, such as clustering and novelty detection? This way, we avoid the need to calculate a definitive and meaningful dependent variable. Data can be naively grouped and partitioned, and then the meaning of the groups and patterns can be interpreted by the researcher. Text mining techniques may be applied to the interview transcripts as well.
- **Rich data collection**: Another approach is to measure the participants more closely, including biometrics such as EEG (brain), ECG (heart), EDA (skin) and EMG (skin) (see Nacke et al. 2010). A noted by Stowell et al. (2009), this is an exciting possibility for evaluating DMIs, but work needs to be done to provide justification for the meaningfulness of the obtained measures.

5.6 Conclusion

The Viscotheque DMI was has been developed with careful consideration of the musical and experiential context of jamming. Preliminary field trials suggest that the potential is there for the interface to support rich jamming experiences, and we continue to pursue those goals.

Music interface research in HCI has long felt the need to justify its design decisions with techniques more suited to technologies in the workplace. As HCI continues to explore issues of experience and technology, music interaction designers are increasingly liberated to affirm the real reasons we build the tools that we build—the ability of music to bring joy to the heart. We have not forgotten *why* we jam, hopefully we are increasingly able to justify our design decisions in mainstream HCI discourse.

References

Ashley, R. (2009). Musical improvisation. In *The oxford handbook of music psychology*. Oxford: Oxford University Press.

Bakker, A. (2005). Flow among music teachers and their students: The crossover of peak experiences. *Journal of Vocational Behavior, 66*(1), 26–44.

Bardzell, J., & Bardzell, S. (2008). Interaction criticism: A proposal and framework for a new discipline of HCI. In *CHI '08 extended abstracts on human factors in computing systems*. New York: ACM Request Permissions.

Berliner, P. (1994). Thinking in Jazz: The infinite art of improvisation. In *Chicago studies in ethnomusicology* (1st ed.). Chicago: University of Chicago Press.

Bryan-Kinns, N., & Hamilton, F. (2009). Identifying Mutual Engagement. *Behaviour & Information Technology, 31*, 1–25.

Csikszentmihalyi, M. (1991). *Flow: The psychology of optimal experience*. New York: Harper Collins.

Dobrian, C., & Koppelman, D. (2006). The 'E' in NIME. In *Proceedings of the 2006 international conference on new interfaces for musical expression (NIME06)*. Paris: IRCAM.

Doffman, M. (2009). Making it groove! Entrainment, participation and discrepancy in the 'conversation' of a Jazz Trio. *Language & History, 52*(1), 130–147.

Essl, G., & Rohs, M. (2009). Interactivity for mobile music-making. *Organised Sound, 14*(02), 197–207.

Fallman, D. (2011). The new good: Exploring the potential of philosophy of technology to contribute to human-computer interaction. In *CHI '11: Proceedings of the 2011 annual conference on Human factors in computing systems*. New York: ACM Press.

Flores, L., Pimenta, M., Miranda, E., Radanovitsck, E., & Keller, D. (2010). Patterns for the design of musical interaction with everyday mobile devices. In *IHC '10: Proceedings of the IX symposium on human factors in computing systems*. Porto Alegre: BrazilianComputerSociety.

Forlizzi, J., & Battarbee, K. (2004). Understanding experience in interactive systems. In *DIS '04: Proceedings of the 5th conference on designing interactive systems* (pp. 261–268). New York: ACM.

Gifford, T. (2013). Appropriate and complementary rhythmic improvisation in an interactive music system. In S. Holland, K. Wilkie, P. Mulholland, & A. Seago (Eds.), *Music and human-computer interaction* (pp. 271–286). London: Springer. ISBN 978-1-4471-2989-9.

Glaser, B., & Strauss, A. (1967). *The discovery of grounded theory: Strategies for qualitative research*. New York: Aldine Transaction.

Gurevich, M., Stapleton, P., & Marquez-Borbon, A. (2010, June 7–11). Style and constraint in electronic musical instruments. In *Proceedings of the 2010 Conference on New Interfaces for Musical Expression (NIME 2010)* (pp. 106–111). Sydney.

Lamont, A. (2009). Strong experiences of music in university students. In *Proceedings of the 7th triennial conference of European Society for the Cognitive Sciences of Music (ESCOM 2009)* (pp. 250–259). https://jyx.jyu.fi/dspace/handle/123456789/20886?show=full.

MacDonald, R., & Wilson, B. (2006). Constructions of jazz: How jazz musicians present their collaborative musical practice. *Musicae Scientiae, 10*(1), 59–83.

Mazzola, G. (2008). Jazz and the creative flow of collabortive gesturtes. In *Annäherungen und Grenzüberschreitungen*. http://www.uni-due.de/imperia/md/content/ekfg/sb_mazzola.pdf.

McDermott, J., Sherry, D., & O'Reilly, U. (2013). Evolutionary and generative music informs music HCI—and *vice versa*. In S. Holland, K. Wilkie, P. Mulholland, & A. Seago (Eds.), *Music and human-computer interaction* (pp. 222–240). London: Springer. ISBN 978-1-4471-2989-9.

McPherson, A., & Kim, Y. (2013). Piano technique as a case study in expressive gestural interaction. In S. Holland, K. Wilkie, P. Mulholland, & A. Seago (Eds.), *Music and human-computer interaction* (pp. 123–138). London: Springer. ISBN 978-1-4471-2989-9.

Miranda, E., & Wanderley, M. (2006). *New digital musical instruments: Control and interaction beyond the keyboard* (Computer Music and Digital Audio Series 1st ed.). Middleton: A-R Editions, Inc.

Monson, I. (1996). *Saying something: Jazz improvisation and interaction*. Chicago: University of Chicago Press.

Nacke, L., Grimshaw, M., & Lindley, C. (2010). More than a feeling: Measurement of sonic user experience and psychophysiology in a first-person shooter game. *Interacting with Computers, 22*(5), 336–343.

O'Modhrain, S. (2011). A framework for the evaluation of digital musical instruments. *Computer Music Journal, 35*(1), 28–42.

Paine, G. (2010, June 7–11). Towards a taxonomy of realtime interfaces for electronic music performance. In *Proceedings of the International Conference on New Interfaces for Musical Expression (NIME)* (pp. 436–439). Sydney.

Sawyer, R. K. (2006). Group creativity: Musical performance and collaboration. *Psychology of Music, 34*(2), 148.

Sawyer, R. K. (2007). *Group genius: The creative power of collaboration*. New York: Perseus Books Group.

Sawyer, R. K., & DeZutter, S. (2009). Distributed creativity: How collective creations emerge from collaboration. *Psychology of Aesthetics, Creativity, and the Arts, 3*(2), 81–92.

Sorensen, A., & Gardner, H. (2010). Programming with time: Cyber-physical programming with impromptu. In *OOPSLA '10: Proceedings of the ACM international conference on object oriented programming systems languages and applications*. New York: ACM.

Springett, M. (2009). Evaluating cause and effect in user experience. *Digital Creativity, 20*(3), 197–204.

Stewart, D., Shamdasani, P., & Rook, D. (Eds.). (2006). *Focus groups: Theory and practice* (2nd ed.). Newbury Park: Sage.

Stowell, D., & McLean, A. (2013). Live music-making: A rich open task requires a rich open interface. In S. Holland, K. Wilkie, P. Mulholland, & A. Seago (Eds.), *Music and human-computer interaction* (pp. 139–152). London: Springer. ISBN 978-1-4471-2989-9.

Stowell, D., Plumbley, M., & Bryan-Kinns, N. (2008). Discourse analysis evaluation method for expressive musical interfaces. In *Proceedings of the 2008 conference on New Interfaces for Musical Expression (NIME 2008)*, Genova.

Stowell, D., Robertson, A., Bryan-Kinns, N., & Plumbley, M. (2009). Evaluation of live human-computer music-making: Quantitative and qualitative approaches. *International Journal of Human Computer Studies, 67*(11), 960–975.

Swift, B., Gardner, H., & Riddell, A. (2010). Engagement networks in social music-making. In *OZCHI '10: Proceedings of the 22nd Australasian conference on computer-human interaction*.

Tanaka, A. (2006). Interaction, experience and the future of music. In *Consuming music together*. Dordrecht: Springer.

Tanaka, A. (2010, June 7–11). Mapping out instruments, affordances, and mobiles. In *Proceedings of the International Conference on New Interfaces for Musical Expression* (pp. 88–93). Sydney.

Tuedio, J. (2006). "And Then Flew On": Improvisational moments of rhizomatic assemblage in grateful dead musical experience. In *Texas/Southwest Popular Culture Association/American Popular Culture Association Joint National Conference*. http://www.csustan.edu/Philosophy/Tuedio/GratefulDeadPapers/GD-Improvisation.pdf.

Wallis, I., Ingalis, T., Campana, E., & Vuong, C. (2013). Amateur musicians, long-term engagement, and HCI. In S. Holland, K. Wilkie, P. Mulholland, & A. Seago (Eds.), *Music and human-computer interaction* (pp. 48–66). London: Springer. ISBN 978-1-4471-2989-9.

Wanderley, M., & Orio, N. (2002). Evaluation of input devices for musical expression: Borrowing tools from HCI. *Computer Music Journal, 26*(3), 62–76.

Wilkie, K., Holland, S., & Mulholland, P. (2010). What can the language of musicians tell us about music interaction design? *Computer Music Journal, 34*(4), 34–48.

Chapter 6
The Haptic Bracelets: Learning Multi-Limb Rhythm Skills from Haptic Stimuli While Reading

Anders Bouwer, Simon Holland, and Mat Dalgleish

Abstract The Haptic Bracelets are a system designed to help people learn multi-limbed rhythms (which involve multiple simultaneous rhythmic patterns) while they carry out other tasks. The Haptic Bracelets consist of vibrotactiles attached to each wrist and ankle, together with a computer system to control them. In this chapter, we report on an early empirical test of the capabilities of this system, and consider design implications. In the pre-test phase, participants were asked to play a series of multi-limb rhythms on a drum kit, guided by audio recordings. Participants' performances in this phase provided a base reference for later comparisons. During the following passive learning phase, away from the drum kit, just two rhythms from the set were silently 'played' to each subject via vibrotactiles attached to wrists and ankles, while participants carried out a 30-min reading comprehension test. Different pairs of rhythms were chosen for different subjects to control for effects of rhythm complexity. In each case, the two rhythms were looped and alternated every few minutes. In the final phase, subjects were asked to play again at the drum kit the complete set of rhythms from the pre-test, including, of course, the two rhythms to which they had been passively exposed. Pending analysis of quantitative data focusing on accuracy, timing, number of attempts and number of errors, in this chapter we present preliminary findings based on participants' subjective evaluations. Most participants thought that the

A. Bouwer (✉)
Intelligent Systems Lab, Faculty of Science, University of Amsterdam, Amsterdam, The Netherlands
e-mail: andersbouwer@uva.nl

S. Holland (✉)
Music Computing Lab, The Open University, Milton Keynes, Buckinghamshire, UK
e-mail: s.holland@open.ac.uk

M. Dalgleish
Department of Music, SSPAL, University of Wolverhampton, West Midlands, UK
e-mail: m.dalgleish2@wlv.ac.uk

S. Holland et al. (eds.), *Music and Human-Computer Interaction*, Springer Series on Cultural Computing, DOI 10.1007/978-1-4471-2990-5_6,

technology helped them to understand rhythms and to play rhythms better, and preferred haptic to audio to find out which limb to play when. Most participants indicated that they would prefer using a combination of haptics and audio for learning rhythms to either modality on its own. Replies to open questions were analysed to identify design issues, and implications for design improvements were considered.

6.1 Introduction

The acquisition and refinement of rhythm skills is generally vital for musicians. One particularly demanding aspect of rhythmic skills concerns multi-limb rhythms, i.e., multi-stream rhythms that require the coordinated use of hands and feet. The mastery of such rhythms is essential for drummers, but can also be highly beneficial to other musicians, for example piano and keyboard players (Gutcheon 1978). Dalcroze (Juntunen 2004) and others further suggest that the physical enaction of rhythms is essential even for the development of non-performance rhythm skills, such as exercised in composition and analysis. Crucially, physical enaction of many basic building blocks of rhythm, such as standard polyrhythms, is difficult without the coordinated use of multiple limbs. More broadly, it has been claimed that these skills may be able to contribute to general well-being, for example in improving mobility (Brown 2002) and alertness, and helping to prevent falls for older people (Juntunen 2004; Kressig et al. 2005). The development of skills of this nature may also be relevant in rehabilitation, for example from strokes or injury (Huang et al. 2010).

In recent experiments, we demonstrated that the use of haptics (vibrotactile devices) can support the learning of multi-limb rhythms of various kinds (Holland et al. 2010). These experiments featured a system called the Haptic Drum Kit. This system consists of: haptic devices (standard vibrotactiles in the original version, and more specialised tactors in the revised version) attached to the wrists and ankles; a computer system that feeds signals to the haptic devices; and a midi drum kit, which is played by the person while wearing the haptic devices, and which allows accurate data collection. These experiments showed that:

(a) haptic guidance alone can be used with similar success compared to audio guidance to support the acquisition of multi-limb rhythms,
(b) the combination of the two kinds of guidance is preferred to either kind alone, and
(c) haptic guidance has advantages for certain tasks (e.g. knowing which event goes with each limb) but disadvantages for other tasks (energetic body movement can mask the haptic signals).

These experiments also suggested a wide range of other applications. The current experiment aims to examine whether *passive* learning of multi-limb rhythms can occur when haptic rhythmic stimuli are applied away from a drum kit, or any other instrument, when the wearer is performing non-musical tasks, such as reading comprehension. That is to say, we are investigating the acquisition of skills enabled by experiencing haptic stimuli while distracted by another activity.

6.2 Background

In the case of at least some musical skills, learning via haptic systems is known to be possible. For example, Grindlay (2008) created a mechanical installation that employs haptic guidance by automatically moving a single drumstick that the learner was holding, and showed that this supported learning of rhythms which can be played with one hand. This contrasts in significant respects with the focus of the present study, in that we are interested specifically in multi-limb skills, for reasons outlined earlier, and we are particularly keen to explore the possibilities of passive learning with hands and feet free for other tasks.

Passive learning of at least one related musical skill has been demonstrated. Huang et al. (2008) built a system using a wireless haptic glove with vibrotactile effectors for each finger and demonstrated that users wearing the glove improved their performance at playing simple piano tunes after passive exposure to combined audio and haptic playback, while focused on another task. Participants in their study considered the haptic glove as uncomfortable to wear, however. Furthermore, the results of a later study indicated poor performance related to rhythm (Huang et al. 2010). The focus on fingers of one hand rather than multiple limbs also makes their system unsuitable for our purposes.

More details on the above research and other related work is discussed in Sect. 6.5.

6.3 The Haptic Bracelets

The vision behind the present study is of a portable haptic music player, i.e., a "Haptic iPod",[1] which can be worn all day while the wearer performs other tasks. Such an envisaged system would play music, like any other music player, while also transmitting associated rhythms to all four limbs as haptic pulses delivered via lightweight, wireless comfortable bracelets worn on wrists and ankles.

[1] In earlier work, we referred to a prototype of the family of systems we have designed and built, as the "Haptic iPod". We have now changed the name to the Haptic Bracelets, to avoid any confusion with products of Apple Inc. The Haptic Bracelets have numerous non-musical applications, for example in three-dimensional navigation, fitness, sports and rehabilitation. When it helps to emphasise the specific application to learning multi-limb rhythms, we sometimes use the alternative name "Rhythm Bracelets". The conception, overall design and theory of the Haptic Bracelets are due to Holland. The implementation and design of the current experiment is due to Bouwer. The design and implementation of the static design featured in this chapter is due to Dalgleish.

Fig. 6.1 The static lab-bench version of the Haptic Bracelets, used for passively learning multi-limb rhythms. Four tactors and straps are shown

For practical reasons, the version of the Haptic Bracelets chosen for this experiment is wired and stationary, as opposed to one of our prototype mobile versions. This conservative choice reflected the greater power and reliability of the stationary version at the time of the study. The version used here is essentially a modified version of the Haptic Drum Kit (Holland et al. 2010) without the drums.

The Haptic Bracelets as used in the current experiment employs four 'tactor' vibrotactile devices as the haptic transducers (see Fig. 6.1). These are secured to limbs, as needed, using elastic velcro bands. The tactors are driven by multi-channel audio signals controlled from a laptop via a firewire audio interface, amplified by two Behringer high-powered headphone amplifiers.

The theory behind the Haptic Bracelets draws on three principal areas: sensory motor contingency theory (O'Regan and Noe 2001), human entrainment theory (Clayton et al. 2004), and Dalcroze Eurhythmics (Juntunen 2004). For a detailed discussion, see Holland et al. (2010).

6.4 Evaluation of the Haptic Bracelets

To explore the potential of the Haptic Bracelets for passive learning of multi-limb rhythm patterns, an evaluation study was carried out. Preliminary findings based on participants' subjective evaluations are presented below.

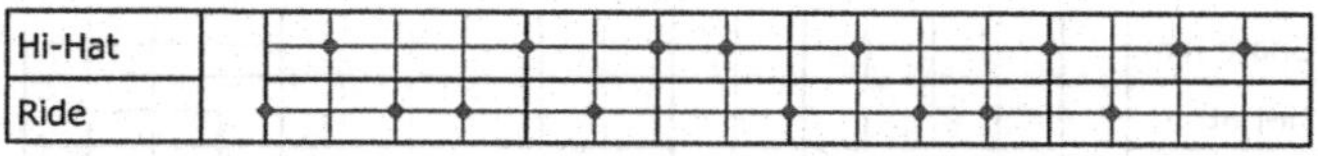

Fig. 6.2 A paradiddle

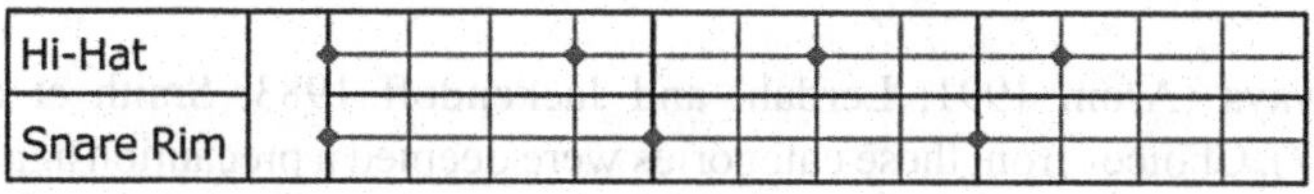

Fig. 6.3 A two-handed polyrhythm: three against four

6.4.1 Participants

Fifteen people participated in the experiment (eight men and seven women), aged 15–51. Three were experienced drummers (with approximately 10 years of experience playing the drums), five had a little drumming experience, and seven had no experience with drumming.

6.4.2 Materials: Selection of Reference Rhythms

To act as reference rhythms, six multi-limb rhythms were drawn from three technical categories. All of these rhythms are challenging for beginners, and some are challenging even for experienced musicians. Each category incorporates multi-limb coordination in a different way. Examples from a fourth category, pure metrical rhythms, were excluded as these are generally the easiest multi-limb patterns to play. The three categories used were as follows:

- linear rudiments, i.e., regular beats rendered figural by the way events are distributed across limbs (i.e., paradiddle);
- cross-rhythms (i.e., systematic polyrhythms);
- syncopated figural rhythms, based on the Cuban clave.

The six specific rhythms were as follows:

- a two handed paradiddle, i.e., RLRRLRLL (see Fig. 6.2);
- a two handed paraparadiddle, i.e., RLRLRRLRLRLL;
- a three against four polyrhythm (see Fig. 6.3);
- a five against four polyrhythm;
- a seven against four polyrhythm;
- a three-two clave combined with a quarter-note beat on the hi-hat, and a tumbao bass pattern (see Fig. 6.4).

Taking representative rhythms from these categories was motivated by evidence from music psychology that the human perception system deals with them in

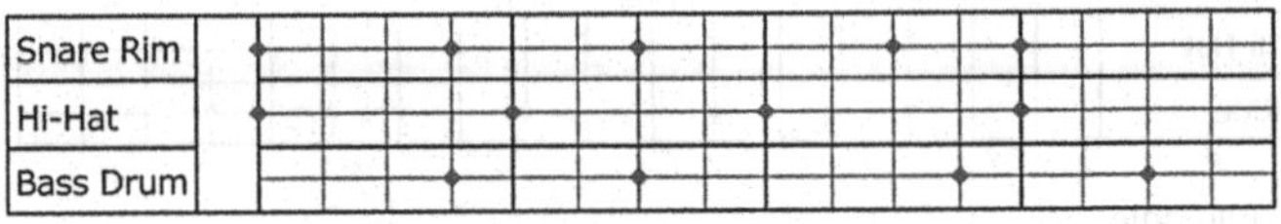

Fig. 6.4 A Cuban rhythm based on the clave pattern

different ways (Arom 1991; Lerdahl and Jackendoff 1983; Smith et al. 1994; Upitis 1987). Choices from these categories were deemed a precaution against over-generalisation of findings based on an overly narrow class of rhythms.

Viewed globally, a paradiddle is just a regular uniform beat, consisting of a continuous stream of notes assigned to two different limbs. However, viewed from the perspective of each individual limb, it requires a complex figural pattern to be played, involving single and double strokes and pauses lasting different time intervals. This is more difficult than simply alternating single strokes, where one limb can lead and the other can follow. The paradiddle and paraparadiddle (also called double paradiddle) are very common in instruction for drummers as they form part of the set of basic drumming rudiments. When played on one drum, the alternation of single and double strokes results in subtle variation in emphasis and tone color. As played aurally to subjects in the pre-test (see below), the pattern was distributed over the ride and hi-hat cymbals, to make it easier to discern what the individual limbs should play.

Cross-rhythms are systematic polyrhythms that combine two regular pulses played against each other. By nature they are polyphonic and generally played using two limbs. They are built from completely regular layered elements, but they are not hierarchical. That is to say, the periods in slower layers need not coincide with beats in faster layers (because the periods are relatively prime) except at the beginning of complete cycles. Because it is difficult to conceive of multiple meters running at the same time, learning to understand and play such rhythms can be done by counting the lowest common multiple, (e.g., 12 in the case of three against four), and determining which of these beats are played by which limb. The simplest cross-rhythm, two against three, is quite common in many styles of music, and was therefore left out of this study, but more complicated cross-rhythms such as the ones used here are not often found in western musics (although clear examples occur in jazz, fusion, metal, and classical genres). Cross-rhythms are more common in certain Indian, African, and Afro-Cuban music traditions (e.g., see Arom 1991).

The Cuban rhythm based on the Son three-two clave (see Fig. 6.4) is a predominantly figural rhythm, where the patterns played by a given limb are irregular due to syncopation (see the top and bottom line, which are played by a hand and a foot, respectively). Furthermore, the combination of syncopated patterns into a polyphonic (multi-limb) orchestration, as in this example, increases the complexity of the rhythm because the combinations of limbs played synchronously differ for different points in time (i.e., some limbs are played simultaneously at certain points in time, while other combinations of limbs co-occur at other points in time). This kind of organization tends to make challenging demands on memorization, analysis, retention and reproduction.

6.4.3 Setup: Experimental Tasks and Methods

1. The first phase of the experiment was a pre-test phase, in which subjects were asked to play, as best they could, a series of six multi-limb rhythms on a midi drum kit, based on audio playback of each rhythm. These performances served as base reference levels for comparing performances in the post-test phase.
2. The second phase of the experiment was a passive learning phase, away from the drum kit and in a different room. For this phase, subjects had rhythms silently played back haptically via tactors attached to their wrists and/or ankles while they were engaged in a distraction task. The distraction task was a 30-min reading comprehension test. During this task, only two rhythms from the set of six in the first phase were 'played' to each subject: different pairs of rhythms were chosen for different subjects, so that clear distinctions could be made in the third phase. Within that constraint, choices were also made to accommodate for different levels of playing experience. In each case, the two different rhythms were repeated and then alternated every few minutes until the end of the task.
3. The third phase was a post-test phase, in which subjects were asked again to play on the midi drum kit the complete set of rhythms from the pre-test (Fig. 6.5). Clearly, this included the two rhythms to which the subject had been given passive haptic exposure in the second phase. Each subject's performance for all rhythms was compared to the corresponding baseline performances in the pre-test, in terms of accuracy, timing, the number of attempts and the number of errors in their best attempt.
4. Finally, a questionnaire was administered that asked about subjects' experiences during the experiment, and their attitudes towards the Haptic Bracelets technology.

Clearly, a key outcome will be to determine whether there were measurably greater improvements between pre-test and post test in the case of rhythms for which subjects experienced passive exposure, as compared with the other rhythms. As already noted, these results are still undergoing analysis, so in this chapter we present preliminary results based on participants' subjective evaluations from the questionnaire.

6.4.4 Questionnaire Results

In this section, we present participants' responses to the 14 closed items on the questionnaire in turn. A summary of these responses is given at the end of this section.

Do you like the idea of being able to feel the beat, using haptic technology?
(The possible answers were: 1: I dislike the idea very much, 2: I dislike the idea a little, 3: I feel neutral about the idea, 4: I like the idea a little and 5: I like the idea very much)

Fig. 6.5 Subjects were asked to play the test rhythms without the Haptic Bracelets in pre-test and post-test phases

The idea of haptically feeling rhythms is clearly appealing, since all participants answered positively to this question. Seven subjects answered "I like the idea a little", and eight subjects answered "I like the idea a lot" (Median = 5, Min = 4, Max = 5). However, we should note that the volunteers coming to participate in this study are likely to be more positive towards the technology than people in general.

How comfortable was it to wear the technology?
(1: very uncomfortable, 2: slightly uncomfortable, 3: neutral, 4: slightly comfortable, 5: very comfortable)

Although the scores were generally more positive than neutral (Median = 4, Min = 1, Max = 4), scores varied among participants, with ten participants scoring 4 (reasonably comfortable), one participant scoring 3 (neutral), two participants scoring 2 (a little uncomfortable), and two participants scoring 1 (very uncomfortable). Seven participants indicated it became slightly more comfortable over the course of the experiment, whereas three participants indicated it became slightly less comfortable over time; the rest indicated it didn't change.

Do you think this technology helped you to play any of the rhythms better?
(1: not at all, 2: a little, 3: a lot)

Eight participants answered 2 (a little) (Median = 2, Min = 1, Max = 3). Three participants reported a score of 1 (not at all), whereas one reported the maximum score of 3 (A lot). Two participants did not answer this question, indicating that they did not feel that they could answer it after experiencing the haptics for only a brief period.

Do you think this technology helped you to understand any of the rhythms?
(1: not at all, 2: a little, 3: a lot)

Seven of the participants scored a 2 (a little) for this question (Median = 2, Min = 1, Max = 3). Five people scored 3 (a lot), which is a more positive reply than for the previous question. Nevertheless, three people scored 1 (not at all).

When you started reading, how much attention did you pay to the pattern of the beat, compared with the reading task?
(1: no attention to the pattern, 2: some attention to the pattern, 3: about evenly split, 4: more than half on the pattern, 5: mostly on the pattern)

When they started reading, the participants reportedly paid slightly less attention to the haptic rhythmic stimuli compared to the reading task (Median = 2, Min = 2, Max = 5). Nine participants scored 2 (Some attention to the pattern), two participants scored 3 (About evenly split), three participants scored 4 (More than half on the pattern), and one scored 5 (Mostly on the pattern). The fact that none of the participants scored 1 (No attention to the pattern) indicates that it is hard to completely ignore the haptic stimuli.

When you had been reading for a while, how much attention did you pay to the pattern of the beat, compared with the reading task?
(1: no attention to the pattern, 2: some attention to the pattern, 3: about evenly split, 4: more than half on the pattern, 5: mostly on the pattern)

After reading for a while, reported attention levels to the haptic stimuli dropped slightly (Median = 2, Min = 1, Max = 4). Two participants now reported a score of 1 (No attention to the pattern).

Which type of information helps most to find out which drum to play when?
(1: audio is much better, 2: audio is slightly better, 3: no preference, 4: haptic is slightly better, 5: haptic is much better)

The participants' scores indicated a slight preference for the haptic information (Median = 4, Min = 1, Max = 5). Five people scored 5 (haptic is much better), whereas two people scored 1 (audio is much better), indicating a wide variety in personal preferences. One person did not answer this question.

Which type of information helps most to find out which limb to play when?
(1: audio is much better, 2: audio is slightly better, 3: no preference, 4: haptic is slightly better, 5: haptic is much better)

For this question, the preference for haptics was even stronger (Median = 5, Min = 2, Max = 5). Eight participants scored 5 (haptic is much better), while only one scored 2 (audio is slightly better). One person did not answer this question.

Which type of information helps most to find out when the pattern repeats?
(1: audio is much better, 2: audio is slightly better, 3: no preference, 4: haptic is slightly better, 5: haptic is much better)

To find out when the pattern repeats, participants only have a slight preference for the haptic information (Median = 3, Min = 1, Max = 5). Three persons indicated a score of 5 (haptic is much better), whereas one indicated a score of 1 (audio is much better). One person did not answer.

Which type of information helps most to understand a rhythm?
(1: audio is much better, 2: audio is slightly better, 3: no preference, 4: haptic is slightly better, 5: haptic is much better)

To understand a rhythm, participants have a slight preference for haptics (Median = 4, Min = 2, Max = 5). Four participants scored a 5 (haptic is much better), against two participants scoring a 2 (audio is slightly better). Two persons left this blank.

Which type of information helps most to play a rhythm?
(1: audio is much better, 2: audio is slightly better, 3: no preference, 4: haptic is slightly better, 5: haptic is much better)

To play a rhythm, there was also a slight preference for haptics (Median = 4, Min = 2, Max = 5). Two people scored a 5 (haptic is much better), against one person scoring a 2 (audio is slightly better). Two people did not answer this question.

How easy was it to play in time with the audio playback?
(1: very difficult, 2: a little difficult, 3: neutral, 4: reasonably easy, 5: very easy)

Most participants found it at least a little difficult to play in time with the audio feedback (Median = 2, Min = 1, Max = 4). Seven people even found it very difficult (a score of 1), but on the other hand, three participants found it a little easy (a score of 4). Of these last three, one was an experienced drummer, and the two others had some experience with rhythms. The other two experienced drummers scored a 2 (a little difficult), indicating that the materials were not straightforward, not even for experienced drummers.

Would you prefer audio, haptics, or both for learning rhythms?
(1: I prefer audio only, 2: I prefer both audio and haptics, 3: I prefer haptics only)

With a large majority of 11 participants scoring 2 (I prefer both audio and haptics), there is a clear preference for having both audio and haptics (Median = 2, Min = 2, Max = 3). Two participants scored 3 (I prefer haptics only), and nobody indicated a preference for audio only. Two persons did not answer this question. Taken together, this suggests that haptics offer a clear added value, especially when provided together with audio.

Did you enjoy the experiment?
(1: I disliked it very much, 2: I disliked it a little, 3: I feel neutral about it, 4: I liked it a little, 5: I liked it very much)

Overall, the majority of participants enjoyed taking part in the experiment (Median = 5, Min = 2, Max = 5), with eight participants scoring the maximum score of 5 (I liked it very much). However, two participants scored a 2 (I disliked it a little), and one scored a 3 (neutral), indicating that the positive feeling was not universal.

6.4.5 Open Questions

There were six open questions, which are listed below, followed by all replies from participants. A summary of the responses can be found later in the chapter.

Are there things that you liked about using the technology in the training session?

1. "Unfamiliar feeling, tickle. Friendly appearance of the hardware – they beep slightly." (P1)
2. "It was fun to play the electronic drums." (P2)
3. "I did not perceive it as 'training'. My instruction was to read the text. It was nice to feel the rhythm through haptic." (P3)
4. "Fun to use new technology in novel ways." (P4)
5. "No. Interesting to find out about another way of learning though." (P5)
6. "I had to concentrate harder in order to be able to read the text. Of course it was a matter of decision to set the reading task as the priority." (P7)
7. "Understanding the complexity of different rhythms like learning a language." (P8)
8. "Clarity of the haptics. 'seeing' the repeated foot figure in the son clave. 'seeing' how the 4/5 inter plays." (P9)
9. "I had never played a drum kit like that, so was exciting." (P10)
10. "The buzzers were strong enough to feel." (P11)
11. "It helped to differentiate between the limbs, whereas using audio feedback it is often hard to separate limb function." (P13)
12. "That it helped me understand the rhythm." (P14)
13. "Being able to flawlessly distinguish between which limb to use. The audio is more confusing." (P15)

Are there things that you didn't like about using the technology in the training session?

14. "The way the cables were soldered made it feel like one has to be very careful not to move too much. Wireless would be nice, I can imagine." (P1)
15. "I wish I had a chance to play with haptic on." (P3)
16. "The comprehension test. Give me some maths." (P4)
17. "Maybe a bit annoying after some time." (P7)
18. "Started to get a little irritating after a while due to the repetitive nature." (P8)
19. "Having to do the reading. Let's have a portable one." (P9)
20. "No dislike." (P10)
21. "I was useless!" (P12)
22. "That it didn't allow for me to physically practice much, because I find it difficult to play a polyrhythm; I have to build a physical memory." (P13)
23. "That the audio made it difficult to differentiate between which drums needed to be played." (P14)
24. "The wrist/ankle strap/haptics cables are unwieldy – but that can't be helped." (P15)

Are there things that you like about the haptic playback?

25. "It makes the playing of complex patterns easier to understand." (P2)
26. "I can feel the rhythm better." (P3)
27. "Helps to concentrate on individual limbs." (P4)
28. "Being able to distinguish right and left more easily." (P5)
29. "I like the technology cause (it) assists you (to) embody the rhythm in a new promising way." (P7)
30. "Knowing your left from your right." (P8)
31. "Clarity of timing. Clarity of assignment of limb to time stream." (P9)
32. "Easier to concentrate on the particular rhythms within a polyrhythm (than audio only)." (P10)
33. "The haptic allows you to think the process through before you actually play. It may reduce the likelihood of learning wrong patterns." (P13)
34. "That you could easily feel which drums you needed to play when and how quickly it went on to the next beat." (P14)
35. "The distinction between instruments (limbs)." (P15)

Are there things that you don't like about the haptic playback?

36. "Might be annoying or distracting or boring to use in everyday life. Would rather listen to actual music." (P5)
37. "(Neutral) repetition gets irritating 'under the skin'" (P8)
38. "Just initially strapping on the legs. Portability." (P9)
39. "The ankle vibrations felt weak on me and I had to concentrate hard to feel them." (P10)
40. "On the paradiddle it felt that when the 2 hand buzzers coincided the right one was weaker than the left one." (P11)
41. "That I didn't hear the audio at the same time." (P13)
42. "That at times they got a bit annoying." (P14)
43. "Slightly disorientating when a new rhythm starts playing." (P15)

Do you have any suggestions to improve the haptics as used in this study?

44. "I would have liked to try the haptics while playing the drums." (P2)
45. "Use it while playing." (P3)
46. "Sounds are distracting -> Hard to work out where sound is coming from. Need pure vibrations." (P4)
47. "None that I can think of… end of play brain drain." (P8)
48. "Please go portable and wireless!" (P9)
49. "Have ankle vibrodetectors that have stronger vibrations." (P10)
50. "Feeling the rhythm whilst listening to the audio would be a lot better to create a more holistic understanding of the polyrhythm and the interaction needed by the limbs." (P13)
51. "Vary the strength of the vibrations for different limbs." (P14)

Do you have any other comments?

52. "The laptop mouse pad (used to scroll text and select answers in the reading comprehension test) was hard to use." (P5)

53. "There was too much to take in – i.e. sequences too long + too many + too complex." (P5)
54. "Subject's familiarity with playing from score/improvising is probably a key variable." (P6)
55. "Music is a universal language that can have profound impact on learning and collaboration, building community as part of an oral tradition. The most ancient form of meditation." (P8)
56. "Quality of haptic 4/5 was more clear than [merely] audio signal." (P9)
57. "I think participants may need a little time to practice after the haptics without the audio playback on." (P13)

6.4.6 Summary of Findings from the Closed Responses

The responses to closed items on the questionnaire demonstrated a wide range of attitudes. The system did not meet with universal approval. However, the views of the 15 participants towards the haptic bracelets as used in the training session were generally positive. The principal findings from this section of the questionnaire can be summarized as follows:

- All users liked the idea of being able to feel the beat using haptic technology.
- 12 of 15 participants thought the technology helped them to *understand* rhythms.
- 9 of 15 participants thought the technology helped them to *play* rhythms better.
- Most participants preferred haptic to audio to find out which *limb* to play when.
- There was a slight preference for haptic to find out which *drum* to play when.
- All participants paid some attention to the haptic stimuli initially while reading.
- After a while, only two participants reported paying no attention at all.
- A clear preference was stated for learning rhythms with *both haptic and audio.*

6.4.7 Summary of Issues Emerging from the Open Questions

Several of the responses to open items on the questionnaire suggest design issues, and reflect ways in which the current prototype could be improved. The relevant responses are summarised in four broadly related groups.

The first group of comments identified miscellaneous limitations and annoyances of the system, centered around two aspects: irritation and boredom felt or expected after repeated use (see quotes 17, 18, 36, 37, and 42), and the desire to combine feeling the haptics with listening to audio (quote 41 and 50). Some of these comments may be specific to the current implementation; others may apply to any implementation of the core idea.

One of the most obvious potential benefits of a multi-limb haptic system, the ease of assigning rhythm streams to limbs was noted by several participants (see quote 11, 12, 13, 27, 28, 30, and 31).

The passive haptic stimuli appear to have prompted some participants to reflect insightfully on the rhythms, as evidenced by quotes 8, 27, 28, 32, and 33.

Some comments pointed to options for improved designs, in particular combining the sensation of haptics with playing the drums (quote 15, 44, and 45), as we employed in the Haptic Drum Kit (Holland et al. 2010), using a portable wireless version (quote 48), and more control over the strength of the haptic signals on particular limbs (quote 39 and 40).

For a detailed discussion of the implications of these considerations, see Sect. 6.6 on design issues and further work.

6.5 Related Work

The potential of using haptics in learning and training motor skills has been acknowledged in many domains, leading to applications for a diverse range of task types, including learning complex 3D motions (Feygin et al. 2002), learning of force skills (Morris et al. 2007), sensory substitution (Bird et al. 2008), training in snowboarding skills (Spelmezan et al. 2009), and posture for violin players (van der Linden et al. 2011). In most of these systems, the goal is to support learning the desired movement patterns necessary for carrying out the specific task, involving the detection of mistakes and giving haptic signals to correct suboptimal movements. For example, Morris et al. (2007) demonstrated that haptic feedback can enhance the learning of force skills, and Bird et al. (2008) reviewed research in sensory substitution, where one sensory modality is used to facilitate performance in tasks usually guided by another sensory modality. Examples include flight suits that communicate warning information to pilots using puffs of air. Spelmezan et al. (2009) considered a wireless prototype vibrotactile system for real-time snowboard training. This system detected common mistakes during snowboarding and gave students immediate feedback suggesting how to correct their mistakes.

Although some of this work also relates to the movement of multiple limbs, these systems are in general not particularly concerned with timing skills in coordinated multi-limb movement, as in the current study. One finding of relevance to timing skills came from Feygin et al. (2002). In this study, subjects learned to perform a complex motion in three dimensions by being physically guided through the ideal motion. The finding was that although trajectory shape was better learned by visual training, temporal aspects of the task were more effectively learned from haptic guidance.

Within the domain of music, there are numerous systems which incorporate haptic feedback into virtual or physical musical instruments. Examples can be found in O'Modhrain (2000), Collicutt et al. (2009), Sinclair (2007), and Miranda and Wanderley (2006). A project that aims to direct feedback to the players arms, rather than the instrument, was carried out by Van der Linden et al. (2011), who showed that haptic feedback can be used for training in the posture and bowing of violin students.

Work that shares our focus on learning polyphonic rhythms includes the following projects: LapSlapper (Andresen et al. 2010), the Programmable Haptic Rhythm Trainer (Ni 2010), and Polyrhythm Hero (McNulty 2009).

LapSlapper (Andresen et al. 2010) allows players to create midi drum sounds by striking their hands on any available surface, such as the player's own body. This is achieved by using piezo microphones attached to gloves, and optionally in a shoe. Outputs from the microphones are converted by Max/MSP into triggers for midi events with midi velocity information. Different microphones may be mapped to different midi instruments. This simple idea, which echoes earlier systems developed by Zimmerman et al. (1987) with just such an aim, and other systems developed by musicians such as Kraftwerk, does not involve technologically mediated haptic feedback, However, drumming varied rhythms on one's own body as method for improving rhythm skills has been long recommended by musicians (Gutcheon 1978). This was one motivation for both the Haptic Drum kit and the Haptic Bracelets.

The Programmable Haptic Rhythm Trainer (Ni 2010) consists of a demo board with a 4×4 keypad and an LCD display. The keypad may be used to enter two rhythms, in a notation reminiscent of a drum machine, as well as other information such as tempo, time signature and number of repeats. The user then rests two fingertips on plastic fittings that cap each of two servomotors. These caps wiggle in time to the two rhythms. The time signature is indicated by a regular clicking sound synchronized with blinks of the LCD. The first beat of each bar is emphasised by a click at a different pitch, as in many electronic metronomes. The imposition of a single time signature seems to make this system less suitable for dealing with polyrhythms, and the encoding of the wiggles appears to encode durations rather than onsets, which may not be ideal for the clear communication of rhythms (though this could be tested empirically). The need to hold fingertips to the motors seems to obviate the possibility of drumming while feeling rhythms.

Polyrhythm Hero (McNulty 2009) is a mobile rhythm training game for the iPhone, with two large buttons labelled 'left' and 'right'. The game challenges users to tap the two rhythms of a polyrhythm simultaneously, one on the left button, and the other on the right button. Any two-voice uniform polyrhythm specifiable by an integer ratio $m{:}n$ can be created as a target rhythm, where m and n are integers between 1 and 16. The rhythms to be tapped are played to the user as audio using two contrasting percussion timbres. Two optional hints about the rhythm are also available. These are a single periodic pulse from the phone's vibrator at the beat where the two rhythms coincide, and a static graphical illustration showing two lines side by side subdivided into m and n sections respectively. Based on participants subjective evaluation, the audio and visual clues queues were helpful but the haptic downbeat indicator was more problematic. The author suggests that the nature of the vibration was at fault rather than its conception. From our design experience with various haptic effectors (Holland et al. 2010), we suspect that the haptic pulse produced by the iPhone may have been too blurred to permit the needed temporal resolution for the desired purpose.

Reflecting on these three systems, the Haptic Bracelets share a focus on multi-limbed rhythm skills with Lapslapper, but contrast in that the bracelets provide multi-limbed haptic guidance, and can teach passively as well as actively. The Haptic Bracelets share a common interest in polyrhythm training with Polyrhythm Hero, but differ in several ways: the Haptic Bracelets involve all four limbs; they use haptic stimuli to communicate all rhythmic events, not just common downbeats; the use of haptics in the Haptic Bracelets appears to be better liked and more effective; and the Haptic Bracelets can be used passively as well as actively. Various limitations of the Programmable Haptic Rhythm Trainer as currently reported were noted earlier. To the best of our knowledge, the use of four limb haptic stimuli, especially for teaching rhythm skills, is unique to the Haptic Bracelets and Haptic Drum Kit.

Work that addresses the use of haptics to support (passive) learning of musical tasks involving temporal sequencing includes the work by Grindlay (2008), Lewiston (2008), and Huang et al. (2008, 2010). As already mentioned in Sect. 6.2, Grindlay (2008) focused on monophonic rhythms where the system physically moved a single hand of a human subject to train in playing monophonic rhythms. Haptics were shown to help significantly to improve performance of playing rhythmic patterns with one hand, and haptic plus audio guidance was found to work best.

Lewiston's (2008) five-key keyboard was designed for a single hand in a fixed position. The keyboard uses computer-controlled electromagnets to guide finger movements during sensorimotor learning of tasks involving sequential key presses, such as typing or playing the piano. Preliminary data suggested that this form of haptic guidance is more effective at teaching musical beginners to perform a new rhythmic sequence, when compared with audio-only learning.

As also noted earlier, Huang et al. (2008) explored the passive learning of rhythmic fingering skills for piano melodies. Later work by Huang et al. (2010) similarly considered a lightweight wireless haptic system with a single fingerless glove containing one vibrotactile per finger. The system was used to teach sequences of finger movements to users haptically, while they performed other tasks. A set of finger movements, if executed correctly and transferred to a musical keyboard, played a monophonic melody. In experiments, target melodies were typically restricted to five pitches, so that no movement of the hand (as opposed to the fingers) was needed. Sample melodies contained rests and notes of different durations. A study demonstrated that passive learning with audio and haptics combined was significantly more effective than audio only. Interestingly, in a second study that compared the amount of time required for subjects to learn to play short, randomly generated passages using passive training versus active training, participants with no piano experience could repeat the passages after passive training alone, while subjects with piano experience often could not.

One item of related research arguably in a category of its own is The Possessed Hand (Tamaki et al. 2011). This system employs a forearm band with 28 electrode pads, which, without any invasive technology, i.e. without penetrating the wearer skin, allows a computer to take fine control of the wearers finger movements for a limited period. This research is perhaps unique for the test subjects' comments, which include "Scary… just scary" and "I felt like my body was hacked".

Two beginners were able to play short Kyoto passages making fewer mistakes when their hands were externally controlled using Possessed Hand technology. The designers note that this technology may have future musical applications, but also that issues of reaction rate, accuracy, and muscle fatigue need to be investigated. We would like to stress an important difference between the work by Grindlay (2008) and Tamaki et al. (2011), and our work. They both use a system that physically (and to different degrees involuntarily) controls human movements, while in our work (as well as most other related work) the haptics are only used to communicate signals to guide movement, and the decision to physically act upon these signals remains with the user. This distinction between guidance and involuntary control was blurred in one interesting case described by Huang et al. (2010, p. 798), where one of the 16 participants reported "an involuntary twitch in response to the vibration motors resting just below his second knuckle".

From the above broadly related work, the two projects with most relevant similarities to the present study are the work by Grindlay (2008) and Huang et al. (2008, 2010). We will briefly compare these with the Haptic Bracelets. Grindlay's work shares our focus on the use of haptics for passive learning of drumming skills, but contrasts in at least two ways: firstly, the form of support (vibrotactile guidance in our case vs. physically controlled movement in Grindlay's work) and secondly, and perhaps most importantly, our specific focus on multi-limb movement and multiple parallel streams of rhythmic patterns, as opposed to a single rhythmic line. In the case of Huang et al., similarities with our approach include a common focus on haptics, passive learning, and multiple body parts. Major contrasts include the use of four limbs vs. the fingers of one hand, and multiple parallel rhythms vs. monophonic melodies. Whereas Grindlay (2008) found that passive haptic training benefited learning of rhythms, Huang et al. (2010) found their participants to perform poorly on rhythm, presumably because they focused on performing the melodic note sequence correctly, slowing down when needed. In our work, the presented preliminary results indicate that the Haptic Bracelets have strong potential for learning multi-limb rhythmic skills. Like in our study, Huang et al. also used a reading comprehension task as distraction. Interestingly, the participants in Huang's study noted that perception of the tactile stimuli was (almost) subconscious, while in our study, many participants found it hard to ignore the haptics while reading. To what extent this difference relates to the position (fingers vs. wrists and ankles) or signal strength of the haptics is unclear at this stage.

6.6 Design Issues and Further Work

In this section, we relate the design issues emerging from participants' subjective experiences as noted earlier, to the design vision of the Haptic Bracelets, and consider the implications for further work.

Recall that the vision behind the Haptic Bracelets is of a portable music player for both active and passive learning, able to be worn all day while working on other tasks. This system should optionally play music while also optionally transmitting associated rhythms as haptic pulses delivered via lightweight, wireless, easy to don bracelets worn on wrists and ankles.

For the purposes of the research presented in this chapter, we have focused exclusively on passive learning via haptics, without accompanying music. However, future versions of the Haptic Bracelets are intended to allow stereo audio to be played back via headphones while limb-specific information is played back in exact synch via four haptic channels. This change will address many of the miscellaneous issues raised by participants, as follows.

Repetitiveness. Where music and haptic signals are synchronized, playback may not have to be so repetitive in order to support active and passive learning as when haptic stimuli are used alone. A case for this view could be made as follows. When listening to tonal, metrical music (i.e. most traditional and popular western music) there is much empirical evidence (Sloboda 1985) that beginners and experts, composers and listeners alike, all tend to be able to perceive the same wide variety of structural boundaries, using combined markers including pitch, timbre, volume and rhythm. Music is readily perceived by listeners as structured quasi-hierarchically, and this helps to make the accurate memorization and reproduction of such music far easier than the memorization or reproduction of equally long periods of arbitrary sound (Sloboda 1985). When providing haptic playback alone, much of this structuring information is not present, so that frequent repetition of short sections of material is an important aid to learning. By contrast, with accompanying music, the needed structuring and framing and context for the rhythms is far more readily provided, so that more efficient learning may be possible with less repetition. For now this argument remains speculative, and further work is required to test it empirically.

Locating the start and end points of rhythms. When a repeated haptic stimulus is used without audio, it can be hard to locate the start and end points of the rhythm. This matters because two identical repeated rhythms played with different start and end points may not be recognised as the same rhythm (Sloboda 1985). One obvious way to indicate the starting point of a haptically repeated rhythm would be to play the starting pulse more "loudly". However, this solution is not always possible, since in order to deliver clearly recognized pulses (a problem noted by participants in the study) haptic systems may play all pulses as "loudly" as possible. Another problem with such an approach is that some rhythms are most usefully conceptualized as starting on a rest. A different solution to all of these problems would be to deliver a framing pulse haptically at a different point on the body. Fortunately, however, for our purposes, this whole class of problems can be solved more easily simply by synchronizing haptic delivery with the musical context via audio. Thus, this particular design issue becomes moot.

"Holistic... less boring". More generally, likely benefits of adding synchronized musical context in the manner discussed above are well expressed by two of the participants, P5: "Might be annoying or distracting or boring to use in everyday life.

Would rather listen to actual music.", and P13: "Feeling the rhythm whilst listening to the audio would be a lot better to create a more holistic understanding of the polyrhythm and the interaction needed by the limbs."

Haptic Balance. Some users found haptic stimuli harder to perceive as clearly on one limb as on another. Although the current system already allowed the experimenter to control the balance of individual tactors, this was done only once, at the beginning of each session. A straightforward refinement in future versions will be to provide a balance control for users to adjust the levels of the different vibrotacticles themselves whenever they want to.

"Use it while playing". From previous work (Holland et al. 2010), it is clear that Haptic Bracelets have diverse applications for drummers and other musicians while they are playing their instruments (for example, hierarchical click-tracks that leave the ears free, an inter-musician communication system that leaves the eyes free, rhythm section synchronization where foldback is inadequate, and training applications). Equally, the vision of learning rhythms and gaining rhythmic insights while commuting or carrying out non-music related chores is compelling. One way in which the Haptic Bracelets could have their cake and eat it in this regard would be simply to add an accelerometer to each bracelet, so that it may optionally be used to trigger chosen midi or sampled instruments. Such an 'air drum' or 'body drum' feature follows a long line of previous systems such as Zimmerman et al.'s (1986) data glove, explicitly motivated by a desire to play 'air guitar', and some Kraftwerk stage systems. See also (Andresen et al. 2010) discussed earlier, for a more recent and pleasingly simple approach to the body drum idea.

"A bit annoying... maybe a bit irritating after some time". Even if we imagine a system with all of the above design issues addressed, and even with very light, wireless comfortable and easy-to-put-on bracelets, and (crucially) appropriate off-switches, it is clear that the Haptic Bracelets may still not be for everyone.

Future empirical work. In parallel to our current development work, empirical work is planned. Key experiments will involve active and passive learning using a mobile system with synchronized music, as well as experiments with possible medical applications. Such applications could address areas as diverse as rehabilitation, conductive education, Parkinsons, Stroke, and other conditions which affect limb movement and co-ordination.

6.7 Conclusions

In this chapter we have presented the Haptic Bracelets and the design vision and theoretical rationale behind them; presented and analysed findings based on users' subjective evaluations; presented and analysed design implications from the evaluation; and proposed design solutions.

Results from users' subjective evaluations suggest that the passive learning of multi-limb rhythms is a promising approach that may help both in learning to play and to understand complex rhythms. All participants in our study had a positive to very positive attitude towards this use of haptic technology. They indicated several advantages of the system, including increased support for distinguishing between limbs, increased understanding of the complexity of rhythms, and 'fun to use'. An important negative finding was that the haptic buzzers got slightly irritating after a while for some participants. Many participants noted that they would like to feel the haptics in combination with hearing audio, and/or while playing the drums. Some participants commented that they did not enjoy the reading task, so in further studies, we might consider alternative distraction tasks, including tasks chosen by participants. Other interesting findings include the fact that all participants paid at least some attention to the haptics while reading. If the passive learning phase is not perceived as training, as one participant noted, this might explain why the haptics are considered to facilitate learning difficult rhythms and making the process more enjoyable. More research is necessary to determine exactly under which circumstances haptics can be used most effectively, in passive and active modes of learning.

Design issues emerging from participants' subjective experiences were noted and analysed, including repetitiveness, locating the start and end points of rhythms, holistic understanding of polyrhythms, and possible sources of irritation.

Design solutions were proposed, including provision for adjusting haptic balance, provision of air drum capabilities and an off-switch for the haptic channel. One family of design solutions that appears to address several identified problems reflects the notion of the Haptic Bracelets as resembling a portable music player, suitable for both active and passive learning, and able to be worn all day while working on other tasks. Such a system should optionally play music while also optionally transmitting associated rhythms as haptic pulses delivered via lightweight, comfortable, easy to take on and off, wireless bracelets worn on wrists and ankles. Arguments from musical psychology were detailed which suggest ways in which this arrangement might address problems including context, start and end points, and excessive repetition: it is proposed to test these arguments empirically.

Dealing with multiple parallel rhythmic streams is a central skill for drummers, but it is also vital for other musicians, for example piano, keyboard, guitar and string players. Even for the full development of rhythm skills to be exercised away from performance, such as in composition and analysis, the previous physical enaction of rhythms appears to be an essential precursor (Holland et al. 2010). Multi-limb rhythms are of particular importance to this process, because the physical enaction of many basic building blocks of rhythm, such as standard polyrhythms, is difficult without the co-ordinated use of multiple limbs. To the best of our knowledge, the use of rhythmic haptic stimuli delivered to four limbs is unique to the Haptic Bracelets and Haptic Drum Kit.

Diverse active and passive applications for drummers and other musicians were identified. These include hierarchical click-tracks that leave the ears free, inter-musician communication systems that leaves the eyes free, rhythm section synchronization systems to encourage 'tight' playing, and training applications.

In addition, several non-musical applications of the Haptic Bracelets were identified. These include three-dimensional navigation when ears and eyes are busy elsewhere, fitness, sports and rehabilitation, for example from strokes or injury (Huang et al. 2010). Improved rhythmic skills may be able to contribute to general well being, for example in improving mobility (Brown 2002) and alertness, and helping to prevent falls for older people (Juntunen 2004; Kressig et al. 2005).

In general terms, the present work may help, for example, to identify areas where haptics are underused in mainstream HCI. While it has always been clear that haptics can be useful where eyes and ears are focused elsewhere, the present work may help to emphasise the possible value of haptics in applications where spatial movements or temporal sequencing of movements need to be learned or communicated. It is interesting to note that specifically rhythmic applications of haptics have been very little explored in HCI. Some of the more intricate aspects of interaction with rhythm may, by their nature, be of special value to applications in Music Interaction. However, we speculate that there are applications of the rhythmic use of haptics in health, entertainment, security, safety, and other areas yet to be identified and explored.

References

Andresen, M. S., Bach, M., & Kristensen, K. R. (2010). The LapSlapper: Feel the beat. In *Proceedings of HAID 2010, international conference on Haptic and Audio Interaction Design* (pp. 160–168). Berlin, Heidelberg: Springer.

Arom, S. (1991). *African polyphony and polyrhythm, musical structure and methodology*. England: Cambridge University Press. ISBN 052124160x.

Bird, J., Holland, S., Marshall, P., Rogers, Y., & Clark, A. (2008). Feel the force: Using tactile technologies to investigate the extended mind. In *Proceedings of DAP 2008, workshop on devices that alter perception*, 21 September 2008, Seoul, South Korea, pp 1–4.

Brown, M. (2002). Conductive education and the use of rhythmical intention for people with Parkinson's disease. In I. Kozma & E. Balogh (Eds.), *Conductive education occasional papers, no. 8* (pp. 75–80). Budapest: International Peto Institute.

Clayton, M., Sager, R., & Will, U. (2004). In time with the music: The concept of entrainment and its significance for ethnomusicology. *ESEM CounterPoint, 1*, 1–82.

Collicutt, M., Casciato, C., & Wanderley, M. M. (2009). From real to virtual: A comparison of input devices for percussion tasks. In B. Dannenberg, & K. D. Ries (Eds.), *Proceedings of NIME 2009*, 4–6 June 2009, (pp. 1–6). Pittsburgh: Carnegie Mellon University.

Feygin, D., Keehner, M., & Tendick, F. (2002). Haptic guidance: Experimental evaluation of a haptic training method for a perceptual motor skill. In *Proceedings of Haptics 2002, the 10th International Symposium of Haptic Interfaces for Virtual Environment and Teleoperator Systems*, March 24–25, 2002, Orlando, FL (pp. 40–47). New York: IEEE.

Grindlay, G. (2008). Haptic guidance benefits musical motor learning. In: *Proceedings of symposium on haptic interfaces for virtual environments and teleoperator systems 2008*, March, Reno, Nevada, USA, 978-1-4244-2005-6/08, pp. 13–14.

Gutcheon, J. (1978). *Improvising rock piano*. New York: Consolidated Music Publishers. ISBN 0-8256-4071-7.

Holland, S., Bouwer, A. J., Dalgleish, M., & Hurtig, T. M. (2010). Feeling the beat where it counts: Fostering multi-limb rhythm skills with the haptic drum kit. In *Proceedings of the 4th international conference on Tangible, Embedded, and Embodied Interaction (TEI'10)*, January 25–27, 2010, Cambridge, MA (pp. 21–28). New York: ACM, ISBN: 978-1-60558-841-4.

Huang, K., Do, E. Y., & Starner, T. (2008). PianoTouch: A wearable haptic piano instruction system for passive learning of piano skills. In *Proceedings of ISWC 2008, the 12th IEEE International Symposium on Wearable Computers*, September 28–October 1, 2008, Pittsburgh, PA (pp. 41–44).

Huang, K., Starner, T., Do, E., Weiberg, G., Kohlsdorf, D., Ahlrichs, C., & Leibrandt, R. (2010). Mobile music touch: Mobile tactile stimulation for passive learning. In *Proceedings of the 28th international conference on human factors in computing systems (CHI '10)* (pp. 791–800). New York: ACM.

Juntunen, M. L. (2004). *Embodiment in Dalcroze Eurhythmics*. PhD thesis, University of Oulu, Finland.

Kressig, R. W., Allali, G., & Beauchet, O. (2005). Long-term practice of Jaques-Dalcroze eurhythmics prevents age-related increase of gait variability under a dual task. *Letter to Journal of the American Geriatrics Society*, April 2005, *53*(4), 728–729.

Lerdahl, F., & Jackendoff, R. (1983). *A generative theory of tonal music*. Cambridge, MA: MIT Press.

Lewiston, C. (2008). *MaGKeyS: A haptic guidance keyboard system for facilitating sensorimotor training and rehabilitation*. PhD thesis, MIT Media Laboratory, Massachusetts.

McNulty, J. K. (2009). Polyrhythm hero: A multimodal polyrhythm training game for mobile phones. Unpublished, Retrieved on 6 May 2012, from the word-wide web at http://robotmouth.com/papers_files/Polyrhythm_Hero.pdf

Miranda, E. R., & Wanderley, M. (2006). *New digital musical instruments: Control and interaction beyond the keyboard*. Middleton: A-R Editions.

Morris, D., Tan, H., Barbagli, F., Chang, T., & Salisbury, K. (2007). Haptic feedback enhances force skill learning. In: *Proceedings of World Haptics 2007, the 2nd Joint EuroHaptics Conference and Symposium on Haptic Interfaces for Virtual Environment and Teleoperator Systems*, March 22–24, 2007 (pp. 21–26). Tsukuba: IEEE Computer Society.

Ni, L. G. (2010). The programmable haptic rhythm trainer. In *Proceedings of HAVE 2010, IEEE international symposium on Haptic Audio-Visual Environments and Games*, 16–17 Oct. 2010, Phoenix, Arizona.

O'Modhrain, S. (2000). *Playing by feel: Incorporating haptic feedback into computer-based musical instruments*. PhD thesis, Stanford University.

O'Regan, K., & Noe, A. (2001). A sensorimotor account of vision and visual consciousness. *Behavioral and Brain Sciences, 24*(5), 883–917.

Sinclair, S. (2007). *Force-feedback hand controllers for musical interaction*. MSc thesis, Music Technology Area, Schulich School of Music, McGill University, Montreal, Canada.

Sloboda, J. (1985). *The musical mind: The cognitive psychology of music*. Oxford: Clarendon.

Smith, K. C., Cuddy, L. L., & Upitis, R. (1994). Figural and metric understanding of rhythm. *Psychology of Music, 22*, 117–135.

Spelmezan, D., Jacobs, M., Hilgers, A., & Borchers, J. (2009). Tactile motion instructions for physical activities. *CHI, 2009*, 2243–2252.

Tamaki, E., Miyaki, T., & Rekimoto, J. (2011). PossessedHand: Techniques for controlling human hands using electrical muscles stimuli. In *Proceedings of the 2011 annual conference on human factors in computing systems (CHI '11)* (pp. 543–552). New York: ACM.

Upitis, R. (1987). Children's understanding of rhythm: The relationship between development and musical training. *Psychomusicology, 7*(1), 41–60.

van der Linden, J., Johnson, R., Bird, J., Rogers, Y., & Schoonderwaldt, E. (2011). Buzzing to play: Lessons learned from an in the wild study of real-time vibrotactile feedback. In *Proceedings of the 29th international conference on human factors in computing systems*, Vancouver, BC, Canada.

Zimmerman, T. G., Lanier, J., Blanchard, C., Bryson, S., & Harvill, Y. (1987). A hand gesture interface device. In J. M. Carroll, & P. P. Tanner (Eds.), *Proceedings of the SIGCHI/GI conference on human factors in computing systems and Graphics Interface (CHI '87)* (pp. 189–192). New York: ACM.

Chapter 7
Piano Technique as a Case Study in Expressive Gestural Interaction

Andrew P. McPherson and Youngmoo E. Kim

Abstract There is a longstanding disconnect between mechanical models of the piano, in which key velocity is the sole determinant of each note's sound, and the subjective experience of trained pianists, who take a nuanced, multidimensional approach to physical gestures at the keyboard (commonly known as "touch"). We seek to peel back the abstraction of the key press as a discrete event, developing models of key touch that link qualitative musical intention to quantitative key motion. The interaction between performer and instrument (whether acoustic or electronic) can be considered a special case of human-machine interaction, and one that takes place on far different terms than ordinary human-computer interaction: a player's physical gestures are often the result of intuitive, subconscious processes. Our proposed models will therefore aid the development of computer interfaces which connect with human users on an intuitive, expressive level, with applications within and beyond the musical domain.

7.1 Introduction

The piano-style keyboard remains the most commonly used interface for many computer music tasks, but it is also notable for a different reason: it is the object of a persistent disconnect between musicians and computer scientists, whose differing approaches to understanding expressive keyboard performance have important implications for music computing and human-computer interaction generally.

A.P. McPherson (✉)
Centre for Digital Music, School of Electronic Engineering and Computer Science, Queen Mary, University of London, Mile End Road, London E1 4NS, UK
e-mail: andrewm@eecs.qmul.ac.uk

Y.E. Kim
Music Entertainment Technology Laboratory, Department of Electrical and Computer Engineering, Drexel University, 3141 Chestnut St, Philadelphia, PA 19104, USA
e-mail: ykim@drexel.edu

S. Holland et al. (eds.), *Music and Human-Computer Interaction*, Springer Series on Cultural Computing, DOI 10.1007/978-1-4471-2990-5_7,

Expression on the acoustic piano, considered from a mechanical perspective, seems straightforward: the speed of a key press determines the velocity with which a hammer strikes a string, which in turn determines nearly all acoustic features of a note. In the mechanical view, expression at the piano is a function of the velocity and timing of each key press (with secondary contributions from the pedals). Accordingly, digital keyboards are essentially discrete interfaces, sensing only the onset and release of each note, with a single velocity metric associated with each onset.

On the other hand, pianists often swear by a rich, multidimensional gestural vocabulary at the keyboard. To the pianist, key "touch" is a critical component of any expressive performance, and though pianists differ on the ideal approach, there is a consensus that expressive keyboard gesture goes well beyond mere key velocity. Consider pianist Alfred Brendel on emulating orchestral instruments at the piano (Berman 2000):

> The sound of the oboe I achieve with rounded, hooked-under, and, as it were, bony fingers, in poco legato. The flute … whenever possible, I play every note with the help of a separate arm movement. The bassoon … the touch is finger-staccato. The noble, full, somewhat veiled, 'romantic' sound of the horn demands a loose arm and a flexible wrist.

Another common thread in piano pedagogy is the value of achieving a "singing" touch. Reginald Gerig, in summarising his historical survey of famous pianists' techniques, writes, "the pianist with the perfect technique is also a singer, a first-rate vocalist! The singing voice is the ideal tonal model and aid to phrasing, breathing, and interpretation" (Gerig 2007, p. 520).

Perhaps symptomatic of these diverging views, very few pianists would choose even the most sophisticated digital piano over an acoustic grand of any quality. Pianist Boris Berman (2000) offers this advice to students: "Often overlooked is the need to work on an instrument that responds sufficiently to the nuances of touch. (No electronic keyboard will do, I'm afraid.)"

7.1.1 Quantifying Expressive Keyboard Touch

Our work seeks to reconcile mechanical and expressive views of piano performance by developing quantitative models of keyboard technique. We deliberately leave aside the question of how key touch affects the sound of the piano, instead focusing on the *performers themselves*. Topics of interest include:

- How does expressive musical intent translate into physical motion at the keyboard?
- Can we identify general relationships between musical character and key motion?
- Which aspects of touch are common across performers, and which are part of an individual player's style?
- Can we use detailed measurements of a player's finger motion to predict the musical qualities of a performance?

These questions have important implications for both musical performance and HCI. Like many forms of human-computer interaction, the notion of a "key press" is an abstraction which reduces a potentially complex series of motions into one or two discrete quantities. In this chapter, we will show how looking beyond this abstraction can reveal new details of a performer's intentions; similar abstraction-breaking approaches can potentially yield insight into other computer interfaces.

7.2 Background

7.2.1 Measurement of Piano Performance

Numerical measurement of piano performance has a long history, detailed summaries of which can be found in Goebl et al. (2008) and Clarke (2004). The percussive nature of the piano action has encouraged models of expressive performance focused primarily on velocity and timing. Classical performances in particular are often evaluated by tempo and loudness deviations from a printed score, e.g. (Repp 1996).

In the past decade the field of performance studies has flourished (Rink 2004), bringing with it an emphasis on the performing musician as equal partner with the composer in realising a musical product. However, even as attention has shifted to the unique role of the performer, a bias remains toward analyses of tempo and dynamics, which Rink suggests may be "because these lend themselves to more rigorous modelling than intractable parameters like colour and bodily gesture" (p. 38).

It is true that conventional analyses largely discard any sense of the performer's physical execution beyond the resulting hammer strikes. Acoustically speaking, though, this approach has merit: in the 1920s, Otto Ortmann (1925) demonstrated that keys played percussively (in which a moving finger strikes the key) exhibit a different pattern of motion than those played non-percussively (when the finger begins at rest on the key surface), but Goebl et al. (2004) showed that apart from a characteristic noise of the finger striking the key, percussive and non-percussive notes of the same velocity are indistinguishable by listeners. A similar study by Suzuki (2007) showed very little spectral difference between tones played in each manner.

7.2.2 Beyond Velocity and Timing

If velocity and timing (along with pedal position) are sufficient to reproduce a piano performance with high accuracy, what then is the value of studying additional dimensions of performer motion? Doğantan-Dack (2011, p. 251) argues that the performer's conception of a performance is inseparable from its physical execution:

> I would indeed hypothesize that performers do not learn, represent and store rhythmic-melodic units without their accompanying gestural and expressive dimensions. As distinct from the listener's experience and knowledge of such local musical forms, the performer, in order to be able to unfold the dynamic shape of the musical unit from beginning to end as in one single, unified impulse, needs a kind of continuous knowledge representation that

> is analogue and procedural rather than declarative.... The performer does not come to know the rhythmic-melodic forms they express in sound separately from the physical gestures and movements required to bring them about. Any gesture made to deliver a unit of music will inevitably unify the structure and expression, as well the biomechanical and affective components, which theory keeps apart.

From this perspective, measurements of piano mechanics alone will fail to capture important details of the performance's original expressive conception. Measuring key touch as a continuous gestural process rather than a sequence of discrete events may better preserve some of these details. Of course, gesture measurement can be carried further still, even beyond the keyboard: for example, Castellano et al. (2008) found links between pianists' emotional expression and their body and head movements. For our present purposes, measuring continuous motion at the keyboard provides an appropriate amount of expressive detail while retaining links to traditional methods of analysing piano performance.

Some authors have previously examined touch as a continuous entity. Parncutt and Troup (2002) discuss mechanical constraints in playing complex multi-note passages, and also examine the contribution of auxiliary contact noises (finger-key, key-keybed, hammer-string) to the perception of piano sound; the amplitude and timing of these noises often depends heavily on the type of touch used. Goebl and Bresin (2001), in examining the reproduction accuracy of MIDI-controlled acoustic pianos, contrast the continuous velocity profile of a human key press with its mechanical reproduction. On the commercial side, Bösendorfer CEUS pianos have the ability to record continuous key position (Goebl et al. 2008), but thus far few detailed studies have made use of this data.

7.3 Measuring Gesture Within a Key Press

To better understand the expressive dimensions of key touch, it is necessary to break the abstraction of a key press as discrete event. To this end, we have developed a new hardware and software system which can be retrofitted to any piano to measure the continuous position of each key.

7.3.1 Optical Sensor Hardware

Our sensor system (McPherson and Kim 2010) is based on a modified Moog Piano Bar, a device which installs atop an acoustic piano keyboard to provide MIDI data. Internally, the Piano Bar uses optical reflectance sensors on the white keys and beam interruption sensors on the black keys to measure the position of each key (Fig. 7.1). The Piano Bar generates discrete key press and release events from this information, but we instead sample the raw sensor values to provide a continuous stream of position information. The position of each key is recorded 600 times per second with 12-bit resolution (closer to 10 bits in practice due to limited signal range).

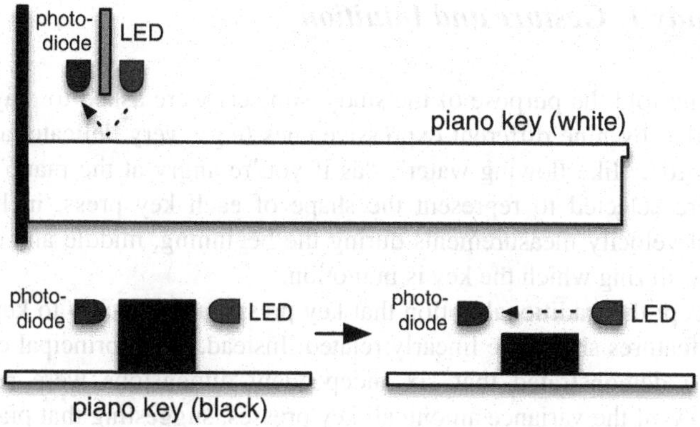

Fig. 7.1 Optical reflectance and break-beam sensors measure continuous key position

7.3.2 Data Segmentation and Analysis

The 600 Hz sample rate is sufficient to capture several position values during the brief interval the key is in motion, recording not just its velocity but its *shape* (continuous time-position profile). Key press events can be extracted in real time from the position data stream by simple thresholding to identify the start of a press, followed by peak detection to identify the point of impact with the key bed. Once the start and end points of the press have been identified, higher-level features can be extracted, including (MIDI-like) velocity, peaks and troughs in the continuous velocity curve (indicating percussively-played notes), and the position of the key immediately following the key bed impact (which is proportional to the force exerted by the player). See McPherson and Kim (2011) for further details.

Beyond measuring traditional key presses, continuous key position can identify fingers resting lightly on a key surface, changes in weight over the course of a long-held note, and details of the overlap between notes in a phrase. Section 7.5 will show that measurements of weight in particular may have important correlations with expressive musical intent.

7.4 Multidimensional Modelling of Key Touch

Our sensor system takes an important step toward reconciling pianists' nuanced, multidimensional view of keyboard technique with the mechanical realities of the instrument. In recent work (McPherson and Kim 2011) we show that, regardless of whether different forms of key touch produce different sounds on the acoustic piano, pianists can and do vary the shapes of their key presses in multiple independent dimensions. Two user studies conducted on an acoustic piano with continuous position sensing support this result:

7.4.1 Study 1: Gesture and Intuition

Without being told the purpose of the study, subjects were asked to play a simple melody guided by nine different expressive cues (e.g. "very delicate, as if afraid of being heard", "like flowing water", "as if you're angry at the piano"). Twelve features were selected to represent the shape of each key press, including key position and velocity measurements during the beginning, middle and end of the brief window during which the key is in motion.

If we accept the traditional notion that key presses reduce only to key velocity, then all 12 features should be linearly related. Instead, using principal component analysis, we demonstrated that six independent dimensions were required to represent 90% of the variance among all key presses, suggesting that pianists' rich picture of key touch has a strong mechanical foundation.

We further trained classifier systems to predict the expressive cue from key motion. We showed that classifiers trained on all 12 features performed on average 25% better than those trained on MIDI velocity alone, indicating that key motion in multiple dimensions correlates meaningfully with expressive intent. The detailed nature of this correlation is a primary topic of continuing investigation.

7.4.2 Study 2: Multidimensional Performance Accuracy

In pilot studies with professional pianists, we identified five dimensions of key motion for further investigation (Fig. 7.2):

- **Velocity:** Speed of the key in the traditional MIDI sense, related to hammer speed.
- **Percussiveness:** Whether the finger is at rest or in motion when it strikes the key.
- **Rigidity:** For percussively-played notes, whether the finger joints are rigid or loose when the finger-key collision occurs.
- **Weight:** Force into the key-bed immediately after a press.
- **Depth:** Whether a press reaches the key bed or stops midway through its range of motion.

Our main study evaluated whether subjects were able to accurately control each dimension, independently or in combination. Each dimension was divided into two or three discrete classes, and decision tree classifiers were trained using key presses performed by the investigators. Ten subjects (all novice or intermediate pianists[1]) played a series of isolated key presses, attempting to match particular target classes (Fig. 7.3). Subject accuracy is shown in Fig. 7.4; with the exception of rigidity, subjects were able to control each individual dimension with greater than 75% accuracy. Multidimensional accuracy was lower, but still significantly above random chance for each task.

[1]By evaluating non-professional pianists, our results suggest that the ability to control a press gesture in multiple dimensions is not dependent on advanced training.

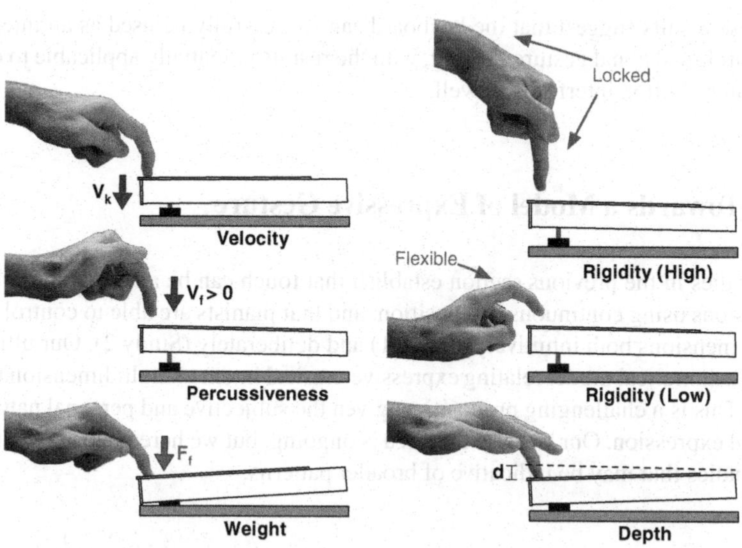

Fig. 7.2 Five dimensions of a piano key press (Reprinted from McPherson and Kim (2011) with kind permission from ACM)

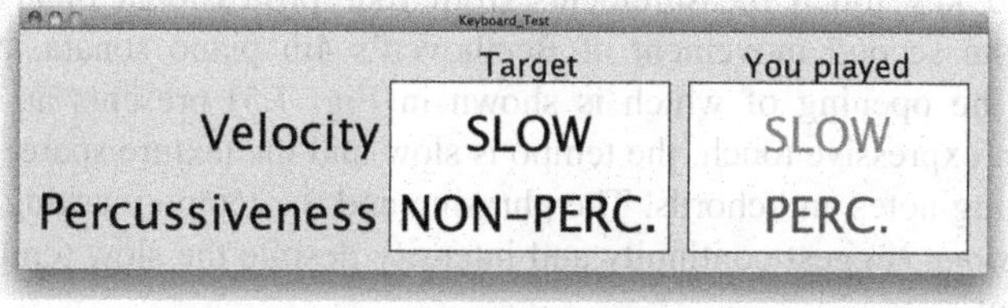

Fig. 7.3 Multidimensional key touch testing environment

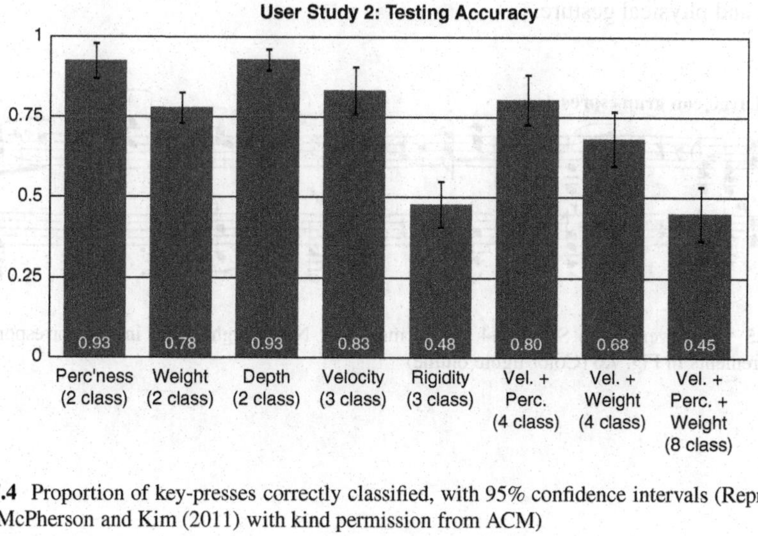

Fig. 7.4 Proportion of key-presses correctly classified, with 95% confidence intervals (Reprinted from McPherson and Kim (2011) with kind permission from ACM)

These results suggest that the keyboard can successfully be used as an interface for multidimensional gesture sensing, with the results potentially applicable to other mechanical button interfaces as well.

7.5 Towards a Model of Expressive Gesture

The studies in the previous section establish that touch can be analysed in multiple dimensions using continuous key position, and that pianists are able to control multiple dimensions both intuitively (Study 1) and deliberately (Study 2). Our ultimate goal is a numerical model relating expressive musical intent to multidimensional key touch. This is a challenging proposition, given the subjective and personal nature of musical expression. Our work in this area is ongoing, but we here present two initial case studies that may be indicative of broader patterns.

7.5.1 Touch in Beethoven's Piano Sonata #4

We collected key touch measurements from four professional pianists' performances of the second movement of Beethoven's 4th piano sonata, op. 7. This movement (the opening of which is shown in Fig. 7.5) presents an interesting case study in expressive touch: the tempo is slow and the texture spare, employing long-sustaining notes and chords. The phrasing and the tempo marking *largo, con gran espressione* suggest continuity and intensity despite the slow tempo and soft dynamic level.

Though each pianist's interpretation differed, we observed some notable patterns of key touch in the opening measures that suggest a relationship between expressive intent and physical gesture.

Fig. 7.5 Beethoven Piano Sonata #4, op. 7, mm. 1–7. Notes highlighted in *red* correspond to measurements in Fig. 7.6 (Color figure online)

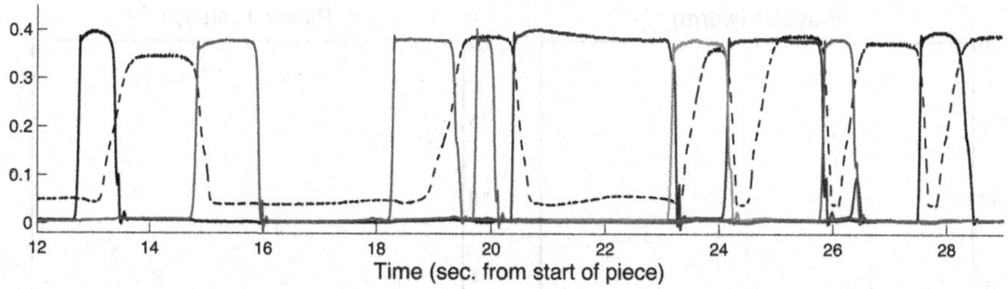

Fig. 7.6 Key position for Beethoven sonata #4, mm. 3–5, topmost line only. *Vertical axis* indicates deviation from key rest position in inches. *Dashed line* indicates (scaled) damper pedal position. Colours by pitch: A (*magenta*), B (*green*), C (*blue*), D (*red*), E (*black*) (Color figure online)

7.5.1.1 Weight and Musical Intensity

Figure 7.6 shows one pianist's performance of mm. 3–5. For clarity, only the top notes in the right hand are shown. In contrast to traditional MIDI representations, the pianist's action over the entire course of each note is shown. Because a felt pad separates the key from the key bed, weight on a pressed key effects a slight change in position. Examining the pattern of weight over the course of each note suggests interesting musical correlations:

1. The first note (corresponding to m. 3) has a rounded position profile indicating that the pianist increased the force into the key bed over the course of the note, rather than exerting maximum force at the time of impact. A similar effect can be seen in the last two notes of the passage (m. 5). Subjectively, we observed that these notes tended to be played with greater emphasis and continuity; the phrase in m. 5 in particular was typically played with a crescendo across the measure.
2. The long note in m. 4 (shown in blue in Fig. 7.6), marked *sforzando* in the score, exhibits a particularly telling weight profile. After the initial impact, the pianist exerts an exaggerated force into the key which diminishes over the course of the note. This is a direct parallel to the typical musical shape of the passage, where the *sf* note marks the strong point of the phrase, with a diminuendo for the rest of the measure.

These observations indicate that force into the key bed may correlate with the intended intensity or direction of a musical phrase. Since the piano's decay cannot be altered, conventional analyses typically do not consider the performer's intended shape within a note; however, the body language of most pianists indicates that they shape phrases both across and *within* notes. Indeed, a recent study found that nearly half of keyboard players agreed with the statement "I think about musical shape when thinking about how to perform a single note" (Prior 2011).

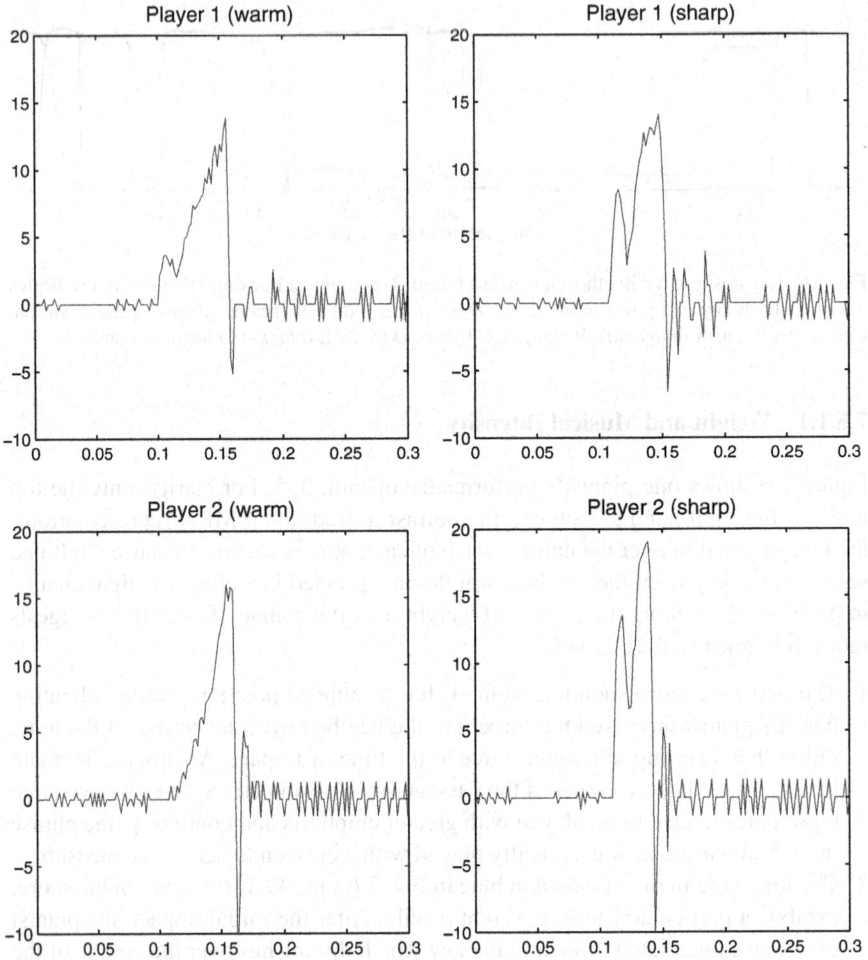

Fig. 7.7 Key velocity (in/s) versus time for the *sforzando* note in m. 4. Four players (two shown here) were asked to play a "warm" and a "sharp" sforzando, with most players demonstrating a more percussive touch on the latter

7.5.1.2 Articulation and Touch

Figure 7.7 shows key velocity over time for the note marked *sf* in m. 4, highlighting the shape of the key onset itself. Each pianist was asked to play the entire phrase twice, the first time playing a "warm" sforzando, the second time a "sharp" sforzando. Such distinctions in articulation are common on string instruments, where they relate to the motion of the bow. Though their application on the piano is less obvious, pianists routinely employ similar vocabulary.

Fig. 7.8 Schubert D. 960 movement IV opens with a forte-piano that has no direct mechanical realisation on the piano

Our measurements showed that three of four pianists played the "sharp" sforzando with a more percussive stroke than the "warm" sforzando.[2] The fourth pianist played both notes identically. Peak key velocity tended to be similar in both versions, suggesting that the expressive descriptors influenced the shape of each pianist's gesture independently of its overall speed.

7.5.2 *Touch in Schubert's Piano Sonata D. 960*

The fourth movement of Schubert's Piano Sonata in B-flat Major D. 960 opens with a curious marking: *forte-piano*, implying a note that begins strongly and immediately becomes soft (Fig. 7.8). This dynamic profile is impossible on the acoustic piano, yet the marking recurs frequently throughout the movement. We interviewed the four pianists in our study about their approach to this passage and collected continuous key position measurements, not only of the Schubert's *fp* marking, but also several "re-compositions" substituting other dynamic markings: *forte, forte* with diminuendo, *mezzo-forte, mezzo-forte* with an accent, *mezzo-forte* with a *sforzando*, and *piano*.

Three of the four pianists indicated specific gestural approaches to playing *forte-piano*. To one pianist, the marking implied "a sharp attack, but without the follow-up weight." Another interpreted it as "forte, [with] piano body language," adding that in his teaching, body language is important and that he encourages students to "apply expression to non-keystroke kinds of events." A third explained in more detail:

> When I teach people, there are a number of different ways I tell them they can vary the tone color.... There's the speed of the attack, there's the weight of the attack, there's the firmness of the fingers, and there's how direct or how much of an angle you play at. So when I see an fp ... I want a very fast attack and probably a shallow attack.

Given the consistency and specificity of the pianists' responses, we expected to find a marked difference in key motion for notes played *forte-piano* compared to

---

[2]Percussive strokes are characterised by an initial spike in key velocity, versus a continuous ramp (McPherson and Kim 2011).

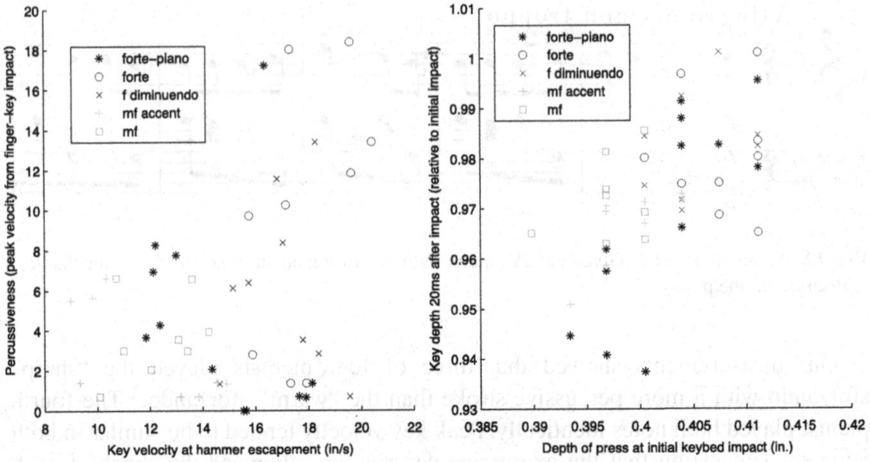

Fig. 7.9 Comparison of four features of the opening G key press in Schubert D. 960, labelled according to the initial dynamic marking. Plots reflect several repetitions by four pianists

other dynamic markings. However, the numerical data is less clear-cut. Figure 7.9 shows key presses for the top G for all pianists, scored according to key velocity, percussiveness, maximum key depth and follow-up position (weight) several milliseconds after impact with the key bed. The data exhibits some clustering according to playing style, indicating at least moderate consistency across pianists and repetitions. Velocity shows clear differentiation among playing styles, but few other dimensions show any substantial, independent correlation. The results were similar for the bottom G, and did not change when considering only the three pianists who indicated a consciously different technique.

One hypothesis for this result is that, though the pianists may perceive each marking differently, their physical execution is identical. Another is that the pianists do indeed use different body language for different dynamics, but that this is not manifested in different profiles of key motion. Either way, this excerpt demonstrates the limitations of key touch in encompassing all aspects of expression at the piano.

7.5.3 Discussion

The preceding examples lend initial support to the notion that expression on the piano extends beyond discrete metrics of key velocity, and that in certain cases, expressive intent has a direct effect on the profile of motion within a single key press. Further studies are needed to definitively establish the nature and scope of the expression-gesture link. In addition to studying larger numbers of performers, the use of narrowly-defined expressive tasks (for example, to emulate a carefully

Fig. 7.10 The magnetic resonator piano, an electronically-augmented acoustic piano. Electromagnets induce the strings to vibration in response to continuous gestural input sensed from the motion of the piano keys

constructed audio example, or to play an excerpt emphasising specific emotional qualities) will help clarify the ways that key touch is shaped by expressive intent. Augmenting future studies with video motion capture could allow further exploration of the way body language reflects the expressive qualities of a performance.

7.6 Implications

7.6.1 Computationally Augmenting the Acoustic Piano

Piano touch and HCI naturally converge in the creation of new digital musical instruments. We have created a system of electromagnetic augmentation of the acoustic piano which uses information from the performer's key touch to shape the sound of each note (McPherson 2010). The acoustic piano, for all its versatility, has a notable limitation: a note, once struck, cannot be further shaped by the performer before it is released. Our system (Fig. 7.10) uses electromagnets inside the instrument to induce the strings to vibration independently of the hammer mechanism, allowing notes with no attack and indefinite sustain, as well as harmonics, pitch bends and new timbres.

Continuous measurements of key touch are used to control signals to the electromagnets; continuous key position measurement also enables new types of gestures that have no meaning on the traditional keyboard (McPherson and Kim 2010). For example:

- Slowly moving a key from its rest position to fully pressed creates a crescendo effect.
- Exerting a heavy force on a pressed key elicits a timbre change by altering the harmonic content of the electromagnet waveform.
- Periodic variations in key pressure generate vibrato on a note.
- Lightly vibrating a key near its rest position creates a glissando up the harmonic series of the corresponding string.
- Holding one key while lightly pressing the adjacent key bends the pitch of a note.

All of these effects are rendered acoustically by the strings and soundboard, promoting integration between traditional and extended piano sounds. Relationships between keyboard gestures and acoustic features are adjustable in software, allowing the instrument to serve as a laboratory for the *mapping problem*: how do we map the performer's physical actions to sound in a way that is flexible and intuitive?[3] Studying the expressive aspects of piano touch, as in Sect. 7.5, may assist in developing mappings that build on the intuition of trained pianists.

In McPherson and Kim (2011), we showed that novice and intermediate pianists were successfully able to control the volume of electromagnetically-induced notes by manipulating continuous key position, both for passages played at a constant dynamic level and passages containing crescendos within individual notes. Acoustic feedback appeared to be highly important for user accuracy: when the electromagnetic system was switched off and the pianists were asked to silently control the depth of each key press, they exhibited significantly lower consistency.

7.6.2 Broader Implications for HCI

Even beyond the creation of musical interfaces, piano touch can potentially offer lessons for HCI researchers.

7.6.2.1 The Value of Breaking Abstractions

Most input devices rely on abstractions: keyboards, mice, trackpads and touchscreens each capture a few salient dimensions of a more complex human motor process. In this chapter, we have shown how breaking down a similar abstraction at the piano keyboard can yield additional insight into the performer's intention. We are interested not only in which keys are pressed and when, but *how* the keys are pressed. Despite the apparent irrelevance of many of the additional dimensions of motion to sound production at the piano, interviews and the pedagogical literature

[3]See Wanderley and Depalle (2004) for more background on musical mapping strategies.

show that pianists feel strongly about them, with certain patterns appearing common across performers and others serving as hallmarks of personal style.

Correspondingly, HCI researchers may find value in considering the broader gestural parameters of common devices. Examples of such approaches include pressure-sensitive computer keyboards (Dietz et al. 2009) and mice (Cechanowicz et al. 2007) and touch-screen interaction which considers the orientation of the user's finger in addition to traditional XY contact location (Wang et al. 2009). A potentially interesting area of exploration would employ such systems in common interaction scenarios without alerting the user to the presence of additional dimensions, looking for patterns in users' gestures which could guide the development of future interfaces.

7.6.2.2 Interaction on an Intuitive Level

The piano can be considered as a human-machine interface whose parameters of interaction are quite different from normal computer systems. Playing a musical instrument involves a great deal of internalised, subconscious motor control, and correspondingly, expressive musical intent and physical gesture are connected on an intuitive level. Though piano technique reflects considerable specialised training, we believe that patterns of expression at the piano can potentially generalise to other gestural interfaces.

Designing interfaces to specifically capture expressive information is a challenge; even defining the nature of "expression" is no easy task. A notable recent example of such a system is EyesWeb (Camurri et al. 2004), which analyses motion profiles from video data to assess expressive intent. Our experience with piano technique suggests that expressive cues can be found in many places, and that bridging the qualitative and quantitative creates potential for new computer interfaces that permit intuitive, expressive interaction, with applications to the creative arts and beyond.

Acknowledgments This material is based upon work supported by the US National Science Foundation under Grant #0937060 to the Computing Research Association for the CIFellows Project.

References

Berman, B. (2000). *Notes from the pianist's bench.* New Haven/London: Yale University Press.

Camurri, A., Mazzarino, B., & Volpe, G. (2004). Analysis of expressive gesture: The EyesWeb expressive gesture processing library. In A. Camurri & G. Volpe (Eds.), *Gesture-based communication in human-computer interaction* (Vol. 2915, pp. 469–470). Berlin/Heidelberg: Springer.

Castellano, G., Mortillaro, M., Camurri, A., Volpe, G., & Scherer, K. (2008). Automated analysis of body movement in emotionally expressive piano performances. *Music Perception, 26*(2), 103–120.

Cechanowicz, J., Irani, P., & Subramanian, S. (2007). Augmenting the mouse with pressure sensitive input. In *Proceedings of the 25th ACM Conference on Human Factors in Computing Systems (CHI)*. San Jose, CA, USA.

Clarke, E. F. (2004). Empirical methods in the study of performance. In E. F. Clarke & N. Cook (Eds.), *Empirical musicology: Aims, methods, prospects* (pp. 77–102). Oxford: Oxford University Press.

Dietz, P., Eidelson, B., Westhues, J., & Bathiche, S. (2009). A practical pressure sensitive computer keyboard. In *Proceedings of the 22nd Symposium on User Interface Software and Technology (UIST)*. Victoria, BC, Canada.

Doğantan-Dack, M. (2011). In the beginning was gesture: Piano touch and the phenomenology of the performing body. In A. Gritten & E. King (Eds.), *New perspectives on music and gesture* (pp. 243–266). Farnham: Ashgate.

Gerig, R. (2007). *Famous pianists & their technique*. Bloomington: Indiana University Press.

Goebl, W., & Bresin, R. (2001). Are computer-controlled pianos a reliable tool in music performance research? Recording and reproduction precision of a Yamaha Disklavier grand piano. In *Proceedings of the MOSART workshop*, Barcelona.

Goebl, W., Bresin, R., & Galembo, A. (2004). Once again: The perception of piano touch and tone. Can touch audibly change piano sound independently of intensity? In *Proceedings of the International Symposium on Musical Acoustics*. Nara, Japan.

Goebl, W., Dixon, S., De Poli, G., Friberg, A., Bresin, R., & Widmer, G. (2008). Sense in expressive music performance. In P. Polotti & D. Rocchesso (Eds.), *Sound to sense – sense to sound: A state of the art in sound and music computing* (pp. 195–242). Berlin GmbH: Logos.

McPherson, A. (2010). The magnetic resonator piano: Electronic augmentation of an acoustic grand piano. *Journal of New Music Research, 39*(3), 189–202.

McPherson, A., & Kim, Y. (2010). Augmenting the acoustic piano with electromagnetic string actuation and continuous key position sensing. In *Proceedings of the International Conference on New Interfaces for Musical Expression (NIME)*. Sydney, Australia.

McPherson, A., & Kim, Y. (2011). Multidimensional gesture sensing at the piano. In *Proceedings of the 29th ACM conference on human factors in computing systems (CHI)*. Vancouver, BC, Canada.

Ortmann, O. (1925). *The physical basis of piano touch and tone*. London: Kegan Paul, Trenc, Trubner & Co.

Parncutt, R., & Troup, M. (2002). Piano. In R. Parncutt & G. McPherson (Eds.), *Science and psychology of music performance: Creative strategies for teaching and learning* (pp. 285–302). Oxford: Oxford University Press.

Prior, H. (2011). Links between music and shape: Style-specific, language-specific, or universal? In *Proceedings of Topics in Musical Universals: 1st International Colloquium*. Aix-en-Provence, France.

Repp, B. (1996). Patterns of note onset asynchronies in expressive piano performance. *Journal of the Acoustical Society of America, 100*, 3917–3932.

Rink, J. (2004). The state of play in performance studies. In J. W. Davidson (Ed.), *The music practitioner: Research for the music performer, teacher, and listener* (pp. 37–51). Aldershot: Ashgate.

Suzuki, H. (2007). Spectrum analysis and tone quality evaluation of piano sounds with hard and soft touches. *Acoustical Science and Technology, 28*, 1–6.

Wanderley, M., & Depalle, P. (2004). Gestural control of sound synthesis. *Proceedings of the IEEE, 92*(4), 632–644.

Wang, F., Cao, X., Ren, X., & Irani, P. (2009). Detecting and leveraging finger orientation for interaction with direct-touch surfaces. In *Proceedings of the 22nd Symposium on User Interface Software and Technology (UIST)*. Vancouver, BC, Canada.

Chapter 8
Live Music-Making: A Rich Open Task Requires a Rich Open Interface

Dan Stowell and Alex McLean

Abstract In live human-computer music-making, how can interfaces successfully support the openness, reinterpretation and rich signification often important in live (especially improvised) musical performance? We argue that the use of design metaphors can lead to interfaces which constrain interactions and militate against reinterpretation, while consistent, grammatical interfaces empower the user to create and apply their own metaphors in developing their performance. These metaphors can be transitory and disposable, yet do not represent wasted learning since the underlying grammar is retained. We illustrate this move with reflections from live coding practice, from recent visual and two-dimensional programming language interfaces, and from musical voice mapping research. We consider the integration of the symbolic and the continuous in the human-computer interaction. We also describe how our perspective is reflected in approaches to system evaluation.

8.1 Introduction

In this chapter we discuss themes of our research, strands of which reflect our title's assertion in various ways. Our focus here is on live music-making, in particular improvised or part-improvised performances which incorporate digital technologies.

D. Stowell (✉)
Centre for Digital Music, Queen Mary University of London, London, UK
e-mail: dan.stowell@eecs.qmul.ac.uk

A. McLean (✉)
Interdisciplinary Centre for Scientific Research in Music, University of Leeds, Leeds, UK
e-mail: a.mclean@leeds.ac.uk

S. Holland et al. (eds.), *Music and Human-Computer Interaction*, Springer Series on Cultural Computing, DOI 10.1007/978-1-4471-2990-5_8,

Is music-making rich and open? Rich, yes, as evident from the many varieties of emotional and social content that a listener can draw out of music, meaningful from many (although not all) perspectives (Cross and Tolbert 2008). Even unusually constrained music styles such as minimalism often convey rich signification, their sonic simplicity having a social meaning within wider musical culture. Music is particularly rich in its inner relationships, with musical themes passed between musicians both consciously and subconsciously, weaving a complex tapestry of influence. And open, yes: the generative/composable nature of musical units means a practically unbounded range of possible music performances. While musical genres place constraints on music-making, such constraints are often seen as points of departure, with artists celebrated for pushing boundaries and drawing a wide range of cultural and meta-musical references into their work. As a result, new musical genres spring up all the time.

We will start by considering the role of computers in music-making and the interfaces that facilitate this, before focusing on live music-making explored through approaches such as gestural interaction and live coding, and strategies that may combine their advantages. Finally, we will consider the evaluation question in relation to our position, and with respect to evaluation approaches we have developed.

8.2 Rich Interfaces

Against the rich and open background of music as a whole, we examine the use of computers in live music making. Famously, computers do nothing unless we tell them to. We can think of them as lumps of silicon, passively waiting for discontinuities amongst the electric and magnetic signals, which provide the on/off states of digital representation. Computers operate somewhat like a mechanical music box, where pins on a cylinder are read by tuned teeth of a steel comb. In particular, computers are controlled by performative language, where describing something causes it to happen. Beyond this, the magic of computation comes when such sequences of events describe operations upon themselves, in other words perform higher order, abstract operations. We can describe computers then as providing an active system of formal language for humans to explore. Musicians may choose to work directly in this system of discrete language, on the musical level of notes and other discrete events such as percussive strikes. Alternatively, they may use computer language to describe analogue systems such as traditional musical instruments, and expressive movements thereof. As such, computers allow us to engage with music either on the level of digital events or analogue movements, but we contend that the greatest potential for a musically rich experience lies in engaging with both levels, simultaneously.

8.2.1 Interfaces and Metaphors

Many computer music interfaces are based on pre-existing music technology: the mixing desk, the step-sequencer grid, the modular synth patchbay. These are sometimes called *design metaphors* (Carroll et al. 1988), though they may often behave more like similes, especially in interfaces which inherit features from multiple prior technologies. Design metaphors have an advantage of providing a good leg-up for those users who are familiar with the original technologies, but can lead to problems: such users may get unpleasant surprises when the analogy is incomplete, while unfamiliar users may face what seems like inexplicably-motivated design decisions. In particular, these interfaces are full of *skeuomorphic* design elements, originating in physical constraints which no longer apply. The user may be left feeling as though they are dealing with a nonsensical metaphor, which induces unneeded limitations (such as running out of display space), and embeds now-irrelevant design decisions (e.g. based on wiring considerations).

Rigorous attempts to base computer interface design around coherent metaphors have consistently met with failure (Blackwell 2006b). From this it would seem that structuring software design around fixed metaphors does not hold cognitive advantage, beyond helping users adjust to software interfaces in the short term. It seems likely that this is because such metaphors typically reflect neither the "problem space" (the target music domain) nor the breadth of possibilities provided by the computer. The target music domain is in any case hard to specify and may vary from genre to genre or track to track. If we assume that everyone has their own systems of metaphor (Cognitive Semantics; Lakoff and Johnson 1980), then we should instead develop interfaces that let people apply their *own* metaphors. This is an important part of our definition of an open interface.

Runciman and Thimbleby (1986) state a slightly more general version of this requirement: "premature design commitments must be avoided" (p. 440). They give examples from programming language design and from spreadsheet interfaces, arguing in particular that interfaces should allow the user to assign input and output roles to parts of the interface at will, rather than having the roles pre-defined by the designer. (It is interesting to consider how that idea might be incorporated into music programming interfaces.) The cells of a spreadsheet can indeed be flexibly allocated as input or output, and this flexibility and freedom of spatial arrangement is one aspect of spreadsheets which allows users to construct their own metaphors on top of the basic architecture (Hendry and Green 1994). Spreadsheets also provide a "low-viscosity" interface particularly suited to incremental or exploratory working (ibid.). Spreadsheets are a central focus of research in the field of *end-user programming*, essentially being programming environments targetted at those writing code for their own use. Spreadsheets are not designed for professional programmers, but are widely used by professionals in a wide range of other domains (Blackwell 2006a), and so must be taken seriously as programming environments.

Spreadsheet interfaces were originally motivated by a design metaphor for paper worksheets, but they now have standard features (such as absolute and relative cross-referencing) which are not constrained by the metaphor, instead providing a reusable toolset for users to build and edit their own structures. They are however oriented towards static data representations rather than temporal forms such as music. In the following subsections we describe some of our work which strives towards similar openness in a sound/music context, toward musical interfaces which allow the user to define and repurpose their own metaphors.

8.2.2 Mapping Vocal Gestures

A specific musical example comes from one of our (DS's) research into interfaces based on extended vocal techniques – in particular, beatboxing, which is a genre of vocal percussion (Stowell 2010, Section 2.2). Vocal expression is potentially a very rich source of information that could be used by musical interactive systems – pitch, loudness, timbre, linguistic content (if any) – and traditions such as beatboxing demonstrate a wide variety of timbral gestures, rich in signification.

One way to connect such a vocal signal to a computer system is by detecting vocal "events" in real time and classifying them (Stowell and Plumbley 2010, and citations within). However, vocal events can be robustly classified into only a small number of classes (especially in real time, where only the start of the event's sound is known), so the end result is a system which can learn to trigger one of a small number of options – like playing a drum machine with only three or four buttons. Much of the richness of the audio input is discarded. This can create a system which is accessible for immediate use by amateurs, but does not lead to long-term engagement as a tool for musical expression, certainly not for experienced beatboxers.

A more expressive way to make use of the vocal source is to treat the timbral input data as a continuous space, and to try to recreate some of the nuance of performers' continuous timbral gestures; for example by controlling a synthesiser such that it performs analogous gestures (Stowell and Plumbley 2011). Any "classification" is deferred to the perception of the listener, who can understand nuances and significations in a way that is beyond at least current technology. In a user study with beatboxers (discussed further below), this approach was found useful. Further, we informally observed the interface's openness in the fact that the participating beatboxers found new sounds they could get out of the system (e.g. by whistling, trilling) that had not been designed in to it!

The classification approach is not exactly enforcing a metaphor but pre-judging what variation in the input is musically salient, which has a similar channeling, constraining effect on creative options (a premature design decision). This research is one example in which designing for an open musical interaction can allow for richer musical possibilities. Similar lessons might be drawn about physical gesture interfaces, for example – should one discretise the gestures or map them continuously? The continuous-mapping approach has been used by some performers to achieve detailed expressive performance, even when the mappings are simple.[1]

8.2.3 *Shape in Notation*

When we fix gesture as marks on a two dimensional surface, we call it a notation. In Western culture these marks generally represent discrete events, but may also represent continuous mappings. Indeed, precursors to staff notation include cheironomic neumes, which notate the articulation of melody with curved lines. In both discrete and continuous notations, one dimension is generally dedicated to time, and the other to a quality, classically pitch. The time dimension, or timeline, is also present in notation interfaces in much music software, from the commercial offerings of sequencers to the experimental drawn sound interfaces such as Xenakis's UPIC. In effect this software constrains users to considering just one dimension at a time to describe the state of a musical moment. This allows the evolution of a musical quality in detail, but makes cross-parameter relationships difficult to describe.

The *Acid Sketching* system was developed by one of the present authors (AM) to explore the use of geometric forms and relationships in a music interface beyond standard dimensional mappings. The Acid Sketching interface consists of an ordinary pen and paper, where the latter also acts as a projection surface. When shapes are drawn on the paper with an ink pen, they are identified and analysed using computer vision. These shapes are translated to sound synthesis parameters, and their relative positions translated into a polyphonic sequence, using a minimum spanning tree algorithm. This use of a minimum spanning tree turns a visual arrangement into a linear sequence of events, a kind of dimensionality reduction. The path along the minimum spanning tree is traced, as shown in Fig. 8.1. We claim for a richness from using this graph structure, as it is built from the highly salient perceptual measure of relative distance in 2D space. After all when we view a picture, our eyes do not generally read from left to right, but instead jump around multiple fixation points, influenced by the structure of the scene (Henderson 2003).

Each shape that is drawn on the page represents a particular sound event. The nature of each sound event is given by morphological measurements of its corresponding shape, where each measurement is mapped to sound synthesis parameters. Specifically, *roundness* is calculated as the ratio of a shape's perimeter length to its area, and maps to envelope modulation; *angle* is that of the shape's central axis relative to the scene, and maps to resonance; and finally, the shape's *area* maps to pitch, with larger shapes giving lower pitched sounds.

[1] http://ataut.net/site/Adam-Atau-4-Hands-iPhone.

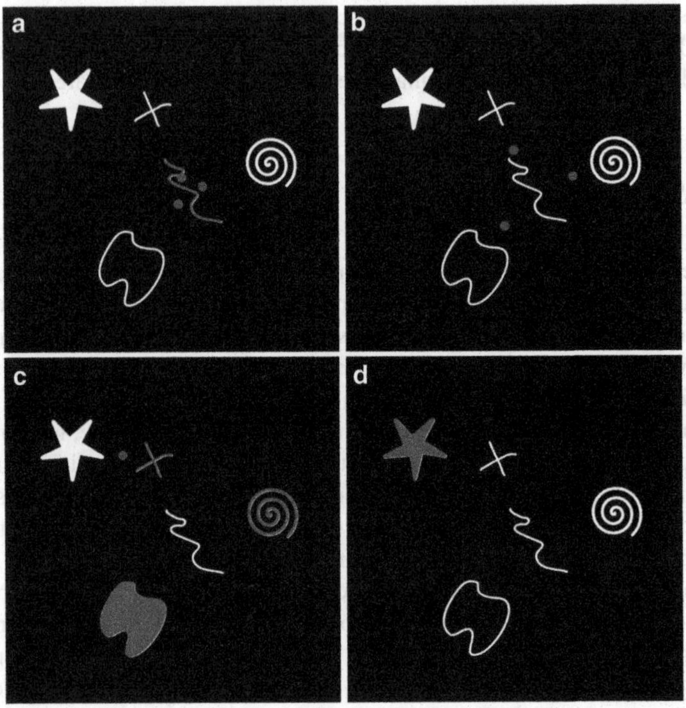

Fig. 8.1 Sequencing of shapes in Acid Sketching. Each shape is drawn to represent a different sound, given by its size, angle and roundness. Shapes are shown with a darker hue when they are 'played'. (**a**) Central shape is 'played', *circles* shown moving towards nearest neighbours. (**b**) *Circles* continue to trace line towards nearest neighbours. (**c**) Nearest neighbour shapes are 'played', with *circle* moving between the cross shape and the final neighbouring shape. (**d**) The final shape is 'played', and the process repeated (Color figure online)

Visual feedback is projected on to the paper using a standard data projector. This feedback takes the form of moving dots, tracing the path from one shape to the next along the edges of the minimum spanning tree, flood-filling each shape as its corresponding sound event is triggered. The geometric relationships employed by the Acid Sketching prototype are not formally tested, but we assert them to be perceptually salient. The correspondence between shape and timbre appear to be straightforwardly learnable, suggesting that this prototype system could be developed further into an engaging interface for live music.

Acid sketching demonstrates a use of analogue symbols which have morphological properties continuously mapped from those of what is represented. Further work by Stead (2011) demonstrates a similar system which allows mappings to be user controlled in a straightforward manner, in effect allowing the user to create their own vision-sound metaphors. A further challenge is to integrate analogue and discrete symbols in a mutually supporting manner. In particular, we look forward to the development of programming languages which are enriched with analogue symbols, in much the same way that language is enriched with prosodic speech.

8.3 Programming Languages

How would one design a computer music interface that can allow for a rich, structured yet open-ended musical expression? One answer is to design for an interaction pattern that makes use of human abilities to represent ideas in a structured but unbounded way, to abstract, to make meta-references – all well-represented in the linguistic faculty. A grammatical interface is a consistent and so learnable interface. Many different levels of musical expression find a representation in formalised language, from music-theoretic abstractions, through pattern manipulations such as modulations and L-systems, down to sample-by-sample structures for audio synthesis and effects. Hence the grammatical interface represented by programming/scripting languages is used in some of the more open sound-and-music systems (SuperCollider, CMusic, ChucK, SAOL).

8.3.1 The Skeuomorph vs. The Abstract Grammar

A grammatical interface is consistent, and so both learnable and powerful, but perhaps it achieves this at some cost. It sits well with our linguistic faculty but may be in tension with some other faculties: an abstract grammar lacks anchoring in familiar relations such as physical spatial arrangement, relationship to external entities, or signification by reference to common understandings. This is the converse of the situation with the skeuomorph, whose cognitive benefit is anchored in some experiential memory which provides signification and is useful for recall – but only if the user shares this prior experience, and if they are unlikely to be overly constrained by habits learned from it.

Hence our proposal that interfaces should let people apply their own metaphors, providing a more transitory use of metaphor than that often baked in to an interface by its designers. The signification and accumulated knowledge assumed by a skeuomorph becomes outdated over time, from year to year or even gig to gig, yet the relationship between performer and audience is rich in signification. One question is then how to support this without requiring users to build their own user interface afresh for each new situation, and without discarding the learning they have already acquired. A grammatical interface goes a long way toward satisfying this, since most of the learning is invested in the underlying composable structure; but there is work still to be done on managing the relationship between the language and the referential aspects of a music performance (both for the performer and the audience).

Fig. 8.2 Solo performance by Stowell as MCLD, combining beatboxing with live coded audio processing

8.3.2 Live Coding

Live coding (Collins et al. 2004) is an emerging practice of creative public programming, used to make music and other art forms in a live context. It renders digital performance in some sense more transparent to the audience, allowing them to share in the creative process.

Improvised performance with a tightly-constrained system (such as a simple drum machine) can be expressive; but improvised performance with an open system (such as an audio-oriented programming environment) allows for an interaction that coherently gives access to many of the different levels of music-making in the digital system, from high-level structure to phrasing to sound design and effects.

Most current livecoders are using performance systems that have not been around for long enough to reach the well-publicised figure of 10,000 h of practice for mastery; the virtuoso livecoder might not yet have been encountered. However, many people spend many hours typing and/or programming in their daily lives, and one advantage of a programming interface over a skeuomorphic interface might be that it can recruit skills developed in neighbouring arenas.

A livecoder, like any improvising performer, is under pressure to do something interesting in the moment. Livecoders can use abstraction and scheduling so the notion of "in the moment" may be a little different to that for more traditional instrumental improvisers. It can lead to a lack of immediacy in how the performer's actions relate to the music, which can sometimes deny the more raw physiological expressionism that some people seek in music. Hence it may be useful to combine the symbolic interaction of livecoding with open gesture-based expression; one of us (AM) has been doing this in collaboration with vocalists, guitarists, drummers and banjo players. The other (DS) has taken both roles in solo live performance by combining livecoding with beatboxing (Fig. 8.2). The cognitive load for one performer carrying out both roles is high, but the combination of continuous organic expression with symbolic abstraction helps to provide immediate multimodal access to the multiple levels of musical ideas. Compare this situation with dual-task experiments such as that of Dromey and Bates (2005) which found evidence of cognitive competition between manual and speech tasks performed concurrently. In the beatboxing-and-livecoding scenario, the vocal and typing tasks are not independent since they both work towards a common goal, but are only loosely coupled since they tend to operate on different timescales. We argue (from experience not experiment) that the skill gained from learning such a multimodal interaction allows confluence rather than competition of the modalities.

Connecting livecoding with performers' sounds and gestures is one way to integrate the organic and continuous into the programming interaction. As we will see in the following section, it is possible to cast programming itself in terms such that the symbolic and the continuous are both part of the ontology of the language.

8.3.3 Visual Programming Notation

Programming language source code is generally considered as discrete, one dimensional text constrained by syntactical rules. Myers (1990, p. 2) contrasts *visual* programming languages as "any system that allows the user to specify a program in a two (or more) dimensional fashion." This definition is highly problematic, for a number of reasons. First, several text based languages, such as Haskell and Python have two dimensional syntax, where vertical alignment is significant. Second, amongst those systems known as visual programming languages, it is rare that 2D arrangement has any real syntactical significance, including Patcher languages such as Puredata and Max/MSP (Puckette 1988). Indeed lines and boxes in visual programming languages allow non-visual, high dimensional syntax graphs of hypercubes and up.

The significance of visual notation then is generally as secondary notation (Blackwell and Green 2002), in that it is not syntactical but still of key importance to human readability. We can relate this to Dual Coding theory (Paivio 1990), in treating visuospatial and linguistic representations as not being in opposition, but rather supporting one another, with humans able to attend to both simultaneously, experiencing an integrated whole. Visual layout therefore not only supports readability, but supplements code with meaningful expression that is in general ignored by the software interpreter.

Some computer music interfaces, such as the ReacTable by Jordà et al. (2007), Nodal by Mcilwain et al. (2006) and Al-Jazari by Dave Griffiths (McLean et al. 2010) use visual layout in primary syntax. In the case of the ReacTable, Euclidean proximity is used to connect functions in a dataflow graph, and proximity and relative orientation are used as function parameters. In the case of Nodal and Al-Jazari, city block distance maps to time, in terms of the movements of agents across a grid. Inspired by the ReacTable in particular, one of us (AM) is developing a visual, pure functional programming notation based on Haskell, designed for live coding of musical pattern. This is a work in progress, but feedback from preliminary workshops with non-programmers has already been highly encouraging (McLean and Wiggins 2011). All four of the aforementioned visual programming languages allow, and with the exception of Nodal are designed primarily for live coding. Whereas research from the live coding field has mainly been concerned with time, we can think of this research as extending computer music notation into space.

We assert that integration between linguistic and spatial representations is what makes a musical experience rich. We can relate this to beatboxing, which is experienced both in terms of discrete instrumental events via categoral perception, and continuous expression within spatial experience. This is much like the relationship between the perception of words and prosody, respectively discrete and continuous, but both symbolic and integrated into a whole experience. By considering a programming notation as necessarily having both linguistic and visuospatial significance, we look to find ways of including both forms of representation in the human-computer interaction.

8.4 Rich and Open Evaluation

This attitude towards musical interface design must be reflected in our approach to evaluation. Much development of new musical interfaces happens without an explicit connection to HCI research, and without systematic evaluation. Of course this can be a good thing, but it can often lead to systems being built which have a rhetoric of generality yet are used for only one performer or one situation. With a systematic approach to HCI-type issues one can learn from previous experience and move towards designs that incorporate digital technologies with broader application – e.g. enabling people who are not themselves digital tool designers.

Wanderley and Orio (2002) made a useful contribution to the field by applying experimental HCI techniques to music-related tasks. While useful, their approach was derived from the "second wave" task-oriented approach to HCI, using simplified tasks to evaluate musical interfaces, using analogies to Fitts' Law to support evaluation through simple quantifiable tests. This approach leads to some achievements, but has notable limitations. In particular, the experimental setups are so highly reduced as to be unmusical, leading to concerns about the validity of the test. Further, such approaches do not provide for creative interactions between human and machine.

For live music-making, what is needed is more of a "third wave" approach which finds ways to study human-computer interaction in more musical contexts in which real-time creative interactions can occur. And live music-making can feed back into HCI more generally, developing HCI for expressive and ludic settings and for open interactions.

One of us (DS) developed a structured qualitative evaluation method using discourse analysis (DA) (Stowell et al. 2009). DA originates in linguistics and sociology, and means different things to different people: at its core, it is a detailed analysis of texts (here, transcribed participant interviews) to elucidate the structured worlds represented in those texts. In the context of a user of a new interface, it can be used to explore how they integrate that interface into their conceptual world(s), which gives a detailed impression of affordances relatively uncontaminated by the investigator's perspective.

This approach is useful and could benefit from further exploration, perhaps in different contexts of interface use. The approach bears an interesting comparison against that of Wilkie et al. (2010), who analyse musicians' language using an embodied cognition approach, which differs in that it decomposes text using a set of simple metaphors claimed to be generally used in abstract thought. As in any exploratory domain, the approach which attempts to infer structure "directly" from data and the approach which applies *a priori* structural units each have their advantages.

Such rich and open evaluation approaches sit well with the nature of creative musical situations. Alternative approaches may be worthwhile in some cases, such as controlled experimental comparisons, but often risk compromising the musical situation. As one example from a slightly different domain, Dubnov et al. (2006) conduct a numerical analysis of an audience's self-evaluated response to a composed piece of music over time. The study went to great lengths to numerically explore audience response in an authentic musical context – commissioning a composed piece whose structure can take two configurations, attracting a concert audience willing to be wired up to continuous rating system, etc. Their results were fairly inconclusive, demonstrating mainly that such a scientistic approach is at least possible if logistically difficult. (Simpler approaches in the same mould exist in the computer-games literature, where the audience can often be only one person (Mandryk and Atkins 2007).) In evaluating systems for music-makers we have the added complication that gathering concurrent data is generally not possible: self-reports would distract from the music-making process, while physiological measures (including brain activity sensors) are generally disrupted by the muscle movement impulses (and sweating) that occur in most music-making. Thus we see little prospect in the immediate future for concurrent protocols, hence the use of retrospective protocols in e.g. Stowell et al. (2009).

Music-making HCI evaluation is still very much an unfinished business: there is plenty of scope for development of methodologies and methods. Evaluation of music-making, like that of computer games, fits well with the developments in the HCI field that are called "third paradigm" (non-task-focused, experiential, ludic). But further: music-making is a key area in which the development of rich and open, yet structured, HCI approaches are crucial to the development of the field.

8.5 Rich and Open Questions

In relating the above themes we have provided a particular view on music interaction, extrapolating from existing analog and digital interactions to try to look towards what could be possible. We conclude then by outlining the themes we have touched upon, and proposing directions we might take in our search for new, rich and open music interactions.

Firstly, in a research field in which the study of embodied interaction is beginning to mature (e.g. through gestural and tablet interfaces), we highlight the role of computer languages and grammatical interfaces. This aspect is represented by the small but growing community of live coding researchers, and we argue it allows for a productive, creative repurposing for musical expression. This focus is not mainstream in musical interface research: in presenting their paper for the New Interfaces for Musical Expression conference, Aaron et al. (2011) noted that the word *language* was conspicuously missing from the top 200 keywords for the conference. In sympathy we take the view that programming languages give us an opportunity to explore music that we have only begun to comprehend. We add to the argument well made by Patel (2007), that music and natural language share close family resemblances, by considering computer language as a third category with its own unique properties. The research theme, ongoing for many years in many guises, is in how to address the properties of computer language to music, towards expressive, higher-order music notations.

An issue we have not discussed is that of learning to program, and whether the strategies we propose could enable (or hinder) the use of programming-type musical systems more widely. We have argued that a grammatical interface is flexible and learnable, and also that such a music interface can productively combine symbolic and continuous aspects; but we have also noted the tension with the anchored accessibility offered by more skeuomorphic designs.

However our argument for rich and open interfaces does not rest on computer languages alone, but in greater integration between abstract language, and embodied gesture. The expressive power of natural language lies in its close integration with prosodic gesture when it is communicated, and accordingly the full potential for computer language can only be unlocked when it is fully integrated with visual and gestural interfaces.

References

Aaron, S., Blackwell, A. F., Hoadley, R., & Regan, T. (2011). A principled approach to developing new languages for live coding. *Proceedings of New Interfaces for Musical Expression, 2011*, 381–386.

Blackwell, A. F. (2006a). Psychological issues in end-user programming. In H. Lieberman, F. Paternò, & V. Wulf (Eds.), *End user development* (Human-computer interaction series 9th ed., pp. 9–30). Dordrecht: Springer. doi:10.1007/1-4020-5386-X_2. chap 2.

Blackwell, A. F. (2006b). The reification of metaphor as a design tool. *ACM Transactions on Computer-Human Interaction, 13*(4), 490–530. doi:10.1145/1188816.1188820.

Blackwell, A., & Green, T. (2002). Notational systems – the cognitive dimensions of notations framework. In J. M. Carroll (Ed.), *HCI models, theories, and frameworks: Toward a multidisciplinary science* (pp. 103–134). San Francisco: Morgan Kaufmann.

Carroll, J. M., Mack, R. L., & Kellogg, W. A. (1988). Interface metaphors and user interface design. In M. Helander (Ed.), *Handbook of human-computer interaction* (pp. 67–85). New York: Elsevier.

Collins, N., McLean, A., Rohrhuber, J., & Ward, A. (2004). Live coding in laptop performance. *Organised Sound, 8*(03), 321–330. doi:10.1017/S135577180300030X.

Cross, I., & Tolbert, E. (2008). Music and meaning. In *The Oxford handbook of music psychology*. Oxford: Oxford University Press.

Dromey, C., & Bates, E. (2005). Speech interactions with linguistic, cognitive, and visuomotor tasks. *Journal of Speech, Language, and Hearing Research, 48*(2), 295–305.

Dubnov, S., McAdams, S., & Reynolds, R. (2006). Structural and affective aspects of music from statistical audio signal analysis: Special topic section on computational analysis of style. *Journal of the American Society for Information Science and Technology, 57*(11), 1526–1536. doi:10.1002/asi.v57:11.

Henderson, J. (2003). Human gaze control during real-world scene perception. *Trends in Cognitive Sciences, 7*(11), 498–504. doi:10.1016/j.tics.2003.09.006.

Hendry, D. G., & Green, T. R. G. (1994). Creating, comprehending and explaining spreadsheets: A cognitive interpretation of what discretionary users think of the spreadsheet model. *International Journal of Human Computer Studies, 40*(6), 1033–1066. doi:10.1006/ijhc.1994.1047.

Jordà, S., Geiger, G., Alonso, M., & Kaltenbrunner, M. (2007). The reacTable: Exploring the synergy between live music performance and tabletop tangible interfaces. In *Proceedings of tangible and embedded interaction* (pp. 139–146). doi:10.1145/1226969.1226998.

Lakoff, G., & Johnson, M. (1980). *Metaphors we live by* (2nd ed.). Chicago: University of Chicago Press.

Mandryk, R. L., & Atkins, M. S. (2007). A fuzzy physiological approach for continuously modeling emotion during interaction with play technologies. *International Journal of Human Computer Studies, 65*(4), 329–347. doi:10.1016/j.ijhcs.2006.11.011.

Mcilwain, P., Mccormack, J., Lane, A., & Dorin, A. (2006). Composing with nodal networks. In T. Opie & A. Brown (Eds.), *Proceedings of the Australasian Computer Music Conference 2006* (pp. 101–107).

McLean, A., & Wiggins, G. (2011). Texture: Visual notation for the live coding of pattern. In *Proceedings of the International Computer Music Conference 2011* (pp. 612–628). Huddersfield.

McLean, A., Griffiths, D., Collins, N., & Wiggins, G. (2010, July 5–7). Visualisation of live code. In *Proceedings of Electronic Visualisation and the Arts London 2010* (pp. 26–30). London.

Myers, B. (1990). Taxonomies of visual programming and program visualization. *Journal of Visual Languages and Computing, 1*(1), 97–123. doi:10.1016/S1045-926X(05)80036-9.

Paivio, A. (1990). *Mental representations: A dual coding approach (Oxford psychology series)*. USA: Oxford University Press, New York.

Patel, A. D. (2007). *Music, language, and the brain* (1st ed.). USA: Oxford University Press, New York.

Puckette, M. (1988). The patcher. In C. Lischka & J. Fritsch (Eds.), *Proceedings of the 1988 International Computer Music Conference*, Cologne, September 20–25, 1988 (pp. 420–429).

Runciman, C., & Thimbleby, H. (1986). Equal opportunity interactive systems. *International Journal of Man–machine Studies, 25*(4), 439–451. doi:10.1016/S0020-7373(86)80070-0.

Stead, A. G. (2011). User configurable machine vision for mobiles. In *Proceedings of psychology of programming interest group*. York: University of York. http://www.ppig.org/papers/23/15%20Stead.pdf.

Stowell, D. (2010). *Making music through real-time voice timbre analysis: machine learning and timbral control*. PhD thesis, School of Electronic Engineering and Computer Science, Queen Mary University of London. http://www.mcld.co.uk/thesis/.

Stowell, D., & Plumbley, M. D. (2010). Delayed decision-making in real-time beatbox percussion classification. *Journal of New Music Research, 39*(3), 203–213. doi:10.1080/09298215.2010.512979.

Stowell, D., & Plumbley, M. D. (2011). Learning timbre analogies from unlabelled data by multivariate tree regression. *Journal of New Music Research*. doi:10.1080/09298215.2011.596938.

Stowell, D., Robertson, A., Bryan-Kinns, N., & Plumbley, M. D. (2009). Evaluation of live human-computer music-making: Quantitative and qualitative approaches. *International Journal of Human Computer Studies, 67*(11), 960–975. doi:10.1016/j.ijhcs.2009.05.007.

Wanderley, M. M., & Orio, N. (2002). Evaluation of input devices for musical expression: Borrowing tools from HCI. *Computer Music Journal, 26*(3), 62–76. doi:10.1162/014892602320582981.

Wilkie, K., Holland, S., & Mulholland, P. (2010). What can the language of musicians tell us about music interaction design? *Computer Music Journal, 34*(4), 34–48.

Chapter 9
A New Interaction Strategy for Musical Timbre Design

Allan Seago

Abstract Sound creation and editing in hardware and software synthesizers presents usability problems and a challenge for HCI research. Synthesis parameters vary considerably in their degree of usability, and musical timbre itself is a complex and multidimensional attribute of sound. This chapter presents a user-driven search-based interaction style where the user engages directly with sound rather than with a mediating interface layer. Where the parameters of a given sound synthesis method do not readily map to perceptible sonic attributes, the search algorithm offers an alternative means of timbre specification and control. However, it is argued here that the method has wider relevance for interaction design in search domains which are generally well-ordered and understood, but whose parameters do not afford a useful or intuitive means of search.

9.1 Introduction

Much recent research in music HCI has concerned itself with the tools available for real time control of electronically generated or processed sound in a musical performance. However, the user interface for so-called 'fixed synthesis' – that part of the interface which allows the design and programming of sound objects from the ground up (Pressing 1992) – has not been studied to the same extent. In spite of the migration that the industry has seen from hardware to software over the last 20 years, the user interface of the typical synthesizer is, in many respects, little changed since the 1980s and presents a number of usability issues. Its informed use typically requires an in-depth understanding of the internal architecture of the instrument and of the methods used to represent and generate sound. This chapter

---

A. Seago (✉)
Sir John Cass Faculty of Art, Architecture and Design, London Metropolitan University, London, UK
e-mail: a.seago@londonmet.ac.uk

S. Holland et al. (eds.), *Music and Human-Computer Interaction*, Springer Series on Cultural Computing, DOI 10.1007/978-1-4471-2990-5_9,

proposes a system which essentially removes the mediating synthesis controller layer, and recasts the problem of creating and editing sound as one of search. The search strategy presented here has wider HCI applications, in that it provides a user-driven method of exploring a well-ordered search space whose axes may either be unknown, or else not connected uniquely to any one parameter. This will be considered further in the conclusion.

We begin, however, by summarising usability problems associated with sound synthesis methods and with the building of intuitive controllers for timbre. Approaches to the problem which have used visual representations of sound or sought to bridge the semantic gap between sound and language are briefly reviewed. The discussion goes on to consider timbre space and its use in sound synthesis, and then describes the operation of the weighted centroid localization (WCL) search method in three contrasting timbre spaces. The chapter concludes by considering the extent to which the WCL algorithm could be applied in other application domains, and discusses relevant issues arising from the building and testing of the system. Finally, directions for future work are proposed.

9.2 Synthesis Methods

Synthesis methods themselves present varying degrees of difficulty to the uninformed user. Some, like subtractive synthesis, offer controllers which are broadly intuitive, in that changes to the parameter values produce a proportional and predictable change in the generated sound. Other methods, however, are less easily understood. FM synthesis, for example, is a synthesis method that may be viewed as essentially an exploration of a mathematical expression, but whose parameters have little to do with real-world sound production mechanisms, or with perceived attributes of sound. However, all synthesis methods require a significant degree of understanding of the approach being employed, and therefore present usability problems for the naïve user, to a greater or lesser extent. The mapping of the task language familiar to musicians – a language which draws on a vocabulary of colour, texture, and emotion – is not easily mapped to the low-level core language of any synthesis method. In other words, the design of intuitive controllers for synthesis is difficult because of the complex nature of musical timbre.

9.3 Timbre

The process of creating and editing of a synthesized sound typically involves incremental adjustments to its various sonic attributes – pitch, loudness, timbre, and the way that these evolve and change with respect to time. Regardless of architecture or method of synthesis, the last of these three attributes – timbre – presents the most intractable usability issues.

The difficulties attached to the understanding of timbre have been summarised in a number of studies; notably by Krumhansl (1989) and Hajda et al. (1997). It has variously been defined as the 'quality' or 'character' of a musical instrument (Pratt and Doak 1976), or that which conveys the identity of the originating instrument (Butler 1992). However, most recent studies of timbre take as their starting point the ANSI standards definition in which timbre is stated as being "that attribute of auditory sensation in terms of which a listener can judge that two sounds similarly presented and having the same loudness and pitch are dissimilar" – that is to say, timbre is what is left, once the acoustical attributes relating to pitch and loudness are accounted for. This definition, of course, raises the question of how timbral differences are to be defined in isolation from loudness and pitch when these qualities are not dissimilar.

Timbre has been traditionally presented as an aspect of sound quite distinct from and orthogonal to pitch and loudness. This 'three axis' model of musical sound is reflected in the design of commercial subtractive synthesizers, where the user is provided with 'handles' to these three nominal attributes in the form of voltage-controlled oscillators (for pitch), amplifiers (for loudness) and filters (for timbre). However, it has long been understood that timbre is a perceptual phenomenon which cannot be simply located along one axis of a three dimensional continuum. Instead, it arises from a complex interplay of a wide variety of acoustic elements, and is itself multidimensional; to a great extent, it subsumes the uni-dimensional vectors of pitch and loudness (which map, more or less linearly, to frequency and amplitude respectively).

9.4 Sound Synthesis Using Visual Representations of Sound

A number of sound synthesis systems offer a user interface in which the user engages with a visual representation of sound in either the time or frequency domain. A good example of such a system is *Metasynth*, by U and I Software. However, audio-visual mapping for sound visualisation presents problems (Giannakis 2006). It is difficult to make an intuitive association between the waveform and the sound it generates – the information is simply at too low a level of abstraction. No user is able to specify finely the waveform of imagined sounds in general, either in the time or frequency domains. In other words, there is no 'semantic directness' (Hutchins et al. 1986) for the purpose of specifying any but the most crudely characterized sounds (Seago et al. 2004).

9.5 Sound Synthesis Using Language

Much research has been focussed on the design of systems whose interfaces connect language with synthesis parameters (Ashley 1986; Ethington and Punch 1994; Vertegaal and Bonis 1994; Miranda 1995, 1998; Rolland and Pachet 1996; Martins et al. 2004). Many of these systems draw on AI techniques and encode rules and heuristics for synthesis in a knowledge base. Such systems are based on explicitly encoded rules and heuristics which relate to synthesis expertise ('bright sounds have significant energy in the upper regions of the frequency spectrum', 'a whole number modulator/carrier frequency relationship will generate a harmonic sound'), or to the mapping of specific acoustic attributes with the adjectives and adverbs used to describe sound.

While the idea of presenting the user with an interface which mediates between the parameters of synthesis and a musical and perceptual vocabulary is an attractive one, there are a number of problems. There is a complex and non-linear relationship between a timbre space and a verbal space. The mapping of the sound space formed by a sound's acoustical attributes to the verbal space formed by semantic scaling is, as has been noted (Kendall and Carterette 1991), almost certainly not linear, and many different mappings and sub-set spaces may be possible for sounds whose envelopes are impulsive (e.g., xylophone) or non-impulsive (e.g., bowed violin). There are also questions of the cross-cultural validity and common understanding of descriptors (Kendall and Carterette 1993). Most studies of this type make use of English language descriptors, and issues of cultural specificity are inevitably raised by studies of this type where the vocabulary used is in a language other than English (Faure et al. 1996; Moravec and Stepánek 2003). Similarly, it has been found that the choice of descriptors for a given sound is likely to vary according to listener constituency – whether they are keyboard players or wind players, for example (Moravec and Stepánek 2003). Apparently similar semantic scales may not actually be regarded by listeners as similar (Kendall and Carterette 1991); it is by no means self-evident, that, for example, soothing-exciting is semantically identical with calm-restless, or would be regarded as such by most subjects.

9.6 Timbre Space

One approach to timbre study has been to construct timbre spaces: coordinate spaces whose axes correspond to well-ordered, perceptually salient sonic attributes. Timbre spaces can take two forms. The sounds that inhabit them can be presented as points whose distances from each other either reflect and arise from similarity/dissimilarity judgments made in listening tests (Risset and Wessel 1999). Alternatively, the space may be the *a priori* arbitrary choice of the analyst, where the distances between points reflect calculated (as distinct from perceptual) differences derived from, for example, spectral analysis (Plomp 1976).

More recent studies have made use of multidimensional scaling to derive the axes of a timbre space empirically from data gained from listening tests. That such spaces are firstly, stable and secondly, can have predictive as well as descriptive power has been demonstrated (Krumhansl 1989), and this makes such spaces interesting for the purposes of simple synthesis. For example, hybrid sounds derived from combinations of two or more instrumental sounds were found to occupy positions in an MDS solution which were located between those of the instruments which they comprised. Similarly, exchanging acoustical features of sounds located in an MDS spatial solution can cause those sounds to trade places in a new MDS solution (Grey and Gordon 1978). Of particular interest is the suggestion that timbre can be 'transposed' in a manner which, historically, has been a common compositional technique applied to pitch (Ehresman and Wessel 1978; McAdams and Cunible 1992).

9.7 Timbre Space in Sound Synthesis

If timbre space is a useful model for the analysis of musical timbre, to what extent is it also useful for its synthesis? Here, we summarise and propose a set of criteria for an ideal *n*-dimensional attribute space which functions usefully as a tool for synthesis.

- It should have good coverage – that is to say, it should be large enough to encompass a wide and musically useful variety of sounds.
- It should have sufficient resolution and precision.
- It should provide a description of, or a mapping to a sound sufficiently complete to facilitate its re-synthesis.
- The axes should be orthogonal – a change to one parameter should not, of itself, cause a change to any other.
- It should reflect psychoacoustic reality. The perceived timbral difference of two sounds in the space should be broadly proportional to the Euclidean distance between them.
- It should have predictive power. A sound C which is placed between two sounds A and B should be perceived as a hybrid of those sounds.

The first of these criteria – that the number of timbre space dimensions needs to be high – poses clear computational problems. Some studies have sought to address this by proposing data reduction solutions (Sandell and Martens 1995; Hourdin et al. 1997a; Nicol 2005). Other researchers have sought to bridge the gap between attribute/perceptual space and parameter space by employing techniques drawn from artificial intelligence.

9.8 Search Algorithms

The position taken in this chapter is that the problem can usefully be re-cast as one of search – in which a target sound, located in a well-ordered timbre space, is arrived at by a user-directed search algorithm.

A number of such algorithms already exist (Takala et al. 1993; Johnson 1999; Dahlstedt 2001; Mandelis 2001; Mandelis and Husbands 2006). Such methods typically use interactive genetic algorithms (IGAs). The features of IGAs are reviewed by McDermott (2013) in this volume; for our purposes, the main drawback of IGAs is the so-called 'bottleneck'; genetic algorithms take many generations to converge on a solution, and human evaluation of each individual in the population is inevitably slower than in systems where the determination of fitness is automated (Takagi 2001).

We present here another form of search algorithm, called weighted centroid localization (WCL), based, not on the procedures of breeding, mutation and selection characteristic of GAs, but on the iterative updating of a probability table. As with interactive GAs, the process is driven by user selection of candidate sounds; the system iteratively presents a number of candidate sounds, one of which is then selected by the user. However, in this approach, a single candidate solution (rather than a population) is generated; over the course of the interaction, this series of choices drives a search algorithm which gradually converges on a solution.

9.9 Weighted Centroid Localization (WCL)

The search strategy employs an adapted *weighted centroid localisation* (WCL) algorithm, which is used to drive the convergence of a candidate search solution on to a 'best-fit' solution, based on user input. The technique has been shown to be an effective search method for locating individual sensors within wireless sensor networks (Blumenthal et al. 2007).

The structure and function of the system is summarised here before considering it in greater detail. A target sound T is identified or imagined by a user. The target T, which is assumed to be fixed, is unknown to the system. An n-dimensional attribute space is constructed which is assumed to have the ability to generate the target sound T, and in which will be created a number of iteratively generated probe sounds. In addition, the system holds an n-dimensional table P, such that, for each point s in the attribute space, there is a corresponding element p in the probability table. The value of any element p represents the probability, at any given moment, that the corresponding point s is the target sound, based on information obtained so far from the user.

At each step of the user/system dialog, the user is asked to listen to a number of system generated probes, and to judge which of the probes most closely resembles the target sound T. The user's judgement on the probes is used by the system to generate a new candidate sound C, whose coordinates correspond, at generation time, to those of the weighted centroid of the probability table. Two versions of this search strategy were tested; the first of these, referred to here as the WCL-2 strategy, presented two probes to subjects. The second, the WCL-7 strategy, presented seven. We begin by considering the WCL-2 strategy.

For the purposes of a formal test of the system, three sounds, initially chosen randomly from the space, are presented to the subject – a target sound T and two probes A and B. On each iteration of the algorithm, the subject is asked to judge

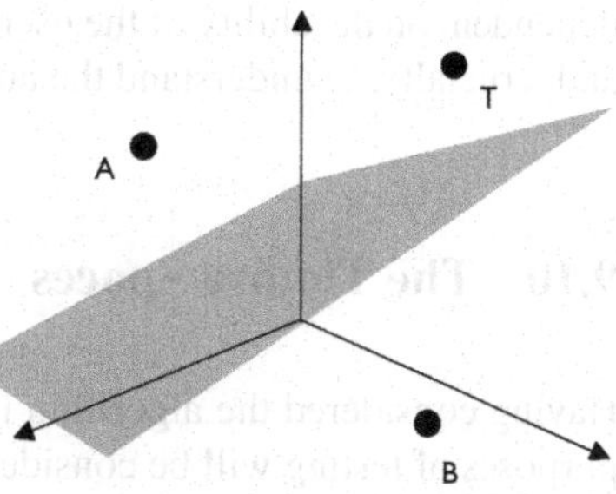

Fig. 9.1 Bisection of probability table P

which of the two probes *A* or *B* more closely resembles *T*. If *A* has been chosen, the values of all cells in *P* whose Euclidean distance from *B* is greater than their distance from *A* are multiplied by a factor of $\sqrt{2}$; the values of all other cells are multiplied by a factor of $1/\sqrt{2}$. Similarly, if *B* has been chosen, the values of all cells in *P* whose Euclidean distance from *A* is greater than their distance from *B* are multiplied by a factor of $\sqrt{2}$; the values of all other cells are multiplied by a factor of $1/\sqrt{2}$. Thus, on each iteration (in the case of a three dimensional space), the space *P* is effectively bisected by a plane which is perpendicular to the line *AB* (see Fig. 9.1). The probability space *P* having been updated, two new probes A_{new} and B_{new} are generated, and the process repeated.

As *P* is progressively updated, its weighted centroid *C* starts to shift. If all, or most, of the subject responses are correct (i.e. the subject correctly identifies which of *A* or *B* is closer to *T*), the position of *C* progressively approaches that of *T*.

The WCL-7 strategy works slightly differently. A target sound *T* and seven probes $A \ldots G$, initially chosen randomly from the space, are presented to the subject. On each iteration of the algorithm, the subject is asked to judge which of the seven probes *A*–*G* more closely resembles *T*. For each cell in the probability table *P*, establish its Euclidean distance *d* from the cell corresponding to the selected probe, and multiply its value by $100/d$. In effect, the value of a cell increases in inverse proportion to its distance from the selected probe. The weighted centroid *C* is recalculated, and a new set of probes $A \ldots G$ generated.

In both cases, the search strategy is user driven; thus, the subject determines when the goal has been achieved. At any point, the subject is able, by clicking on the 'Listen to candidate' button, to audition the sound in the attribute space corresponding to the weighted centroid *C*; the interaction ends when the subject judges *C* and *T* to be indistinguishable. In operational use, T might be a sample or an imagined sound.

In order to have a baseline against which to assess the success of the WCL strategy, another program was developed which provided the user with the means of manually navigating the attribute space. The user interface afforded direct access to the attribute space via individual sliders which control navigation along each axis. This is a form of multidimensional line search (MLS). It has the virtue of simplicity; indeed, for a space of low dimensionality, it may be the most effective search method. However, a successful interaction using this technique is entirely dependent on the ability of the user to hear the individual parameters being modified and, crucially, to understand the aural effect of changing any one of them.

9.10 The Timbre Spaces

Having considered the algorithm itself, the three timbre spaces constructed for the purposes of testing will be considered.

The first timbre space, referred to here as the *formant space*, is fully described in Seago et al. (2005) and is summarized here. It was inhabited by sounds of exactly 2 s in duration, with attack and decay times of 0.4 s. Their spectra contained 73 harmonics of a fundamental frequency (*F0*) of 110 Hz, each having three prominent formants, *I*, *II* and *III*. The formant peaks were all of the same amplitude relative to the unboosted part of the spectrum (20 dB) and bandwidth ($Q = 6$). The centre frequency of the first formant, I, for a given sound stimulus, was one of a number of frequencies between 110 and 440 Hz; that of the second formant, *II*, was one of a number of frequencies between 550 and 2,200 Hz, and that of the third, *III*, was one of a number of frequencies between 2,200 and 6,600 Hz. Each sound could thus be located in a three dimensional space.

The second space, referred to here as the *SCG-EHA space*, was derived from one studied by Caclin et al. (2005). The dimensions of the space are rise time, spectral centre of gravity (SCG) and attenuation of even harmonics relative to the odd ones (EHA). The rise time ranged from 0.01 to 0.2 s in 11 logarithmic steps. In all cases, the attack envelope was linear. The spectral centre of gravity (SCG), or spectral centroid is defined as the amplitude-weighted mean frequency of the energy spectrum. The SCG varied in 15 linear steps between 3 and 8 in harmonic rank units – that is to say, between 933 and 2,488 Hz. Finally, the EHA – the attenuation of even harmonics relative to odd harmonics – ranged from 0 (no attenuation) to 10 dB, and could take 11 different values, separated by equal steps. Again, the sounds used in the space were synthetically generated pitched tones with a fundamental of 311 Hz (E4), containing 20 harmonics.

These two spaces were chosen because a mapping between perceptual and Euclidean distances in the space could be demonstrated; in the case of the formant space, this was shown in Seago (2009) and in that of the SCG-EHA space, in Caclin et al. (2005). The construction of the last of the three spaces – the MDS space – is more complex, and for this reason will be discussed here in greater detail. Based on a space constructed by Hourdin et al. (1997b), it was generated through multi-dimensional scaling analysis of a set of instrumental timbres – e.g. alto flute, bass clarinet, viola etc. Multidimensional scaling (MDS) is a set of techniques for uncovering and exploring the hidden structure of relationships between a number of objects of interest (Kruskal 1964; Kruskal and Wish 1978). The input to MDS is typically a matrix of 'proximities' between such a set of objects. These may be actual proximities (such as the distances between cities) or may represent people's similarity-dissimilarity judgments acquired through a structured survey or exposure to a set of paired stimuli. The output is a geometric configuration of points, each representing a single object in the set, such that their disposition in the space, typically in a two or three dimensional space, approximates their proximity relationships. The axes of such a space can then be inspected to ascertain the nature of the variables underlying these judgments.

However, the technique can also be used as a means of data reduction, allowing the proximity relationships in a multidimensional set of data to be represented using fewer dimensions – notably, for our purposes, by Hourdin et al. (1997a). As already mentioned, both the space and the construction technique used to build it are derived in part from this study, and the list of 15 instrumental timbres is broadly the same. The pitch of all the instrumental sounds was, again, Eb above middle C (311 Hz). Each instrumental sample was edited to remove the onset and decay transients, leaving only the steady state portion, which was, in all cases, 0.3 s.

For the purposes of our test, a multi-dimensional timbre space was constructed. One of its dimensions was attack time, with the same characteristics as those of the SCG-EHA space described in the previous paragraph (i.e. ranging from 0.01 to 0.2 s). The remaining dimensions were derived by MDS techniques, and an initial MDS analysis was performed to determine the minimum number of dimensions required to represent the audio samples with minimum loss of information. This resulted in a seven-dimensional timbre space.

This preparatory process is described fully in Seago (2009); we will summarise it here. The audio files were spliced together and processed using heterodyne filter analysis. Heterodyne filtering resolves periodic or quasi-periodic signals into component harmonics, given an initial fundamental frequency; a fuller account of the technique is given in Beauchamp (1969) and Moorer (1973). After a process of editing, the output was a 15 row by 20 column matrix of data in which each row held the Long Time Averaged Spectrum (LTAS) for one instrumental sound, and the columns contained the amplitude values of each harmonic. This matrix was used to build a dissimilarity matrix which was in turn input to a classical multidimensional scaling function. This generated two outputs: a solution space to the input dissimilarity matrix, and the eigenvalues of each axis of the solution space. The magnitude of each eigenvalue is an indicator of the amount of information associated with that axis. Inspection revealed that 95% of the total information required to reconstruct the spectra was associated with just six axes; thus, MDS can be used to reduce the dimensionality from 20 to 6 with minimal loss of information. A new six-dimensional MDS space was thus generated from the dissimilarity matrix. The following scatter graph (Fig. 9.2) shows the 15 instrumental sounds placed in a three dimensional space (the first three columns of the reduced space dataset).

Sounds represented in the reduced space can be auditioned by means of a data recovery process. The harmonic amplitudes of a given sound can be dynamically generated from a single six-coordinate point in the space and input to an additive synthesis process for playback.

Having considered the three spaces in which the search strategies were tested, we turn now to consider the testing procedure itself.

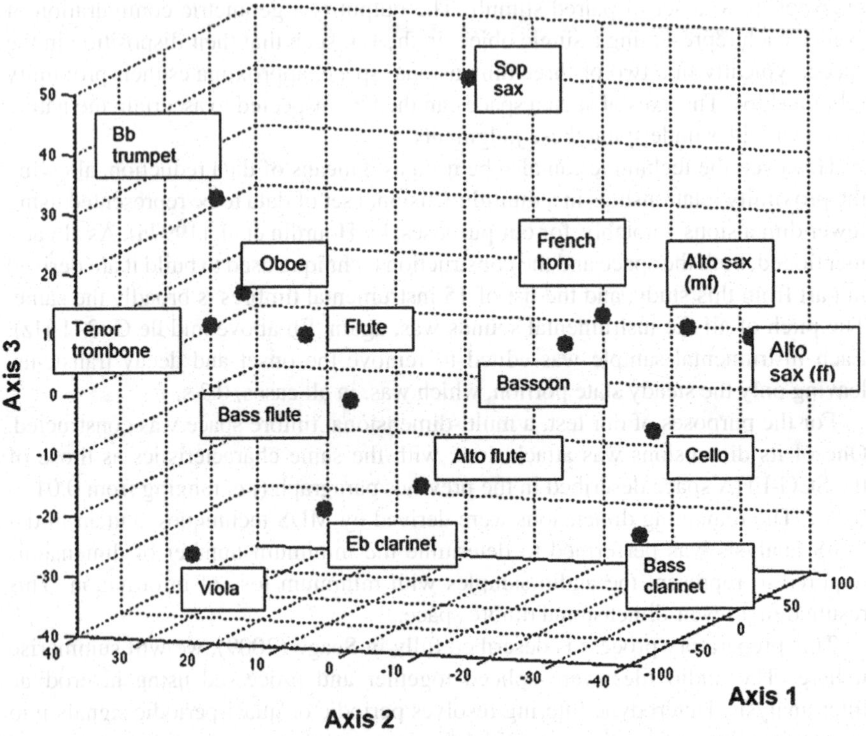

Fig. 9.2 The 15 instrumental sounds located in a three dimensional space following MDS analysis

9.11 Strategy Testing Procedure

The strategy was tested on a number of subjects – 15 in the case of the formant and SCG-EHA space tests, and 20 for the MDS space tests (which were conducted later). The purpose of the test was explained, and each subject given a few minutes to practise operating the interfaces and to become accustomed to the sounds. The order in which the tests were run varied randomly for each subject. Tests were conducted using headphones; in all cases, subjects were able to audition all sounds as many times as they wished before making a decision.

For the multidimensional line search test, each subject was asked to manipulate the three software sliders, listening to the generated sound each time until EITHER the 'Play sound' button had been clicked on 16 times OR a slider setting was found for which the generated sound was judged to be indistinguishable from the target. For the WCL-2 and WCL-7 tests, each subject was asked to listen to the target and then judge which of two sounds A or B (in the case of the WCL-2 strategy) or of seven sounds (in the case of the WCL-7 strategy) more closely resembled it. After making the selection by clicking on the appropriate button, new probe sounds were generated by the software, and the process repeated until EITHER 16 iterations had been completed OR the sound generated by clicking on the 'Candidate' button was judged to be indistinguishable from the target.

Finally, in order to determine whether the strategy was, in fact, operating in response to user input and was not simply generating spurious results, the WCL-2 and WCL-7 strategies was run with a simulation of user input, but where the 'user response' was entirely random.

9.12 Results

Figures 9.3 and 9.4 summarise the mean WCL-2 and WCL-7 weighted centroid trajectories, averaged for all 15 interactions, in the formant and SCG-EHA attribute spaces respectively; in each case, they are compared with the trajectory in the respective spaces of the sound generated by the user on each iteration of the multidimensional line search strategy – again, averaged for all 15 interactions.

In all three strategies deployed in the two attribute spaces, there was considerable variation in individual subject performance. However, the mean trajectories of both the WCL-2 and WCL-7 strategies show a greater gradient (faster convergence on the target) than that of the MLS strategy, with the WCL-7 trajectory being, in both cases, the steepest. It is noticeable that the MLS trajectories, both individually and taken as an average, show no significant convergence in the formant space, but do converge in the SCG-EHA space, suggesting that the parameters of the SCG-EHA space are more perceptually salient (and therefore useful) than those of the formant space.

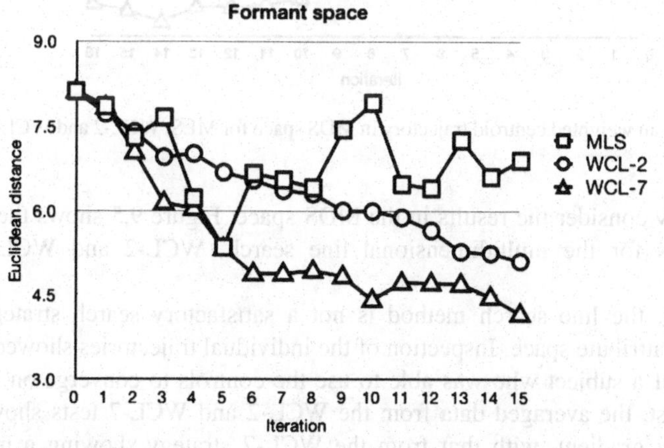

Fig. 9.3 Mean weighted centroid trajectory in formant space for MLS, WCL-2 and WCL-7 strategies

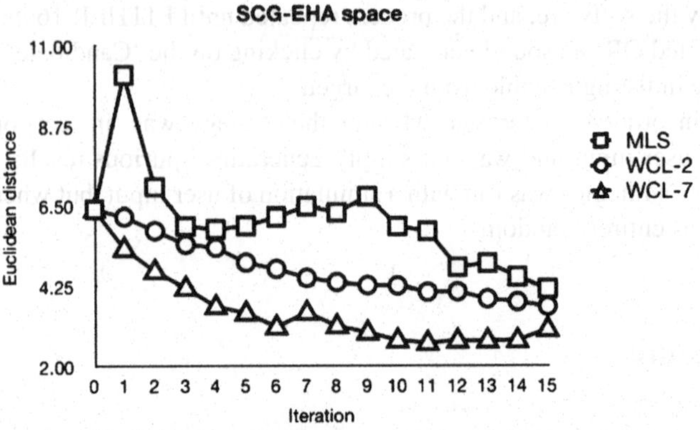

Fig. 9.4 Mean weighted centroid trajectory in SCG-EHA space for MLS, WCL-2 and WCL-7 strategies

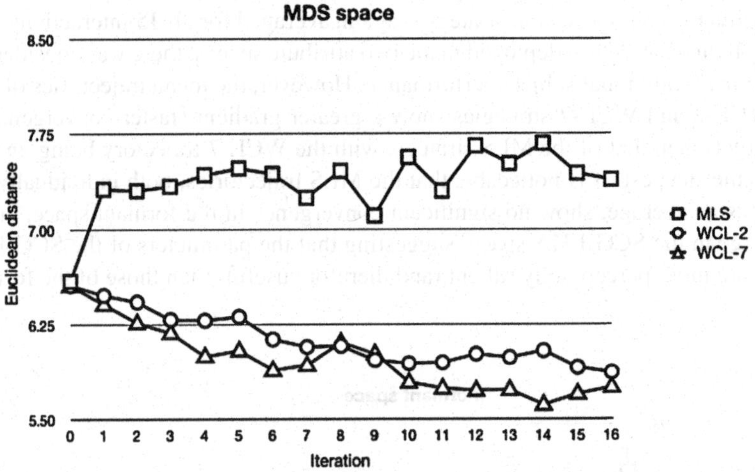

Fig. 9.5 Mean weighted centroid trajectory in MDS space for MLS, WCL-2 and WCL-7 strategies

We now consider the results in the MDS space. Figure 9.5 shows the averaged trajectories for the multidimensional line search, WCL-2 and WCL-7 search strategies.

Overall, the line search method is not a satisfactory search strategy in this particular attribute space. Inspection of the individual trajectories showed only one example of a subject who was able to use the controls to converge on the target. By contrast, the averaged data from the WCL-2 and WCL-7 tests shows a clear and steady gradient, with that from the WCL-7 strategy showing a more rapid convergence.

Finally, the average trajectories of the 'control' strategy (in which 'random' user responses were given) showed no convergence at all.

9.13 Summary of Results

A summary of the results is presented in Fig. 9.6. In order to make possible direct comparison of the results from three attribute spaces that otherwise differed, both in their sizes and in their characteristics, the vertical axis represents the percentage of the Euclidean distance between the target and the initial position of the weighted centroid.

While it should be borne in mind that, in all cases, there was considerable variation in individual subject performance, the six mean weighted centroid trajectories from the WCL-2 and WCL-7 search strategies in the three spaces all show, to a greater or lesser extent, a convergence on the target. Two observations can be made from the above results. Firstly, the gradients of the two traces representing the weighted centroid mean trajectory in the seven-dimensional MDS space are considerably shallower than those in either of the two three-dimensional spaces. One probable reason for this is the greater difficulty of the task; a seven dimensional space is clearly more complex and difficult to navigate than a three dimensional one. Secondly, in each of the three attribute spaces, the WCL-7 strategy (in which subjects were asked to choose from seven probes) produced a swifter convergence (expressed as the number of subject iterations) on the target than the WCL-2

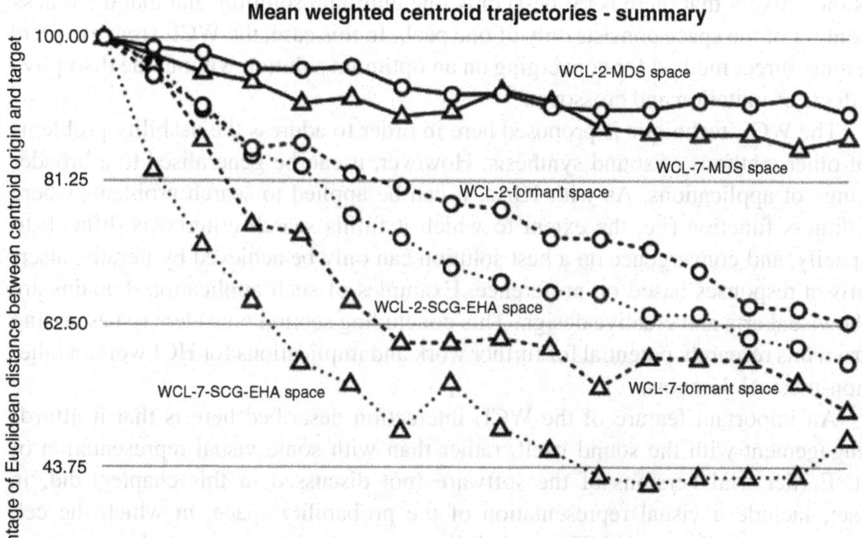

Fig. 9.6 Mean trajectories of weighted centroid for WCL-2 and WCL-7 strategies in three different timbre spaces

strategy, where only two probes were offered. This was observable in a number of individual subject performances, as well as in the overall graph, and is an interesting result. The task of critically evaluating seven, rather than two probes imposes on the subject a greater cognitive load and it had been speculated that this would result in a slower (or even zero) rate of convergence. It should be emphasised, however, that the metric used here is the number of iterations, not the elapsed time or the number of individual actions (i.e. mouse clicks) required to audition the seven probes. Several subjects reported that the WCL-7 task was more difficult than the WCL-2 task; and although this was not measured, it was noticeable that the time required by a number of subjects to complete the task was significantly greater in the case of the WCL-7 task than for either of the other two.

9.14 Conclusion

This paper has presented a discussion of usability in sound synthesis and timbre creation, and the problems inherent in current systems and approaches. Interactive genetic algorithms (IGAs) offer a promising means of exploring search spaces where there may be more than one solution. For a timbre search space which is more linear, however, and whose dimensions map more readily to acoustical attributes, it is more likely that there is (at best) only one optimum solution, and that the fitness contour of the space consists only of one peak. In this case, the WCL strategy offers a more direct method for converging on an optimum solution without the disruptive effects of mutation and crossover.

The WCL technique is proposed here in order to address the usability problems of other methods of sound synthesis. However, it can be generalised to a broader range of applications. As with IGAs, it can be applied to search problems where a fitness function (i.e. the extent to which it fulfils search criteria) is difficult to specify, and convergence on a best solution can only be achieved by iterative user-driven responses based on preference. Examples of such application domains are the visual arts and creative design. This concluding section considers issues arising from this research, potential for further work and implications for HCI work in other non-musical domains.

An important feature of the WCL interaction described here is that it affords engagement with the sound itself, rather than with some visual representation of it. Earlier trial versions of the software (not discussed in this chapter) did, in fact, include a visual representation of the probability space, in which the cell values were colour-coded. The probability space was thus represented as a contour map, from which users were able to see areas of higher probability in the search space. Interestingly, during pilot testing, subjects found the visual element to be a distraction; they stopped listening critically to the sounds and instead, selected those probes which appeared to be closer to these 'high probability' areas. In this way, a dialogue was established in which the software was driving user choices, rather than the other way round, and where convergence on the target was poor. This is not to say that a visual component should or could not be used, but does suggest that visual aids may not always be helpful in interactions of this kind.

The efficacy of the algorithm for sound synthesis, or indeed in any of these domains rests on two assumptions. In order to test the strategies, a target sound was provided for the subjects, whereas the ultimate purpose, as previously noted, is to provide a user interaction which converges on a target which is imaginary. The assumption is, firstly, that the imagined sound actually exists in the space and can be reached; and secondly, that it is stable – the user's imagined sound does not change. Consideration of the efficacy of these, or any other search strategies when the goal is a moving target – that is to say, the user changes his/her mind about the target – is outside the scope of this study, but should be nevertheless noted; it is the nature of interactive search that some searches prove not to be fruitful, or the target changes during the course of the interaction (because the user has changed his/her mind). This being the case, the interface might incorporate a 'backtrack' feature, by use of which previous iterations could be revisited, and new choices made.

Future directions of research are briefly outlined here. First of all, the sounds inhabiting all three spaces are spectrally and dynamically invariant (although the SCG-EHA and MDS spaces include a variable attack time dimension). Clearly, for the strategy to be a useful tool for timbral shaping, this will need to be addressed.

Neither the WCL process itself, nor the spaces in which it was tested took account of the non-linearity of human hearing. That the sensitivity of the hearing mechanism varies with frequency is well known; it would be of interest to establish whether the WCL search strategy performed significantly better in such spaces which incorporated a perceptual model which reflected this.

The number of iterations required to achieve a significant degree of convergence with the target is unacceptably high. Essentially, this is the 'bottleneck' problem, characteristic of interactive GAs. Convergence on the target might be significantly accelerated if the user, instead of being offered two or more probes for consideration, is provided with a slider which offers sounds which are graduated interpolations between two points in the space, or alternatively a two dimensional slider which interpolate between four points. Very much the same technique is described in McDermott et al. (2007) as a means of selection; what is proposed here is an adapted version of it, in which the sliders are dynamically attached to a vector which joins two probes in the MDS space whose positions are updated on each iteration. A two dimensional slider could be similarly used for a vector which joined three probes. Another direction which could prove fruitful is to provide the user with the means of rating two or more probes for perceived similarity to the target (rather than simply selecting one). The probability space could then be given an additional weighting based on the relative rating of the probes, which in turn might result in a swifter convergence of the weighted centroid on the target.

References

Ashley, R. (1986). A knowledge-based approach to assistance in timbral design. In *Proceedings of the 1986 international computer music conference*, The Hague, Netherlands.

Beauchamp, J. (1969). A computer system for time-variant harmonic analysis and synthesis of musical tones. In H. von Foerster & J. W. Beauchamp (Eds.), *Music by computers*. New York: Wiley.

Blumenthal, J., Grossmann, R., Golatowski, F., & Timmermann, D. (2007). Weighted centroid localization in Zigbee-based sensor networks. WISP 2007. In *IEEE international symposium on intelligent signal processing*, Madrid, Spain.

Butler, D. (1992). *The musician's guide to perception and cognition*. New York: Schirmer Books.

Caclin, A., McAdams, S., Smith, B. K., & Winsberg, S. (2005). Acoustic correlates of timbre space dimensions: A confirmatory study using synthetic tones. *Journal of the Acoustical Society of America, 118*(1), 471–482.

Dahlstedt, P. (2001). *Creating and exploring huge parameter spaces: Interactive evolution as a tool for sound generation proceedings of the 2001 international computer music conference*. Havana: ICMA.

Ehresman, D., & Wessel, D. L. (1978). *Perception of timbral analogies*. Paris: IRCAM.

Ethington, R., & Punch, B. (1994). SeaWave: A system for musical timbre description. *Computer Music Journal, 18*(1), 30–39.

Faure, A., McAdams, S., & Nosulenko, V. (1996). Verbal correlates of perceptual dimensions of timbre. In *Proceedings of the 4th International Conference on Music Perception and Cognition (ICMPC4)*, McGill University, Montreal, Canada.

Giannakis, K. (2006). A comparative evaluation of auditory-visual mappings for sound visualisation. *Organised Sound, 11*(3), 297–307.

Grey, J. M., & Gordon, J. W. (1978). Perceptual effects of spectral modifications on musical timbres. *Journal of the Acoustical Society of America, 63*(5), 1493–1500.

Hajda, J. M., Kendall, R. A., Carterette, E. C., & Harshberger, M. L. (1997). Methodological issues in timbre research. In I. Deliège & J. Sloboda (Eds.), *The perception and cognition of music*. London: Psychology Press.

Hourdin, C., Charbonneau, G., & Moussa, T. (1997a). A multidimensional scaling analysis of musical instruments' time varying spectra. *Computer Music Journal, 21*(2), 40–55.

Hourdin, C., Charbonneau, G., & Moussa, T. (1997b). A sound synthesis technique based on multidimensional scaling of spectra. *Computer Music Journal, 21*(2), 40–55.

Hutchins, E. L., Hollan, J. D., & Norman, D. A. (1986). Direct manipulation interfaces. In D. A. Norman & S. W. Draper (Eds.), *User centered system design: new perspectives on human-computer interaction*. Hillsdale: Lawrence Erlbaum Associates.

Johnson, C.G. (1999). Exploring the sound-space of synthesis algorithms using interactive genetic algorithms. In *AISB'99 symposium on musical creativity*, Edinburgh.

Kendall, R. A., & Carterette, E. C. (1991). Perceptual scaling of simultaneous wind instrument timbres. *Music Perception, 8*(4), 369–404.

Kendall, R., & Carterette, E. C. (1993). Identification and blend of timbres as basis for orchestration. *Contemporary Music Review, 9*, 51–67.

Krumhansl, C. L. (1989). Why is musical timbre so hard to understand? In S. Nielzen & O. Olsson (Eds.), *Structure and perception of electroacoustic sound and music*. Amsterdam: Elsevier (Excerpta Medica 846).

Kruskal, J. B. (1964). Multidimensional scaling by optimizing goodness of fit to a nonmetric hypothesis. *Psychometrika, 29*(1), 1–27.

Kruskal, J. B., & Wish, M. (1978). *Multidimensional scaling*. Newbury Park: Sage Publications.

Mandelis, J. (2001). Genophone: An evolutionary approach to sound synthesis and performance. In E. Bilotta, E. R. Miranda, P. Pantano, & P. Todd (Eds.), *Proceedings of ALMMA 2002: Workshop on artificial life models for musical applications*. Cosenza: Editoriale Bios.

Mandelis, J., & Husbands, P. (2006). Genophone: Evolving sounds and integral performance parameter mappings. *International Journal on Artificial Intelligence Tools, 20*(10), 1–23.
Martins, J.M., Pereira, F.C., Miranda, E.R., & Cardoso, A. (2004) Enhancing sound design with conceptual blending of sound descriptors. In *Proceedings of the workshop on computational creativity (CC'04),* Madrid, Spain.
McAdams, S., & Cunible, J. C. (1992). Perception of timbral analogies. *Philosophical Transactions of the Royal Society of London. Series B, Biological Sciences, 336*(1278), 383–389.
McDermott, J. (2013). Evolutionary and generative music informs music HCI—and vice versa. In S. Holland, K. Wilkie, P. Mulholland, & A. Seago (Eds.), *Music and human-computer interaction* (pp. 222–240). London: Springer. ISBN 978-1-4471-2989-9.
McDermott, J., Griffith, N. J. L., & O'Neill, M. (2007). Evolutionary GUIs for sound synthesis. In *Applications of evolutionary computing*. Berlin/Heidelberg: Springer.
Miranda, E. R. (1995). An artificial intelligence approach to sound design. *Computer Music Journal, 19*(2), 59–75.
Miranda, E. R. (1998). Striking the right note with ARTIST: An AI-based synthesiser. In M. Chemillier & F. Pachet (Eds.), *Recherches et applications en informatique musicale*. Paris: Editions Hermes.
Moorer, J. A. (1973). *The heterodyne filter as a tool for analysis of transient waveforms*. Stanford: Stanford Artificial Intelligence Laboratory.
Moravec, O., & Stepánek, J. (2003). Verbal description of musical sound timbre in Czech language. In *Proceedings of the Stockholm Music Acoustics Conference (SMAC'03),* Stockholm.
Nicol, C. A. (2005). *Development and exploration of a timbre space representation of audio*. PhD thesis, Department of Computing Science. Glasgow: University of Glasgow.
Plomp, R. (1976). *Aspects of tone sensation*. New York: Academic.
Pratt, R. L., & Doak, P. E. (1976). A subjective rating scale for timbre. *Journal of Sound and Vibration, 45*(3), 317–328.
Pressing, J. (1992). *Synthesiser performance and real-time techniques*. Madison: A-R Editions.
Risset, J. C., & Wessel, D. L. (1999). Exploration of timbre by analysis and synthesis. In D. Deutsch (Ed.), *The psychology of music*. San Diego: Academic.
Rolland, P.-Y., & Pachet, F. (1996). A framework for representing knowledge about synthesizer programming. *Computer Music Journal, 20*(3), 47–58.
Sandell, G., & Martens, W. (1995). Perceptual evaluation of principal components-based synthesis of musical timbres. *Journal of the Audio Engineering Society, 43*(12), 1013–1028.
Seago, A. (2009). A new user interface for musical timbre design. Ph.D thesis, Faculty of Mathematics, Computing and Technology, The Open University.
Seago, A., Holland, S., & Mulholland, P. (2004). *A critical analysis of synthesizer user interfaces for timbre*. HCI 2004: Design for Life, Leeds, British HCI Group.
Seago, A., Holland, S., & Mulholland, P. (2005). Towards a mapping of timbral space. In *Conference on Interdisciplinary Musicology (CIM05),* Montreal, Canada.
Takagi, H. (2001). Interactive evolutionary computation: Fusion of the capabilities of EC optimization and human evaluation. *Proceedings of the IEEE, 89*(9), 1275–1296.
Takala, T., Hahn, J., Gritz, L., Geigel, J., & Lee, J.W. (1993). Using physically-based models and genetic algorithms for functional composition of sound signals, synchronized to animated motion. In *Proceedings of the International Computer Conference (ICMC'93),* Tokyo, Japan.
Vertegaal, R., & Bonis, E. (1994). ISEE: An intuitive sound editing environment. *Computer Music Journal, 18*(2), 21–29.

Chapter 10
Pulsed Melodic Processing – The Use of Melodies in Affective Computations for Increased Processing Transparency

Alexis Kirke and Eduardo Miranda

Abstract Pulsed Melodic Processing (PMP) is a computation protocol that utilizes musically-based pulse sets ("melodies") for processing – capable of representing the arousal and valence of affective states. Affective processing and affective input/output are key tools in artificial intelligence and computing. In the designing of processing elements (e.g. bits, bytes, floats, etc.), engineers have primarily focused on the processing efficiency and power. They then go on to investigate ways of making them perceivable by the user/engineer. However Human-Computer Interaction research – and the increasing pervasiveness of computation in our daily lives – supports a complementary approach in which computational efficiency and power are more balanced with understandability to the user/engineer. PMP allows a user to tap into the processing path to hear a sample of what is going on in that affective computation, as well as providing a simpler way to interface with affective input/output systems. This requires the developing of new approaches to processing and interfacing PMP-based modules. In this chapter we introduce PMP and examine the approach using three example: a military robot team simulation with an affective subsystem, a text affective-content estimation system, and a stock market tool.

10.1 Introduction

This chapter proposes the use of music as a processing tool for affective computation in artificial systems. It has been shown that affective states (emotions) play a vital role in human cognitive processing and expression (Malatesa et al. 2009):

A. Kirke (✉) • E. Miranda
Interdisciplinary Centre for Computer Music Research, School of Humanities, Music and Performing Arts, Plymouth University, Drake Circus, Plymouth, UK
e-mail: Alexis.Kirke@Plymouth.ac.uk; Eduardo.Miranda@Plymouth.ac.uk

S. Holland et al. (eds.), *Music and Human-Computer Interaction*, Springer Series on Cultural Computing, DOI 10.1007/978-1-4471-2990-5_10,

Fig. 10.1 The valence/arousal model of emotion

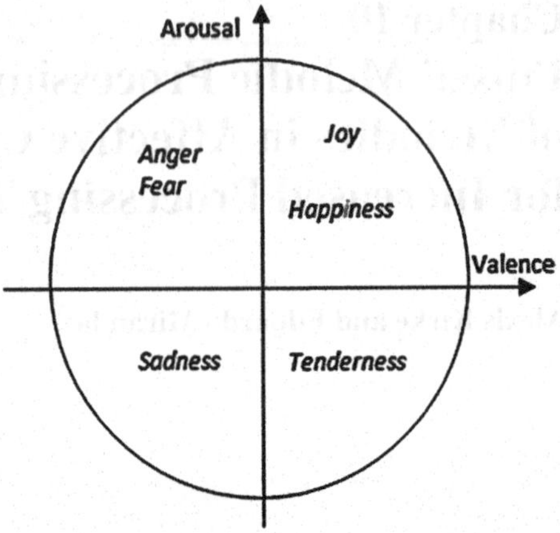

1. Universal and Enhanced Communication – two people who speak different languages can more easily communicate basic states such as happy, sad, angry, and fearful.
2. Internal Behavioral modification – a person's internal emotional state will affect the planning paths they take. For example it can reduce the number of possible strategies in certain situations – if there is a snake in the grass, fear will cause you to only use navigation strategies that allow you to look down and walk quietly. Also pre- and de-emphasising certain responses: for example if a tiger is chasing you, fear will make you keep running and not get distracted by a beautiful sunset, or a pebble in your path.
3. Robust response – in extreme situations the affective reactions can bypass more complex cortical responses allowing for a quicker reaction, or allowing the person to respond to emergencies when not able to think clearly – for example very tired, or in severe pain, and so forth.

As a result, affective state processing has been incorporated into artificial intelligence processing and robotics (Banik et al. 2008). The issue of developing systems with affective intelligence which also provide for greater user-transparency is what is addressed in this chapter. Music has often been described as a language of emotions (Cooke 1959). There has been work on automated systems which communicate emotions through music (Livingstone et al. 2007) and which detect emotion embedded in music based on musical features (Kirke and Miranda 2011). Hence the general features which express emotion in western music are known.

Before introducing these, affective representation will be briefly discussed. The dimensional approach to specifying emotion utilizes an n-dimensional space made up of emotion "factors". Any emotion can be plotted as some combination of these factors. For example, in many emotional music systems (Kirke and Miranda 2009) two dimensions are used: Valence and Arousal. In that model, emotions are plotted on a graph (see Fig. 10.1) with the first dimension being how positive or negative the emotion is (Valence), and the second dimension being how intense the physical arousal of the emotion is (Arousal). For example "Happy" is high valence, high arousal affective state, and "Stressed" is low valence high arousal state.

Previous research (Juslin 2005) has suggested that a main indicator of valence is musical key mode. A major key mode implies higher valence, minor key mode implies lower valence. For example the overture of The Marriage of Figaro opera by Mozart is in a major key; whereas Beethoven's melancholy "Moonlight" Sonata movement is in a minor key. It has also been shown that tempo is a prime indicator of arousal, with high tempo indicating higher arousal, and low tempo – low arousal. For example: compare Mozart's fast overture above with Debussy's major key but low tempo opening to "Girl with the Flaxen Hair". The Debussy piano-piece opening has a relaxed feel – i.e. a low arousal despite a high valence.

Affective Computing (Picard 2003) focuses on robot/computer affective input/output. Whereas an additional aim of PMP is to develop data streams that represent such affective states, and use these representations to internally process data and compute actions. The other aim of PMP is more related to Picard's work – to aid easier sonification of affective processing (Cohen 1994) for transparency in HCI, i.e. representing non-musical data in musical form to aid its understanding. Related sonification research has included tools for using music to debug programs (Vickers and Alty 2003).

10.2 PMP Representation of Affective State

Pulsed Melodic Processing (PMP) is a method of representing affective state using music. In PMP the data stream representing affective state is a series of pulses of ten different levels with a varied pulse rate. This rate is called the "Tempo". The pulse levels can vary across 12 values. The important values are: 1,3,4,5,6,8,9,10,11,12 (for pitches C,D,Eb,E,F,G,Ab,A,Bb,B). These values represent a valence (positivity or negativity of emotion). Values 4, 9 and 11 represent negative valence (Eb, Ab, Bb are part of C minor) e.g. sad; and values 5, 10, and 12 represent positive valence (E, A, B are part of C major), e.g. happy. The other pitches are taken to be valence-neutral. For example a PMP stream of say [1,1,4,4,2,4,4,5,8,9] (which translates as C,C,Eb,Eb,C#,Eb,Eb,E,G,Ab) would be principally negative valence since most of the notes are in the minor key of C.

The pulse rate of a stream contains information about arousal. So [1,1,4,4,2,4,4,5, 8,9] transmitted at maximum pulse rate, could represent maximum arousal and low valence, e.g. "Anger". Similarly [10,8,8,1,2,5,3,1] (which translates as A,G,G,C,D,E,C,C) transmitted at a quarter of the maximum pulse rate could be a positive valence, low arousal stream, e.g. "Relaxed" (because it is in the major key of C). If there are two modules or elements both with the same affective state, the different note groups which go together to make up that state representation can be unique to the object generating them. This allows other objects, and human listeners, to identify where the affective data is coming from.

In performing some of the initial analysis on PMP, it is convenient to utilize a parametric form, rather than the data stream form. The parametric form represents a stream by a Tempo-value variable and a Key-value variable. The Tempo-value is a real number varying between 0 (minimum pulse rate) and 1 (maximum pulse rate). The Key-value is an integer varying between −3 (maximally minor) and 3 (maximally major).

10.3 Musical Logic Gate Example

Three possible PMP gates will now be examined based on AND, OR and NOT logic gates. The PMP versions of these are respectively: MAND, MOR and MNOT (pronounced "emm-not"), MAND, and MOR. So for a given stream, the PMP-value can be written as $m_i = [k_i, t_i]$ with key-value k_i and tempo-value t_i. The definitions of the musical gates are (for two streams m_1 and m_2):

$$\mathrm{MNOT}(m) = [-k, 1 - t] \tag{10.1}$$

$$m1\ \mathrm{MAND}\ m2 = [minimum(k1, k2), minimum(t1, t2)] \tag{10.2}$$

$$m1\ \mathrm{MOR}\ m2 = [maximum(k1, k2), maximum(t1, t2)] \tag{10.3}$$

These use a similar approach to Fuzzy Logic (Marinos 1969). MNOT is the simplest – it simply reverses the key mode and tempo – minor becomes major and fast becomes slow, and vice versa. The best way to get some insight into what the affective function of the music gates is it to utilize music "truth tables", which will be called Affect Tables here. In these, four representative state-labels are used to represent the four quadrants of the PMP-value table: "Sad" for [−3,0], "Stressed" for [−3,1], "Relaxed" for [3,0], and "Happy" for [3,1]. Table 10.1 shows the music tables for MAND and MNOT.

Taking the MAND of two melodies, the low tempos and minor keys will dominate the output. Taking the MOR of two melodies, then the high tempos and major keys will dominate the output. Another way of viewing this is that MAND requires all inputs to be "optimistic and hard-working" whereas MOR is able to "ignore" inputs which are "pessimistic and lazy". Another perspective: the MAND of the melodies from Moonlight Sonata (minor key, low tempo) and the Marriage of Figaro Overture (major key, high tempo), the result would be mainly influenced by Moonlight Sonata. However if they are MOR'd, then the Marriage of Figaro Overture would dominate. The MNOT of Marriage of Figaro Overture would be a slow minor key version. The MNOT of Moonlight Sonata would be a faster major key version. It is also possible to construct more complex music functions. For example MXOR (pronounced "mex-or"):

$$m_1\ \mathrm{MXOR}\ m_2 = (m_1\ \mathrm{MAND}\ \mathrm{MNOT}(m_2))\ \mathrm{MOR}\ (\mathrm{MNOT}(m_1)\ \mathrm{MAND}\ m_2) \tag{10.4}$$

Table 10.1 Music tables for MAND and MNOT

MAND						MNOT			
State label 1	State label 2	KT-value 1	KT-value 2	MAND value	State label	State label	KT-value	MNOT value	State label
Sad	Sad	−3,0	−3,0	−3,0	Sad	Sad	−3,0	3,1	Happy
Sad	Stressed	−3,0	−3,1	−3,0	Sad	Stressed	−3,1	3,0	Relaxed
Sad	Relaxed	−3,0	3,0	−3,0	Sad	Relaxed	3,0	−3,1	Stressed
Sad	Happy	−3,0	3,1	−3,0	Sad	Happy	3,1	−3,0	Sad
Stressed	Stressed	−3,1	−3,1	−3,1	Stressed				
Stressed	Relaxed	−3,1	3,0	−3,0	Sad				
Stressed	Happy	−3,1	3,1	−3,1	Stressed				
Relaxed	Relaxed	3,0	3,0	3,0	Relaxed				
Relaxed	Happy	3,0	3,1	3,0	Relaxed				
Happy	Happy	3,1	3,1	3,1	Happy				

The actual application of these music gates depends on the level at which they are to be utilized. The underlying data of PMP (putting aside the PMP-value representation used above) is a stream of pulses of different heights and pulse rates. At the digital circuit level this can be compared to VLSI hardware spiking neural network systems (Indiveri et al. 2006) or VLSI pulse computation systems. A key difference is that the pulse height varies in PMP, and that specific pulse heights must be distinguished for computation to be done. But assuming this can be achieved, then the gates would be feasible in hardware. It is probable that each music gate would need to be constructed from multiple VLSI elements due to the detection and comparison of pulse heights necessary.

The other way of applying at a low level, but not in hardware, would be through the use of a virtual machine. So the underlying hardware would use standard logic gates or perhaps standard spiking neurons. The idea of a virtual machine may at first seem contradictory, but one only needs to think back 20 years when the idea of the Java Virtual Machine would have been unfeasible given current processing speeds then. In 5–10 years current hardware speeds may be achievable by emulation; and should PMP-type approaches prove useful enough, would provide a practical implementation.

A simple application is now examined. One function of affective states in biological systems is that they provide a back-up for when the organism is damaged or in more extreme states (Cosmides and Tooby 2000). For example an injured person who cannot think clearly, will still try to get to safety or shelter. An affective subsystem for a robot who is a member of a military team is now examined; one that can kick in or over-ride if the higher cognition functions are damaged or deadlocked. Figure 10.2 shows the system diagram. A group of mobile robots with built-in weapons are placed in a potentially hostile environment and required to search the environment for enemies; and upon finding enemies to move towards them and fire on them. The PMP affective sub-system in Fig. 10.2 is designed to keep friendly robots apart (so as to maximize the coverage of the space), to make them move towards enemies, and to make them fire when enemies are detected.

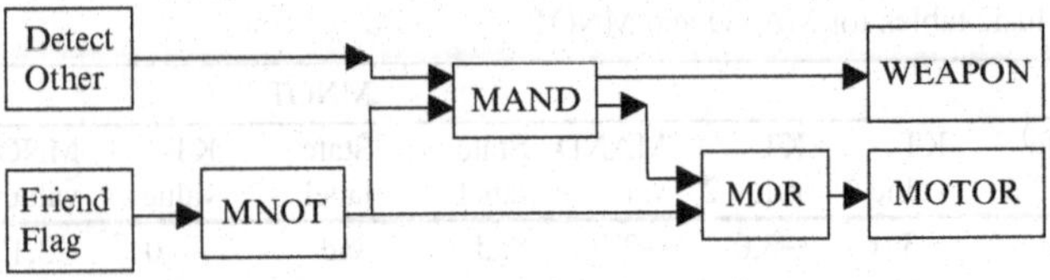

Fig. 10.2 Affective subsystem for military multi-robot system

The modules in Fig. 10.2 are "DetectOther", "FriendFlag", "MOTOR", and "WEAPON". "DetectOther" emits a regular minor mode melody; then every time another agent (human or robot) is detected within firing range, a major-key mode melody is emitted. This is because detecting another agent means that the robots are not spread out enough if it is a friendly, or it is an enemy if not. "FriendFlag" emits a regular minor key mode melody except for one condition. Other friends are identifiable (visually or by RFI) – when an agent is detected within range, and if it is a friendly robot – this module emits a major key mode melody. "MOTOR" – this unit, when it receives a major key note, moves the robot forward one step. When it receives a minor key note, it moves the robot back one step. "WEAPON" – this unit, when it receives a minor key note, fires one round. The weapon and motor system is written symbolically in Eqs. (10.5) and (10.6):

$$\text{WEAPON} = \textit{DetectOther}\ \text{MAND}\ \text{MNOT}(\textit{FriendFlag}) \quad (10.5)$$

$$\text{MOTOR} = \text{WEAPON}\ \text{MOR}\ \text{MNOT}(\textit{DetectOther}) \quad (10.6)$$

Using Eqs. (10.1) and (10.2) gives the theoretical results in Table 10.2. The five rows have the following interpretations: (a) if alone continue to patrol and explore; (b) If a distant enemy is detected move towards it fast and start firing slowly; (c) If a distant friendly robot is detected move away so as to patrol a different area of the space; (d) If enemy is close-by move slowly (to stay in its vicinity) and fire fast; (e) If a close friend is detected move away. This should mainly happen (because of row c) when robot team are initially deployed and they are bunched together, hence slow movement to prevent collision.

To test in simulation, four friendly robots are used, implementing the PMP-value processing described earlier, rather than having actual melodies within the processing system. The robots using the PMP affective sub-system are called "F-Robots" (friendly robots). The movement space is limited by a border and when an F-Robot hits this border, it moves back a step and tries another movement. Their movements include a perturbation system which adds a random nudge to the robot movement, on top of the affectively-controlled movement described earlier. The simulation space of is 50 units by 50 units. An F-Robot can move by up to 8 units at a time backwards or forwards. Its range (for firing and for detection by others) is 10 units. Its PMP minimum tempo is 100 beats per minute (BPM), and its maximum is 200 BPM. These are encoded as a tempo value of 0.5 and 1 respectively. The enemy robots are placed at fixed positions (10,10), (20,20) and (30,30).

Table 10.2 Theoretical effects of affective subsystem

Detect other	Friend flag	Detect other- value	Friend flag- value	MNOT (friend flag)	MAND detect other	WEAPON	MNOT (detect other)	MOR WEAPON	MOTOR
Sad	Sad	−3,0	−3,0	3,1	−3,0	Inactive	3,1	3,1	Fast forwards
Relaxed	Sad	3,0	−3,0	3,1	3,0	Firing	−3,1	3,1	Fast forwards
Relaxed	Relaxed	3,0	3,0	−3,1	−3,0	Inactive	−3,1	−3,0	Slow back
Happy	Stressed	3,1	−3,1	3,0	3,0	Firing	−3,0	3,0	Slow forwards
Happy	Happy	3,1	3,1	−3,0	−3,0	Inactive	−3,0	−3,0	Slow back

Table 10.3 Results for robot affective subsystem

Range	Average distance between F-Robots	Std deviation	Average distance of F-Robots from enemy	Std deviation
0	7.6	0.5	30.4	0.3
10	13.1	0.5	25.2	0.4

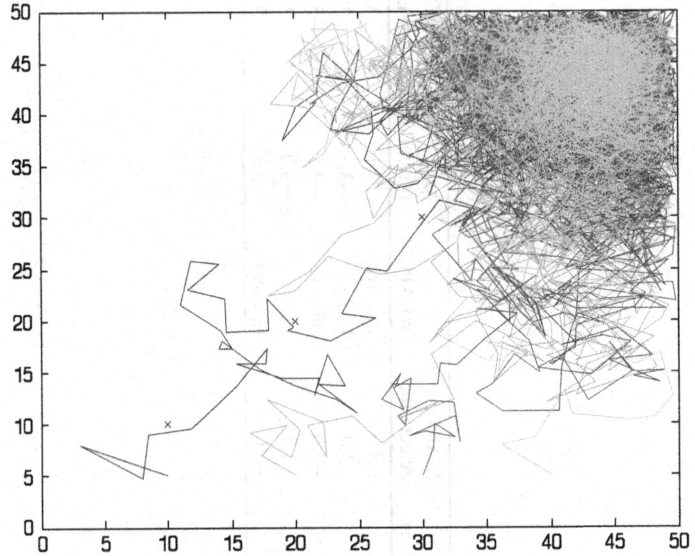

Fig. 10.3 Simulation of military robots without pulsed melodic processing

The F-robots are placed at initial positions (10,5), (20,5), (30,5), (40,5), (50,5)– i.e. they start at the bottom of the space. The system is run for 2,000 movement cycles – in each movement cycle each of the 4 F-Robots can move. Thirty simulations were run and the average distance of the F-Robots to the enemy robots was calculated. Also the average distances between F-Robots was calculated. These were done with a range of 10 and a range of 0. A range of 0 effective switches off the musical processing. The results are shown in Table 10.3. It can be seen that the affective subsystem keeps the F-Robots apart encouraging them to search different parts of the space. In fact it increases the average distance between them by 72%. Similarly the music logic system increases the likelihood of the F-Robots moving towards enemy robots. The average distance between the F-Robots and the enemies decreases by 21% thanks to the melodic subsystem. These results are fairly robust with coefficients of variation between 4 and 2% respectively across the results. Figures 10.3 and 10.4 show two simulation runs, with each F-Robots' trace represented by a different colour, and each fixed enemy robot shown by an "X".

It was also found that the WEAPON firing rate had a very strong tendency to be higher as enemies were closer. Robot 1's tempo value when it is within range

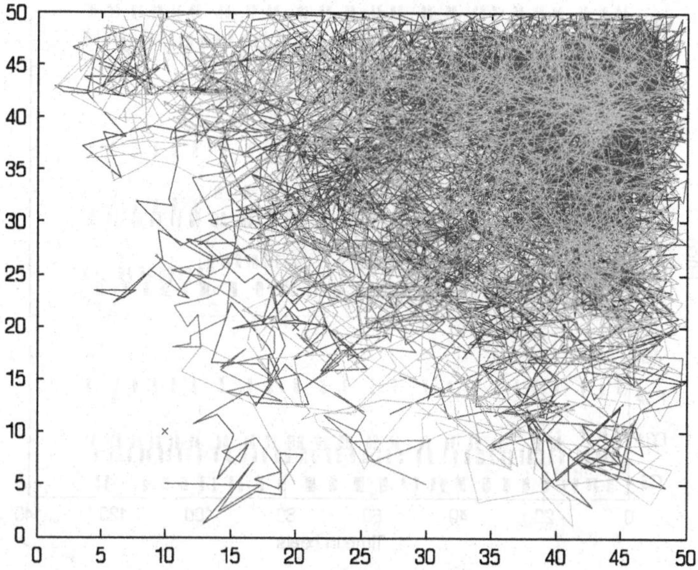

Fig. 10.4 Simulation of military robots with PMP system and range of 10 units

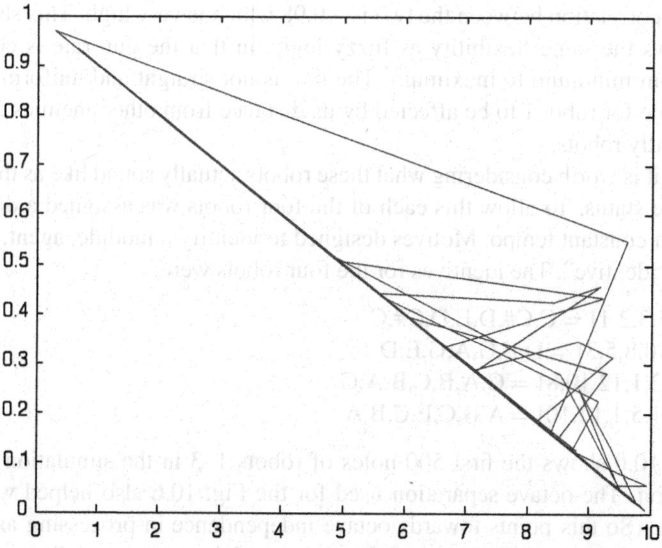

Fig. 10.5 Plot of distance of R1 from enemy when firing + weapon tempo value

of an enemy and firing is shown in Fig. 10.5. The x-axis is the distance from the closest enemy, and the y-axis is tempo. It can be seen that the maximum tempo (just under maximum tempo 1) or firing rate is achieved when the distance is at its minimum. Similarly the minimum firing rate occurs at distance ten in most cases.

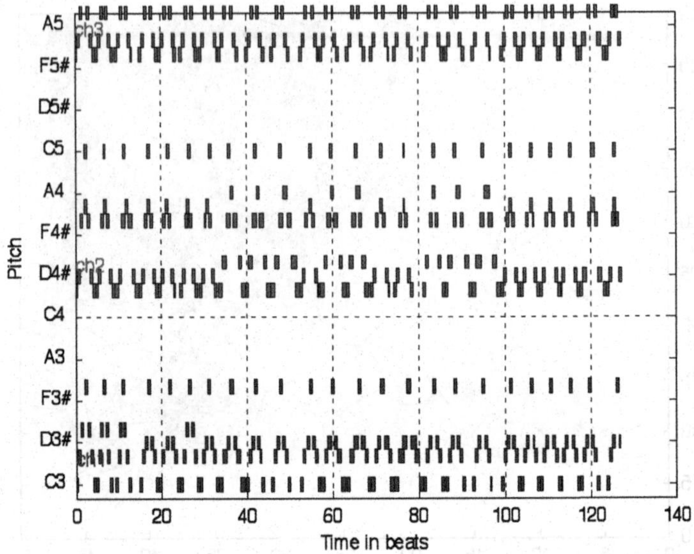

Fig. 10.6 A plot of 500 notes in the "motor" processing of robots 1–3 (octave separated)

In fact the correlation between the two is –0.98 which is very high. This shows that PMP allows the same flexibility as fuzzy logic, in that the gun rate is controlled fuzzily from minimum to maximum. The line is not straight and uniform because it is possible for robot 1 to be affected by its distance from other enemies and from other friendly robots.

Finally it is worth considering what these robots actually sound like as they move and change status. To allow this each of the four robots was assigned a distinctive motif, with constant tempo. Motives designed to identify a module, agent, etc. will be called "Identive". The identives for the four robots were:

1. [1,2,3,5,3,2,1] = C,C#,D,E,D,C#,C
2. [3,5,8,10,8,5,3] = D,E,G,A,G,E,D
3. [8,10,12,1,12,10,8] = G,A,B,C,B,A,G
4. [10,12,1,5,1,12,10] = A,B,C,E,C,B,A

Figure 10.6 shows the first 500 notes of robots 1–3 in the simulation in piano roll notation. The octave separation used for the Fig. 10.6 also helped with aural perception. (So this points towards octave independence in processing as being a useful feature.) It was found that more than three robots were not really perceivable. It was also found that transforming the tempo minimums and maximums to between 100 and 200 beats per minute and quantizing by 0.25 beats seemed to make seem to make changes more perceivable as well.

An extension of this system is to incorporate rhythmic biosignals from modern military suits (Stanford 2004; Kotchetkov et al. 2010). For exampleif "BioSignal" is a tune generating module whose tempo is a heart rate reading from a military body suit, and whose key mode is based on EEG valence readings, then the MOTOR system becomes:

$$MOTOR = WEAPON\ MOR\ MNOT(DetectOther)\ MOR\ MNOT(BioSignal) \tag{10.7}$$

The music table for (10.7) would show that if a (human) friend is detected whose biosignal indicates positive valence, then the F-Robot will move away from the friend to patrol a different area. If the friendly human's biosignal is negative then the robot will move towards them to aid them.

10.4 Musical Neural Network Example

We will now look at a form of learning artificial neural network which uses PMP. These artificial networks take as input, and use as their processing data, pulsed melodies. A musical neuron (muron – pronounced MEW-RON) is shown in Fig. 10.7. The muron in this example has two inputs, though it can have more than this. Each input is a PMP melody, and the output is a PMP melody. The weights on the input w_1 and w_2 are two element vectors which define a key mode transposition, and a tempo change. A positive R_k will make the input tune more major, and a negative one will make it more minor. Similarly a positive D_t will increase the tempo of the tune, and a negative D_t will reduce the tempo. The muron combines input tunes by superposing the spikes in time – i.e. overlaying them. Any notes which occur at the same time are combined into a single note with the highest pitch being retained. This retaining rule is fairly arbitrary but some form of non-random decision should be made in this scenario (future work will examine if the "high retain" rule adds any significant bias). Murons can be combined into networks, called musical neural networks, abbreviated to "MNN". The learning of a muron involves setting the weights to give the desired output tunes for the given input tunes. Applications for which PMP is most efficiently used are those that naturally utilize temporal or affective data (or for which internal or external sonification is particularly important).

One such system will now be proposed for the estimation of affective content of real-time typing. The system is inspired by research by the authors on analysing QWERTY keyboard typing, in a similar way that pianokeyboard playing is analyzed

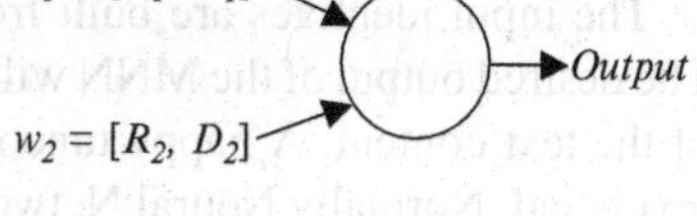

Fig. 10.7 A Muron with two inputs

Fig. 10.8 MNN for offline text affective analysis

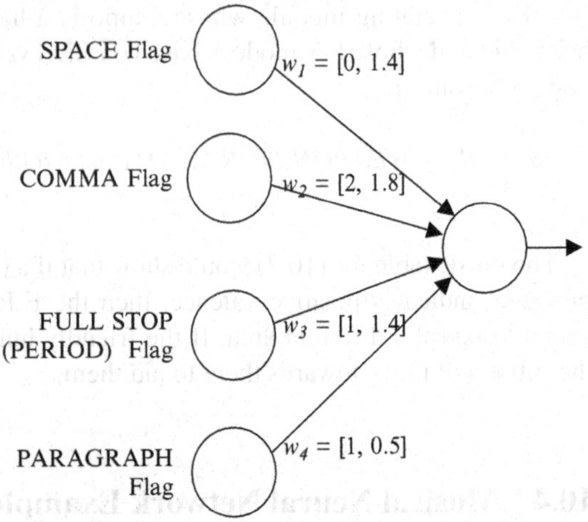

to estimate the emotional communication of the piano player (Kirke et al. 2011). In this a real-time system was developed to analyse tempo of typing and estimate affective state. The MNN/PMP version demonstrated in this chapter is not real-time, and does not take into account base typing speed. This is to simplify simulation and experiments here. The proposed architecture for offline text emotion estimation is shown in Fig. 10.8. It has two layers known as the Input and Output layers. The input layer has four murons – which generate notes. Every time a Space character is detected, then a note is output by the Space Flag. If a comma is detected then a note is output by the comma flag, if a full stop/period then the Period Flag generates a note, and if an end of paragraph is detected then a note is output by the Paragraph flag. The idea of these four inputs is they represent four levels of the timing hierarchy in language. The lowest level is letters, whose rate is not measured in the demo, because offline pre-typed data is used. These letters make up words (which are usually separated by a space). The words make phrases (which are often separated by commas). Phrases make up sentences (separated by full stops), and sentences make up paragraphs (separated by a paragraph end). So the tempo of the tunes output from these four murons represent the relative word-rate, phrase-rate, sentence-rate and paragraph rate of the typist. (Note that for data from a messenger application, the paragraph rate will represent the rate at which messages are sent). It has been found by researchers that the mood a musical performer is trying to communicate effects not only their basic playing rate, but also the structure of the musical timing hierarchy of their performance (Bresin and Friberg 2002). Similarly we propose that a person's mood will affect not only their typing rate (Kirke et al. 2011), but also their relative word rate and paragraph rate, and so forth.

The input identives are built from a series of simple rising semitone melodies. The desired output of the MNN will be a tune which represents the affective estimate of the text content. A happy tune means the text structure is happy, sad means the text is sad. Normally Neural Networks are trained using a number of methods, most

Table 10.4 Mean error of MNN after 1920 iterations of gradient descent

	Key target	Mean key error	Tempo target (BPM)	Mean tempo error (BPM)
Happy docs	3	0.8	90	28.2
Sad docs	−3	1.6	30	0

commonly some variation of gradient descent. A gradient descent algorithm will be used here. w_1, w_2, w_3, w_4 are all initialised to [0,1] = [Key mode sub-weight, Tempo sub-weight]. So initially the weights have no effect on the key mode, and multiply tempo by 1 – i.e. no effect. The final learned weights are also shown in Fig. 10.8. Note, in this simulation actual tunes are used (rather than PMP-value parameterization used in the robot simulation). In fact the Matlab MIDI toolbox is used. The documents in the training set were selected from the internet and were posted personal or news stories which were clearly summarised as sad or happy stories. Fifteen sad and fifteen happy stories were sampled. The happy and sad tunes are defined respectively as the targets: a tempo of 90 BPM and a major key mode, and a tempo of 30 BPM and a minor key mode.

At each step the learning algorithm selects a training document. Then it selects one of w1, w2, w3, or w4. Then the algorithm selects either the key mode or the tempo sub-weight. It then performs a single one-step gradient descent based on whether the document is defined as Happy or Sad (and thus whether the required output tune is meant to be Happy or Sad). The size of the one step is defined by a learning rate, separately for tempo and for key mode. Before training, the initial average error rate across the 30 documents was calculated. The key mode was measured using a modified key finding algorithm (Krumhansl and Kessler 1982) which gave a value of 3 for maximally major and −3 for maximally minor. The tempo was measured in Beats per minute. The initial average error was 3.4 for key mode, and 30 for tempo.

After the 1920 iterations of learning the average errors reduced to 1.2 for key mode, and 14.1 for tempo. These results are described more specifically in Table 10.4 split by valence – happy or sad. Note that these are in-sample errors for a small population of 30 documents. However what is interesting is that there is clearly a significant error reduction due to gradient descent. This shows that it is possible to fit the parameters of a musical combination unit (a muron) so as to combine musical inputs and give an affectively representative musical output, and address a non-musical problem. (Though this system could be embedded as music into messenger software to give the user affective indications through sound). It can be seen in Table 10.4 that the mean tempo error for Happy documents (target 90 BPM) is 28.2 BPM. This is due to an issue similar to linear non-separability in normal artificial neural networks (Haykin 1994). The Muron is approximately adding tempos linearly. So when it tries to approximate two tempos then it focuses on one more than the other – in this case the Sad tempo. Hence adding a hidden layer of murons may well help to reduce the Happy error significantly (though requiring some form of melodic Back Propagation).

10.5 Affective Market Mapping

The Affective Market Mapping (AMM) involves mapping stock movements onto a PMP representation. One mapping that was initially considered was a risk/return mapping – letting risk be mapped onto arousal/tempo, and return be mapped onto valence/key mode. However this does not give an intuitively helpful result. For example it implies that a high arousal high valence stock (high risk/high return) is "happy". However, this entirely depends on the risk profile of the investor/trader. So a more flexible approach – and one that is simpler to implement – for the AMM is:

1. Key mode is proportional to Market Imbalance.
2. Tempo is proportional to Number of Trades per Second.

These can refer to a single stock, a group of stocks, or a whole index. Consider a single stock S. The Market Imbalance Z in a time period dT is the total number of shares of buying interest in the market during dT minus the total number of shares of selling interest during dT. This information is not publically available, but can be approximated. For example it can be calculated as in Kissell and Glantz (2003) – the total number of buy-initiated sales minus the total number of sell-initiated trades (normalized by the Average Daily Volume for S); with a trade is defined as buy initiated if it happens on an uptick in the market price of stock S, and sell-initiated if it happens on a downtick. If there are as many buyers as sellers in stock S then it is balanced and its market imbalance Z will be 0. If there are a large number of buyers and not enough sellers (e.g. in the case where positive news has been released about the stock) the imbalance will become positive.

To generate a melody from a stock, simply have a default stream of non-key notes at a constant or uniformly random rate; and every time there is a trade add a major key note for a buy initiated trade and a minor key note for a sell initiated trade. So for example, if a stock is being sold off rapidly due to bad news, it will have a negative market imbalance and a high trading rate – which will be represented in PMP as a minor key and high tempo – previously labelled as "angry". Stocks trading up rapidly on good news will be "happy", stocks trading up slowly in a generally positive market will be "relaxed". The resulting PMP stream matches what many would consider their affective view of the stock.

For algorithmic trading, affective strategies can be investigated. An example might be "affective arbitrage". In this case the affective content of current news stories about a company could be automatically ascertained by text scanning algorithms (either using an MNN of the type in the previous section, or by keyword analysis that utilizes the various word-affective databases available). These could be compared to the affective state of the company's stocks, bonds etc. If there is a sufficient disparity, then an opportunity may exist for arbitrage. Suppose we define a measure of PMP called the "Positivity":

$$positivity(X) = keyValue(X) + tempoValue(X) \tag{10.8}$$

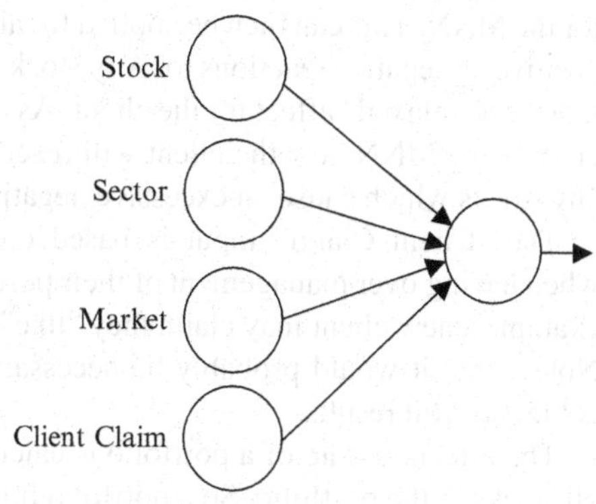

Fig. 10.9 MNN for offline learning client preferences

Then happy stocks would have a higher positivity than sad ones, and relaxed would have a slightly lower positivity than happy ones. An algorithmic trading rule could be:

$$\text{If } positivity(newsStoriesAboutX \ MXOR \ stockX) > k \text{ Then } Flag(stockX) \quad (10.9)$$

The MXOR function will give a low key/tempo (valence/arousal) output for valence and arousal as long as the news story and the stock's affectivity are similar enough. However if the news story becomes very emotionally positive while the stock is more negative, or vice versa, then the MXOR value will begin to increase. Data mining for "affective arbitrage" opportunities could be done by investigating various functions of stocks and seeing if they allow profits; for example rules such as:

$$positivity(Stock1 \ MAND \ stock2) > x$$

$$positivity(Stock1 \ MXOR \ Market) > y$$

$$positivity(Stock1) + postivity \ MNOT(Market) < z$$

could be investigated. Trader "feeling" about the market sentiment could also be incorporated. "I've got a good feeling", "Slow market", etc.

Emotions are considered to be particularly relevant in the field of behavioural finance (Subrahmanyam 2008). In behavioural finance a client's emotional reaction to stock movements may be different to the actual rational implications of the stock movements. Hence an investment professional needs to optimize a client's affective reactions as well as their portfolio. Figure 10.9 shows a possible approach to learning a client's behaviour biases for investing using PMP. In the past a client may have said they are happy to invest in stocks S1 to Sn. However in reality they may show different affective responses to the movements of these stocks over the time they are held. The MNN in Fig. 10.9 is trained based on past client reactions. For example if they were happy about the performance of MSFT (Microsoft) which is part of the tech sector in the S&P 500 market, then that can be used as training date for the MNN. This can then be applied for all stocks the client has reported particular positive or negative reactions to. Any stocks they do not report on could be assumed to have a "relaxed" affect for the client. As data is collected it will gradually become clear to the MNN how the client will react. Then when the portfolio is rebalanced, any stocks which cause an excessive negative reaction can be optimized out.

The "Client Claim" input is based on any questionnaire a client was given when having over management of their portfolio to the investment professional. For example a new client may claim they "like" tech stocks, and dislike utility "stocks". Note – that it would probably be necessary to add a hidden layer to the MNN to achieve useful results.

The affective state of a portfolio is calculated as the average PMP values across all stocks in the portfolio. So a portfolio full of frequently trading stocks will have a higher tempo. A portfolio where stocks are being sold off will tend to have a minor key/low valence.

As well as considering the affectivity of a stock or a market, we can consider the affectivity of a trading strategy. A "happy" strategy is buying fast, an "angry" strategy is selling fast. For example, consider investment implementations: the Market Impact (Kissell and Glantz 2003) of a stock trade can be viewed as a form of affective influence – moving the key/valence of the stock's market towards that of the trader and thus incurring a cost. So minimizing market impact involves minimizing the effect of the trader's key/valence on the market's key/valence. Minimizing trading risk involves maximising tempo/arousal so the market does not have time to move against you. So minimizing these sorts of trading costs for a single stock involves maximizing tempo in your trading, while keeping the key/valence-influence minimal.

As well as the processing potential of PMP in the markets, it is interesting to note that the melodies provide a natural sonification of stock movements and processing – a useful factor for traders whose eyes are already too busy. One can also consider the harmonic relationship between two stocks, or between a stock and the market. If they start to create dissonance where once was consonance (e.g. one becomes more major as the other stays minor) then this indicates a divergence in any correlated behaviour.

So there are four elements which suggest PMP may have potential in the stock markets: the simple Market Mapping, the incorporation of trader, client and news article "feelings" into what is an art as well as a science, a unified framework for affectivity across short and long-term investments and trading implementation, and a natural sonification for eyes-free HCI in busy environments.

10.6 Conclusions

This chapter has introduced the concept of pulsed melodic processing, a complementary approach in which computational efficiency and power are more balanced with understandability to humans (HCI); and which can naturally address rhythmic and affective processing. As examples music gates and murons have been introduced; as well as potential applications for this technology in robotics, real-time text analysis and financial markets. This chapter is by necessity a summary of the research done, leaving out much of the detail and other application ideas; these include the use of biosignals, sonification experiments, ideas for implementing PMP in a high level language, programming by music, etc. However it demonstrates that music can be used to process affective functions either in a fixed way or via learning algorithms. The tasks are not the most efficient or accurate solutions, but have been a proof of concept of a sound-based unified approach addressing HCI and processing.

There are a significant number of issues to be further addressed with PMP, a key one being is the rebalance between efficiency and understanding useful and practical, and also just how practical is sonification – can sonification more advanced than Geiger counters, heart rate monitors, etc. really be useful and adopted? The valence/arousal coding provides simplicity, but is it sufficiently expressive while remaining simple? Similarly it needs to be considered if a different representation than tempo/key mode be better for processing or transparency. PMP also has a close relationship to Fuzzy Logic and Spiking Neural Networks – so perhaps it can adapted based on lessons learned in these disciplines. And finally, most low level processing is done in hardware – so issues of how PMP hardware is built need to be investigated.

References

Banik, S., Watanabe, K., Habib, M., Izumi, K. (2008). Affection based multi-robot team work. *Lecture Notes in Electrical Engineering, 21*, 355–375.

Bresin, R., & Friberg, A. (2002). Emotional coloring of computer-controlled music performances. *Computer Music Journal, 24*(4), 44–63.

Cohen, J. (1994). Monitoring background activities. In *Auditory display: Sonification, audification, and auditory interfaces* (pp. 499–531). Reading: Addison-Wesley.

Cooke, D. (1959). *The language of music*. Oxford: Oxford University Press.

Cosmides, L., & Tooby, J. (2000). Evolutionary psychology and the emotions. In M. Lewis & J.M. Haviland-Jones (Eds.), *Handbook of emotions* (pp. 91–115). New York: Guilford.

Haykin, S. (1994). *Neural networks: A comprehensive foundation*. New York: Prentice Hall.

Indiveri, G., Chicca, E., & Douglas, R. (2006). A VLSI array of low-power spiking neurons and bistable synapses with spike-timing dependent plasticity. *IEEE Transactions on Neural Networks, 17*(1), 211–221.

Juslin, P. (2005). From mimesis to catharsis: Expression, perception and induction of emotion in music. In *Music communication* (pp. 85–116). Oxford: Oxford University Press.

Kirke, A., & Miranda, E. (2009). A survey of computer systems for expressive music performance. *ACM Surveys, 42*(1), 1–41.

Kirke, A., & Miranda, E. (2011). Emergent construction of melodic pitch and hierarchy through agents communicating emotion without melodic intelligence. In *Proceedings of 2011 International Computer Music Conference (ICMC 2011)*, International Computer Music Association. Huddersfield, UK.

Kirke, A., Bonnot, M., & Miranda, E. (2011). Towards using expressive performance algorithms for typist emotion detection. In *Proceedings of 2011 international computer music conference (ICMC 2011)*, International Computer Music Association. Huddersfield, UK.

Kissell, R., & Glantz, M. (2003). *Optimal trading strategies*. New York: Amacom.
Kotchetkov, I., Hwang, B., Appelboom, G., Kellner, C., & Sander Connolly, E. (2010). Brain-computer interfaces: Military, neurosurgical, and ethical perspective. *Neurosurgical Focus, 28*(5), E25.
Krumhansl, C., & Kessler, E. (1982). Tracing the dynamic changes in perceived tonal organization in a spatial representation of musical keys. *Psychological Review, 89*(4), 334–368.
Livingstone, S. R., Muhlberger, R., Brown, A. R., & Loch, A. (2007). Controlling musical emotionality: An affective computational architecture for influencing musical emotions. *Digital Creativity, 18*(1), 43–53.
Malatesa, L., Karpouzis, K., & Raouzaiou, A. (2009). Affective intelligence: The human face of AI. *Artificial Intelligence, 5640*, 53–70. Springer-Verlag.
Marinos, P. (1969). Fuzzy logic and its application to switching systems. *IEEE transactions on computers C, 18*(4), 343–348.
Picard, R. (2003). Affective computing: Challenges. *International Journal of Human Computer Studies, 59*(1–2), 55–64.
Stanford, V. (2004). Biosignals offer potential for direct interfaces and health monitoring. *Pervasive Computing, 3*(1), 99–103.
Subrahmanyam, A. (2008). Behavioural finance: A review and synthesis. *European Financial Management, 14*(1), 12–29.
Vickers, P., & Alty, J. (2003). Siren songs and swan songs debugging with music. *Communications of the ACM, 46*(7), 87–92.

Chapter 11
Computer Musicking: HCI, CSCW and Collaborative Digital Musical Interaction

Robin Fencott and Nick Bryan-Kinns

Abstract We are interested in the design of software to transform single user devices such as laptop computers into a platform for collaborative musical interaction. Our work draws on existing theories of group musical interaction and studies of collaboration in the workplace. This chapter explores the confluence of these domains, giving particular attention to challenges posed by the auditory nature of music and the open-ended characteristics of musical interaction. Our methodological approach is described and a study is presented which contrasts three interface designs for collaborative musical interaction. Significant results are discussed, showing that the different interface designs influenced the way groups structured their collaboration. We conclude by proposing several design implications for collaborative music software, and outline directions for future work.

11.1 Introduction

Novel systems for group musical interaction such as touch surfaces (Jordà et al. 2007) and multi-player instruments (Fels and Vogt 2002) represent an exciting insight into the future of music technology; however many of these systems rely on bespoke hardware which prevents them being widely available. An alternative to developing new physical interfaces is to design software that transforms single user devices such as personal computers into a platform for collaboration. We believe that there are wide and under-explored possibilities for such environments; however at present the majority of music software is designed for single user operation, and there are few readily available technologies to support musical collaboration beyond the synchronisation of single user devices. MIDI and NINJAM are examples of

R. Fencott (✉) • N. Bryan-Kinns
Queen Mary University of London, London, UK
e-mail: RobinFencott@eecs.qmul.ac.uk; NickBK@eecs.qmul.ac.uk

S. Holland et al. (eds.), *Music and Human-Computer Interaction*, Springer Series on Cultural Computing, DOI 10.1007/978-1-4471-2990-5_11,

synchronisation-based technologies. MIDI is a serial communication protocol that enables multiple devices to be slaved to a single timing source, while NINJAM enables audio to be synchronised over the Internet to facilitate geographically distributed collaboration (Mills 2010).

Systems for musical collaboration can extend beyond synchronisation by allowing more complex sharing of musical contributions, ideas and representations within a group of musicians. For instance, distributed graphical interfaces can allow multiple users to interact simultaneously with a collection of shared on-screen virtual instruments, or collaboratively arrange items on a shared timeline. In addition to facilitating more complex interrelations between musicians' contributions, a distributed software environment could provide support and scaffolding for collaboration by, for instance, displaying information about the authorship of specific contributions, allowing annotations to be attached to the shared workspace or allowing individuals to work with varying degrees of privacy. The technical challenges of this approach have been explored by laptop and mobile phone orchestra projects (Dannenberg et al. 2007; Wang et al. 2009; Trueman et al. 2006) and geographically distributed software environments such as the Daisyphone (Bryan-Kinns and Hamilton 2009), LNX Studio[1] and Ohm Studio[2]. However less attention has been paid to the way people use these environments, or to the effect different interface designs have on collaborative group processes.

Our research deals with co-located interaction where groups of musicians create music using a shared software interface distributed across multiple computer terminals. Some of the issues we are particularly interested in are illustrated by the following examples. Firstly, when musicians can edit each other's musical contributions the issues of ownership, territory and privacy become important. Questions arise such as whether users should be able to edit each other's work at any point or should the interface provide mechanisms that give authors control over sharing and access to their musical contributions? Secondly, in a shared interface where musicians are not tied to specific instruments or equipment, the roles they play within the group may become more fluid. How does this freedom impact on the way groups structure their collaboration? Third is the issue of awareness, or knowledge of others' activities within the shared workspace. If musicians can work on musical ideas privately, or transition between different roles and activities, how do they maintain awareness of each other's actions and how might an interface support maintenance of such awareness. These issues are fundamental to the design of group musical environments as they define the way groups collaborate, however at present there is limited research investigating the way groups of people engage in musical collaboration using computers, and consequently there are few existing guidelines for the design of future systems.

We propose the term Collaborative Digital Musical Interaction (CDMI) to describe the phenomenon of technologically supported group musical interaction.

---

[1]http://lnxstudio.sourceforge.net/

[2]http://www.ohmstudio.com/

This term bounds the concept in three ways. Firstly, it stresses the collaborative nature of group musical interaction. Secondly, it emphasises the process of musical interaction rather than concentrating on a particular musical activity such as performance, composition or improvisation. Finally, CDMI focuses on the use of digital technology to support collaboration, but does not commit to a specific device or platform. This chapter outlines CDMI by drawing on research from within Human Computer Interaction (HCI) and Computer Supported Collaborative Work (CSCW). Our understanding of music is informed by studies of conventional musical interaction, the theory of Musicking (Small 1998) and studies of group creativity (Sawyer 2003). Our methodological approach to studying CDMI is described, and illustrated through the presentation of an experimental study. We conclude with a number of design concerns for CDMI and more general reflection on how studying CDMI can contribute to HCI and CSCW.

11.1.1 Music and Collaboration

Computer Supported Cooperative Work (CSCW) is a specialised branch of HCI focused on understanding the nature of group work and designing appropriate technology to support collaboration between people (Bannon and Schmidt 1991). Although generally not concerned with musical interaction, CSCW represents a substantial body of research into the nature of group-work and the design of technology to augment collaboration. CSCW can be viewed as an umbrella term for all HCI research concerning multiple users, however Hughes et al. (1991) stress that all work, no matter how individual, occurs within a wider social context, and therefore CSCW might usefully be regarded as a paradigm shift within the Computer Science community away from the view of HCI as interaction between individual people and computers, and towards a social view of work and interaction as a collective phenomena.

Key research themes for CSCW are the design and evaluation of collaborative and multi-user software termed ‘groupware’, and the study of group interaction in workplaces. Workplace studies often employ ethnographic techniques (Heath et al. 2002) and draw on frameworks such as distributed cognition (Furniss and Blandford 2006; Hutchins 1996) to develop rich accounts of group work activities in work settings which feature intense group coordination. These studies typically present detailed analysis of a number of specific incidents within the observed interaction to characterise the relationships and processes that take place. Controlled experimental studies in CSCW typically investigate specific aspects of group activity by presenting work teams with simplified tasks such as completing jigsaw puzzles (Scott et al. 2004) or work-like activities such as designing a post-office (Dourish and Bellotti 1992). This type of study environment provides more flexibility in data collection and control over the activities participants engage in. Groupware evaluation is often based on an experimental approach where groups engage in an activity using interfaces with different features or support for collaboration. Typical observations are time to complete the task, quality of the solution, ease of collaboration and user satisfaction. Gutwin and Greenberg (1999) describe these features as *Product* (the result or outcome of a task), *Process* (the activity of the group while developing their solution), and *Satisfaction* (feelings about the work and interaction with the system).

Workplace studies in CSCW often base observations in high-risk environments such as control rooms. In these environments full concentration is needed, and peoples' activities are time-critical, highly interdependent and potentially life threatening. While musical interaction is clearly a lower risk activity, for the musicians involved the interaction may exhibit similar attributes to those found in other workplace activities. Real-time musical interaction is typically time-critical, and musicians are especially sensitive to timing accuracy on many different musical time scales. Group musical interaction can also be highly interdependent, with musicians using and broadcasting cues for changes and transitions (Gratier 2008; Healey et al. 2005), adapting their own contributions in response to what they hear from others in the group (Sawyer 2003) and helping each other recover from mistakes (Gratier 2008).

As well as similarities, there are existing points of confluence between CSCW and music technology research. Gates et al. (2006) uses the theory of Workspace Awareness (Gutwin and Greenberg 2002) to discuss the ways in which DJs maintain awareness of their audience while performing. Merritt et al. (2010) explore visualization techniques to promote awareness in collocated musical interaction. Bryan-Kinns and Hamilton (2009) and Fencott and Bryan-Kinns (2010) draw on aspects of CSCW to explore interface design issues for collaborative music software. Gurvich (2006) discusses privacy and awareness in an online music environment and Klugel et al. (2011) draws on studies of co-located collaboration to inform the design of a tabletop music interface.

The aspects of CSCW research we apply to CDMI are those associated with awareness, coordination, and the analysis of communication. Our research takes the Workspace Awareness framework (Gutwin and Greenberg 2002) as a starting point for understanding the interrelationship between people engaged in co-located musical interaction using a shared software environment. Their framework is informed by observational studies of co-located workplace activities, and identifies the types of information people hold or may attempt to gather while collaborating in work tasks.

11.1.2 Musical Interaction

This section draws on theories and observational studies of musical interaction to highlight the ways in which group musical interaction can be regarded as distinct from other forms of group work and collaboration. This in turn leads to implications for both design and evaluation of new CDMI systems.

Small (1998) proposes that music is constructed by those who engage in the act of 'Musicking', a social ritual through which participants explore their identity and relation to others. Small argues that activities such as listening to a personal stereo, playing in a rock band, dancing and attending a classical music concert can all be regarded as acts of Musicking. Musicking is an activity commonly associated with Flow (Csikszentmihalyi 1990) and Group Flow (Sawyer 2003), while the acknowledgement that all Musicking is a social and cultural phenomenon parallels the assertion that all work activities are social (Hughes et al. 1991).

Small argues that traditional philosophies and theories of music mistakenly value musical artifacts such as scores and recordings, while ignoring both the actions of creation and perceptions or responses to it. Sawyer (2003) illustrates the importance of the creative process by stressing that artists frequently modify their work, that inspiration does not always precede execution, and that creators do not share all their acts of creativity with the world. For this reason music has been described as a problem-seeking activity (Holland 2000) where the product is the process (Makelberge 2010; Sawyer 2003) and those involved are concerned with exploring the medium, discovering new ideas and finding a creative problem to resolve. In a group context the individuals may also be interested in exploring their creative relationship to others in the group.

An association has frequently been drawn between musical interaction and face-to-face conversation (Healey et al. 2005; Gratier 2008; Small 1998; Bryan-Kinns and Hamilton 2009). Healey et al. (2005) identifies a turn-taking process used by participants to introduce new musical themes. Sawyer (2003) argues that improvisational music making exhibits many of the same properties as everyday conversation, including emergence, contingency, and a reliance on intersubjectivity. Sawyer (2003) also notes that while musicians frequently use conversation as a metaphor for describing improvisation, in musical improvisation there is no turn-taking as all musicians perform simultaneously.

Although there are traditions for which notation is a central aspect of musical culture and understanding, music is primarily an auditory domain. This represents a key distinction between CDMI and research in CSCW concerned with the generation of visual artifacts such as documents, drawings and diagrams. We believe working with sound has a number of implications for the way people collaborate. One crucial implication relates to Clark and Brennan's theory of communicative grounding (Clark and Brennan 1991), where it is noted that 'indicative gestures' such as looking, pointing and touching are important means by which interlocutors arrive at an understanding that they are both referring to the same object. In a purely auditory situation these visual gestures may not be as useful as it is not possible to point at sounds.

Coughlan and Johnson (2007) identify many forms of representation used by musicians to convey ideas and refer to aspects of the music. These include playing their instruments, vocalising, gesture and verbal communication. This illustrates the idea that a musical gesture is both an act of communication and an aesthetic product in its own right (Gratier 2008; Bryan-Kinns and Hamilton 2009). Coughlan and

Johnson (2007) argue that an understanding of how musicians represent and convey ideas is crucial to the design of new musical interfaces and software environments, while Nabavian and Bryan-Kinns (2006) note that musicians often successfully collaborate while holding entirely different cognitive representations of the music they are co-creating.

Healey et al. (2005) describe the way musicians use the physical space around them as a collaborative resource, arguing that musicians use the orientation of their bodies and musical instruments towards the physical 'interaction space' as a sign of their (dis)engagement with the ongoing improvisation. However the role of this physical interaction space may be reduced when musicians are seated at computers using a shared software interface, as the musicians may be less free to move while still in reach of their computer. Compared to acoustic instruments, the abstracted nature of the shared software interface and generic physical input devices may provide less opportunity to gesture.

To summarise, our conception of music draws on the theory of Musicking, and views music as an activity in which the participants may be equally concerned with the process of creating and exploring as they are with arriving at a musical outcome. As a domain, music is in many ways distinct from visual and spatial mediums, and this has implications for the way people go about discussing, referring to and representing ideas within and about it. CSCW provides some insights into observable features of collaboration, however the tasks used in CSCW research are often more aligned to product outcomes.

11.2 Approach

We use a controlled experimental approach to investigate interface design considerations for CDMI. During experiment sessions groups of musicians make music using collaborative music software developed specifically for our research. We present the groups with different software interface designs and observe how this impacts on the way they use the software, their approach to organising collaborative activities and their subjective preferences. This approach is inspired by studies such as Gutwin and Greenberg (1999), where interface based awareness mechanisms are manipulated to assess their impact on group collaboration usability. Our additional focus on qualitative measures extends the traditional CSCW approach to account for some of the distinct experiential properties of CDMI. Typical research questions driving our studies are:

- How does manipulating the degree of privacy individuals have in a shared musical interface alter the way they work together?
- How do different forms of audio presentation influence the way groups coordinate and organise the shared workspace?
- How do mechanisms for gathering authorship information alter the way groups discuss the music they are creating?

We collect and analyse interaction features using log data captured by the software. We use video observation to study participants' discussions during the interaction, and we hold group discussions with the participants to discover their interpretations of the experience. Finally, we employ multiple choice questionnaires to capture demographic and preference information. Observations include:

- The amount of musical contributions participants make during the interaction
- The amount of editing and participants perform on contributions
- The degree musical contributions are co-edited by multiple participants
- The topics of conversations participants engage in
- Spatial use and arrangement of the software interface by participants
- The emergence and negotiation of roles within the interaction

As illustrated by the study presented subsequently in Sect. 11.3, these features can tell us a lot about the way participants used the software and structured their collaboration. Many of the quantitative log measures can be directly compared between different interface conditions to reveal the effects brought about by different interface designs, although features such as roles and conversation require analysis of video and audio recordings.

The software used in our studies has been designed specifically for our research, and our approach is therefore in line with others who develop musical interfaces specifically to conduct experiments, rather than applying posteriori evaluation techniques to previously developed artifacts of new musical technology (Marquez-Borbon et al. 2011). Creating software specifically for performing research has several advantages over attempting to apply evaluation techniques to existing software. Primarily, as noted in Sect. 11.1, there are few existing collaborative music making applications which support the type of interaction we are interested in studying. Secondly, using bespoke software provides us with complete control over every aspect of the functionality, appearance and behavior of the software. This is beneficial as it allows us to implement multiple interface designs for the same underlying software model, and enables us to explore interface and interaction possibilities that might not be present in existing third party applications. Furthermore, using bespoke software allows us to limit the capabilities of the software so as to be suitable for short experimental sessions. This is important as the sessions are time-constrained and it is essential for participants to reach a competent level with the software in a short amount of time. Finally, using novel software introduces control over the influence of participants' previous experience by ensuring that all participants are using the software for the first time.

However, there are several considerations to using bespoke software. One such concern is that participants need to be trained in the use of the software. Where appropriate using interaction metaphors from existing music software may help people familiarise themselves, although time must still be allocated to training in each experiment session. Secondly, the design and affordances of the software will direct participants towards specific interactions, and generalisations about study findings must be balanced against the idiosyncrasies of the experimental software. Thirdly, ordering effects may be introduced as participants become more experienced and familiar with the software over the course of the experiment session.

We use mailing lists and forums to recruit participants. Our recruitment seeks to find people with an interest in making music and/or experience using computer music software. While social and musical rapport are important aspect of group musical interaction (Sawyer 2003; Small 1998) several factors have motivated us to study groups of people who have not previously worked together. Firstly, established groups will arrive with a history of experiences to draw upon, a shared musical repertoire and established working strategies. These working strategies and means of communication may be obtuse and difficult to interpret or study. Secondly, studying musicians who have previously worked together may introduce bias between groups, as not all groups will have an equal level of experience working together. Thirdly, the group's musical repertoire, group musical knowledge and established working strategies may be stronger than or resilient to the effects brought about by the experimental conditions under investigation. Studying groups of individuals who are not familiar with each other introduces control over differences in the level of group experience, as all participants will have an equal level of familiarity with one another. We acknowledge that participants will need to build a social and musical rapport and although it is less common for musicians to play with people they have not previously worked with, this is not an entirely unnatural situation. Finally, recruiting groups of strangers simplifies the process of recruitment and allows us to use a larger sample of participants.

11.3 Study

To demonstrate the practical application of the methodology outlined above, this section describes a study focusing on how varying the amount of privacy and awareness provided by a software interface impacts on the process of musical collaboration. The study design uses three experimental conditions, each providing participants with different level of privacy. This design is intended to reveal the different approaches taken by collaborators when given varying degrees of information about each other's activities. For instance introducing the ability for someone to work in isolation from the group creates a situation where collaborators have potentially heterogeneous representations of the music, with each participant listening to a mixture of personal and group-level contributions. Given this situation, participants may need to work harder to maintain awareness of one another, or may develop alternative strategies for managing the collaborative process. Specific features addressed in our analysis are how awareness information is gathered and exploited by collaborators, the emergence of roles, and how musical contributions are introduced to the group.

Participants used a bespoke software environment that allows for the creation of 'electronica' style music based on synthesised sounds, drum beats and melodic loops. Music is made by deploying 'Music Modules' within an on-screen workspace

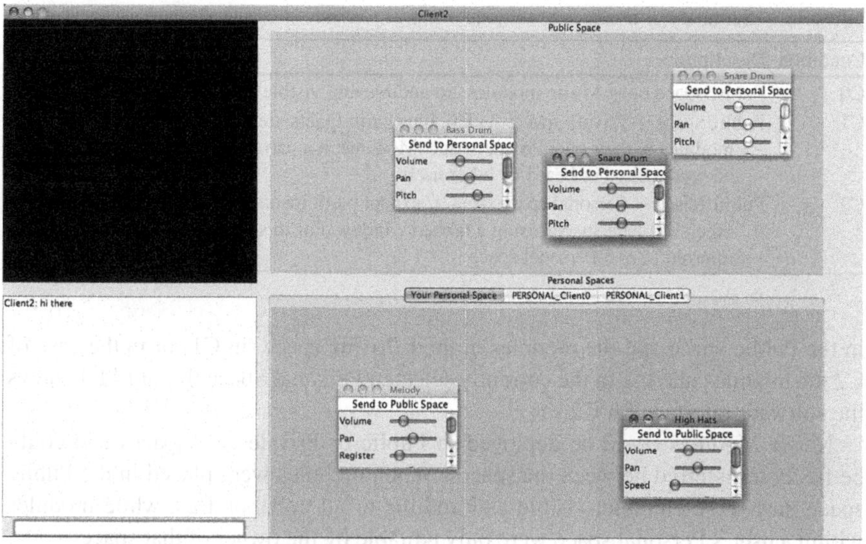

Fig. 11.1 User interface for condition C2

mirrored across multiple computers connected via a local network. Music Modules are windows containing controls to manipulate their musical behavior (see Fig. 11.1). Changes to module controls are immediately reflected to all connected clients via a server application which logs all events and maintains a database of the music being created. Each module offers control over volume and stereo pan position, plus a number of module specific controls. By using the 'music module' metaphor the software is similar to commercial music applications which feature 'virtual instruments', however it is important to stress that our software does not use the timeline metaphor common to digital audio workstations. Although the software presents participants with a shallow learning curve it does require a degree of domain knowledge, for instance an understanding basic music technology terminology.

The study had three experimental conditions. In the first interface condition (C0), participants worked in a shared and public workspace where all music was audible to their collaborators and all changes in the graphical interface were immediately visible to others. In the second condition (C1), each participant was provided with a private workspace in addition to the public workspace. The private workspace could not be accessed by their collaborators. In the third condition (C2), an additional interface feature allowed participants to view and listen to the contents of their collaborators' private workspaces. Switching workspace 'views' was achieved using a tabbed window that allowed users to select either their own personal space or the personal space of one of their collaborators. C2 therefore weakened the level of privacy provided and increases the potential for participants to gather information about the activities of their collaborators. Table 11.1 summarises the interface conditions. Participants received a personalised audio mix of the modules currently

Table 11.1 Summary of interface conditions

Condition	Description
C0	Public space only. Music modules are audible and visible to all participants at all times
C1	Public space + Private space. As C0, plus participants are able to create or place modules in their own Private space. Modules in a participant's Private space cannot be seen, edited or heard by other users
C2	Public space + Personal space. As C1, except participants can view and hear each others' Private spaces using a tabbed window. For this reason the Private space is referred to as a Personal space

in the Public space and the modules in their Private space (in C1) or in the case of C2 the modules playing in the currently selected Personal Space. Figure 11.1 shows the software interface for C2.

Music Modules could be deployed in Public or Private workspaces and could be freely transferred between the spaces. When modules were placed in the Public space they were editable, visible and audible to all collaborators, while modules within a user's Personal space were only editable by the owner of that space.

Participants were given 15 min with each condition plus an initial training session. The presentation order of conditions was permuted to control for ordering effects. Audio was presented individually to each participant through headphones, thus ensuring that private audio was not audible to others. The software included a text-chat tool for communication, although participants were free to communicate verbally. Participants were each seated around a table and provided with a personal computer.

11.4 Results

Twenty seven participants were recruited into nine groups of three people. Participants received financial compensation for taking part in the experiment. A multiple choice questionnaire was used to collect demographic information. Twenty-four participants could play a musical instrument. Two participants described their level of proficiency as 'beginner', eight participants described their level of proficiency as 'intermediate', nine participants described themselves as 'semi-professional', four described themselves as 'professional' and four gave no response. Twenty-four had written musical compositions by themselves and 19 had written musical compositions with other people. When describing their level of computer literacy 2 participants selected 'beginner', 12 participants chose 'intermediate' and 13 chose 'expert'. Sixteen participants had previously used multi-user computer software such as collaborative document editors or online games.

Table 11.2 presents a simplified summary of the interaction log data collected automatically during the participants' interaction with the software. To save space the totals have been summed across groups for each experimental condition. Column C0 contains n/a for features which were not observable in that interface condition.

Table 11.2 Log file data grouped by feature

Feature	C0	C1	C2
Total module creations	220	339	333
Public module creations	220	43	59
Private/personal module creations	n/a	296	274
Public module deletions	138	51	97
Private/personal module deletions	n/a	103	101
Total module edits	3,752	4,527	4,497
Public module edits	3,752	2,152	2,277
Private/personal module edits	n/a	2,375	2,220
Module transfers to public	n/a	237	232
Module transfers to personal	n/a	74	96

The Friedman Test was applied on per-participant totals to compare the absolute amount of module creations, deletions and edits:

- Significantly more Public Creations occurred in C0 than in C1 or C2 ($p < 0.0001$, $df = 2$ $csq_r = 25.8$).
- Significantly fewer creations occurred in total for C0 ($p = 0.0029$, $df = 2$, $csq_r = 11.69$).
- Significantly less Editing in total took place in condition C0, compared to conditions C1 and C2 ($p = 0.0344$, $df = 2$, $csq_r = 6.75$).
- Significantly more Public Module Deletions took place in condition C0 than in conditions where participants also had a Personal Space ($p = 0.0293$, $df = 2$, $csq_r = 7.06$).

Co-editing was counted where one participant edited a module they had not initially created, and was calculated per participant as a proportion of all edits made by that participant. Significantly more co-editing took place in condition C0 (where participants only had a Public Space) compared to conditions C1 or C2 ($p = 0.0019$, $df = 2$, chi-squared $= 12.57$).

The Wilcoxon Signed-Ranks Test was used to compare between conditions where a Private Space was made available to participants (Conditions C1 and C2):

- In C1 and C2 significantly more module creations took place in the Personal Space than in the Public space (for C1 $p = 0.0001, w = -331$, $z = 3.97$, for C2 $p = 0.0002$, $w = -307$, $z = -3.68$).
- There was no significant effect on the number of times modules were transferred between workspaces in either C1 or C2.

A post-test questionnaire was used to collect quantitative preference data from participants. Participants were asked to choose which condition they felt most applied to a series of statements. Bold indicates statistically significant statements using the Chi-test (Table 11.3).

Dialog was transcribed from video recordings. Space prevents us from presenting entire transcripts, however the following vignettes demonstrate typical exchanges between participants while working together. In these extracts individual participants are identified by a letter.

Table 11.3 Questionnaire responses

Statement	C0	C1	C2	Total	Chi-test P value
The best music?	5	12	8	25	0.23
I felt most involved with the group	6	9	10	25	0.59
I enjoyed myself the most	5	13	8	26	0.07
I felt out of control	12	2	8	22	**0.04**
I understood what was going on	6	10	7	23	0.51
I worked mostly on my own	3	10	13	26	**0.05**
We worked most effectively	6	11	9	26	0.16
Other people ignored my contributions	10	6	4	20	0.22
The interface was most complex	7	3	14	24	**0.01**
I knew what other people were doing	8	2	11	21	0.06
I felt satisfied with the result	5	9	9	23	0.5
We edited the music together	4	11	8	23	0.2

Participants sometimes ran into problems identifying the cause of specific features within the music:

B: it's really difficult to single out what's doing what
A: exactly, yeah
C: yeah
A: there's someone somewhere that's, there's one of them there that's making the
A: *repeatedly clicks mouse* how about this one down here?

There are two points to draw from this extract. Firstly, B expresses the problem of identifying the music module responsible for a certain sound within the musical mix, stating it is difficult to single out what is doing what. B is attempting to gather awareness information about the source of a sound, and in doing so draws attention to the way graphical interfaces for music detach the means of visually defining a musical event from the auditory result; the two operate in different modalities. The second point about this incident relates to the way A draws Bs attention to a specific item within the interface. Participant A uses both the spatially consistent workspace layout across all users' screens and the knowledge that his actions are immediately reflected on all other screens as a resource to make an indexical reference to a music module by repeatedly modifying a parameter (the repeated mouse clicks) and verbally referring to the module as 'down here'.

It is important to note that B is not at this stage trying to ascertain who created the music module he is searching for, and this highlights a situation that the Workspace Awareness framework (Gutwin and Greenberg 2002) cannot fully describe, as it does not take into account awareness of authorship by non-human entities. It would therefore be feasible to suggest a What-Authorship element to account for an awareness of which non-human agent is responsible for which sounds within the unfolding music.

Participants rarely moved around the table or attempted to view each other's screens, except when assisting each other in the use of the software interface. The following excerpt provides such an example:

B: *Removes headphones from one ear.* "How do you"
B: *Places headphones around neck.* "get it into the public space?"
A: *Looks over and removes headphones.*
C: *Looks over and removes headphones.* "How do you what?"
B: "How do you get your thing into the public space?"
C: *while replacing headphones.* "Click on send to pub. Send to public space"
A: *Pointing with finger but looking at own screen.* "Erm, click on Personal space"
C: "Below the title there"
C: *leans over and points to something on B's screen.*
A: *leans over to point at B's screen.*
B: "Oh, ss, yeah, yeah."
A: *Replaces headphones*
B: *Replaces headphones*

Group interviews were conducted at the end of each session. The discussions were structured around a set of pre-prepared topics including the use of personal, private and public spaces, approaches to gathering awareness of others and the emergence of roles. To save on space, extracts from the group discussions are incorporated into the following section.

11.5 Discussion

Video of the interaction suggests participants engaged in improvisation type activities, as there was rarely any initial discussion about the musical direction of the piece or formulation of an overall plan for how the music should sound. This suggests that their style of working, and the music they created, was emergent and contingent on the group interaction. During group interviews some participants described the activity as like a 'jam', although the majority of participants did not describe the nature of the activity or liken it to other musical experiences.

The log analysis reveals that participants made extensive use of the Private Space and Personal Space when they were made available. When a Personal Space or Private Space was included in the interface (conditions C1 and C2) music modules were almost always created within it, rather than in the Public space, and significantly more editing took place when participants had a Personal or Private space. Participants noted working least on their own in condition C0, which did not feature a private or public workspace. In interview the public space was described as the 'actual composition' or the 'main space', while participants often described the Personal and Private spaces as places to experiment, test ideas and formulate contributions, as illustrated in the following statement:

> I quite liked to try things out there, so instead of just adding a [music module] in, I'd try it out and then tweak it a little bit and then move it up, afterwards

Post-test questionnaire responses show that the C2 interface was seen as the most complex, however during interviews participants did not express concern over it being too difficult to use. One frequently raised issue was the problem of distinguishing between audio in the public and private spaces. The interface provided no explicit mechanism for separating audio from the two spaces, leading to confusion about which music modules were responsible for which sounds and which sounds were audible to other participants. This is demonstrated by the dialog extracts in Sect. 11.4, and statements made in group discussions, such as:

> and it's, and it's, it's hard to , you can't isolate, a element, or a sound

The groups adopted a variety of working strategies, which appeared to be influenced by the inclusion of Personal and Public spaces. For instance some groups exploited the ability to create contributions in private by agreeing initially to work individually and then share their ideas with the group. One participant suggested during the interaction:

> why don't we, erm, like start off just a simple little thing looping at the top, and then we each build a little section each and then, to bring in

The results of this study pose a number of design implications for CDMI. Firstly, the plurality of approaches to collaboration adopted by the groups suggests that interfaces should not enforce a particular style of working, but instead should be flexible and adaptable to the working style of the group. Secondly, where interfaces offer degrees of privacy this needs to be balanced with mechanisms to provide appropriate levels of awareness to others, or the increased potential for private work may interfere with the group members' ability to formulate coherent musical contributions. Given the extent to which participants exploited the private and personal spaces to formulate contributions, and the role this played in shaping the way groups collaborated, we argue that this is a key design consideration. Thirdly, the way audio is presented, and the ways in which it can be interrogated need to be considered by designers. In particular interfaces could provide an auditory means of distinguishing between music contributions that are shared and private, and interfaces could provide mechanisms for identifying or highlighting specific contributions within the audio mix. These features may aid individuals in identifying specific musical elements, and may also contribute to collaborative activities such as establishing indexical references.

11.6 Summary

Our research draws on CSCW literature and studies of group creativity in musical improvisation to compare software interface designs for Collaborative Digital Musical Interaction. We have identified a number of distinctions between CDMI and CSCW type activities. Some of these distinctions are related to the problem seeking nature of musical interaction. Other distinctions are due to the auditory nature of music, and the implications this has for the design of collaborative systems.

A study was presented in which nine groups of three musicians used three software interfaces to make music together using networked computers. Each interface variant provided users with different degrees of privacy. Changes in the interface design caused significant differences to the way the participants used the software and the way the groups worked together. Specifically, when given the opportunity, participants made extensive use of the ability to work individually and control access to, and release of their musical contributions. When made available, the ability to work privately was exploited by participants from all groups to formulate ideas in isolation before making them available for others in the group to hear and edit. This impacted on the way the groups worked as a whole by facilitating more varied working strategies, for instance the inclusion of privacy allowed groups to adopt a strategy that encouraged isolated work initially, followed by a period where ideas from different people were combined.

While the graphical interface made a clear distinction between private and public contributions, our design did not reflect this distinction through the way audio was delivered to users. This caused a breakdown in awareness at individual and group level, as participants encountered difficulties establishing which musical elements were publicly available, which were personal to them, and which graphical interface elements were responsible creating these sounds.

Questionnaire based measures produced statistically significant results. Participants consistently identified C2 as the most complex, and C0 as least conducive to individual work. In interview some participants stated preference for interfaces that incorporated aspects of privacy, however subjective preferences are difficult to attribute to any single experimental factor, as they may be associated with many aspects of the experience, such as the music being made or the flow and coherence of the group.

We believe there are many ways the study of CDMI can inform our understanding of work and collaboration. The auditory nature of musical interaction distinguishes it from the visual and spatial activities typically studied in groupware evaluation, and therefore an understanding of this distinction may inform the development of collaborative systems for less spatial or visually oriented tasks. Compared to primarily visual domains, there is at present limited research directed towards human interaction and collaboration in auditory domains, and this is clearly an area music interaction research can contribute to. Additionally, Sawyer (2003) posits that group creativity in music is in some ways similar to group activities in the workplace, and consequently studying the design of technological support for group music making and understanding the human interaction associated with CDMI may have implications for the design of real-time groupware to support activities that involve problem-seeking creativity or the generation of novel ideas and design solutions.

References

Bannon, L. J., & Schmidt, K. (1991). CSCW: Four characters in search of a context. In J. M. Bowers & S. D. Benford (Eds.), *Studies in computer supported cooperative work: Theory, practice and design*. The Netherlands: North-Holland Publishing Co. Amsterdam.

Bryan-Kinns, N., & Hamilton, F. (2009). Identifying mutual engagement. Behaviour & information technology. http://www.tandfonline.com/doi/abs/10.1080/01449290903377103. Accessed 11 Sept 2011.

Clark, H. H., & Brennan, S. A. (1991). Grounding in communication. In L. B. Resnick, J. M. Levine, & S. D. Teasley (Eds.), *Perspectives on socially shared cognition*. Washington: APA Books.

Coughlan, T., & Johnson, P. (2007). Support for creativity in musical collaboration and creator/technologist interaction. Position paper for CHI 2007 workshop: HCI and New Media Arts. http://www.cs.bath.ac.uk/~tc225/papers/CHIWorkshopPosition.pdf. Accessed 11 Sept 2011.

Csikszentmihalyi, M. (1990). *Flow: The psychology of optimal experience*. New York: Harper & Row. New York, USA.

Dannenberg, R., Cavaco, S., Ang, E., Avramovic, I., Aygun, B., Baek, J., Barndollar, E., Duterte, D., Grafton, J., Hunter, R., Jackson, C., Kurokawa, U., Makuck, D., Mierzejewski, T., Rivera, M., Torres, D., & Yu, A. (2007, August). The Carnegie Mellon Laptop Orchestra. In *Proceedings of the 2007 international computer music conference* (Vol. II, pp. II-340–343). San Francisco: The International Computer Music Association. http://en.scientificcommons.org/43303028. Accessed 11 Sept 2011.

Dourish, P., & Bellotti, V. (1992). Awareness and coordination in shared workspaces. CSCW '92: In *Proceedings of the 1992 ACM conference on computer-supported cooperative work*. http://doi.acm.org/10.1145/143457.143468. Accessed 11 Sept 2011.

Fels, S., & Vogt, F. (2002). Tooka: Explorations of two person instruments. In *Proceedings of the 2002 conference on new interfaces for musical expression*. http://citeseerx.ist.psu.edu/viewdoc/summary?doi=10.1.1.19.9365. Accessed 11 Sept 2011.

Fencott, R., & Bryan-Kinns, N. (2010). Hey man, you're invading my personal space! Privacy and awareness in collaborative music. In Proceedings of the 10th international conference on New Interfaces for Musical Expression (NIME 2010). http://www.educ.dab.uts.edu.au/nime/PROCEEDINGS/papers/Paper%20J1-J5/P198_Fencott.pdf. Accessed 11 Sept 2011.

Furniss, D., & Blandford, A. (2006). Understanding emergency medical dispatch in terms of distributed cognition: A case study. *Ergonomics Journal*. http://www.scientificcommons.org/27796749. Accessed 11 Sept 2011.

Gates, C., Subramanian S., & Gutwin, C. (2006). DJs' perspectives on interaction and awareness in nightclubs. DIS '06: In *Proceedings of the 6th conference on designing interactive systems*. http://doi.acm.org/10.1145/1142405.1142418. Accessed 11 Sept 2011.

Gratier, M. (2008) Grounding in musical interaction: Evidence from jazz performances. *Musicae Scientiae*. http://msx.sagepub.com/content/12/1_suppl/71.abstract. Accessed 11 Sept 2011.

Gurevich, M. (2006). JamSpace: Designing a collaborative networked music space for novices. NIME '06:In *Proceedings of the 2006 conference on new interfaces for musical expression*. http://dl.acm.org/citation.cfm?id=1142245. Accessed 11 Sept 2011.

Gutwin, C., & Greenberg, S. (1999). The effects of workspace awareness support on the usability of real-time distributed groupware. *ACM Transactions On Computer-Human Interaction (TOCHI)*. http://dl.acm.org/citation.cfm?doid=329693.329696. Accessed 11 Sept 2011.

Gutwin, C., & Greenberg, S. (2002). A descriptive framework of workspace awareness for real-time groupware. *Computer supported cooperative work*. Kluwer Academic Publishers. Norwell, MA, USA. http://dx.doi.org/10.1023/A:1021271517844. Accessed 11 Sept 2011.

Healey, P. G. T., Leach, J., & Bryan-Kinns, N. (2005). Inter-Play: Understanding group music improvisation as a form of everyday interaction. In *Proceedings of less is more – Simple computing in an age of complexity*. Microsoft Research Cambridge. http://www.eecs.qmul.ac.uk/~joel/writing/Inter-Play_Understanding_Group_Music_Improvisation_as_a_form_of_Everyday_Interaction.pdf. Accessed 11 Sept 2011.

Heath, C., Svensson, M. S., Hindmarsh, J., Luff, P., & vom Lehn, D. (2002). Configuring awareness. *Computer supported cooperative work*. http://dx.doi.org/10.1023/A:1021247413718. Accessed 11 Sept 2011.

Holland, S. (2000). Artificial intelligence in music education: A critical review. In E. Miranda (Ed.), *Readings in music and artificial intelligence, contemporary music studies* (Vol. 20). The Netherlands: Harwood Academic Publishers.

Hughes, J., Randall, D., & Shapiro, D. (1991). CSCW: Discipline or paradigm? A sociological perspective. In *Proceedings of the second conference on European conference on computer-supported cooperative work*. http://portal.acm.org/citation.cfm?id=1241910.1241933. Accessed 11 Sept 2011.

Hutchins, E. (1996). *Cognition in the wild*. Cambridge, MA: MIT Press. Massachusetts, USA.

Jordà, S., Geiger, G., Alonso, M., & Kaltenbrunner, M. (2007). The reactable: Exploring the synergy between live music performance and tabletop tangible interfaces. TEI '07: In *Proceedings of the 1st international conference on tangible and embedded interaction, ACM*. New York, NY, USA. http://doi.acm.org/10.1145/1226969.1226998. Accessed 11 Sept 2011.

Klügel, N., Frieß, M. R., Groh, G., & Echtler, F. (2011). An approach to collaborative music composition. In *Proceedings of the international conference on new interfaces for musical expression*. Oslo, Norway. http://www.nime2011.org/proceedings/papers/B02-Klugel.pdf. Accessed 11 Sept 2011.

Makelberge, N. (2010). Le concert, c'est moi. In *Proceedings of the 1st DESIRE network conference on creativity and innovation in design*. Lancaster, UK. http://portal.acm.org/citation.cfm?id=1854969.1854991. Accessed 11 Sept 2011.

Marquez-Borbon, A., Gurevich, M., Fyans, A. C. , & Stapleton, P. (2011). Designing digital musical interactions in experimental contexts. In *Proceedings of the international conference on new interfaces for musical expression*. Oslo, Norway. http://www.nime2011.org/proceedings/papers/K02-Marquez-Borbon.pdf. Accessed 11 Sept 2011.

Merritt, T., Kow, W., Ng, C., McGee, K., & Wyse, L. (2010). Who makes what sound?: Supporting real-time musical improvisations of electroacoustic ensembles. In *Proceedings of the 22nd conference of the computer-human interaction special interest group of Australia on computer-human interaction*. New York, NY, USA. http://dl.acm.org/citation.cfm?id=1952245. Accessed 26 Oct 2011.

Mills, R. (2010). Dislocated sound: A survey of improvisation in networked audio platforms. http://www.educ.dab.uts.edu.au/nime/PROCEEDINGS/papers/Paper%20J1-J5/P186_Mills.pdf. Accessed 11 Sept 2011.

Nabavian, S., & Bryan-Kinns, N. (2006). Analysing group creativity: A distributed cognitive study of joint music composition. In *Proceedings of cognitive science*. Vancouver, British Columbia, Canada. http://csjarchive.cogsci.rpi.edu/proceedings/2006/docs/p1856.pdf. Accessed 11 Sept 2011.

Sawyer, R. K. (2003). *Group creativity: Music, theatre*. Collaboration: Psychology Press.

Scott, S. D., Sheelagh, M., Carpendale, T., & Inkpen, K. M. (2004). Territoriality in collaborative tabletop workspaces. In *Proceedings of the 2004 ACM conference on computer supported cooperative work*. http://doi.acm.org/10.1145/1031607.1031655. Accessed 11 Sept 2011.

Small, C. (1998). *Musicking: The meanings of performing and listening*. Hanover: Wesleyan University Press. Middletown, Connecticut, USA.

Trueman, D., Cook, P., Smallwood, S., & Wang, G. (2006). PLOrk: The Princeton Laptop Orchestra, Year 1. In *Proceedings of the international computer music conference*. New Orleans, USA. http://citeseerx.ist.psu.edu/viewdoc/download?doi=10.1.1.65.8861&rep=rep1&type=pdf. Accessed 11 Sept 2011.

Wang, G., Bryan, N., Oh, J., & Hamilton, R. (2009). Stanford Laptop Orchestra (Slork). In *Proceedings of the International Computer Music Conference (ICMC 2009)*. Montreal, Quebec, Canada. https://ccrma.stanford.edu/~ge/publish/slork-icmc2009.pdf. Accessed 11 Sept 2011.

Chapter 12
Song Walker Harmony Space: Embodied Interaction Design for Complex Musical Skills

Anders Bouwer, Simon Holland, and Mat Dalgleish

Abstract Tonal Harmony is widely considered to be the most technical and complex part of music theory. Consequently harmonic skills can be hard to acquire. Furthermore, experience of the flexible manipulation of harmony in real time generally requires the ability to play an instrument. Even for those with instrumental skills, it can be difficult to gain clear insight into harmonic abstractions. The above state of affairs gives rise to substantial barriers not only for beginners but also for many experienced musicians. To address these problems, Harmony Space is an interactive digital music system designed to give insight into a wide range of musical tasks in tonal harmony, ranging from performance and composition to analysis. Harmony Space employs a principled set of spatial mappings to offer fluid, precise, intuitive control of harmony. These mappings give rise to sensory-motor and music-theoretic affordances that are hard to obtain in any other way. As a result, harmonic abstractions are rendered amenable to concrete, visible control by simple spatial manipulation. In the language of conceptual metaphor theory, many relationships in tonal harmony become accessible to rapid, universal, low-level, robust human inference mechanisms using image schemata such as containment, contact, centre-periphery, and source-path-goal. This process is more rapid, and imposes far less cognitive load, than slow, abstract symbolic reasoning. Using the

---

A. Bouwer (✉)
Faculty of Science, Intelligent Systems Lab, University of Amsterdam, Amsterdam, The Netherlands
e-mail: andersbouwer@uva.nl

S. Holland (✉)
Music Computing Lab, Centre For Research in Computing, The Open University, Milton Keynes, UK
e-mail: s.holland@open.ac.uk

M. Dalgleish
Department of Music, SSPAL, University of Wolverhampton, West Midlands, UK
e-mail: m.dalgleish2@wlv.ac.uk

S. Holland et al. (eds.), *Music and Human-Computer Interaction*, Springer Series on Cultural Computing, DOI 10.1007/978-1-4471-2990-5_12,

above principles, several versions of Harmony Space have been designed to exploit specific interaction styles for different purposes. We note some key variants, such as the desktop version, the camera tracked version, while focusing principally on the most recent version, Song Walker, which employs whole body interaction. Preliminary results from a study of the Song Walker system are outlined, in which both beginners and expert musicians undertook a range of musical tasks involving the performance, composition and analysis of music. Finally, we offer a discussion of the limitations of the current system, and outline directions for future work.

12.1 Introduction

One potential source of insights about tonal harmony comes from rhythm. The Victorian music educator Emil Dalcroze (1865–1950) noticed that his students showed little insight into musical rhythm if they lacked experience of enacting rhythms with their own bodies. Dalcroze proposed that students needed to become competent in physically enacting representative rhythms before they could achieve mastery of rhythm. Dalcroze's findings seem to be a special case of a more general phenomenon. Sensory motor contingency theory (O'Regan and Noë 2001) suggests that, in order to learn how to organize and respond appropriately to sensory input in some new domain or context, it is typically an essential precursor that the individual learner's motor actions should have the power to affect relationships in the domain being sensed. In this way, the learner can repeatedly experience diverse outcomes that they have themselves influenced. In situations where this very specific kind of active engagement coupled with feedback is absent, competency has been observed to fail to develop. This principle has been demonstrated in many different contexts and time scales (O'Regan and Noë 2001).

We posit that a similar situation exists for musical harmony. Skills in harmony are generally difficult to acquire, and are often taught abstractly via symbolic notation. Explicit understanding of harmony involves knowledge of many abstract entities, categories and relationships, which are associated with an extensive specialised vocabulary. We assert that students have little opportunity to gain insight into musical harmony if they lack experience of enacting and manipulating those harmonies with their own bodies – an experience which is scant or non-existent for many students. As with rhythms, simply hearing harmonies repeatedly, or studying them on paper, does not appear to be adequate preparation for insightful skill.

The conventional way to enact full musical harmony with one's body is by learning to play a polyphonic musical instrument. However, learning to play a conventional polyphonic instrument (e.g. a piano) competently typically takes months or years. Thus, there are substantial barriers to achieving the prerequisites for mastery of harmony, not only for beginners but also for many musicians. But not even polyphonic skills invariably grant the experience of flexibly manipulating harmony at will. For example, players who focus solely on playing from written notation do not typically develop the ability to manipulate harmonic sequences at will in real time.

A related point is that only a minority of musicians appears to gain a working insight into larger scale harmonic abstractions. There are numerous open-ended harmonic structures and strategies, some of which are generic, others which are specific to particular scales, tunings, idioms, composers, or pieces – yet few musicians gain mastery of manipulating such structures – i.e. composing or improvising insightfully with harmonic materials. Reflecting on the achievements of musicians as diverse as Bach and the Beatles, both of whom manipulated harmony in highly original ways (Pedler 2001), to miss out on creative manipulation of harmony is arguably to miss out on one of the deepest joys of music.

In this chapter, we address these issues by presenting a system that enables creative experiences with tonal harmony, facilitates the understanding of harmonic concepts and relationships, and promotes insights into how specific pieces work. More specifically, we consider ways in which interaction design can be harnessed to help both novices and musicians to get experience of shaping and manipulating harmonic sequences in real time, and to gain awareness of higher-level harmonic abstractions.

12.2 The Song Walker System Design

Harmony Space (Holland 1989, 1994) is an interactive digital music system designed to give beginners and experts insight into a wide range of musical tasks ranging from performance and analysis to composition. The interaction design, as we will outline below, exploits mappings from spatial movement to musical abstractions, through the mechanisms of conceptual metaphor (Lakoff and Núñez 2000; Zbikowski 1997; Wilkie et al. 2013) and conceptual blending (Fauconnier and Turner 2002). The specific principled spatial mappings employed offer novices precise intuitive control of harmony by exploiting intuitions about bodily movement and navigation. The result is that a wide range of harmonic abstractions are rendered amenable to concrete, visible manipulation via spatial navigation in different layers of the interface. In the language of conceptual metaphor theory (Hurtienne and Blessing 2007), relationships in tonal harmony become accessible to rapid, universal, low-level, robust human inference mechanisms using image schemata such as containment, contact, centre-periphery, and source-path-goal. This process is rapid, and imposes far less cognitive load, than slow, abstract symbolic reasoning. While keeping the above principles invariant, different versions of Harmony Space have been designed to exploit different detailed interaction styles for different purposes. The most recent version, Song Walker (Holland et al. 2011), employs a variant of whole body interaction. In short, this encourages users to engage spatial intuitions by physically enacting the control of complex harmonic phenomena.

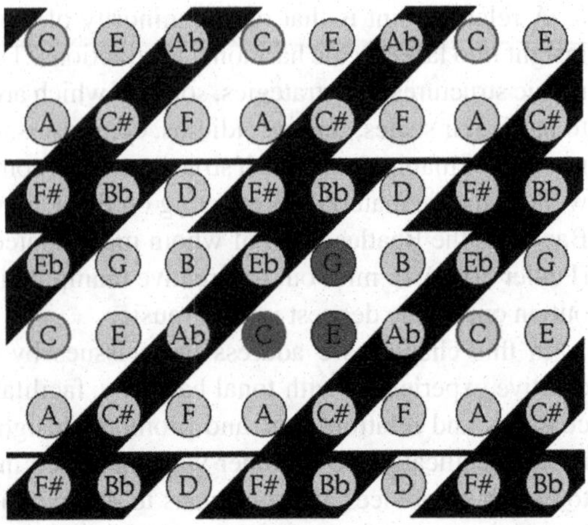

Fig. 12.1 Fragment of Harmony Space grid, highlighting a C major triad

12.2.1 Conceptual Metaphors

Harmony Space exploits a set of conceptual metaphors[1] that link concepts in tonal harmony to spatial concepts (Wilkie et al. 2009, 2010). The principal metaphors can be outlined as follows.

12.2.1.1 Pitch

- Different musical interval classes (octaves, semitones, perfect fifths, major thirds, minor thirds) correspond to steps in different directions in space.
- In particular, semitones, fifths, and octaves are at right angles to each other in the plane, and octaves lie vertically (i.e., on the z-axis).

These conceptual metaphors employ extensions of Longuet-Higgins' (1962) and Balzano's theories (1980) of harmonic perception, which may be seen as positing a three-dimensional image schema for tonal harmony.

12.2.1.2 Scales, Keys and Modes

- Common scales can be formed from the notes occurring in contiguous strips seven steps long in the fifths direction. Due to the repeating nature of the plane, these strips group into irregularly shaped two-dimensional areas (as illustrated in Fig. 12.1).

[1]Only the principal conceptual metaphors are noted here. For a more detailed discussion see Holland et al. (2011). An alternative but related kind of analysis uses conceptual integration (Fauconnier and Turner 2002).

- Key areas are scales spatially situated to represent "preferred territory" for journeys and chord elements within the diatonic scale (see the white area in Fig. 12.1).
- A modal centre is a privileged location within preferred territory, typically where journeys start, end or rest. In Fig. 12.1, the major or Ionian modal centre is ringed in red.

12.2.1.3 Chords

- Chord qualities are oriented geometrical shapes. Preservation of chord quality requires retention of shape and orientation. Altering the pitch of a fixed quality is change of location of the shape without rotation.
- The most common chord qualities, major and minor, correspond to the most frequent three-element chord shapes formed by the most compact shapes possible within the geometry of the most common scales.

12.2.1.4 Harmonic Movement

- Harmonic movement of a chord sequence is spatial trajectory.
- Composition is navigation, which may involve targets, directions, inertia, oscillatory movement and preferred territories.
- Tonal movement corresponds to trajectories along the diagonal from top right to bottom left or vice versa.
- Modal movement corresponds to trajectories along the diagonal from top left to bottom right or vice versa.

12.2.2 System Details and Interface

The Song Walker system employs whole body interaction through the use of dance mats, wireless controllers (Wii remotes and nunchuks), optional foot pedals, a large projection screen and a synthesizer. These are coordinated by a Harmony Space Server receiving data from controllers via HSP (Harmony Space protocol), a layer on top of OSC (Open Sound Control).

When played by a solo player (see Fig. 12.2), one dance mat is used to navigate a proxy for the player represented by a marker in the projected display. Squeezing the trigger on the Wii remote visibly and audibly plays the chord associated with the current location and situation.[2] When multiple players collaborate, additional

[2]The word "situation" here refers to the prevailing key and mode, but also to the default size of chords (e.g., triads, seventh, and ninth chords – also single notes and dyads) and to the particular chord vocabulary and voicing that is in play, and other factors. Players may choose which aspects of the situation to control dynamically during play. Other aspects are typically set for the duration of a piece.

Fig. 12.2 A solo activity, controlling Song Walker with dance mat and Wii remote

Fig. 12.3 Two players playing asymmetrical roles

dance mats and controllers (up to four) may be used in a variety of roles, e.g., to navigate key changes, to create harmonic inversions or otherwise alter the chords (see Fig. 12.3).

The Song Walker interaction design appears to offer affordances for experiencing and enacting the conceptual metaphors embodied in the multi-layered representation more directly than desktop versions of Harmony Space.

12.2.3 Asymmetrical Collaboration

Besides the potential advantages of whole body interaction for physical engagement with spatial phenomena, there are also potential advantages for the support of collaborative roles. Conventionally, when musicians collaborate to produce harmony, each musician contributes a single sounding part. For many purposes, this approach works well. However, in cases where players are novices, or where there is a desire to gain insights into the abstract structures of tonal harmony, an important drawback of this approach is that it leaves these abstractions intangible and invisible.

By contrast, in the case of Harmony Space, collaborative roles do not have to be split voice-wise (though this is readily supported), but may be split asymmetrically into heterogeneous spatial navigation and selection tasks, corresponding to abstractions of interest. For example, contrasting simultaneous asymmetrical roles available include the navigation of: the root path; changes of key; inversions and voicing; chord size; chord maps; altered chords; and bass lines. For playing many pieces of music, typically only two or three of these roles are required at a time. The combinatorial interplay of these factors yields the detail of harmonic sequences. When multiple dance mats are used, different colours are assigned to the visualization, so that each player can readily see what other players are doing.

12.3 Evaluation of Song Walker

To explore the potential of the Song Walker system for learning about tonal harmony, an evaluation study has been carried out. The focus of this study was on questions related to the embodied interface design, and issues related to collaborative learning.

12.3.1 Participants

16 people participated in the study. One participant did not fill in the questionnaire, so we present data of 15 participants – 8 women and 7 men, all adults aged 28–62, with an average of 36. Of these participants, ten were experienced musicians (with 5 or more years of experience), and five were beginners (with zero or very little experience). Participants varied widely in their self-reported knowledge of harmony, covering the whole range from absolute beginner (1) to expert (5), with a median of 3 on this scale of 1–5.

12.3.2 Setup

To support people using the system collaboratively, and to take advantage of the most important interface features, we developed specific musical tasks and instructions. The participants were asked to carry out three different tasks with the Song Walker system, working in pairs, with task instructions projected on the wall next to the Harmony Space projection. The tasks included the following:

1. Playing a chord sequence of a song;
2. Composing a new chord sequence;
3. Reharmonizing a chord sequence;
4. Analyzing chords and chord sequences;
5. Finding out about key tonality.

All participants were assigned task 1, and at least two other tasks. The exact number and types of tasks assigned depended on musical experience, user interest, and time available. Each session lasted at least 45 min, with approximately equal time allotted to each task. While this means that participants did not receive the same treatment, which may have affected the resulting experience, we believe the tasks had enough in common for all participants to get a working impression of the main functionality, interface, and conceptual basis of the system.

12.3.3 Results

12.3.3.1 Playing a Chord Sequence of a Song

After only a few minutes of training, all participants were able to play chord sequences of at least one well-known song to a recognizable degree (i.e., typically about four to eight chords per song). Songs played included Ticket to Ride (The Beatles, see Fig. 12.4), Isn't She Lovely (Stevie Wonder), Pachelbel's Canon, Giant Steps (John Coltrane), and Billie Jean (Michael Jackson). Many people had to resort to a tempo slower than the original song, though, and some had trouble with playing accidentally triggered chords, especially in the beginning. Participants were able to describe quite clearly what they had learned from this task, as the following quotes illustrate[3]:

"That harmonic structure can be realised in physical movements"

"Movements in chord sequences create very [definite] visual patterns"

[3]Note: wherever participants' handwriting was hard to read, we have indicated our most likely interpretation in square brackets.

Fig. 12.4 Performing the Beatles' "Ticket To Ride"

12.3.3.2 Composing a New Chord Sequence

Regarding the open-ended collaborative composition task, all the participants who received this task succeeded in creating a chord sequence that they felt sounded good. Although part of the chord sequence was given, all pairs came up with unique chord sequence compositions. One pair of beginners spontaneously focused on inversions and explored these carefully, with much discussion. Another pair of users deployed altered chords in a similarly careful way to musically positive effect. Participants noted that they had learned the following from this task, among other things:

"Using economy of movement to great effect."

"Mainly that you can create interesting chord (sequences) substitutions by thinking about what visual/spatial movements you want to make in Harmony Space (i.e. Diagonal vs. Vertical vs. Horizontal: each creating their own kind of substitution possibilities)"

One person had drawn several shapes (i.e., two triangles, and a triangle with a vertical line upwards) to illustrate spatial movement of chords that she had learned as sounding good.

This task seemed to offer opportunities for musical experimentation, as suggested by the following quotes:

"To try stuff out to see what works"

"Feeling free to really try and move from one chord to another"

"Experimentation!"

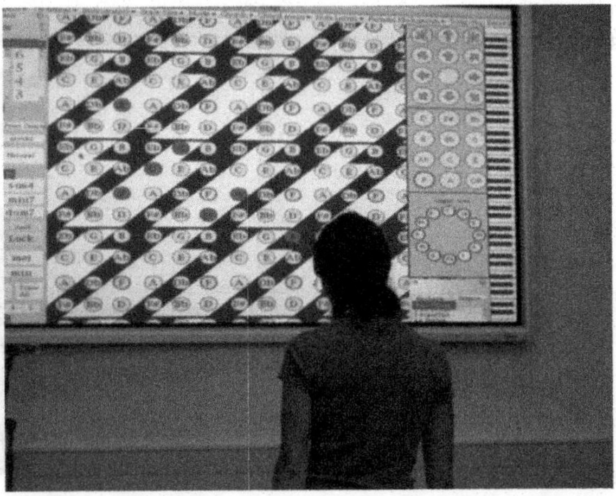

Fig. 12.5 Analyzing David Bowie's "Suffragette City"

12.3.3.3 Reharmonizing a Chord Sequence

All participants who received this task were able to create variations on the chord sequence (a common harmonic sequence in jazz) given below:

||: Cmaj7 | Am7 | Dm7 | G7 :||

This resulted in many (20) different variations overall, and led to lively discussions among the participants about strategies for which chord to change and how to search for possible substitutions.

The participants mentioned having learned the following from this task, among other things:

> *"The combination of both the visual + auditory input helped me understand how chords relate to each other."*

> *"The main point is that the spatial movements in the Harmony Space give me new metaphors, new ways of understanding relationships between chords"*

> *"Chord sequences can be [composed] as paths in a grid [system]"*

12.3.3.4 Finding Out About Key Tonality

Participants who were asked to harmonically analyse a piece, such as Suffragette City by David Bowie, were able to do so. This task required two steps. The first step was to identify the possible modes of the piece by physically shifting "territory" (the space-filling pattern of white and black areas underneath the chord roots played) by means of a dance mat (see Fig. 12.5). This allowed the visual identification of placements where the trace of the harmonic journey fell entirely within "permitted" (i.e. white) territory. The second step involved observing where chord journeys tended to start and finish relative to the shape of the permitted (white) territory. These steps are complicated to describe verbally, but are straightforward to carry out as a practical, spatial task. One participant with some previous musical knowledge noted the following learning effect for this task:

"Reminded me that songs can sound both major + minor if the chord sequences leave out the 3rd (i.e. The main note that determines it as either major or minor)."

Another participant noted having learned the following:

"Can see puddles of sound much more easily – cluster chords."

12.3.3.5 General Comments

Several users commented on the degree of physical engagement they brought to the tasks. To illustrate this, one initially skeptical user was able to learn to play the complete harmony of Pachelbel's canon after about 10 min. Initially he said variously *"I haven't got this musically in my head at all"*, *"I don't have a sense of what's going on cognitively – how the visual representation is helping me remember it"*, and *"visually overwhelming"*. However, about 30 min later, having played several more songs, he commented, *"Love the kinaesthetic quality"* and *"Once you're used to it, you could dance songs"* (in the sense that Song Walker allows one to generate the harmony for a song by dancing to it).

Comments on the degree of physical engagement might be unremarkable in the case of, for example, arcade games, but are unusual in the context of tasks that are generally taught in knowledge-intensive ways using rule-based, symbolic, and quasi-mathematical approaches. Also, conventional approaches to learning these tasks generally take one or two orders of magnitude longer (i.e. weeks instead of minutes).

12.3.3.6 Questionnaire

To find out if people's views on harmony changed after interacting with the Song Walker system, the questionnaire included the following question:

Before/After the experiment, did you consider the concept of harmony to be ... theoretical, practical, abstract, spatial, relating to physical movement, entertaining, dry, visual? (tick all that apply).

Compared to before the experiment, after the experiment, eight more people associated harmony with "relating to physical movement", seven with "spatial", five with "visual", and four with "entertaining".

To find out to what extent people liked the various tasks, we asked:

How much did you like the task of ... using Harmony Space Song Walker? (1: I disliked it very much, 2: I disliked it a little, 3: I feel neutral about it, 4: I liked it a little, 5: I liked it very much)

Table 12.1 Likert scale results for the various musical tasks

Task	Median	Min	Max	N
1. Playing a chord sequence of a song	5	4	5	14
2. Composing a new chord sequence	5	3	5	15
3. Reharmonizing a chord sequence	4.5	3	5	14
4. Analyzing chords and chord sequences	4	3	5	7
5. Finding out about key tonality	4	4	5	5

This question was asked for the five different activities. The results are shown per activity in Table 12.1. The number of N differs per activity because not all participants carried out the same tasks (tasks 4 and 5 were only performed by seven and five people, respectively), and two participants did not fill in a score for tasks 1 and 3, respectively.

The results in Table 12.1 show that the participants liked all tasks more than a little, on average, with the first two tasks scoring highest (median score of 5), and the other tasks slightly lower (median scores of 4–4.5). Interestingly, the scores for how much they had liked a task were positively related to how much they felt they had learned from the task.

With respect to the interface, we asked how comfortable it was to use the interface. Participants scored a little above neutral, on average, although there was much variation for this question (Median = 4, Min = 1, Max = 4, on the following scale: 1: very uncomfortable, 2: a little uncomfortable, 3: neutral, 4: reasonably comfortable, 5: very comfortable). They responded that the feeling of comfort generally became a little better during the experiment.

They felt that the dance mat interface was a reasonably usable way to move around, change key, and play bass notes in Harmony Space, and they felt that the Wii remote interface was a more than reasonable way to carry out actions and make settings.

On the other hand, participants encountered several problems interacting with the dance mat, as indicated by reported issues related to keeping balance, changing feet, overshooting due to the small size of the mat, accidental presses, not being able to move fast enough to move smoothly, the mat becoming buckled up, and (sometimes) jumping notes or no response to the tapping.

With respect to the Wii remote and nunchuck, most participants did not encounter problems, except one, reporting on oversensitivity of the joystick.

The participants reported thinking this technology helped them in their understanding of harmony (Median = 2, Min = 2, Max = 3, on a scale of 1: Not at all; 2: A little; 3: A lot).

Participants' suggestions for improving the system included the following, indicating individual differences in preference for the interface modalities:

- adding a metronome (at a slow tempo);
- for a beginner, hide complexity;
- increase the size of the mat and move more functionality to it;

– interact directly with the representation, e.g., using a tabletop;
– move as much functionality as possible to the Wii remote and nunchuck;
– improve the visualization of "where you are";
– use the keyboard to the right of the screen to display chord inversions.

Overall, 13 out of the 15 participants enjoyed the experiment very much (Median = 5, the maximum score), with two participants scoring 4 (I liked it a little), on a scale of 1: I disliked it very much, 2: I disliked it a little, 3: I feel neutral about it, 4: I liked it a little, 5: I liked it very much.

12.4 Work in Progress

In order to further explore how experience of physically enacting and manipulating harmony can be linked to appropriate conceptual metaphors, we are in the process of developing versions of Harmony Space that will employ gesture-tracking devices such as Microsoft Kinect. Although frame rate and resolution are limited, the Kinect offers a useful complement to the architectural scale of the camera tracked Harmony Space system (Holland et al. 2009) and the detailed expressivity of Song Walker, while offering improved portability.

12.5 Conclusions

Implications of this work relate to the themes of this book in a variety of ways. Song Walker Harmony Space demonstrates in detail how spatial reasoning can be used to carry out complex tasks in tonal harmony that generally require formal symbol systems for their description, explanation and teaching. In this way, Song Walker suggests a candidate model for how the human cognitive system might take cognitive resources for dealing with the movement of the body or movements in the environment and reappropriate them to undertake the creation, manipulation and understanding of tonal harmony. Whether or not the human cognitive system generally approaches tonal harmony in this way, the present case study demonstrates in concrete terms that, with the right scaffolding, people can rapidly learn to reappropriate spatial skills to perform a range of harmonic tasks. More specifically, there are three implications for Music and Human-Computer Interaction. Firstly, Song Walker Harmony Space offers a useful case study in extended uses of conceptual metaphor in interface design (Hurtienne and Blessing 2007; Hurtienne et al. 2008) that is applicable to mainstream interaction design. This is noteworthy because the design makes extensive use of conceptual metaphors (Lakoff and Núñez 2000) and conceptual integration (Fauconnier and Turner 2002), two theories which have been relatively neglected as systematic tools for interaction design. Secondly, the work is suggestive of ways in which whole body interaction can help users to operationalize spatial intuitions to take advantage of spatial metaphors applied in an interaction design. Finally, the work provides a case study of a family of tools for a complex symbolic domain where the interaction design is able to transform symbolic entities, relationships and rules into relatively simple spatial tasks amenable to low level spatial inference (Bird et al. 2008). Other case studies exist, but the present example is notable because of the highly complex, layered and abstract nature of tonal harmony.

References

Balzano, G. J. (1980). The group-theoretic description of 12-fold and microtonal pitch systems. *Computer Music Journal, 4*(4), 66–84.

Bird, J., Holland, S., Marshall, P., Rogers, Y., & Clark, A. (2008). Feel the force: Using tactile technologies to investigate the extended mind. In *Proceedings of DAP 2008, Workshop on Devices that Alter Perception*, 21 September 2008, Seoul, South Korea, pp. 1–4.

Fauconnier, G., & Turner, M. (2002). *How we think: Conceptual blending and the mind's hidden complexities*. New York: Basic Books. ISBN 978-0-465-08786-0.

Holland, S. (1989). *Artificial intelligence, education and music*. Ph.D. thesis, Institute of Educational Technology, The Open University, Milton Keynes, UK. Published as OU IET CITE Report No. 88, July 1989.

Holland, S. (1994). Learning about harmony with harmony space: An overview. In M. Smith & G. Wiggins (Eds.), *Music education: An artificial intelligence approach* (pp. 24–40). London: Springer.

Holland, S., Marshall, P., Bird, J., Dalton, S.N., Morris, R., Pantidi, N., Rogers, Y., & Clark, A. (2009). Running up Blueberry Hill: Prototyping whole body interaction in harmony space. In *Proceedings of TEI 2009, the 3rd conference on tangible and embodied interaction* (pp. 92–98). ISBN 978-1-60558-493-5. New York: ACM.

Holland, S., Wilkie, K., Bouwer, A., Dalgleish, M., & Mulholland, P. (2011). Whole body interaction in abstract domains. In D. England (Ed.), *Whole body interaction* (Human–computer interaction series). London: Springer. ISBN 978-0-85729-432-6.

Hurtienne, J., & Blessing, L. (2007). Design for intuitive use-testing image schema theory for user interface design. In J.-C. Bocquet (Ed.), *Proceedings of ICED 07, international conference on engineering design, Paris, France*, 28–31 August 2007, pp 1–12.

Hurtienne, J., Israel, J. H., & Weber, K. (2008). Cooking up real world business applications combining physicality, digitality, and image schemas. In *Proceedings of the 2nd international conference on tangible and embedded interaction (Bonn, 2008)* (pp. 239–246). New York: ACM.

Lakoff G, & Núñez, R. E. (2000). Conceptual metaphor. *Where mathematics comes from: How the embodied mind brings mathematics into being* (pp. 39–48). New York: Basic Books.

Longuet-Higgins, H. C. (1962). Letter to a musical friend. *Music Review*, August 1962. pp. 244–248.

O'Regan, J. K., & Noë, A. (2001). A sensorimotor account of vision and visual consciousness. *Behavioral and Brain Sciences, 24*(5), 939–973.

Pedler, D. (2001). *The songwriting secrets of the Beatles*. London: Omnibus Press. ISBN 13: 978-0711981676.

Wilkie, K., Holland, S., & Mulholland, P. (2009). Evaluating musical software using conceptual metaphors. In A. Blackwell (Ed.), *Proceedings of BCS HCI 2009*, September 1–5, 2009 (pp. 232–237). Cambridge, UK: EWIC. ISSN 1477–9358. Oro ID 17967.

Wilkie, K., Holland, S., & Mulholland, P. (2010). What can the language of musicians tell us about music interaction design? *Computer Music Journal, 34*(4), 34–48.

Wilkie, K., Holland, S., & Mulholland, P. (2013). Towards a participatory approach for interaction design based on conceptual metaphor theory: A case study from music interaction. In S. Holland, K. Wilkie, P. Mulholland, & A. Seago (Eds.), *Music and human computer interaction* (pp. 259–270). London: Springer. ISBN 978-1-4471-2989-9.

Zbikowski, L. M. (1997). Conceptual models and cross-domain mapping: new perspectives on theories of music and hierarchy. *Journal of Music Theory, 41*(2), 193–225.

Chapter 13
Evolutionary and Generative Music Informs Music HCI—And *Vice Versa*

James McDermott, Dylan Sherry, and Una-May O'Reilly

Abstract This chapter suggests a two-way influence between the field of evolutionary and generative music and that of human–computer interaction and usability studies. The interfaces used in evolutionary and generative music can be made more effective and more satisfying to use with the influence of the ideas, methods, and findings of human–computer interaction and usability studies. The musical representations which are a focus of evolutionary and generative music can enable new user-centric tools for mainstream music software. Some successful existing projects are described and some future work is proposed.

13.1 Introduction

Interactive evolutionary computation (EC) refers to a class of human–computer collaborative algorithms in which the computer simulates a population of designs undergoing evolution and the human designer evaluates them according to aesthetic or other criteria. Interactive EC affords the user an alternative workflow which is iterative, passive and creative. The user's role is said to be closer to that of a gardener than that of a sculptor (Whitelaw 2002).

In the case of musical composition, interactive EC systems do not produce any music which could not have been produced through manual use of a sequencer, but can make certain compositional tasks easier or more pleasant. As such, it implicitly recognises the importance of interfaces which are well-suited to their task and to their users. However few researchers in the field of interactive EC have been explicitly influenced by the methods or ideas of the field of human–computer interaction and usability studies.

J. McDermott (✉) • D. Sherry • U.-M. O'Reilly
EvoDesignOpt Group, CSAIL, MIT, 32-D540, Stata Center, Vassar St., Cambridge, MA 02139, USA
e-mail: jmmcd@csail.mit.edu

S. Holland et al. (eds.), *Music and Human-Computer Interaction*, Springer Series on Cultural Computing, DOI 10.1007/978-1-4471-2990-5_13,

Much evolutionary and generative music research has instead focussed on representations for music. In contrast with the note-by-note (i.e. MIDI-style) representation typical of mainstream music tools, these representations are often generative, grammatical, process-based, or algorithmic. They often have the property that they impose structure on the music in a natural way (Marsden 2005). Small changes in such a representation may lead to many changes at the surface of the music, even though structure is retained. Such alternative representations have the potential to be used in computer-aided composition tools in mainstream music software and to improve this software from the point of view of usability or HCI.

This chapter is therefore divided into two main parts, reflecting a two-way influence between HCI and interactive EC. For simplicity, we will use the term *HCI* as an umbrella term for the relevant fields and sub-fields of human–computer interaction, usability studies, and interaction design; and we will use the term *evo/gen* music to mean evolutionary and generative music. In Sect. 13.3, existing evo/gen music systems are examined from a HCI point of view. The influence (and lack thereof) of HCI on evo/gen music is discussed. In Sect. 13.4, several musical representations used in existing evo/gen systems are described, leading to a proposal for new tools which could make mainstream music software more usable. We begin with some brief background on evolutionary computation and generative music. We assume familiarity with HCI issues.

13.2 Background

13.2.1 Evolutionary Computation

Evolutionary computation (EC) is a class of algorithms modelled after the biological processes of natural and artificial selection, as described by Darwin. In biological evolution, some individuals are more likely than others to survive and mate, and pass on their (presumably more highly-fit) genes to the next generation. As a result the continuously updating population tends over many generations to include more highly-fit genes and individuals, and to exclude others. In a certain simplified sense, these are optimisation processes, in that the population will tend towards optima in the space of genes.

EC is deliberately simplified and abstracted from real-world biological evolution. Each individual in the population has a *genotype*, which is simply a data structure drawn from a well-defined class. Genotypes are mapped to *phenotypes*, seen as potential solutions to the problem at hand. Every phenotype is associated with a *fitness*, a numerical value which represents how good that phenotype is as a solution. *Crossover* (also known as recombination or mating) and *mutation* take place over genotypes, while *selection* takes place over fitness (see Fig. 13.1).

For example, a genotype might be a list of floating-point numbers, and might be input as control parameters to a synthesizer, to produce a phenotype consisting of the

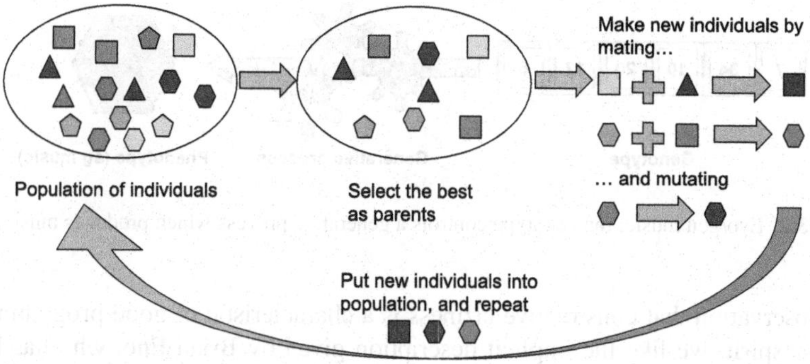

Fig. 13.1 EC schematic, showing selection, recombination, mutation, and iteration

output timbre. Its fitness represents how aesthetically appealing it is to a user (this is interactive EC, as in McDermott et al. (2010)), or how well it scores on a suite of computational aesthetic measures (this more typical situation is non-interactive EC, as in McDermott et al. (2007a)). Either way, some of the best timbres will be selected, and then mated in pairs by recombining the elements of their floating-point array genotypes. Two new genotypes will be the result, and they may be mutated by making small random changes to the genotypes. By inputting these new genotypes as control parameters to the synthesizer, the corresponding new timbres (i.e. phenotypes) are created. Gradually, the population tends towards more aesthetically appealing timbres.

Both interactive and non-interactive uses of EC in aesthetic domains have become very popular: see for example the *EvoMUSART* community.[1]

13.2.2 Generative Music

Generative music is music which is not specified by a score, but by an algorithm, a set of rules, a set of processes, a mapping from randomness, or some other such method. Collins (2008) provides a good introduction, quoting a definition of generative art as art that is "generated, at least in part, by some process that is not under the artist's direct control" (Boden 2007). Of course this requires a definition of "direct". Collins also quotes Sol LeWitt's explicit indirection: "the idea becomes a machine that makes the art". This brings to mind a famous remark, attributed to Richard Sites, in the context of meta-programming: "I'd rather write programs that write programs than write programs." Generative art is "meta", in the same sense: the artist creates not a single instance of the work, but instructions with the potential to create a family of instances. Meta-programming is also an example of

[1] http://evostar.dei.uc.pt/programme/evoapplications/#evomusart

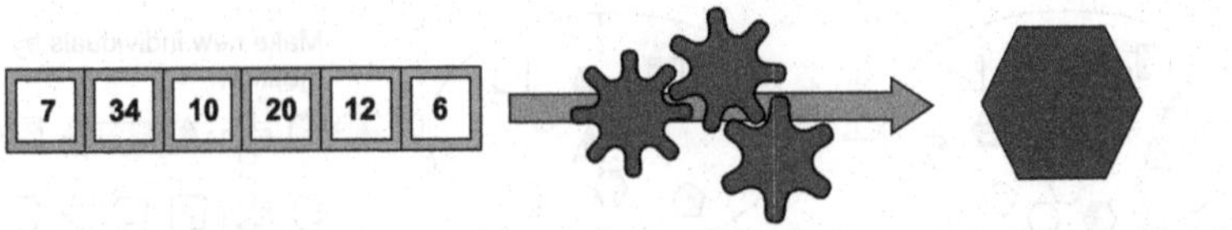

Fig. 13.2 Evo/gen music: the genotype controls a generative process which produces music

the observation that constructive laziness is a characteristic of good programmers. In this spirit, we like the implicit description given by Brian Eno, who has been responsible for popularising both the term "generative art" and the musical genre: "[. . .] I've always been lazy, I guess. So I've always wanted to set things in motion that would produce far more than I had predicted" (Eno 1996).

A great variety of techniques have been used in generative music. Apart from those discussed in this chapter, some common techniques include *Markov models* (Collins et al. 2010) and *cellular automata* (McAlpine et al. 1999).

Generative music is not very far from being mainstream. Eno's work is very well-known as a set of recordings. But relatively mainstream music software is making the techniques available to many more composers. Software such as Ableton *Live*, *Max/MSP* and *Pure Data* allows generative approaches. Eno used *Koan*, now known as *Noatikl*,[2] to produce *Generative Music 1*. There is a community of users of *Jeskola Buzz*[3] who compose using low-frequency oscillators and random-number generators to control the parameters of synthesizers and effects. In such work, it is common to see music *as a function of time*. The first author has contributed a small part to this software, by writing a *Note-Pool* plugin[4] which constrains random choices of notes to within specified scales or chords.

In this chapter, generative ideas are of interest because of their use in evolutionary music. In our evo/gen systems, the genotype acts as a set of parameters for a generative process which creates music, as in Fig. 13.2. This is in contrast to a *direct* representation, in which (for example), each element of the genotype might correspond directly to a single note.

13.3 HCI Informs Evo/Gen

Evo/gen methods do not produce any music which could not have been produced using more typical methods. In choosing to provide an alternative workflow for composition, evo/gen research implicitly recognises the importance of HCI

[2] http://intermorphic.com/tools/noatikl/

[3] http://buzzmachines.com/

[4] http://buzzmachines.com/viewreview.php?id=1053

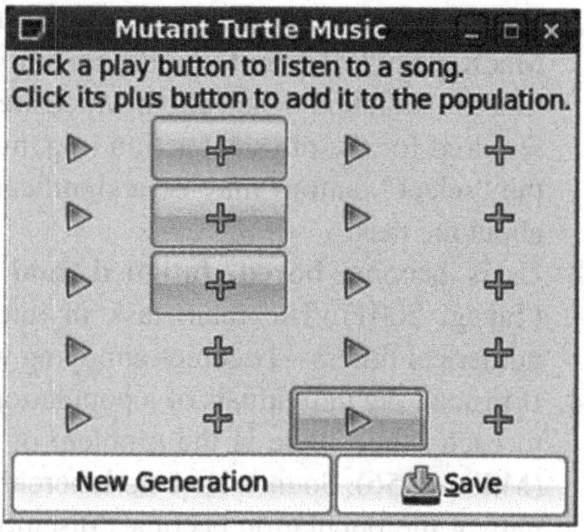

Fig. 13.3 GUI for the *Mutant Turtle Music* system. The population size is 10: the user auditions the music produced by each individual, and either selects or de-selects it. The "new generation" button iterates the algorithm

ideas. However few evo/gen researchers have explicitly used HCI ideas, methods or findings. It is more common to use a minimal evo/gen GUI such as that described next.

13.3.1 The Basic Evolutionary Interface

Figure 13.3 shows the GUI for the *Mutant Turtle Music* system. (The representation used in this system is described in more detail in Sect. 13.4.2.) For each individual in a small population, there is a "play" button for auditioning the individual and a "plus" button for selecting or de-selecting it, i.e. marking it as good or bad. There is also a button which commands the algorithm to produce a new population, using the currently selected individuals as parents.

This GUI is simple and discoverable, given a basic understanding of the evolutionary process. The controls are just about the bare minimum for an interactive EC system. It is entirely closed, allowing the user no method of self-expression or working outside the system. In all these respects, it is quite typical of the GUIs reported in the evo/gen music literature.

13.3.2 Problems in Evo/Gen Music

Many of the main problems in evo/gen music are distinctively HCI issues.

1. Human evaluation of fitness is much slower than computer evaluation. This is the **fitness evaluation bottleneck** (Biles 1994). Interactive EC is therefore restricted to small populations and few generations. In particular, a 60-second piece of music cannot be auditioned in less than 60 s, nor can multiple pieces be auditioned simultaneously. This is in contrast to (e.g.) evolutionary graphics, where many individuals can generally be shown on-screen simultaneously and evaluated at a glance.

2. **Badly-designed GUI elements** make interaction slower. Fitts' law (Fitts 1954; MacKenzie 1992) and similar are important considerations for tasks, such as fitness evaluation or selection, which are repeated many times and where the time required for the physical action (e.g. moving the mouse into place and clicking the "select" button) may be a significant fraction of the time required to think about the task.
3. Users become **bored, fatigued, and annoyed** over long evolutionary runs (Takagi 2001). The main task in interactive EC—the awarding of absolute numerical fitness—becomes annoying with repetition.
4. If instead the individuals of a population must be ranked or otherwise compared to each other, there is the problem of **limits on human short-term memory** (Miller 1956). Sounds have no inherent graphical representation, so the individuals of the population become "disembodied" with respect to the GUI and it is difficult for users to recall the correct association between GUI elements and half-remembered sounds.
5. Users sometimes feel that **the system is not responsive** to their expressed wishes, particularly in the short term. For example the user may feel that the system "should have known" that a particular individual would not be preferred in the light of previous choices in the same generation; but the typical system's incorporation of user feedback happens all at once, at the end of each generation.
6. As in most machine-learning and evolutionary methods, in interactive EC learning happens by sampling randomly from a very large space and gradually improving. This means that users encounter **many bad individuals**, especially in early generations.
7. In aesthetic domains there is no global optimum, and evolution is not guaranteed to find one even if it does exist. Populations can converge (reach uniformity) prematurely; good individuals can be lost; users can change their minds. In all these cases, users may be faced with a **dead end**: a population of individuals all of which seem useless. Yet users are naturally reluctant to scrap all existing work and re-start.
8. The typical fitness-evaluation interaction paradigm is **closed**. It does not afford flexibility and creative use.

13.3.3 Some Solutions

If the problems of evo/gen music can be described as principally those of HCI, then so can their potential solutions. Even the best evo/gen interfaces cannot be said to match the power, flexibility, and usability of successful interfaces in areas such as instrumental or laptop performance (see Stowell and McLean 2013, in this volume; McDermott et al. 2013, in this volume). However some research has shown awareness of HCI issues, with some successes as described next.

1. **Simple GUIs**, with sensible default values and unnecessary controls removed, make the user's job faster and easier.
2. **Archives of good individuals** allow the user to move confidently through the generations without fear of losing important material, and to recombine individuals from different generations, giving a stronger sense of user control (Dahlstedt 2009).
3. **Combining human and computer strengths** can help by removing some menial tasks from the user's workload. For example, sometimes very bad individuals can be easily recognised computationally, even if good ones are more difficult to classify (Baluja et al. 1994). Thus it can be useful to program a filter for bad individuals, or to run a second evolution in the background (with fitness defined computationally) occasionally migrating good results to the user's foreground (McDermott et al. 2007b).
4. **Keyboard shortcuts** make some repetitive tasks much faster.
5. **Expressive interfaces** allow the user more control in addition to the standard evaluation of fitness. "A rich open task requires a rich open interface" (Stowell and McLean 2013, in this volume). For example, **interactive genetic operators with real-time feedback** can take advantage of our ability to recognise and reject bad sounds quickly. The "sweeping" crossover operator (McDermott et al. 2007b) allowed the user to control the relative magnitude of contribution of each parent to the offspring, while hearing the offspring in real-time. It can also be useful to allow the user to **manually modify individuals directly**.
6. **Mnemonic visualisations** help the user to associate individuals with their associated GUI controls (Dahlstedt 2007).
7. With **better representations**, the user's task becomes far more pleasant. Sections 13.4.1 and 13.4.2 give detailed descriptions of higher-level representations which enrich the search space with more good individuals and fewer bad ones. In some cases, for example the work of Seago (2013, in this volume), an alternative search space might be more easily navigable.

13.3.4 Case Study: The XG Interface

The XG ("executable graph") system (McDermott and O'Reilly 2011) is a quite different evo/gen system. The GUI is shown in Fig. 13.4. The "time-lapse" panel on the left displays a realtime plot of pitches and input variables versus time. (See Sect. 13.4.1.2 for information on the input variables and the underlying musical representation.) Below are the audition controls labelled "a0" to "a9": selecting an audition control activates the corresponding individual. An individual is selected or deselected using the selection controls labelled "s0" to "s9". The mouse or keyboard shortcuts can be used to quickly audition, select and deselect individuals. The "next generation" button iterates the algorithm.

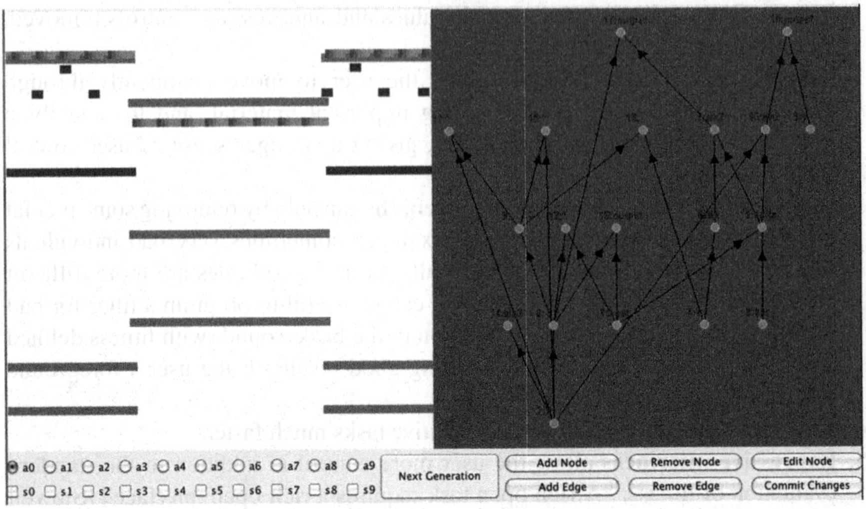

Fig. 13.4 *XG* GUI. The time-lapse panel at *top-left* displays numerical input variables in *green* (*darker bars*, in print) and output pitches in *red* (*lighter bars*). The user can audition or select individuals using the buttons at *bottom-left*. The current individual's graph is displayed on the *top right*, and can be edited using the controls at *bottom-right* (Color figure online)

The "graph editor" panel on the right allows the user to view and edit the current individual's graph. Nodes and edges can be added or deleted; node labels can also be edited. Any changes are put into effect after the user clicks "commit changes", which is only enabled when the edited graph is determined to be valid.

The *XG* GUI addresses some of the issues presented in Sect. 13.3.2. *XG*'s simple layout and keyboard shortcuts allow the user to focus on the evaluation of individuals instead of engaging in repetitive physical tasks. Since selection is binary (good/bad) and individuals are deselected by default, some time is saved. In each generation, *XG* filters out the ten individuals of lowest variety, and hides them from the user, saving some time and tedium. The user is free to select as many or as few individuals as desired, rather than a pre-determined number. The graphs of most individuals are visually distinctive, granting a visual component to the selection process. The ability to edit a graph helps the user to escape from dead ends and allows a more powerful, active form of control. *XG* also uses a generative representation which tends to lead to interesting, coherent-sounding music (as described in more detail in the next section).

There are also several areas where *XG* could be improved. Audition of individuals is unavoidably slow. Users may still become bored over long runs, although the editable graph feature helps to alleviate this. Users may still encounter consecutive undesirable individuals. *XG* does not currently use archiving or similar techniques to preserve distinct, positive results. The *XG* GUI also raises new issues of information visualisation, in both the time-lapse panel and the graph editor, and issues of interaction with information in the graph editor. The GUI is likely far from optimal in these respects and would benefit from further HCI-informed study. However, overall the system has been found to be quite usable and successful in creating new music.

13.4 Evo/Gen Informs HCI

The note-by-note representation used in MIDI sequencers is quite low-level. It is well-suited to the way some composers work: they are able to conceptualise large parts of the music by listening "with the mind's ear", or with the aid of a piano or other instrument, before transcribing to paper. But many composers work quite differently. The process of imagining large amounts of music is beyond many untrained composers, and anyway is made unnecessary since the sequencer can play music back immediately. Similarly there is no need for an external instrument. For some users, the sequencer has replaced the external instrument, the mental playback, and the paper.

Although the sequencer is well-suited to some of these tasks, it does not provide an easy way to imagine coherent variations to the music. If one uses a MIDI sequencer to edit a typical piece, say a pop song in A major, changing a single C sharp to a C natural, it will sound like a wrong note. But if one changes the entire piece to A minor, it will sound strange, certainly, but it will sound like a coherent transformation. Considering such transformations (and many more intelligent ones) seems an indispensable part of the process of producing good music. But MIDI sequencers do not offer good ways of quickly and non-destructively auditioning a broad range of transformations of this type (there are some exceptions, such as simple transposition). Instead they typically require composers to edit many notes manually.

We suggest that the ideas of evo/gen music can provide at least a partial solution to this problem. Research in these areas often focusses on the *representation* of the music (Marsden 2005). When stochastic processes are involved, as in most evo/gen music, good representations are necessary to produce good music.

Several types of representations have been used with some success by the authors in evolutionary approaches to music. Grammatical representations use sets of re-writing rules as a representation either for music directly, or for programs which generate music. Functional representations take advantage of functional abstraction for re-use of musical material. Sometimes music is represented as a function of time. These representations are relatively abstract or high-level, compared to the note-by-note representation of MIDI. A single edit, in such a representation, is likely to change many parts of the musical output; but all these changes are likely to be in some sense consistent. Instead of hearing the same piece with a wrong note, we hear a coherent transformation or variation of the piece. In the ideal case, all such transformations are worth considering, and are easily available in the sequencers' interface, and so the composer's work becomes more fruitful and efficient. In the following two sections, previous work using high-level representations for music is described, leading to a proposal for new user-centric sequencer tools.

13.4.1 *Music as a Function of Time*

In some types of generative music, the music is seen as a function of time. In the simplest possible case, time is a discrete, increasing variable. It is possible to impose some structure, for example using time variables like *bar* and *beat*. Each of these increases (at different rates) over time and periodically resets to zero. By feeding such numerical variables into an arithmetic function, and mapping the numerical output at each time-step to a MIDI note, one is guaranteed to produce a piece of generative music which conforms to some abstract temporal structure. The key question is then the creation of arithmetic functions which lead to interesting music. In this section we describe a line of research in which interactive EC is used to create interesting mappings. A seminal work in this area is by Hoover and Stanley (2009), which used pre-existing MIDI music, as well as time variables, as inputs.

13.4.1.1 Jive

Jive (Shao et al. 2010) is a "generative, interactive, virtual, evolutionary" music system. Music is represented as an input–output mapping. The inputs are a time variable, and several variables which are interactively controlled by the user. Either a mouse can be used to provide x and y values, or a Nintendo Wii Remote can provide x, y and z values. All of these, and the time variable t are fed into a set of arithmetic expressions, with the output of each being mapped in real-time to a MIDI voice. When performing, therefore, the user has some control over how the music behaves, but not over the low-level details of choice of notes. It is somewhat analogous to conducting, though there is no direct control of expressive details such as tempo and dynamics. In another sense it is more like a virtual "hyper-instrument".

The input–output mappings are crucial. They are created using interactive grammatical evolution (GE: see O'Neill and Ryan 2003). GE uses a context-free grammar to specify a language—in this case, a simple language of arithmetic operators such as plus, multiply, sine, and exponential. The grammar specifies a language, but the genotype (an integer array) specifies a particular derivation and thus a string within that language. This string is interpreted as an arithmetic function which maps the input variables to an output variable, as specified above. In addition to producing a MIDI note, it specifies whether that note should be played, or the system should be silent, at each time-step. When pitches and silences are patterned in time, the result is (simple) music. During evolution, the user will audition a population of input–output mappings, always selecting those which are most aesthetically appealing and which have most scope for interactive performance. After many generations, a single input–output mapping is chosen and is used to perform a piece.

The *Jive* software and demo pieces are available for download.[5]

---

[5]http://sites.google.com/site/odcsssjian2009/

13.4.1.2 Executable Graphs

In the *XG* generative music system (McDermott and O'Reilly 2011), we again use a set of control variables and time variables, feeding them into a mapping to produce a MIDI output. In this case, interactive control of real-time parameters is not needed (though is optional): instead, an abstract structure for these parameters (such as the ABABAB structure typical of pop songs, or something more complex) is specified in an input file. Instead of an arithmetic function created by GE, the input–output mapping is represented as an executable directed acyclic graph. The motivation for this choice is that we wish to produce pieces of music consisting of multiple voices which should sound coherent together. A directed acyclic graph can have multiple inputs and multiple outputs, all sharing some common computations in the interior parts of the graph. Therefore, we hypothesize that the outputs will tend to sound related, though not identical. The *XG* system is summarised in Fig. 13.5. One advantage over the *Jive* system is a more sophisticated mapping from the output values to MIDI: as a result of patterns of note-on and note-off signals, and realistically varying dynamics, voices sound more musical than in *Jive*.

13.4.2 Higher-Level Grammatical Representations

In the Mutant Turtle Music system (McDermott and O'Neill 2010), each piece was represented as a string derived from a context-free grammar, again evolved using GE. However, here the string was interpreted as a command program in a language reminiscent of turtle graphics, though adapted for music. Such languages are common in the field of interactive EC art (McCormack 2008) and music (Worth and Stepney 2005). In a sense, the "turtle" (a cursor storing the current pitch, orientation, and position in time) moves about the score, "painting" notes as it goes, as driven by the command program. Commands cause it to add a note or chord, to move, to go up or down in pitch or in note-length, or to change orientation (forward or backward in time). Thus the music is not seen as a function of time.

The *Mutant Turtle Music* GUI has been shown and described in Sect. 13.3.1. Some demo pieces are available for download.[6]

The functional aspects of the representation are of most interest here. In EC, one popular technique for re-use of components and imposing structure and pattern on solutions is *automatically-defined functions* (ADFs). An ADF is a function, composed of multiple primitives, created automatically during the evolutionary process, and available for re-use by later individuals. In this way, useful functionality can be re-used multiple times by the same individual or by multiple individuals, without requiring that evolution re-discover the functionality each time. ADFs

[6]http://skynet.ie/~jmmcd/software/mtm_demos_cec2010.tgz

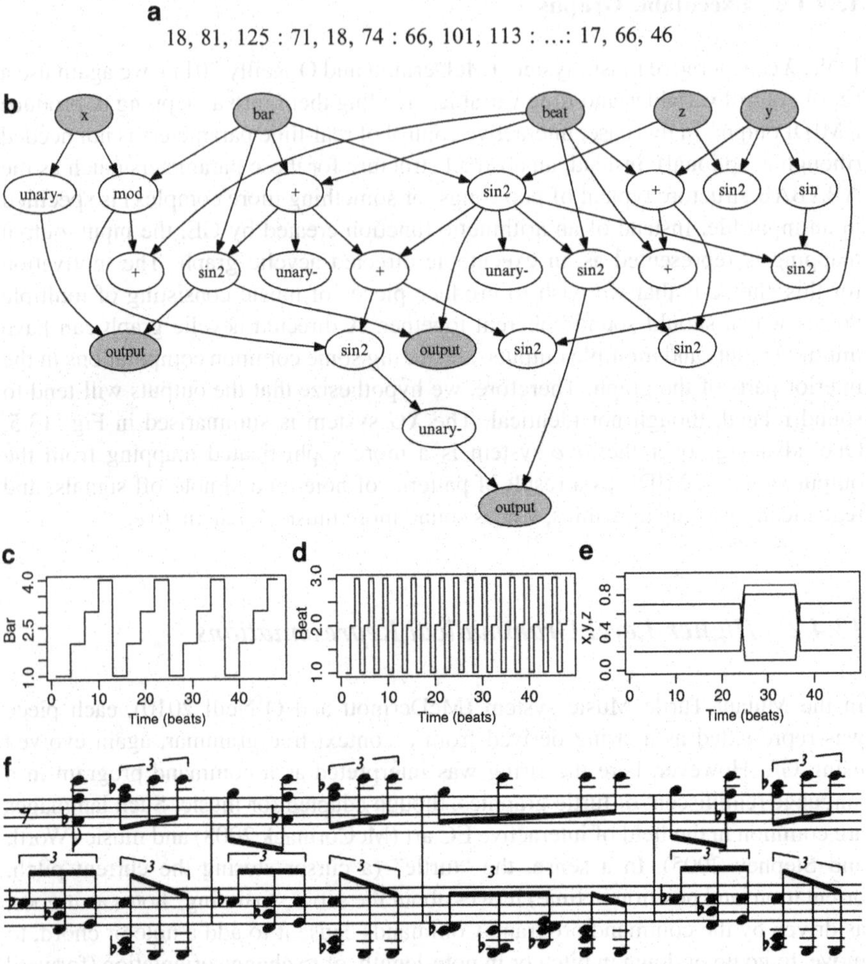

Fig. 13.5 The *XG* representation consists of an integer-array genotype, mapped to an executable graph phenotype, and five time-series of variables (*bar*, *beat*, *x*, *y*, and *z*) which serve as inputs to the graph. The output is one MIDI voice per output. (**a**) The integer-array genotype is divided into chunks of 3. Each chunk creates a new node in the graph, specifying its label and incoming connections. (**b**) The corresponding executable graph phenotype. Node labels are function names. Input and output nodes are highlighted. (**c**) Input variable *bar*. 4 bars per section; 4 sections. (**d**) Input variable *beat*. 3 beats per bar. (**e**) Control variables *x*, *y*, and *z* impose an AABA structure. (**f**) Output in three voices, reflecting the AABA structure

have been shown to be useful in genetic programming (GP) tasks where solutions typically require pattern or structure (Koza 1994).

The advantage of ADFs in the context of music is that they allow re-use. The turtle representation alone might produce a good musical motif, but in order to repeat the motif a few bars later, it would be necessary to re-evolve the same material—a very unlikely event. In the turtle representation, then, most pieces will sound highly disordered and random. When ADFs are introduced, each ADF may correspond to a motif, and each re-use of an ADF will impose obvious structure on the music. Because the turtle representation allows state to be stored, it is possible for a motif to be re-played at a higher pitch, or using a longer note-length, or in reverse—all common and useful musical transformations.

Higher-order functions (HOFs) have a similar advantage. A higher-order function is a function one of whose arguments is itself a function. This is common and easy in languages such as Lisp and Python, but relatively rare and difficult in Java and C. In a representation featuring HOFs, *abstract structure* can be imposed on pieces of music. For example, a HOF could express an abstract motif like "do something three times, then do a variation". The "something" could be a lower-level motif, specified by a function, passed-in to the HOF. Different motifs might then be used to play different versions of this higher-order, abstract motif. Composers often carry out such processes mentally, but explicit representation of the process in algorithmic music is rare. Again, the same result might be achieved without HOFs, but would require a very lucky evolution of the same genetic material in multiple places.

When pieces of music are represented using ADFs and HOFs, structure is imposed on pieces in a natural way. Users of interactive EC systems with ADFs and HOFs are required to listen to fewer random-sounding pieces. Small changes to the underlying representation may well lead to changes to many of the notes of the piece, but without breaking their organisation and structure. Small changes at the representational level tend not to *entropic*, i.e. do not lead to gradually more and more broken versions of the original: rather, they lead to potentially useful creative transformations of the original piece. ADFs and HOFs also allow relatively short genotypes to produce good phenotypes. All of these properties are also potentially beneficial if such higher-order grammatical representations are to be used in a non-evolutionary context, as proposed next.

13.4.3 Creative Transformations

In the previous sections we have described two successful representations for evo/gen music. These ideas now lead to a proposal for a way to make many creative, useful musical transformations automatically available in standard music-editing software.

What the representations described above have in common, for our purposes, is that music is not represented in a note-by-note way. In *Jive*, *XG*, and related systems such as *NEAT Drummer* (Hoover and Stanley 2009), there is an underlying process which generates notes as a function of time. In *Mutant Turtle Music* and related systems, there is a command program consisting of a hierarchy of functions, allowing re-use of material.

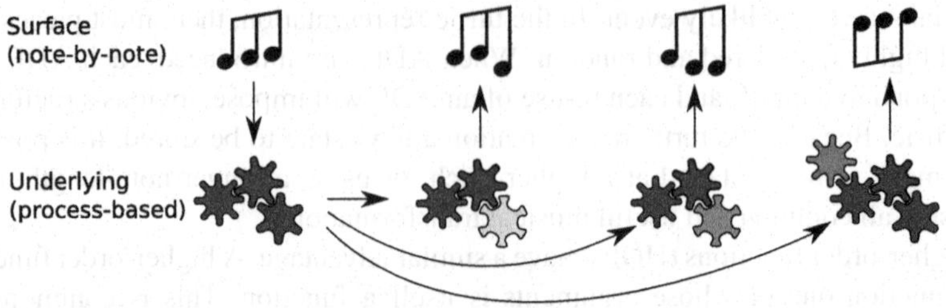

Fig. 13.6 Creative transformation. We begin with a piece of music in note-by-note representation (*top-left*). We find a process or program which can generate that music (*bottom-left*). We make several small mutations to the process (*bottom-centre* to *bottom-right*). Then we run the altered processes to get new pieces of music (*top-centre* to *top-right*) which are well-formed variations of the original

These representations allow a route to creative transformations. A small change to the underlying process may well have effects on many of the elements of the resulting piece of music, but since the new piece will still be produced by a single process, it is likely to sound coherent. Ideally, it will sound like a plausible variation on the original piece. If such representations could be used in our music editors (e.g. MIDI sequencers), users could have easy access to a broad suite of possible transformations. Crucially, the programmer would not need to foresee and implement every possible transformation. Instead, the natural transformations would emerge as those available through small changes to the generative process. Thus, the fundamental idea of *creative transformations* is to take an existing piece of music in a note-by-note representation, *re-represent* it using an evo/gen representation, and then make several slight mutations of the piece available to the user (see Fig. 13.6).

Naturally, most composers will always prefer to begin work by imagining a melody, a set of chords, or a rhythm, and entering it into a sequencer note-by-note. Some will work by playing a MIDI keyboard or other instrument. We cannot recommend that such people switch to an evo/gen workflow in which pieces are only represented in a generative or algorithmic way, in order to take advantage of the possibilities of creative transformations of music.

Therefore, we need a way to take a piece in a typical note-by-note representation, find an (or "the"?) underlying generative process that generates that piece, make a change to the underlying process, and audition the new version. We also want the ability to make manual edits to individual notes in the new version. We want to be able to continue working in either the note-by-note representation, or the underlying generative representation, or both together.

To accomplish these goals, there is one hard problem that needs to be solved. Assume that we have a generative representation, perhaps a grammatical one, which is capable of producing a wide variety of pieces of music. To bring an existing piece of music into this representation, we need to perform an *inverse mapping*.

In grammatical terms, this would be a *parsing* of the piece, as opposed to a *derivation*. By the *parsing problem*, we here mean finding a generative process and its parameters which generate a given piece of music.

Parsing is a hard problem in general. The standard deterministic algorithms for parsing text with context-free grammars are not suitable for the analogous problem in music. It is hypothesized that heuristics such as EC itself can be used to solve instances of the problem: however this is an open question for future work.

Parsing music is also likely to be non-deterministic. A piece may correspond to multiple possible parsings, some of which are better matches than others for the composer's or listener's internal understanding of the piece. There may be information-theoretic and heuristic approaches to deciding on the best parsing: in general the simplest parsing will be the best. This formalised version of Occam's razor is known as the minimum description length principle. It is common in artificial intelligence approaches to art and music (Schmidhuber 1997).

Although the general parsing problem is an open question, in the *XG* project one component of the problem has been solved, as follows. The user usually works by evolving a population of graphs, each of which produces a piece of music. As described in Sect. 13.4.1.2, the user may also edit the graphs manually, by adding, deleting, or changing nodes and edges. In this way the user has control over the music, though this control is indirect by comparison with normal MIDI editing. In order for the user's edits to be made available to the ongoing evolutionary process, it is necessary to perform the inverse mapping from graphs to genotypes. This part of the inverse mapping problem has been implemented in *XG*, and so the user can work either by editing graphs, or by evolving them, or both.

The same methods required to perform natural, creative *transformations* on an existing piece of music would also allow natural, creative *extensions* of an existing piece. A short melody hand-written by the user might be automatically represented using a generative representation, and then this representation might be allowed to run forward in time to produce a consistent extension.

Our proposal for user interaction with the creative transformation and creative extension tools is as follows. A standard MIDI sequencer might incorporate a generative language such as an arithmetic input–output mapping language, as in Sect 13.4.1, or the turtle language with ADFs and HOFs, as in Sect. 13.4.2. As a background process, the system would find generative representations and associated parameters for the existing, user-created music. The user would work as usual in the note-by-note representation, only occasionally moving to a separate window with controls for transformations and extensions. At this point, the system would generate several possible transformations (corresponding to mutations to the generative process and parameters) and an extension (corresponding to running the unaltered generative process forward in time). The user would audition these possibilities as desired, with the note-by-note representation of the music being automatically updated. Good undo functionality would be required. Simpler, hard-coded transformations such as transposition, search-and-replace over notes, inversions, and so on, could be arranged in the same window. Ideally the creative transformations and extensions would be seen as another set of tools of the same type, and from a HCI point of view, would function in the same way. Ultimately MIDI sequencers might become "smarter", and function more as composers' aids than as mere tools for music transcription and playback.

Finally, we note that using computer-aided methods raises interesting questions concerning authorship of the resulting works (Dorin 2001). Certainly some musicians will find that such methods over-step the bounds of legitimate computer assistance and devalue the user's authorship. However others find that samples, pre-programmed beats and synthesizer timbre presets present no such obstacle. In much mainstream music, some aspects are truly original while others are in some sense part of the public artistic commons. Musicians ascribe authorship in a flexible way which depends on the novel contribution of a piece rather than a legalistic interpretation of the authorship of component parts. Beyond these brief comments we prefer to leave this topic open for future discussion.

13.5 Conclusions

This chapter has described the two-way influence between the fields of evo/gen music and music HCI. Evo/gen music benefits when HCI methods and ideas are applied to make the user's job faster, more efficient, and more pleasant. There are also possibilities for augmented evo/gen interfaces, in which the user is given more control over the process. The representational work in evo/gen music can also make a contribution towards music HCI by supporting new user-centric tools in mainstream music editors.

Acknowledgements JMcD gratefully acknowledges *Inspire* funding from the Irish Research Council for Science, Engineering and Technology, co-funded by Marie Curie; DS gratefully acknowledges MIT Undergraduate Research Opportunity (UROP) funding; UMO'R gratefully acknowledges the support of VMWare and USA D.O.E. Grant DE-SC0005288.

References

Baluja, S., Pomerleau, D., & Jochem, T. (1994). Towards automated artificial evolution for computer-generated images. *Connection Science, 6*(2–3), 325–354.

Biles, J. A. (1994). GenJam: A genetic algorithm for generating jazz solos. In *Proceedings of the 1994 international computer music conference* (pp. 131–137). Danish Institute of Electroacoustic Music, Denmark: International Computer Music Association.

Boden, M. (2007). What is generative art? COGS seminar.

Collins, N. (2008). The analysis of generative music programs. *Organised Sound, 13*(3), 237–248.

Collins, T., Laney, R., Willis, A., & Garthwaite, P. (2010). Using discovered, polyphonic patterns to filter computer-generated music. In *Proceedings of the international conference on computational creativity*, Lisbon, Portugal.

Dahlstedt, P. (2007). Evolution in creative sound design. In E. R. Miranda & J. A. Biles (Eds.), *Evolutionary computer music* (pp. 79–99). London: Springer.

Dahlstedt, P. (2009). On the role of temporary storage in interactive evolution. In M. Giacobini, et al. (Eds.), *Applications of evolutionary computing: EvoWorkshops 2009, no. 5484 in LNCS*, (pp. 478–487). New York: Springer.

Dorin, A. (2001). Aesthetic fitness and artificial evolution for the selection of imagery from the mythical infinite library. In J. Kelemen & P. Sosík (Eds.), *ECAL 2001* (Vol. 2159 in LNAI). New York: Springer.

Eno, B. (1996). Generative music. http://www.inmotionmagazine.com/eno1.html. Lecture, San Francisco, USA.

Fitts, P. M. (1954). The information capacity of the human motor system in controlling the amplitude of movement. *Journal of Experimental Psychology, 47*(6), 381–391 (Reprinted in *Journal of Experimental Psychology: General, 121*(3), 262–269, 1992).

Hoover, A. K., & Stanley, K. O. (2009). Exploiting functional relationships in musical composition. *Connection Science, 21*(2), 227–251.

Koza, J. R. (1994). *Genetic programming II: Automatic discovery of reusable programs*. Cambridge, MA: MIT Press.

MacKenzie, I. S. (1992). Fitts' law as a research and design tool in human–computer interaction. *Human–Computer Interaction, 7*, 91–139.

Marsden, A. (2005). Generative structural representation of tonal music. *Journal of New Music Research, 34*(4), 409–428.

McAlpine, K., Miranda, E., & Hoggar, S. (1999). Making music with algorithms: A case-study system. *Computer Music Journal, 23*(2), 19–30.

McCormack, J. (2008). Evolutionary L-systems. In P. F. Hingston, L. C. Barone, Z. Michalewicz, & D. B. Fogel (Eds.), *Design by evolution: Advances in evolutionary design* (pp. 169–196). New York: Springer.

McDermott, J., & O'Neill, M. (2010). Higher-order functions in aesthetic EC encodings. In *CEC 2010: Proceedings of the 12th annual congress on evolutionary computation* (pp. 3018–3025). Barcelona: IEEE Press.

McDermott, J., & O'Reilly, U.-M. (2011). An executable graph representation for evolutionary generative music. In *GECCO '11*. Dublin.

McDermott, J., Griffith, N. J. L., & O'Neill, M. (2007a). Evolutionary computation applied to sound synthesis. In J. Romero & P. Machado (Eds.), *The art of artificial evolution: A handbook on evolutionary art and music* (pp. 81–101). Berlin/Heidelberg: Springer.

McDermott, J., Griffith, N. J. L., & O'Neill, M. (2007b). Evolutionary GUIs for sound synthesis. In M. Giacobini (Ed.), *Applications of evolutionary computing* (vol. 4448 in LNCS, pp. 547–556). New York: Springer.

McDermott, J., O'Neill, M., & Griffith, N. J. L. (2010). EC control of sound synthesis. *Evolutionary Computation Journal, 18*(2), 277–303.

McDermott, J., Gifford, T., Bouwer, A., & Wagy, M. (2013). Should music interaction be easy? In S. Holland, K. Wilkie, P. Mulholland, & A. Seago (Eds.), *Music and human computer interaction* (pp. 29–48). London: Springer.

Miller, G. A. (1956). The magical number seven, plus or minus two: Some limits on our capacity for processing information. *The Psychological Review, 63*, 81–97.

O'Neill, M., & Ryan, C. (2003). *Grammatical evolution: Evolutionary automatic programming in an arbitrary language*. Norwell: Kluwer Academic Publishers.

Schmidhuber, J. (1997). Low-complexity art. *Leonardo, 30*(2), 97–103.

Seago, A. (2013). A new interaction strategy for musical timbre design. In S. Holland, K. Wilkie, P. Mulholland, & A. Seago (Eds.), *Music and human–computer interaction* (pp. 153–169). London: Springer. ISBN 978-1-4471-2989-9.

Shao, J., McDermott, J., O'Neill, M., & Brabazon, A. (2010). Jive: A generative, interactive, virtual, evolutionary music system. In *Proceedings of EvoWorkshops*.

Stowell, D., & McLean, A. (2013). Live music-making: A rich open task requires a rich open interface. In S. Holland, K. Wilkie, P. Mulholland, & A. Seago (Eds.), *Music and human–computer interaction* (pp. 139–152). London: Springer. ISBN 978-1-4471-2989-9.
Takagi, H. (2001). Interactive evolutionary computation: Fusion of the capabilities of EC optimization and human evaluation. *Proceedings of the IEEE, 89*(9), 1275–1296.
Whitelaw, M. (2002). Breeding aesthetic objects: Art and artificial evolution. In D. W. Corne & P. J. Bentley (Eds.), *Creative evolutionary systems* (pp. 129–146). Burlington: Morgan Kaufmann.
Worth, P., & Stepney, S. (2005). Growing music: Musical interpretations of L-systems. In J. Romero & P. Machado (Eds.), *EvoMUSART* (pp. 545–550). Berlin: Springer.

Chapter 14
Video Analysis for Evaluating Music Interaction: Musical Tabletops

Anna Xambó, Robin Laney, Chris Dobbyn, and Sergi Jordà

Abstract There is little evaluation of musical tabletops for music performance, and current approaches tend to have little consideration of social interaction. However, in collaborative settings, social aspects such as coordination, communication, or musical engagement between collaborators are fundamental for a successful performance. After an overview of the use of video in music interaction research as a convenient method for understanding interaction between people and technology, we present three empirical examples of approaches to video analysis applied to musical tabletops; firstly, an exploratory approach to give informal insight towards understanding collaboration in new situations; secondly, a participatory design approach oriented to improve an interface design by getting feedback from the user experience; thirdly, a quantitative approach, towards understanding collaboration by considering frequencies of interaction events. The aim of this chapter is to provide a useful insight into how to evaluate musical tabletops using video as a data source. Furthermore, this overview can shed light on understanding shareable interfaces in a wider HCI context of group creativity and multi-player interaction.

14.1 Introduction

In recent years the number of shareable interfaces for music performance has increased rapidly as is evidenced in conferences in the field such as International Computer Music Conference (*ICMC*), New Interfaces for Musical Expression

---

A. Xambó (✉) • R. Laney • C. Dobbyn
Music Computing Lab, Centre for Research in Computing, The Open University, Milton Keynes, UK
e-mail: anna.xambo@open.ac.uk; robin.laney@open.ac.uk; chris.dobbyn@open.ac.uk
S. Jordà
Music Technology Group, Universitat Pompeu Fabra, Barcelona, Spain
e-mail: sergi.jorda@upf.edu

S. Holland et al. (eds.), *Music and Human-Computer Interaction*, Springer Series on Cultural Computing, DOI 10.1007/978-1-4471-2990-5_14,

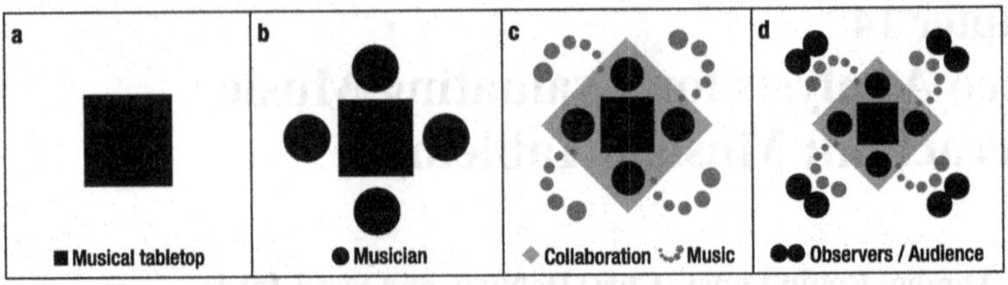

Fig. 14.1 (**a**) A musical tabletop. (**b**) A group of musicians interacting with a musical tabletop. (**c**) Collaboration and musical engagement of a group of musicians interacting with a musical tabletop. (**d**) Understanding music interaction by observing collaboration and musical engagement of a group of musicians interacting with a musical tabletop

(*NIME*) or Sound and Music Computing (*SMC*). A potential problem is how to assess reliably these interfaces, and what are the most appropriate methods to be applied. Assessing music interaction using these shareable interfaces involves understanding musicians interacting with the interface, as well as the social interactions between them when making music. This additional layer of complexity of understanding interactions between collaborators, apart from the interactions of the musicians with the interface, can also be seen as a convenient approach for investigating certain collaborative aspects of interface design such as different usages of the interface from a participatory perspective (Bau et al. 2008) or from a perspective of supporting collective musical engagement (Bryan-Kinns and Hamilton 2012), among others. Musical tabletops are a representative example for understanding these interactions because, in this scenario, musicians can be face-to-face using the same interface. Furthermore, this scenario enables direct observation by the researcher of a focused point of the musical activity (see also Fig. 14.1). In this setting, both verbal communication (e.g., conversations, utterances), and nonverbal communication (e.g., music, gestures, eye-contact, face expressions), can happen and be observed.

Video analysis is a method of human-computer interaction (HCI) research that can help assessing shareable interfaces for music performance because it aims at understanding human interaction with technology, which can be verbally and nonverbally mediated. Video analysis is convenient to overcome the say/do problem of differences between what people say and what they actually do (Jordan 1996). Accordingly, the analysis of video material, in contrast with other methods such as field notes or interviews, provides a more detailed account of what happened compared to what participants report that happened. Thus, even though video analysis can be highly time consuming, results can be richer and more detailed than using other techniques such as note taking, questionnaires or interviews. This method is flexible because, first, it can be qualitative (Heath et al. 2010) and/or quantitative (Martin and Bateson 2007), second, it can record verbal and nonverbal communication (Jordan and Henderson 1995), and, third, it can be analysed both as a single data source or combined with other data sources such as interaction log files (Hagedorn et al. 2008). In the music performance domain, the music/sounds produced can be recorded, and again reproduced, in real time, together with conversations and gestures. Thus, we believe that the use of video in research can be a convenient tool for understanding music interaction in general, and musical tabletops in particular.

In this chapter we first provide a general overview of how the evaluation of novel interfaces for music in general, and musical tabletops in particular, has been tackled so far with an HCI approach. Next, we outline the use of video in music interaction research in terms of visual anthropology and video analysis, and the practical issues implied. Then, we present three examples of video analysis that we conducted on different musical tabletops; firstly, an exploratory approach for giving an initial insight on a minimal and highly constrained interface; secondly, a participatory design approach for documenting users' thoughts about the interface design of TOUCHtr4ck, also with a highly constrained interface; thirdly, a quantitative approach, as complementary of qualitative findings, for measuring frequencies of behaviour patterns when interacting with the Reactable, a commercially popular musical tabletop. We conclude with a discussion on the implications of this approach for the communities of sound and music computing, and, more broadly, HCI.

14.2 Evaluating NIME with HCI Methods

In this section, we overview different approaches undertaken for evaluating new interfaces for musical expression (NIME) that borrow tools from HCI. Then, we present musical tabletops that have been designed and evaluated for collaboration.

14.2.1 Task-based vs. Open Task

In sound and music computing, the evaluation of new interfaces for music is considered a novel field of research: an analysis of the NIME conference proceedings (Stowell et al. 2008) shows that since the beginning of the conference in 2001 (Poupyrev et al. 2001), few of the papers have applied HCI methods thoroughly to evaluate new music instruments. However, the benefits of adapting HCI evaluation to these novel interfaces for music may benefit both the designers who can improve the interface design, and the musicians who can discover or expand on the possibilities of the evaluated tool (Wanderley and Orio 2002). Of those studies which incorporate HCI methods, the majority are task-based, that is, focused on how musical tasks are performed. Possible metrics evaluated might be how precisely musical tasks are performed (Wanderley and Orio 2002); the quality of the user experience and the degree of expressiveness obtained (Bau et al. 2008; Kiefer et al. 2008; Stowell et al. 2008); or the usefulness of the tool (Coughlan and Johnson 2006). Another approach which is more open task-oriented stresses the collaborations among the participants building on empirical studies of mutual engagement (Bryan-Kinns and Hamilton 2012). The recent BCS HCI 2011 Workshop on Music Interaction[1] and this subsequent book illustrate that there is a general interest on the intersections between HCI and sound and music computing, and one of the main issues raised is how to evaluate music interaction as open-ended tasks using HCI methods.

14.2.2 Collaboration with Musical Tabletops

Even though there exists a number of musical tabletops, only a subset is specially designed for multi-player collaboration, which implies a higher level of complexity, such as The Jam-O-Drum (Blaine and Perkis 2000), AudioPad (Patten et al. 2002), Iwai's Composition on the Table (Iwai 1999) or the Reactable (Jordà et al. 2005; Jordà 2008). In general, there is a lack of evaluation, although there have been isolated attempts, such as the assessment of Ensemble (Fiebrink et al. 2009), a task-based study focused on the performance and use of the controllers, and the evaluation of the Reactable, with task-based studies focused on usability assessment (Rauh 2009), or performance and motivation (Mealla et al. 2011).

With the above studies, arguably there is little mention of social interaction, which, as seen earlier, plays a key role in co-located face-to-face settings. In another study (Klügel et al. 2011), a set of terms is borrowed from the computer supported cooperative work (CSCW) discipline, in order to understand collaborations in co-located settings. Some of the terms are group awareness (i.e., mutual understanding about the tasks performed), group coordination, or tailorability (i.e., level of adaptation of the technologies). Nevertheless, the authors adopt a traditional approach of supporting music composition and notation with less consideration to contemporary music practices. A contemporary music approach tends to use alternative musical instructions more focused on the music process (Cox and Warner 2004; Gresham-Lancaster 1998), a practice close to the notion of unpredictability and uncertainty, which arguably tends to be present in music performance with novel interfaces for music. Thus, there is little research on the collaborative aspects of using musical tabletops for music performance.

14.3 Video in Music Interaction Research

In this section, we first introduce the practices of visual anthropology and ethnographic film, which use video for documenting, and we describe how music interaction has been approached. Afterwards, we present the aims, benefits and

[1]BCS HCI 2011 Workshop – *When Words Fail: What can Music Interaction tell us about HCI?*: http://mcl.open.ac.uk/workshop

limitations of video analysis, a research method which uses audiovisual material for studying human interaction with technologies and artefacts, and we then see how video analysis can be appropriate for studying music interaction.

14.3.1 Visual Anthropology: From Film to Digital Media

The use of audiovisual material to capture music interaction phenomena is closely linked to social sciences disciplines such as visual anthropology or ethnomusicology. Visual anthropology refers to the use of audiovisual media such as video to understand social or cultural phenomena (MacDougall 2006; Pink 2006; Ruby 2000), whereas ethnomusicology examines music of different cultures.

Visual anthropology dates back to the 1890s using film and photography to support academic anthropology (Pink 2006), also known as ethnographic film to define one audiovisual method for representing a culture (Ruby 2000). Since the very beginning we find anthropological research that evidence rhythmic and musical activities. An example is the work of Franz Boas, a German-American anthropologist who used film in the 1930s to document native dance while recording sound simultaneously with a wax cylinder sound recorder, with the aim of complementing these data with other materials (Ruby 1980). We also find a number of examples of ethnographic films related to music interaction; among them is the presentation of Canadian Kwakiutl's rituals and cultural aspects in the early 1914 silent film *In the Land of the Head Hunters* by Edward Curtis, so the film documents music aspects of this community only by visual means. The use of film as a scientific tool for research purposes was debated for a long period after these early attempts (Pink 2006). This applied approach to anthropology was accepted again in academia as a reliable method by the 1990s: a subjective reflexive approach was included in the anthropology agenda, and also digital media became more popular (Pink 2006). For example, music, dance and culture of the Alaskan Eskimos Yup'ik is shown in Sarah Elder and Leonard Kamerling's 1988 participatory film *Drums of Winter*, where the subjects of the film were also involved in the editing process. This collaborative filmmaking approach was in tune with other anthropologists and documentary filmmakers such as Jean Rouch or Sol Worth, an approach that addresses ethical and political questions about filmmaking (Ruby 2000).

Rethinking the role and future of visual anthropology has been discussed in recent years. An approach is to combine audiovisual media with new media to represent anthropological knowledge (Pink 2006). Another insight is to build a specific genre of anthropological cinema (Ruby 2000). Furthermore, it is also proposed to explore areas of the social experience that suit well the audiovisual media; those areas related to topographic, temporal, corporeal or personal aspects which can show the implicit from the explicit (MacDougall 2006), such as music interaction. However, as seen in these examples, in visual anthropology the video data is used for documenting, but rarely is used as a data source to be analysed, a practice which is explained next.

14.3.2 Video Analysis

In recent years, the use of video as a research tool for understanding everyday social activity which implies human interaction has increased. We find video used in qualitative research (Heath et al. 2010), as well as in quantitative research (Martin and Bateson 2007). For example, Heath et al. describe how the advent of digital video has facilitated a wider access to and use of this technology in social sciences (e.g., ethnography or sociology). Within this context, collective music performance, as a social activity which implies human interaction with objects or artefacts, can be addressed using video analysis methods.

Video analysis offers advantages when dealing with data: Firstly, it allows multiple reproducibility (i.e., the same source can be watched several times, rewound, shifted forward, or even seen frame by frame). Secondly, it allows multiple views (i.e., different observers, even the subjects of the video, can view and discuss individually or in collaboration, the same source; or multiple cameras can be set to capture the same event from different angles). Nonetheless, video transcription can be highly time-consuming. This can be coped with by transcribing selected extracts only: those more relevant to the defined focus of analysis (Heath et al. 2010). Another issue is that the methodologies of video analysis are not formally established in the social sciences yet (Heath et al. 2010), partly because practitioners are more focused on the practice than on describing the method (Jordan and Henderson 1995).

Having said that, in the mid-1990s, Jordan and Henderson presented a set of interaction analysis principles for analysing video excerpts based on years of practice for studying interaction between humans, and between humans and artefacts in an environment (Jordan and Henderson 1995). The proposed focuses of analysis of this type of audiovisual material are: the timeline of the events (e.g., beginnings and endings, internal structure of events); the temporal organization of the activity (e.g., rhythmicity or periodicity, talk vs. nonverbal activity, low activity vs. high activity, participation patterns); the spatial organization of the activity (e.g., public vs. private space, personal vs. shared space, body distance); whether there are breaches and repairs; and what is the role of artefacts and technologies during the interaction. The authors make a distinction between talk-driven interaction and instrumental interaction related to verbal and nonverbal activities, respectively. The latter refers to activities mainly driven by the manipulation of physical objects (e.g., technologies, artefacts) and where talk may happen as subsidiary to the physical activity.

Audiovisual recordings of music interaction often deal with little verbal communication; thus the instrumental interaction approach may provide a theoretical ground for studying these data. Some researchers have used video analysis in different settings for understanding tabletops and this continuum from talk-driven interaction to instrumental interaction (e.g., Hornecker 2008; Hornecker et al. 2008; Marshall et al. 2009, 2011; Rick et al. 2011; Tuddenham et al. 2010). Evidence has been found which shows that collaborative music performance on musical tabletops can be seen as a clear example of instrumental interaction (see Sect. 14.6.4). Thus, empirical work using video analysis can help an understanding of collaboration with musical tabletops from an instrumental interaction perspective.

Working in a group is a recommended practice in order to discuss the audiovisual material (Heath et al. 2010; Jordan and Henderson 1995). The aim of such research discussions is to confirm the individual findings and develop themes from repetitive patterns. In addition, the participation of the subjects of the video is a recurrent practice (Jordan and Henderson 1995), close to the ethnographic approach of collaborative filmmaking of involving the subjects (Ruby 2000).

14.3.3 Practical Issues

Using video raises a set of practical issues in the three sequential stages of research of, first, collecting audiovisual data; second, analysing these data; and, third, disseminating the results (Heath et al. 2010). When collecting data, depending on the location, permission may be needed. Also, before video-recording participants, an informed consent form is necessary. Furthermore, other decisions have to be taken and justified such as the position of the camera/s, or what period of action will be recorded. As Jordan and Henderson argue, those verbal and nonverbal interactions that precede the official beginning and come after the official ending may have crucial meaning (Jordan and Henderson 1995). At the stage of analysing data, some questions that emerge are: what is the focus of analysis; what are the selection criteria of the extracts to be analysed; or how can the verbal vs. nonverbal activities be transcribed, among others. Finally, when disseminating the results, the question of how to best show video-based results is raised.

In music interaction, when collecting data there exists the additional problem of dealing with music creation and intellectual property rights. In most jurisdictions, musicians have the copyright protection to their music by default. Thus, a question that arises is how to deal with audiovisual material derived from musical sessions when disseminating the results. In this case, a license grant to be signed in the informed consent form could be considered, that could be chosen from the Creative Commons[2] licenses, which provide a varied range of protections and freedoms for creatives. In this case, the license grant in the consent form should permit the researcher using and excerpting (in whole or in part) the music content for research purposes.

14.4 Example 1: Exploratory Research Approach

In this section, we first present the notion of exploratory research as a research method that allows one to acquire preliminary data on an undefined problem. Afterwards, we reveal the video analysis process undertaken in a study of a multi-touch musical tabletop adopting this approach.

[2]http://creativecommons.org

14.4.1 Exploratory Research

Exploratory research allows us to build an initial understanding of an undefined problem with preliminary data, and helps to identify how to further approach that problem (Lazar et al. 2009). Exploratory research is a research method applied in the social sciences (Berg 2001; Murchison 2010). It can be seen as a type of case study where gathering data may be undertaken before defining a research question, which may be useful as a pilot study or as a prelude of longer research (Berg 2001). In ethnographic research, exploratory research may be appropriate when starting a topic with no previous experience, no hypotheses, and no prior research questions, and the research tends to be more open-ended with outcomes more descriptive rather than analytical (Murchison 2010).

14.4.2 The Study

The purpose of this study was to design and evaluate a musical tabletop prototype. The team was formed by people with interdisciplinary backgrounds e.g. computer science, music, education, anthropology, or interaction design. The motivation was to design a simple and collaborative tabletop interface, in order to have a first insight on how beginners, experts, or both, collaborate. For detailed information of the study, refer to Laney et al. (2010).

The design of the prototype was highly constrained. There were four identical areas distributed in each side of a rectangle interface, each area with five buttons, four triggered one different pre-composed sound each, and the fifth switched between speakers and headphones mode. The interface had only discrete parameters, with affordances for up to four players given this strict division by the sides of a rectangle. The interaction was multi-touch.[3]

We worked with 12 participants (beginners and experts), in three groups of four users. The approach was exploratory as an initial step for understanding collaboration and collective musical engagement using this prototype (see Fig. 14.2). The evaluation was task-based, with a final individual questionnaire about the experience. There were three main tasks to be performed with time constraints, which were: sound exploration (3 min), structured composition with a coordinator (seven parts of 1 min each, thus 7 min in total), and free improvisation (5–10 min). Each participant had two signs with the messages of "sounds good" and "sounds bad", which could be raised at any moment of the performance to facilitate participants to give their opinion about the musical results. During the sessions, it was noted that participants tended to use verbal communication for decision

[3]Multi-touch interaction refers to the detection of multiple (two or more) points of contact on a touch sensing surface.

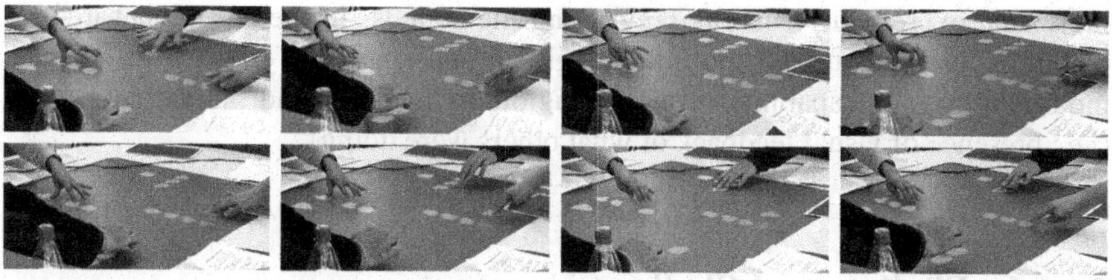

Fig. 14.2 Sequence of gestures when interacting with the multi-touch prototype

Table 14.1 Video transcription sample: free improvisation task performed by a group of four users

TC	User	Verbal	Nonverbal	Codes
00:16:56	#2	Let's go with the bass	–	Roles, decision making
00:17:00	#2	I like it, it has some electronic beats	–	Aesthetics, music results
00:17:26	#2	I think we are improvising	–	Music results
00:17:26	#4	I like the bass	–	Aesthetics
00:17:38	#4	–	"Sounds good" up	Musical engagement
00:17:40	#2	–	"Sounds good" up	Musical engagement

making, mainly to discuss the different musical tasks (before but also during their performance). After the musical tasks performance, we asked them some open questions about the collaborative musical experience, which animated discussion. We videoed all the sessions.

14.4.3 Video Analysis

For building our own coding scheme of themes and as a first insight to the data, we adopted an inductive procedure of, first, transcribing the video interactions identifying key moments (e.g., verbal and nonverbal communication); second, grouping the transcripts by codes; and third, generating themes as general explanations from the categorization of the codes (Laney et al. 2010). This approach was adapted from grounded theory (Glaser and Strauss 1967; Lazar et al. 2009), which is a research method used in the social sciences that derives theoretical explanations from the collected data with no hypotheses in mind. We contrasted these results with existing coding schemes in order to strengthen the emergent themes. Refer to Table 14.1 to see a sample extract of the video transcription and categorization.

We recognised initial themes as concepts and dichotomies present in collaborative music making such as beginners vs. experts' goals; individual vs. shared controls; awareness of others; and private vs. shared spaces. In the case of private vs. shared spaces, for example, participants reported the need of more features for individual expressivity such as previewing the sounds. In the case of awareness of others, users requested the need of global and shareable controls for mutual modifiability (i.e., capability of modifying others' actions) and mutual awareness (i.e., presence of visual feedback of what others were doing).

14.4.4 Findings and Challenges

We found that a minimal and highly constrained musical tabletop prototype can be engaging for beginners, but less for experts, who tended to ask for a broader set of features for promoting their personal musical expressivity. Arguably, video analysis has revealed an initial set of themes related to collaboration and musical engagement between beginners and experts on musical tabletops.

With respect to the evaluation, an exploratory approach with four groups of participants may be useful but vague. Thus, a larger-scale task-based evaluation with varied groups of musicians would help to collect more detailed and significant data. Of the three tasks planned for the evaluation, the structured composition with a coordinator was the most difficult to follow by participants because time was very constrained. Sound exploration and free improvisation were closer to the open-ended task approach, where tasks are less tied to specific actions to be performed with specific time constraints. A further exploratory approach using video analysis could be to just evaluate open tasks less tied to time, and in more realistic settings, named *in situ* or in the wild studies (Marshall et al. 2011; Rogers et al. 2007). This approach could attenuate the stress of finishing tasks on time, and promote more creative and spontaneous interactions, in tune with creative activities such as music.

14.5 Example 2: Participatory Design Approach

In this section, we describe the participatory design approach, which attempts to establish an active collaboration between users and designers. After, we distil from a participatory design perspective, how audiovisual material of users' interactions with the TOUCHtr4ck prototype is used for further video analysis.

14.5.1 Participatory Design

Participatory design is a term that refers to a design approach that invites users—who are not necessarily designers—to become part of the design process of a product (Schuler and Namioka 1993). Participants may be experts or potential users of the product, for example. Participatory design is used in a wide range of disciplines which depend on creative processes, design iterations, and users interactions e.g. software design, product design, graphic design, web design or urban planning, among others. Participatory design dates back to the 1970s in Scandinavian countries with the practice of cooperative design (Bødker et al. 1993). Accordingly, cooperative design tended to happen in trade unions where there was active cooperation between users and designers as part of the design process of computer applications for the workplace, with the notion that designers have to make sure to incorporate users' contributions. In both cooperative design and participatory design, there exists a more decentralised and democratic approach to the design process, when compared to more traditional approaches. This collaborative approach engages different opinions and perspectives which might improve considerably the design of the artefact discussed.

Understanding the interactions between people and computers forms part of the HCI discipline. An example of participatory design in HCI and music technology is the A20 (Bau et al. 2008). The authors collaborated with users in order to design and test the A20 musical device, a prototype with a tangible interface that has audio input and output. The aim of the device is to allow users to explore music and sound. The evaluation consisted of two parts; firstly, there was an assessment of the perceptual characteristics of the device (sonic and haptic) by performing a set of tasks; secondly, users and designers were invited to imagine new interfaces of the instrument based on several interaction mappings of gesture-based interaction. This approach allowed researchers to share with users the iterative design process of their prototypes. Moreover, it was a channel for discovering expected and unexpected functionalities when using the novel device.

14.5.2 The Study

The purpose of this study was to design and evaluate TOUCHtr4ck, a musical tabletop prototype, taking into consideration the lessons learned in the previous exploratory study. The team was formed by people with interdisciplinary backgrounds e.g. computer science, music, anthropology, interaction design, or philosophy. The motivation was to design a simple, collaborative, tabletop interface for creating real-time music, with enough freedom to engage experimentation, and with division of tasks in order to engage egalitarian collaborations between users. For detailed information of the study, refer to Xambó et al. (2011).

The design of TOUCHtr4ck was based on a constrained interface. It consisted of a four track recorder, which allowed musicians to record up to four sounds. It was also possible to modify the musical result adding some effects and/or global controls. The available tasks of recording/playing and transforming/mixing were visually divided into two main circles. The concept of flexible layout was introduced allowing participants to show or hide the different tracks or effects. The interface had both discrete and continuous parameters, with affordances for two to four players mainly because of the presence of these two main circles in a square surface. The interaction was multi-touch.

Fig. 14.3 A group of two people playing the TOUCHtr4ck prototype

We gathered two groups of two people for an informal evaluation: one beginners' group, and one experts' group. The experts' group experimented with an early version of the prototype during ten minutes using pre-built and recorded sounds of their choice, and then they informally commented about the experience with suggestions on interface design close to participatory design practices, and their comments were annotated. For instance, experts indicated the need of more precision for the recording controls. The experts' group also stated the usefulness of the flexible layout approach. Beginners were first introduced to the music technology concept of multiple track recording. Then, they were supplied with a Stylophone, an easy-to-use musical instrument, in order to facilitate the recording of their own sounds, and to let them be focused on the musical tabletop interface. The beginners' group was asked to play, and their musical exploration and spontaneous thinking aloud were videoed with a handheld camera. This group of beginners had the option of comparing between one version with flexible layout vs. one with fixed layout. Beginners also gave feedback about the interface design and using a participatory design approach (see Fig. 14.3).

14.5.3 Video Analysis

We first transcribed the conversations and interactions held during the video recordings of the beginner group, with special attention to interface design comments. From these data, we identified some features that should be changed, improved or added. For example, participants manifested the need of more accuracy when controlling the synchronization of sounds. Also, more graphical precision with the effects knobs was suggested, as shown in Fig. 14.4. Furthermore, when comparing between a fixed and a flexible layout, the beginners chose the flexible option because it facilitated them to adjust the musical interface to their needs.

14.5.4 Findings and Challenges

Video analysis has provided a series of opinions and suggestions about how to improve further iterations of the interface design. In addition, this flexible layout

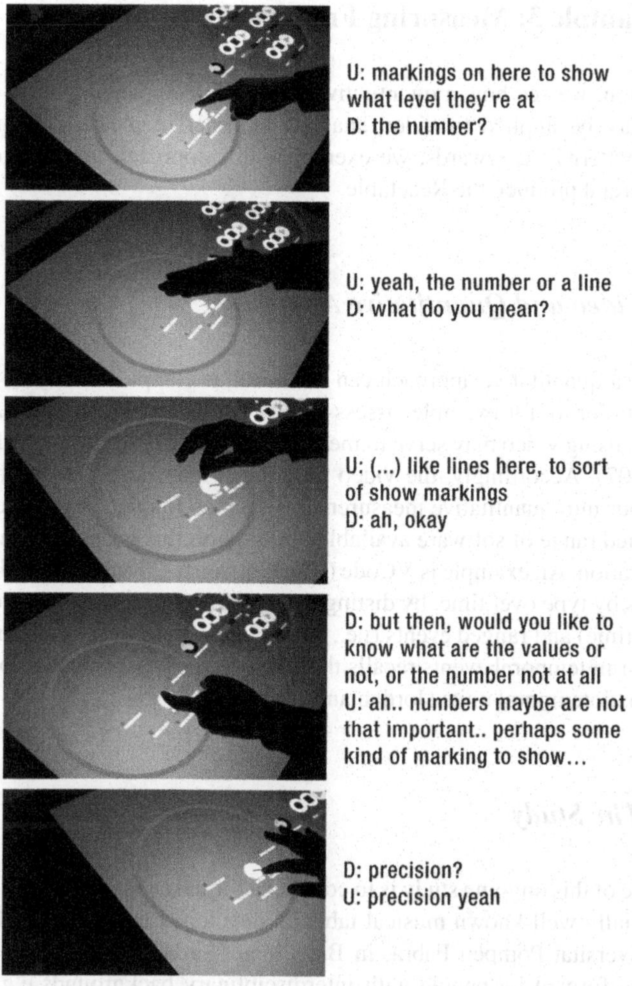

Fig. 14.4 Representative sequence of a user (U) suggesting to the researcher/designer (D) the addition of markings to the effects knobs

approach seems convenient for defining the level of constraint related to the expertise of the user. We conclude that video analysis has informally revealed an insight on what to do next in the design process of the prototype.

As a current methodological challenge, we need to conduct a more formal evaluation of this prototype to confirm our results, with groups of both beginners and experts. This would imply, firstly, the implementation of a minimum of suggested features such as better recording control or track synchronization, in order to fulfil the expectations of the participants, but without losing the experimental character which characterises the actual version. And, secondly, the musical interface should be tested with more participants applying similar conditions (e.g., similar open tasks, data gathering and data analysis).

14.6 Example 3: Measuring Frequencies Approach

In this section, we see how a quantitative approach, complementary to qualitative findings, may be applied to video analysis in order to measure frequencies of behaviour patterns. Afterwards, we exemplify this approach in an ongoing study of a commercial product, the Reactable.

14.6.1 Video and Quantitative Analysis

Sometimes, a quantitative approach can be useful as complementary of qualitative findings in order to, for example, assess results or confirm explanations. From this perspective, using video may serve to measure behaviour quantitatively (Martin and Bateson 2007). Accordingly, the video recordings may be coded by transcribing the behaviour into quantitative measurements such as frequencies of events. There exists a varied range of software available that support this quantitative approach to video annotation. An example is VCode (Hagedorn et al. 2008), which allows one to mark events by type over time, by distinguishing between momentary events (i.e., a moment in time) and ranged events (i.e., a moment in time with a certain duration). This interest in temporal events recalls the focuses of study of interaction analysis, based on spatiotemporal units (Jordan and Henderson 1995).

14.6.2 The Study

The purpose of this ongoing study is to conduct a formal evaluation of the Reactable, a commercially well-known musical tabletop developed in the Music Technology Group–Universitat Pompeu Fabra, in Barcelona (Jordà 2008; Jordà et al. 2005). The team is formed by people with interdisciplinary backgrounds e.g. computer science, music, psychology, anthropology, or interaction design. The motivation of this study is to understand what are the collaboration strategies that happen when using a complex and successful musical interface such as the Reactable in two representative contexts: museums with visitors, and music labs with musicians. So far, we have collected empirical data in both settings, and analysed the data of the latter, which informs this subsection.

The Reactable has a sophisticated design, with both discrete and continuous parameters, and with affordances for one to multiple players given its round shape. The interaction can be both using tangible objects and multi-touch. This use of tangible objects is also known as tangible interaction or tangible user interfaces (TUIs), which refers to the use of physical artefacts which both control and represent digital information on an interactive system (Ullmer and Ishii 2000).

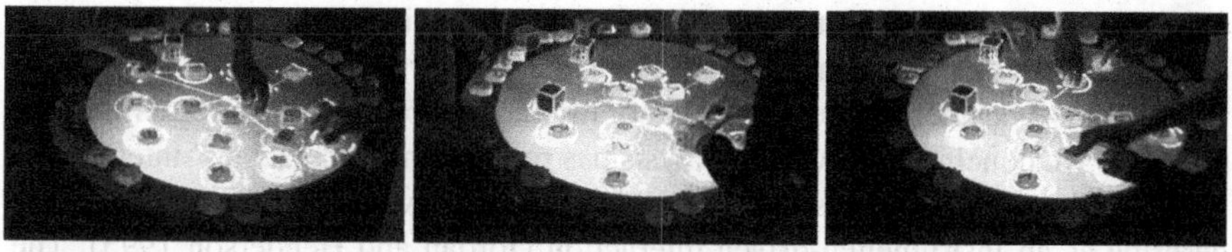

Fig. 14.5 Sequence of a group of three musicians improvising with the Reactable

For the music lab study, we videoed four open-task improvisations performed by four different groups of musicians, from two to four members each group (see Fig. 14.5). The collected audiovisual material consisted of 16 sessions of music improvisation with the Reactable, where the groups tended to play for 45 min, which was the maximum time allocated for each session.

14.6.3 Video Analysis

Since we ended up with ca. 180 min for each group and camera (out of two), we first synchronised the two cameras in a single video source in order to facilitate and reduce the potential time of analysis; where the close-up view was the main data source for the interactions on the table, and the large shot view was used to identify additional data such as people's gestures or eye-contact. For the coding scheme, three of the researchers of the team analysed and discussed the video data in order to develop and iteratively refine the themes, and then confirm them on more extracts, as recommended by Heath et al. (2010) and Jordan and Henderson (1995).

As we were interested in understanding the evolution of collaboration over time, we analysed whether there were significant differences between the sessions. We specifically explored whether collaboration among musicians increased or decreased over time, and whether the proportion of interaction strategies between participants changed over time. For that, we complemented qualitative findings with a quantitative approach of first identifying patterns of events, and then counting their frequencies using VCode. We identified some patterns of events such as invasions (rejected and accepted), takes (active and passive), and shared threads.[4]

14.6.4 Findings and Challenges

We found that the main change between sessions was qualitative. Whilst at the first sessions there was more collaborative exploration and serendipity, at the end there

[4]In the Reactable, each audio thread represents an audio channel, which are all in sync. It is possible to build threads by interconnecting tangible objects.

were more sophisticated interactions, which could be individual or collaborative, depending on the temporal unit of the session. For example, the endings of the sessions became particularly collaborative and sophisticated towards the last sessions. We conclude that video analysis has revealed how musicians' interactions with a tabletop TUI such as the Reactable exemplify what Jordan and Henderson describe as an instrumental-driven interaction (Jordan and Henderson 1995). The evidence has shown that interaction analysis using significant video extracts can help to explain these phenomena of nonverbal interaction, where music is the main channel of communication, and the interaction is artefact-driven by the manipulation of a tabletop musical tangible interface.

With regard to the methodology, using a quantitative approach with a small sample of groups (four in this case), can be useful when complemented with qualitative findings. In order to obtain significant results, though, a large-scale study should be conducted. However, the amount of video evidence can become enormous in that case, so strategies for less time-consuming video analysis techniques are required. Interaction log files may help by providing a complementary layer of information, if they were adapted to provide meaningful and higher-levels of information about collaboration (e.g., users' identification against objects' identification, users' identification against threads' identification).

14.7 Conclusion

In this chapter, we showed that the use of video in music performance can be a convenient and flexible tool for understanding interaction with musical tabletops, which can be used from a range of perspectives (e.g., exploratory, participatory, improvisational, quantitative vs. qualitative). The lessons learned from the examples presented of collaborative music interaction on musical tabletops may be relevant to both the sound and music computing, as well as the HCI communities, about how to deal with multi-player and complex interaction. For the former, a number of reliable HCI methods can help to evaluate and improve the interface design of novel interfaces for music, whilst for the latter the results can inform about how to deal with creative multi-player activities on interactive tabletops, which is currently a major topic of research in HCI. At present, the main corpus of video in music interaction research emerges from the long tradition of video-based studies of interaction in social sciences (Heath et al. 2010), with a wide range of analytic and methodological applications that we can borrow. We believe that a significant number of video-based studies that explore the issues of music interaction in general, and collaboration on shareable interfaces in particular, would help to build a specialised methodology of practice, which could be useful not only for the sound and music computing community, but also for other disciplines related to understanding group creativity and multi-player interaction.

Acknowledgements We wish to thank Eva Hornecker, Paul Marshall and Gerard Roma for lively discussions about several ideas reflected in this chapter. We are also thankful to all the participants of the studies for giving their time and insights. Thanks to Jennifer Ferreira and Minh Tran for their help. And last but not least, thanks to the organisers and participants of the BCS HCI 2011 Workshop for the opportunity to meet and share thoughts with other researchers about this exciting new field of Music Interaction.

References

Bau, O., Tanaka, A., & Mackay, W. E. (2008). The A20: Musical metaphors for interface design. In *Proceedings of NIME'08* (pp. 91–96). Genoa.

Berg, B. L. (2001). *Qualitative research methods for the social sciences*. Boston: Allyn and Bacon.

Blaine, T., & Perkis, T. (2000). The Jam-O-Drum interactive music system: A study in interaction design. In *Proceedings of DIS'00* (pp. 165–173). Brooklyn.

Bødker, S., Grønbæk, K., & Kyng, M. (1993). Cooperative design: Techniques and experiences from the Scandinavian scene. In D. Schuler & A. Namioka (Eds.), *Participatory design: Principles and practices*. Hillsdale: CRC/Lawrence Erlbaum Associates.

Bryan-Kinns, N., & Hamilton, F. (2012). Identifying mutual engagement. *Behaviour and Information Technology, 31*(2), 101–125.

Coughlan, T., & Johnson, P. (2006). Interaction in creative tasks: Ideation, representation and evaluation in composition. In *Proceedings of CHI'06* (pp. 531–540). Montreal.

Cox, C., & Warner, D. (2004). *Audio culture: Readings in modern music*. London: International Publishing Group Ltd.

Fiebrink, R., Morris, D., & Morris, M. R. (2009). Dynamic mapping of physical controls for tabletop groupware. In *Proceedings of CHI'09* (pp. 471–480). Boston.

Glaser, B. G., & Strauss, A. L. (1967). *Discovery of grounded theory: Strategies for qualitative research*. Chicago: Aldine Transaction.

Gresham-Lancaster, S. (1998). The aesthetics and history of the hub: The effects of changing technology on network computer music. *LMJ, 8*, 39–44.

Hagedorn, J., Hailpern, J., & Karahalios, K. G. (2008). VCode and VData: Illustrating a new framework for supporting the video annotation workflow. In: *Proceedings of AVI'08* (pp. 317–321). Naples.

Heath, C., Hindmarsh, J., & Luff, P. (2010). *Video in qualitative research*. London: Sage.

Hornecker, E. (2008). "I don't understand it either, but it is cool" visitor interactions with a multi-touch table in a museum. In *Proceedings of IEEE Tabletop 2008* (pp. 121–128). Amsterdam.

Hornecker, E., Marshall, P., Dalton, N. S., & Rogers, Y. (2008). Collaboration and interference: Awareness with mice or touch input. In *Proceedings of CSCW'08* (pp. 167–176). San Diego.

Iwai, T. (1999). Composition on the table. In *Proceedings of SIGGRAPH'99* (p. 10). Los Angeles.

Jordà, S. (2008). On stage: The reactable and other musical tangibles go real. *International Journal of Arts and Technology, 1*(3/4), 268–287.

Jordà, S., Kaltenbrunner, M., Geiger, G., & Bencina, R. (2005). The reacTable*. In *Proceedings of ICMC 2005* (pp. 579–582). Barcelona.

Jordan, B. (1996). Ethnographic workplace studies and computer supported cooperative work. In D. Shapiro, M. Tauber, & R. Traunmüller (Eds.), *The design of computer-supported cooperative work and groupware systems*. Amsterdam: North Holland/Elsevier Science.

Jordan, B., & Henderson, A. (1995). Interaction analysis: Foundations and practice. *The Journal of the Learning Sciences, 4*(1), 39–103.

Kiefer, C., Collins, N., & Fitzpatrick, G. (2008). HCI methodology for evaluating musical controllers: A case study. In *Proceedings of NIME'08* (pp. 87–90). Genoa.

Klügel, N., Friess, M. R., Groh, G., & Echtler, F. (2011). An approach to collaborative music composition. In *Proceedings of NIME'11* (pp. 32–35). Oslo.

Laney, R., Dobbyn, C., Xambó, A., Schirosa, M., Miell, D., Littleton, K., & Dalton, S. (2010). Issues and techniques for collaborative music making on multi-touch surfaces. In *Proceedings of SMC 2010* (pp. 146–153).

Lazar, J., Feng, J. H., & Hochheiser, H. (2009). *Research methods in human-computer interaction*. Chichester: Wiley.

MacDougall, D. (2006). *The corporeal image: Film, ethnography, and the senses*. Princeton: Princeton University Press.

Marshall, P., Fleck, R., Harris, A., Rick, J., Hornecker, E., Rogers, Y., Yuill, N., & Dalton, N. S. (2009). Fighting for control: Children's embodied interactions when using physical and digital representations. In *Proceedings of CHI'09* (pp. 4–9). Boston.

Marshall, P., Morris, R., Rogers, Y., Kreitmayer, S., & Davies, M. (2011). Rethinking 'multi-user': An in-the-wild study of how groups approach a walk-up-and-use tabletop interface. In *Proceedings of CHI'11* (pp. 3033–3042). Vancouver.

Martin, P., & Bateson, P. (2007). *Measuring behaviour: An introductory guide*. Cambridge: Cambridge University Press.

Mealla, S., Väljamäe, A., Bosi, M., & Jordà, S. (2011). Listening to your brain: Implicit interaction in collaborative music performances. In *Proceedings of NIME'11* (pp. 149–154). Oslo.

Murchison, J. (2010). *Ethnography essentials: Designing, conducting, and presenting your research*. San Francisco: Wiley.

Patten, J., Recht, B., & Ishii, H. (2002). Audiopad: A tag-based interface for musical performance. In *Proceedings of NIME'02* (pp. 1–6).

Pink, S. (2006). *The future of visual anthropology: Engaging the senses*. London: Routledge.

Poupyrev, I., Lyons, M. J., Fels, S., & Blaine, T. (2001). New interfaces for musical expression. In *Proceedings of CHI'01 EA* (pp. 491–492).

Rauh, A. (2009). *Assessing usability and user experience in Tangible User Interfaces. A case study of the Reactable*. Master thesis, Universitat Pompeu Fabra.

Rick, J., Marshall, P., & Yuill, N. (2011). Beyond one-size-fits-all: How interactive tabletops support collaborative learning. In *Proceedings of IDC'11* (pp. 109–117). Ann Arbor.

Rogers, Y., Connelly, K., Tedesco, L., Hazlewood, W., Kurtz, A., Hall, R. E., Hursey, J., & Toscos, T. (2007). Why it's worth the hassle: The value of in-situ studies when designing Ubicomp. In *Proceedings of Ubicomp* (pp. 336–353). Innsbruck.

Ruby, J. (1980). Franz Boas and early camera study of behaviour. *The Kinesis Report, 3*(1), 6–11.

Ruby, J. (2000). *Picturing culture: Explorations of film and anthropology*. Chicago: University of Chicago Press.

Schuler, D., & Namioka, A. (1993). *Participatory design: Principles and practices*. Hillsdale: CRC/Lawrence Erlbaum Associates.

Stowell, D., Plumbley, M. D., & Bryan-Kinns, N. (2008). Discourse analysis evaluation method for expressive musical interfaces. In *Proceedings of NIME'08* (pp. 81–86). Genoa.

Tuddenham, P., Kirk, D., & Izadi, S. (2010). Graspables revisited: Multi-touch vs. tangible input for tabletop displays in acquisition and manipulation tasks. In *Proceedings of CHI'10* (pp. 2223–2232). Atlanta.

Ullmer, B., & Ishii, H. (2000). Emerging frameworks for tangible user interfaces. *IBM Systems Journal, 39*(3–4), 915–931.

Wanderley, M. M., & Orio, N. (2002). Evaluation of input devices for musical expression: Borrowing tools from HCI. *Computer Music Journal, 26*(3), 62–76.

Xambó, A., Laney, R., & Dobbyn, C. (2011). TOUCHtr4ck: Democratic collaborative music. In *Proceedings of TEI'11* (pp. 309–312). Funchal.

Chapter 15
Towards a Participatory Approach for Interaction Design Based on Conceptual Metaphor Theory: A Case Study from Music Interaction

Katie Wilkie, Simon Holland, and Paul Mulholland

Abstract "Music Interaction" is the term for interaction design within the domain of music. In areas such as music, the ability to engage effectively in certain activities tends to be restricted to those who have acquired detailed knowledge of domain-specific theories, terminologies, concepts or processes. It can be challenging to design or enhance user interfaces for software able to support novices in these kinds of musical activities. One promising approach to this challenge involves translating musicians' implicit domain knowledge into patterns known as conceptual metaphors, which are metaphorical extensions of recurring patterns of embodied experience applied to abstract domains, and using this information to inform interaction designs for music. This approach has been applied experimentally with some success to designing user interfaces. However, to the best of our knowledge, this present work is the first to consider in detail the use of Conceptual Metaphor Theory as a key component of a participatory design process. In this chapter we present a participatory approach to Music Interaction design based on the principles of Conceptual Metaphor Theory. We posit that such an approach will facilitate the development of innovative and intuitive interaction designs for both novices and experts alike.

15.1 Introduction

The recent advent of music video games such as Guitar Hero (Activision 2010) and Wii Music (Nintendo 2008) has afforded those with limited knowledge of music the opportunity to experience the pleasure of collaborating with others to produce music, albeit in highly simplified respects through interacting with games

K. Wilkie (✉) • S. Holland • P. Mulholland
Music Computing Lab, Centre for Research in Computing, The Open University, Milton Keynes MK7 6AA, UK
e-mail: k.l.wilkie@open.ac.uk; s.holland@open.ac.uk; p.mulholland@open.ac.uk

S. Holland et al. (eds.), *Music and Human-Computer Interaction*, Springer Series on Cultural Computing, DOI 10.1007/978-1-4471-2990-5_15,

controllers. Although the popularity of such games reflects music's pervasiveness within society, in general they afford limited engagement with the structural properties of the music, focusing instead on note-on note-off accuracy. Thus the ability to engage with, understand and analyze more technical aspects of music such as voice leading and harmonic and rhythmic progressions is generally restricted to those with detailed knowledge of the terminologies, notations and processes used in the domain. Since such knowledge is often only acquired through detailed academic study, many novices who wish to interact with the structural properties of music on a deeper level are excluded from doing so. Furthermore, it can prove challenging to create user interaction designs for music software that can facilitate the exploration and manipulation of the structural properties of music without requiring detailed pre-existing knowledge of the domain. We hypothesize that if we can represent detailed domain knowledge that experienced musicians have acquired in a manner that exploits pre-existing and universally held embodied knowledge, we will be able to lower some of the barriers to structural understanding of musical concepts. Furthermore, we posit that such an approach would result in Music Interaction designs that were intuitively usable to both experts and novices alike.

A promising foundation for this work can be found in the identification of "recurring patterns of our sensory-motor experience" (Johnson 2005) known as image schemas. These image schemas, which it is argued form the basis of our understanding of abstract concepts through the creation of conceptual metaphors (Johnson 2005), are often identified through methods such as the analysis of spoken and written dialog. Exploring the application of image schema, conceptual metaphor and embodied theories in diverse domains have have reported encouraging results. These domains include:

- Music theory (Saslaw 1996, 1997; Zbikowski 1997a, b; Brower 2000; Larson 1997; Johnson 1997; Johnson and Larson 2003; Eitan and Granot 2006; Eitan and Timmers 2010).
- Interaction design (Hurtienne and Blessing 2007; Hurtienne et al. 2008; Treglown 1999).
- Sound Interaction design (Antle et al. 2008, 2009).
- Evaluating Music Interaction designs (Wilkie et al. 2009, 2010).

Applications of image schema, conceptual metaphor and embodied cognition theories to interaction design (Hurtienne and Blessing 2007; Hurtienne et al. 2008; Treglown 1999) and Sound Interaction design (Antle et al. 2008, 2009) to date have focused primarily on using image schemas and conceptual and embodied metaphors as a bridge between the requirements and the user interface controls. However, the use of conceptual metaphors as a tool for facilitating design discussions with domain experts is, to the best of our knowledge, as yet unexplored. In this chapter we present a collaborative approach to interaction design within the domain of music, using domain-specific conceptual metaphors derived from dialog betweeen experts to elicit the functional requirements for a gesture-controlled interactive system. These functional requirements are then used to develop materials for participatory design sessions with musicians, with the aim of designing a wearable instrumented jumpsuit for exploring and manipulating chord progressions.

15.2 Embodied Understanding of Abstract Concepts

As briefly outlined, research into the development of conceptual models has led to the hypothesis that our understanding of melody, harmony, rhythm and other musical concepts is grounded in structures named image schemas (Saslaw 1996, 1997; Zbikowski 1997a, b; Brower 2000). Image schemas may be defined as repeating patterns of our sensory-motor experiences of space, orientation, forces and interactions with other bodies in our environment (Lakoff and Núñez 2000; Johnson 2005; Rohrer 2005, 2007). These image schemas are typically identified through the analysis of linguistic expressions in spoken or written text. In such an analysis, it is important to distinguish between literal or metaphorical uses of images schemas. For example compare the phrase "put the toys in the box" with the superficially similar phrase "the melody is in the key of C". In both examples, the preposition "in" suggests the use of the CONTAINER image schema. However, in the first example the container is a tangible object, while in the second example, the container, the key of C, is an abstraction.

The real power of image schemas in this context is that their inherent structure can give rise to a number of entailments which can then be used to carry out intuitive reasoning operations. For example, if we consider the nested containers shown in Fig. 15.1 below, we can infer quickly and intuitively, without the need for formal reasoning, that if an object is inside a container and that container is itself inside another container, then the object must be inside both containers.

Mapping image schemas onto corresponding aspects of a target domain to create conceptual metaphors enables us to structure our understanding of abstract concepts in other, often unrelated, domains (Johnson 2005) such as music (Saslaw 1996, 1997; Zbikowski 1997a, b; Brower 2000), philosophy (Lakoff and Johnson 1999) or arithmetic (Lakoff and Núñez 2000). For example, analysis of the seemingly simple phrase "the melody starts in C major and moves up to G major", a simplified portrayal of which is shown in musical notation in Fig. 15.2 below, reveals a number of metaphorical mappings, all of which have a corresponding representation in standard music notation:

- The CONTAINER image schema has been mapped onto the target domain of key, resulting in the conceptual metaphor A KEY IS A CONTAINER FOR MELODY. This mapping is demonstrated in standard musical notation by the declaration of the key signature in terms of numbers of flat or sharp notes at the beginning of each stave.
- The UP-DOWN (sometimes referred to as VERTICALITY) image schema has been mapped onto the target domain of pitch, resulting in the conceptual

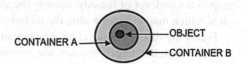

Fig. 15.1 Representation of the relationships between OBJECTS and nested CONTAINERS

Fig. 15.2 Simple melody and bass line, illustrating modulation from the key of C major to G major

Fig. 15.3 Representation of the SOURCE-PATH-GOAL image schema showing LOCATION objects on the PATH

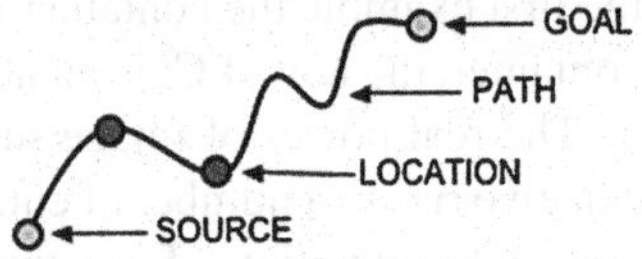

metaphor HIGH PITCH IS UP/LOW PITCH IS DOWN. This mapping is exemplified by the position of the stave lines in standard music notation, as the vertical position of a stave line is directly proportional to the pitch to be sounded.

- The SOURCE-PATH-GOAL image schema, a representation of which is shown in Fig. 15.3 above, has been mapped onto the target domain of melody, resulting in the conceptual metaphor MELODY IS MOVEMENT ALONG A PATH. This mapping is demonstrated in standard music notation by considering each note on a stave to be a location within a path where the final note marks the end of the path.

Furthermore, applying the principles of metaphorical entailment allow us to deduce that, based on the example given above, the key of G major sounds after the key of C major and that G is higher than C with respect to the melody part (assuming octave equivalence).

The Invariance Principle (Zbikowski 1997b) is the cognitive phenomenon whereby only aspects of the source domain which appear to be coherent with the target domain retain their salience. In general, inappropriate aspects of mappings are automatically and tacitly ignored. For example, in the case of the conceptual metaphor defined above, MELODY IS MOVEMENT ALONG A PATH, only the applicable aspects of the SOURCE-PATH-GOAL image schema are perceived to map to the concept of melody, namely the start and finish points and the locations, all of which map to notes within the melody.

Following this principle, although alternative mappings between different image schemas and the target domain are possible, the number of image schematic correspondences between the source and target domains tends to be indicative of the usefulness and likely retention of the mapping. For example, as Zbikowski (1997b) notes, fruits do not readily map to pitch.

The ability to apply image schemas to abstract domains through the process of creating conceptual metaphors via metaphorical mapping makes image schemas and conceptual metaphors extremely useful for intuitive communication and for informal reasoning. Existing applications of these theories to music theory and user interface design will be discussed further in the sections below.

15.2.1 *Embodied Understanding of Musical Concepts*

Previous research into the application of image schema and conceptual metaphor theories to musical concepts to date has typically focused on the analysis of the various musical concepts and phenomena described by music theorists. For example an analysis of Riemann's treatise "Systematic Study of Modulation as a Foundation for the Study of Musical Form" by Saslaw (1996) reveals Riemann's understanding of harmonic progression and modulation to be grounded in the CONTAINER and SOURCE-PATH-GOAL image schemas. Saslaw further claims that Riemann's understanding of modulation hinges on the use of the FORCE image schema to allow movement from one key CONTAINER to the next. In a related example of applying embodied theory to music theory texts, Saslaw (1997) presents a detailed analysis of the text in Schenker's "Free Composition" and Schoenberg's "The Musical Idea and the Logic, Technique, and Art of its Presentation". Arguing that both composers' theories can be attributed to their prior experiences of forces, Saslaw posits that Schenker associates musical progressions with a journey through life, while Schoenberg refers to movement back and forth towards the tonic in terms of a struggle between opposing forces.

Applying the principles of Conceptual Metaphor Theory to the development of a cognitive theory of musical meaning, Brower (2000) identifies the CONTAINER, CYCLE, CENTRE-PERIPHERY, BALANCE and SOURCE-PATH-GOAL image schemas as central to our understanding of harmonic relationships such as the cycle of fifths and the resolution of unstable pitches. By contrast, Larson (1997) focuses on the analysis of short melodic patterns, introducing the concepts of MUSICAL GRAVITY, MUSICAL MAGNETISM and MUSICAL INTERTIA based on the FORCE image schema, arguing that these "musical forces" influence the direction of melodic movement. Larson identifies a series of three and four note stepwise patterns beginning and ending on the notes of the tonic major triad, i.e. "stable" notes, whose formulation was determined by the power exerted on the pattern by each of the three concepts. Through reviewing various texts written by music theorists, Larson identifies a number of hidden repetitions within musical structure that correspond to the patterns he himself identified, suggesting that composition as well as structural analysis is influenced by prior sensory-motor experiences.

In an attempt to establish patterns of association between space and motion and changes in musical parameters such as pitch and tempo, Eitan and Granot (2006) carried out a series of experiments asking participants to specify the movement of an imaginary character in response to various musical stimuli. In general, although the results revealed that a change in a musical parameter was often associated with changing motion, the participants' response to ascending pitch was surprising. Despite associating descending pitch with spatial descent, the association between ascending pitch and spatial ascent was weaker, contrary to the structural inferences of a commonly used conceptual metaphor in Western music, HIGH PITCH IS UP/LOW PITCH IS DOWN (Zbikowski 1997a, b). In summary, the application of conceptual metaphor theory to musical concepts has led to some promising results, but further work is needed to establish the extent to which even widely accepted image schemas and conceptual metaphors are an active mechanism in particular cases.

15.2.2 User Interface Design Using Image Schemas

It is instructive to contrast conceptual metaphors with other kinds of metaphor. The use of what are known as user interface metaphors is a technique frequently recommended to interaction designers (Preece et al. 1994). The aim of this technique is to allow users to readily make inferences about how to operate unfamiliar user interfaces by mapping existing skills and knowledge from some familiar source domain. However, the much narrower use specifically of image schemas and conceptual metaphors to drive user interface design has received relatively little attention.

Discussing the design of a basic file management system, Treglown (1999) concluded that Conceptual Metaphor Theory holds promise as a foundation for user interface design. Echoing his conclusion nearly a decade later, Hurtienne and Blessing (2007) argued that a design could be considered intuitively usable if the user can subconsciously apply prior knowledge when interacting with a design. Exploring the potential of using conceptual metaphors as a technique for developing more intuitive interaction designs, they designed a series of basic user interfaces using slider and button controls. The layout and configuration of the controls were designed variously either to support or contradict basic conceptual metaphors such as GOOD IS UP and MORE IS UP. Participants were asked to select the most appropriate button or move the slider in the most appropriate direction based on their response to a simple phrase employing the conceptual metaphor under investigation. In general, the results of experiments indicated that configuring the controls to support the conceptual metaphors led to a reduction in response times.

Investigating the potential of image schemas as a "meta-language" for the analysis and design of an invoice verification and posting system, Hurtienne et al. (2008) concluded that such an approach encouraged them to focus more on the essential user interface requirements of the system. When taken in conjunction with the encouraging results of Hurtienne and Blessing's (2007) experiments, their conclusion lends further weight to the claim that Image Schema and Conceptual Metaphor Theories hold promise as a foundation for a methodology for Music Interaction design.

15.2.3 Sound Interaction Design Using Embodied Concepts

Investigating the advantages of a system that employed the principles of embodiment to facilitate user interactions with the system, Antle et al. (2008, 2009) designed an interactive system that enabled users to manipulate basic musical parameters such as pitch, tempo and volume simply by moving their bodies. The interactions were based on mapping specific movements with changes in sound parameters, for example equating fast movements with fast tempo. The results of their experiments indicated that an interaction layer employing embodied metaphors led to a system that was easier to learn. This result adds further weight to the claim that the application of embodied theories to interaction designs results in more intuitive interactions. However, the results were inconclusive with respect to enhancing the ability of children to learn musical concepts (Antle et al. 2008).

15.2.4 Using Conceptual Metaphors to Evaluate Music Interaction Designs

Earlier research has demonstrated how conceptual metaphors can be used to evaluate the designs of various interactions within music software, illuminated by two case studies (Wilkie et al. 2009, 2010). Through analysing the transcript of a dialog between experienced musicians discussing the melodic, harmonic and rhythmic structure of a short excerpt of music, we were able to identify a number of conceptual metaphors the musicians used to form their understanding of the musical properties of the excerpt. By comparing the conceptual metaphors with the layout, configuration and behaviour of the Music Interaction designs within two examples of music software, Harmony Space (Holland 1992, 1994; Holland et al. 2009) and GarageBand (Apple Inc 2009), we were able to identify instances where the designs either fully or partially supported the conceptual metaphors or, conversely, contradicted them. In many cases, areas of design tension or contradiction arose due to the desire to enhance support for specific tasks or musical parameters, reducing the support for other tasks or concepts. For example, in Harmony Space, the desire to support tasks associated with harmonic analysis led to less emphasis on the support for voice leading. The results of the evaluation of Harmony Space led to improvements in the design of the tracing functionality to increase support for the conceptual metaphor HARMONIC PROGRESSION IS MOVEMENT ALONG A PATH.

The success of these evaluations provides supportive evidence to the claim that Conceptual Metaphor Theory can be used as a foundation for a methodology for Music Interaction design. The following sections explore how such a methodology can be extended to deal with a participatory approach to design.

15.3 Developing a Participatory Approach to Music Interaction Design

A participatory approach to design generally involves the prospective users of the system in the design process (Kensing and Blomberg 1998; Preece et al. 1994). In our case, we are designing for novices who lack knowledge of the terminology, notations and processes in the domain. Such prospective users have a very limited foundation upon which to base their design decisions. Consequently, although novices are an important target for our interaction designs, our approach focuses primarily on conducting participatory design sessions with experienced musicians. We posit that by encouraging experienced musicians to formulate their design decisions based on conceptual metaphors underpinning their musical knowledge, this will help in the framing of relevant design structures and relationships in ways that afford wider accessibility. In this way, we hope to capitalize on musicians' domain knowledge and thus develop interaction designs for music software that are intuitively usable to novice users.

Despite the use of Conceptual Metaphor Theory as a technique to inform new and redesign existing interactions (Antle et al. 2008, 2009; Hurtienne and Blessing 2007; Hurtienne et al. 2008; Treglown 1999; Wilkie et al. 2009, 2010), to the best of our knowledge, no studies have used this theory as a tool to facilitate design discussions with domain experts. In the following sections we propose a methodology for such a task with respect to Music Interaction design.

15.3.1 Identifying and Validating Task Specific Conceptual Metaphors

A valuable initial step in such a methodology is to validate any relevant domain-specific conceptual metaphors provisionally identified in previous research (such as those noted in Sect. 15.2.1) that the design must address. It is also useful to identify and validate any previously overlooked applications of conceptual metaphors in the domain that may be relevant to the design. All such conceptual metaphors can then be used to develop materials such as functional requirements and scenarios for participatory design sessions and to evaluate any resulting design decisions.

To this end, and following on from the previous study mentioned in Sect. 15.2.4 and discussed in more detail in Wilkie et al. (2009, 2010), two further studies were carried out with a number of groups of musicians as follows. All of the musicians involved in the two studies played at least one instrument regularly and many also had at least some experience of teaching, arranging, conducting or composition.

In the first study, pairs of participants were provided initially with a set of words and subsequently a set of images and asked to use the words or images to describe and discuss short excerpts of music. The set of provided words included pairs of polar opposites, for example "moving" and "static", "up" and "down" and "attracting" and "repelling" and some additional standalone words such as "journey". The words were chosen specifically to encourage the participants to describe aspects of the excerpts in such a way that they might reveal their structural understanding of musical concepts in terms of conceptual metaphors. The images chosen for the second part of the first study were simple clip art drawings, again in some cases representing polar opposites such as a full glass and an empty box, as well as some additional standalone images such as balanced scales. Again, the aim was to encourage participants to discuss aspects of the excerpts, eliciting conceptual metaphors.

In the second study, groups of participants were asked to bring along an excerpt of a piece of music they knew well and to discuss aspects of that music such as the melody, harmony and rhythm with the other participants in the group. The participants were given the opportunity to play or sing the musical excerpt to aid their discussion if they so wished. Following the discussion, a score and an audio recording of a short piece of music was provided to the participants. Again the participants were asked to discuss the structural aspects of the piece with each other. As with the previous study, the aim was to encourage the participants to discuss musical concepts in a manner that would elicit conceptual metaphors associated with the structural aspects of the excerpts they were discussing.

The analysis of the results of the two studies is still being completed. However, a preliminary review of the first study, together with the results of the initial analysis of the transcriptions of the second study indicate that several image schemas and their related conceptual metaphors can be validated, supporting their provisional identification by previous studies (Brower 2000; Eitan and Granot 2006; Eitan and Timmers 2010; Saslaw 1996, 1997; Zbikowski 1997a, b). For example, the image schemas most frequently used by the participants in the second study were SOURCE-PATH-GOAL, PART-WHOLE, CONTAINER, MATCHING, MOMENTUM, UP-DOWN and SCALE in descending order of frequency. Interestingly, despite the BALANCE image schema being identified by Brower (2000) as part of a set of image schemas central to our understanding of harmonic relationships, analysis of the transcriptions did not reveal any instances of this image schema. Subject to further analysis, this could indicate either that the tasks the musicians were asked to carry out did not lend themselves to discussing aspects of the excerpts in terms of balance, or that the musicians did not conceptualise the structural properties of the excerpts in terms of balance. This finding highlights two factors:

- The importance of engaging with participants with appropriate levels of expertise in the topics being discussed in order to ensure conceptual metaphors of a suitable conceptual depth are elicited.

- The importance of designing tasks in such a way as to elicit as wide a coverage of relevant domain-specific conceptual metaphors as possible.

These considerations are important to ensure adequate coverage of conceptual metaphors to support the design of more complex interactions.

15.3.2 *Participatory Music Interaction Design*

Following the identification of relevant image schema and conceptual metaphors as outlined above, the next step will be to establish the extent to which experienced musicians can collaborate to develop music interaction designs based on musical conceptual metaphors. To this end, a participatory design study involving musicians will be carried out. The participants chosen for the study should have knowledge of the principles of harmonic theory and at least some experience of conducting, arranging or composing. During the study, the participants will be asked to work in groups to design a wearable instrumented jumpsuit that would allow wearers with limited knowledge of harmonic theory to create, explore and manipulate simple chord progressions. The participants will be provided with a set of materials to provide input into the design discussions:

- A list of functionality that the jumpsuit will support, for example detecting if the wearer places an object in the pocket or moves their feet.
- A list of musical tasks that the jumpsuit can support, for example playing a chord sequence or adding a chord to an existing chord sequence.
- A series of simple pencil sketches based on musical conceptual metaphors. For example a sketch based on the conceptual metaphor HARMONIC PROGRESSION IS MOVEMENT ALONG A PATH, may involve chord objects moving along a road and fading into the distance.
- A list of mappings between the functionality that the jumpsuit supports and the associated image schema, for example mapping movement of the arms to movement along a path (SOURCE-PATH-GOAL).

The lists of functionality and musical tasks list the functional requirements that the jumpsuit must support, while the sketches and mappings will encourage the participants to link the requirements to the relevant musical conceptual metaphors. We posit that such an approach will not only provide a framework for testing whether conceptual metaphors can be used to drive participatory design discussions but also enable us to determine which musical conceptual metaphors can be mapped to physical gestures in practice.

15.3.3 *Validating Design Decisions*

In order to validate the designs produced during the participatory design sessions, we propose to develop a prototype of the instrumented jumpsuit based on aspects of the design outputs of all of the study sessions. We will evaluate the prototype to determine the degree to which participatory approach based on the principles of Conceptual Metaphor Theory was able to produce a useful design that is usable by novices.

15.4 Conclusion

Previous studies have established that using conceptual or embodied metaphors have at least two clear applications in HCI. Firstly to guide user interaction design (Antle et al. 2008, 2009; Hurtienne and Blessing 2007; Hurtienne et al. 2008; Treglown 1999) and secondly to evaluate, critique and improve existing designs (Wilkie et al. 2009, 2010).

To the best of our knowledge, the present work is the first application of Conceptual Metaphor Theory to drive participatory design discussions in any domain. In interaction design for domains such as music, where it can be particularly hard for novices to articulate concepts, this approach appears particularly well suited to promote the framing of expert knowledge in an accessible form.

References

Activision (2010). Guitar Hero. http://www.guitarhero.com/. Accessed Jan 2013.

Antle, A. N., Droumeva, M., & Corness, G. (2008). Playing with the sound maker: Do embodied metaphors help children learn? In *Proceedings of the 7th international conference on Interaction design and children* (pp. 178–185). Chicago: ACM.

Antle, A. N., Corness, G., & Droumeva, M. (2009). Human-computer-intuition? Exploring the cognitive basis for intuition in embodied interaction. *International Journal of Arts and Technology, 2*(3), 235–254.

Apple Inc. (2009). Garage Band '09. http://www.apple.com/ilife/garageband/. Accessed Sept 2009.

Brower, C. (2000). A cognitive theory of musical meaning. *Journal of Music Theory, 44*(2), 323–379.

Eitan, Z., & Granot, R. Y. (2006). How music moves: Musical parameters and listeners' images of motion. *Music Perception, 23*(3), 221–247.

Eitan, Z., & Timmers, R. (2010). Beethoven's last piano sonata and those who follow crocodiles: Cross-domain mappings of auditory pitch in a musical context. *Cognition, 114*(3), 405–422.

Holland, S. (1992). Interface design for empowerment: A case study from music. In S. Holland & A. Edwards (Eds.), *Multimedia interface design in education*. Heidelberg: Springer.

Holland, S. (1994). Learning about harmony with Harmony Space: An overview. In G. Wiggins & M. Smith (Eds.), *Music education: An artificial intelligence approach*. Heidelberg: Springer.

Holland, S., Marshall, P., Bird, J., Dalton, S. N., Morris, R., Pantidi, N., Rogers, Y., & Clark, A. (2009). Running up Blueberry Hill: Prototyping whole body interaction in harmony space. In *Proceedings of the 3rd conference on tangible and embodied interaction* (pp. 92–98). New York: ACM.

Hurtienne, J., & Blessing, L. (2007). Design for intuitive use – Testing image schema theory for user interface design. In *Proceedings of the 16th international conference on engineering design* (pp. 1–12). Paris, France.

Hurtienne, J., Israel, J. H., & Weber, K. (2008). Cooking up real world business applications combining physicality, digitality, and image schemas. In *Proceedings of the 2nd international conference on tangible and embedded interaction* (pp. 239–246). New York: ACM.
Johnson, M. (1997). Embodied musical meaning. *Theory and Practice, 22–23*, 95–102.
Johnson, M. (2005). The philosophical significance of image schemas. In B. Hampe & J. Grady (Eds.), *From perception to meaning: Image schemas in cognitive linguistics* (pp. 15–33). Berlin: Walter de Gruyter.
Johnson, M. L., & Larson, S. (2003). "Something in the Way She Moves" - Metaphors of Musical Motion. *Metaphor and Symbol, 18*(2), 63–84.
Kensing, F., & Blomberg, J. (1998). Participatory design: Issues and concerns. *Computer Supported Cooperative Work, 7*(3), 167–185.
Lakoff, G., & Johnson, M. (1999). *Philosophy in the Flesh*. New York: Basic Books.
Lakoff, G., & Núñez, R. E. (2000). *Where mathematics comes from*. New York: Basic Books.
Larson, S. (1997). Musical forces and melodic patterns. *Theory and Practice, 22–23*, 55–71.
Nintendo (2008) Wii Music http://www.wiimusic.com/launch/index.html/. Accessed Feb 2012.
Preece, J., Rogers, Y., Sharp, H., Benyon, D., Holland, S., & Carey, T. (1994). *Human–Computer Interaction*. London: Addison-Wesley.
Rohrer, T. (2005). Image schemata in the brain. In B. Hampe & J. Grady (Eds.), *From perception to meaning: Image schemata in cognitive linguistics*. Berlin: Walter de Gruyter.
Rohrer, T. (2007). The body in space: Dimensions of embodiment. In T. Ziemke, J. Zlatev, R. Frank, & R. Dirven (Eds.), *Body, language, and mind: Embodiment* (pp. 339–378). Berlin: Walter de Gruyter.
Saslaw, J. K. (1996). Forces, containers, and paths: The role of body-derived image schemas in the conceptualization of music. *Journal of Music Theory, 40*(2), 217–243.
Saslaw, J. K. (1997). Life forces: Conceptual structures in Schenker's free composition and Schoenberg's the musical idea. *Theory and Practice, 22–23*, 17–34.
Treglown, M. (1999). *The role of metaphor in user interface design*. Unpublished Ph.D. thesis. Milton Keynes, UK: The Open University.
Wilkie, K., Holland, S., & Mulholland, P. (2009). Evaluating musical software using conceptual metaphors. In *Proceedings of the 23rd British Computer Society conference on human computer interaction* (pp. 232–237). British Computer Society.
Wilkie, K., Holland, S., & Mulholland, P. (2010). What can the language of musicians tell us about music interaction design? *Computer Music Journal, 34*(4), 34–48.
Zbikowski, L. M. (1997a). Conceptual models and cross-domain mapping: New perspective on theories of music and hierarchy. *Journal of Music Theory, 41*(2), 193–225.
Zbikowski, L. M. (1997b). Des Herzraums Abschied: Mark Johnson's theory of embodied knowledge and music theory. *Theory and Practice, 22–23*, 1–16.

Chapter 16
Appropriate and Complementary Rhythmic Improvisation in an Interactive Music System

Toby Gifford

Abstract One of the roles that interactive music systems can play is to operate as real-time improvisatory agents in an ensemble. A key issue for such systems is how to generate improvised material that is musically appropriate, and complementary to the rest of the ensemble. This chapter describes some improvisation strategies employed by the Jambot (a recently developed interactive music system) that combine both imitative and 'intelligent' techniques. The Jambot uses three approaches to mediate between imitative and intelligent actions: (i) mode switching based on confidence of understanding, (ii) filtering and elaboration of imitative actions, and (iii) measured deviation from imitative action according to a salient parametrisation of the action space. In order to produce appropriate rhythms the Jambot operates from a baseline of transformed imitation, and utilises moments of confident understanding to deviate musically from this baseline. The Jambot's intelligent improvisation seeks to produce complementary rhythms by manipulating the level of ambiguity present in the improvisation to maintain a balance between novelty and coherence.

16.1 Introduction

Interactive music systems are computer systems for musical performance, with which human performers interact in live performance. A number of interactive music systems operate in what Rowe (1993) describes as the player paradigm, meaning the system has some degree of autonomy, acting as an independent musical agent. Such systems seek to produce improvised material that is, in some sense, musically appropriate, and complementary to the rest of the ensemble. This chapter

T. Gifford (✉)
Queensland Conservatorium of Music, Griffith University, Brisbane, Australia
e-mail: t.gifford@griffith.edu.au

S. Holland et al. (eds.), *Music and Human-Computer Interaction*, Springer Series on Cultural Computing, DOI 10.1007/978-1-4471-2990-5_16,

describes a recently developed interactive music system – the Jambot – and the approaches it employs to produce appropriate and complementary percussive improvisation.

Notions of musical appropriateness and complementarity are difficult to pin down. What is appropriate in a musical setting is contextual; improvisation suited to an experimental computer music concert may not be suitable for a performance in a nightclub for example. The Jambot was designed primarily as a performance tool for Western popular dance music styles. In this discussion I use the term appropriate to mean musically congruent with the rest of the ensemble. My use of the term complementary has an extra nuance, in that it refers to a gestalt property of the combined rhythm of the agent with the rest of the ensemble. So, for example, directly imitating the rest of the ensemble would be appropriate, but not complementary.

The Jambot is a computational music agent that listens to an audio stream and produces improvised percussive accompaniment in real-time, using both imitative and intelligent[1] actions. This chapter describes the mechanisms the Jambot uses to mediate between imitative and musically intelligent actions, and concludes that the use of an imitative strategy as a behavioural baseline is useful for robust interaction.

Human-Agent Interaction (HAI) is a subfield of HCI in which the interface between the human and the computer is a computational agent. Agent interfaces are "shifting users' view of information technology from tools to actors" (Persson et al. 2001:349). From an HCI perspective these interfaces are interesting because they potentially provide a more natural mode of engagement with the computer. Two common paradigms in HAI are identifiable:

1. The use of knowledge representations, symbolic processing, and other techniques of Good Old Fashioned Artificial Intelligence to generate actions based on 'understanding'.
2. The use of imitative actions, where the computational agent mirrors the actions of the human, typically with a twist to obfuscate the direct relationship.

A key issue then is how to seamlessly combine these two paradigms. This chapter describes three abstract approaches to mediating between imitative and intelligent actions, and their implementations in the Jambot.

The Jambot uses imitative actions to produce appropriate rhythms, and intelligent actions to produce complementary rhythms. Complementarity is achieved by striking a balance between novelty and coherence. This balance is altered by manipulating the level of metric ambiguity present in the improvisation.

The rest of this chapter is organised as follows. Section 16.2 gives a brief overview of the Jambot. Interactive music systems are described in Sect. 16.3, focussing on the categorisation of systems as generative, transformative and

[1]The term intelligent is being used here loosely. For the purposes of this chapter, actions taken on the basis of some abstract musical 'understanding' (such as beat-tracking or chord recognition) are termed intelligent.

reflexive. Section 16.4 describes the Jambot's imitative improvisation technique, whilst Sect. 16.5 discusses mechanisms for combining imitation with elements of musical understanding. Sections 16.6 and 16.7 describe the Jambot's intelligent improvisation technique. Section 16.8 concludes.

16.2 The Jambot

The Jambot is a computational music agent, designed for real-time ensemble improvisation. It listens to a musical audio stream, such as an audio feed from a live band or DJ, and improvises percussive accompaniment. Some details of the Jambot have been published in more detail elsewhere (Gifford and Brown 2008, 2009, 2010), so here I give only an overview sufficient to give context for discussion of the Jambot's interaction design. The Jambot's user interface is depicted in Fig. 16.1.

The Jambot listens to the percussive elements of the input signal. It has three percussive onset detection algorithms that are particularly tuned to discriminating between the hi-hat, snare and kick drum sounds of a standard drum-kit.

Once the input signal has been parsed into percussive onsets, these onsets are analysed in terms of some musical attributes. The Jambot performs beat tracking (estimating the period and phase of the beat), metre induction (estimating the number of beats in a bar and the location of the downbeat) and a variety of rhythmic analyses.

The rhythmic analyses used are (i) what periodicities are present in the rhythm, (ii) how consonant the periodicities are, (iii) how well aligned to the metre the

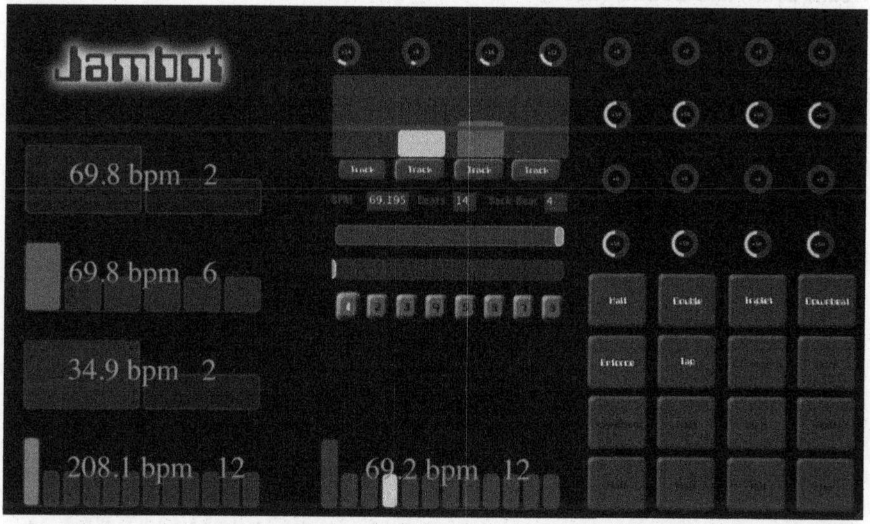

Fig. 16.1 The Jambot user interface

rhythm is, (iv) how syncopated the rhythm is, and (v) how densely the rhythm fills the bar. Together these attributes form a salient parametrisation of rhythm space. More detail on the rhythmic model is given in Gifford and Brown (2010).

The Jambot uses both imitative and musically intelligent strategies of improvisation, and combines these two strategies in several ways, discussed below.

16.3 Interactive Music Systems

The Jambot is an interactive music system. Interactive music systems are computer systems for musical performance, in which a human performer interacts with the system in live performance. The computer system is responsible for part of the sound production, whether by synthesis or by robotic control of a mechanical instrument. The human performer may be playing an instrument, or manipulating physical controllers, or both. The system's musical output is affected by the human performer, either directly via manipulation of synthesis or compositional parameters through physical controllers, or indirectly through musical interactions.

There exists a large array of interactive music systems, varying greatly in type, ranging from systems that are best characterised as hyperinstruments – instruments allowing meta-control over timbral parameters (Machover and Chung 1989) – to those that are essentially experiments in artificial intelligence. The type of output varies from systems that perform digital signal processing on input from an acoustic instrument, through systems that use techniques of algorithmic improvisation to produce MIDI output, to systems that mechanically control physical instruments. More detailed surveys of interactive music systems may be found in Rowe (1993), Dean (2003) and Collins (2006).

16.3.1 Transformative vs. Generative Systems

Rowe (1993) describes a multidimensional taxonomy of interactive music systems. One dimension of this taxonomy classifies systems as transformative or generative. Transformative systems transform incoming musical input (generally from the human performer playing an instrument) to produce output. Generative systems utilise techniques of algorithmic composition to generate output. Rowe also discusses a third category of sequencing, however in this discussion I will consider sequencing as a simple form of generation. This categorisation is somewhat problematic, in that systems may be composed of both transformative and generative elements. None-the-less it provides a useful launching point for discussion.

Transformative systems have the capacity to be relatively robust to a variety of musical styles. They can benefit from inheriting musicality from the human performer, since many musical features of the input signal may be invariant under the transformations used. A limitation of transformative systems is that they tend to produce output that is either stylistically similar (at one extreme), or musically unrelated (at the other extreme), to the input material.

Generative systems use algorithmic composition techniques to produce output. The appropriateness of the output to the input is achieved through more abstract musical analyses, such as beat tracking and chord classification. Generative systems are able to produce output that has a greater degree of novelty than transformative systems. They are often limited stylistically by the pre-programmed improvisatory approaches, and may not be robust to unexpected musical styles.

16.3.2 Reflexive Systems

Within the class of transformative systems is the subclass of reflexive (Pachet 2006) systems. Reflexive systems are transformative in the sense that they manipulate the input music to produce an output. The manipulations that they perform are designed to create a sense of similarity to the input material, but without the similarity being too obvious. Pachet describes reflexive systems as allowing the user to "experience the sensation of interacting with a copy of [themselves]" (ibid:360).

Reflexive systems aim to model the style of the input material, for example using Markov models trained on a short history of the input. Reflexive systems enjoy the benefits of transformative systems, namely inheriting musicality from the human input, and so are robust to a variety of input styles. The use of abstracted transformations means that they can produce surprising and novel output whilst maintaining stylistic similarity to the input. Reflexive systems do not, however, perform abstract musical analyses such as beat tracking.

16.3.3 Beyond Reflexivity

The Jambot is designed to combine transformative and generative approaches. In this way it hopes to achieve the flexibility and robustness of a transformative system, whilst allowing for aspects of abstract musical analysis to be inserted into the improvisation. The idea is to operate from a baseline of transformed imitation, and to utilise moments of confident understanding to deviate musically from this base-line.

Another limitation of many reflexive and generative systems is they model music using statistical/mathematical machinery such as Markov chains, neural nets, genetic algorithms and the like. The difficulty with these models is they do not directly expose salient musical features. This means the parameters of these models do not afford intuitive control over the musical features of their output. The Jambot utilises a representation of musical rhythm that parametrises rhythm space into musically salient features. This way the Jambot's generative processes may be controlled intuitively.

16.4 Transformational Mimesis

Transformational mimesis is the term I use for the Jambot's imitative approach to musical improvisation. Transformational mimesis involves imitating the percussive onsets in the musical stream as they are detected, but with various transformations designed to obfuscate the direct relationship with the input stream.

For transformational mimesis to sound musical it is essential that onsets in the signal are detected with very low latency. This way the Jambot can play a percussive sample as soon as an onset is detected and the timing difference between the actual onset and the Jambot's response will be imperceptible to a human listener.

Transformational mimesis seeks to transform the pattern of onsets, so that the imitation is not too readily identifiable as being an imitation. The Jambot uses several approaches to transforming the detected onsets.

One simple way in which the detected onsets are transformed is by triggering percussive of different timbres from the original onsets. Indeed, the Jambot itself does not have any synthesis capacity, but rather sends out MIDI note-on messages that may be used to fire samples from any synthesiser. Used in this way transformational mimesis may be thought of as a real-time timbral remapping technique.

The timbral remapping is made more effective due to the Jambot's ability to discriminate between three streams of percussive onsets, tuned to the hi-hat, snare and kick drum sounds of a standard drum-kit. Because of this the Jambot is able to selectively highlight any of these streams, which again helps to obscure its direct relationship to the source signal.

Another simple transformation is to filter the onsets in some fashion, such as by a threshold amplitude. This can have the effect of highlighting important musical events. Transformations that select certain events from the original are reminiscent of Aristotle's discussion of mimesis in the context of drama:

> At first glance, mimesis seems to be a stylizing of reality in which the ordinary features of our world are brought into focus by a certain exaggeration ... Imitation always involves selecting something from the continuum of experience, thus giving boundaries to what really has no beginning or end. Mimesis involves a framing of reality that announces that what is contained within the frame is not simply real. Thus the more "real" the imitation the more fraudulent it becomes. (Aristotle in Davis 1999:3)

A limitation of the purely imitative approach is that it is difficult (or musically dangerous) for the Jambot to take any action other than when an onset is detected and still be musically convincing. For music that is very busy (i.e. has a lot of percussive onsets) simple imitation can be quite effective. For music that is more sparse this can render the purely imitative approach ineffective or, at best, musically naive. Transformational mimesis need not, however, be a purely imitative approach. Indeed, the Jambot uses musical understanding gathered from its perceptual algorithms to help transform its imitation.

16.5 Combining Imitative and Intelligent Actions

The Jambot utilises imitation, but also takes actions based on its musical understanding of what would be an appropriate and complementary action. The critical point is an issue of baseline. From the perspective of classical AI, an improvising agent would operate from a blank slate; any actions taken would be on the basis of parsing the incoming music into some higher order understanding, and utilising its musical knowledge to generate an appropriate response.

I suggest, on the other hand, taking direct imitation as a baseline, and utilising musical understanding to deviate artfully from this baseline. This way the agent can communicate its musical understanding in a manner that minimises the cognitive dissonance with the human performer(s). Imitation also provides an engineering efficiency as an aesthetically meaningful fallback when computational resources exceed the real-time demands during performance. The Jambot utilises three approaches to combining imitative and intelligent interaction strategies:

1. Switching based on confidence.
2. Filtering and elaborating imitative actions.
3. Measured deviation from imitative actions according to the dimensions of a salient parametrisation of action space.

In the next sections I describe these approaches in more detail.

16.5.1 Switching Based on Confidence

The first approach is a simple switching mechanism according to the Jambot's confidence in its understanding of the musical context. Below a confidence threshold the Jambot operates entirely by transformational mimesis, and above the threshold it uses intelligent generation.

A QuickTime video example of the Jambot using this approach is demonstrates this approach.[2] The example is a recording of the Jambot jamming live to a pre-recorded audio loop. The loop is the infamous Amen Break, a short recording of a few bars of a rhythm played on a standard drum-kit. The Jambot is improvising accompaniment on percussion.

The improvisation uses mode switching based on confidence – if the Jambot is confident of its beat-tracking then it improvises using intelligent generation. When it loses confidence, it switches to imitative improvisation until confidence is regained.

The Jambot maintains a continually updating measure of confidence to enable this behaviour. The confidence measure is incremented (up to a maximum of one) when an onset occurs at an expected time, and is decremented (down to a minimum of zero) when an onset occurs at an unexpected time.

[2] http://dr.offig.com/research/chapters/MusicInteraction/ModeSwitching.mov

Through the jam, the playback speed of the loop was manually altered. When the playback speed is altered drastically, for a period of time the Jambot loses confidence in its beat tracking, and switches to imitative improvisation. Usually within a few seconds it adjusts to the new tempo, regains confidence, and switches back to intelligent generation. The result is a relatively seamless improvisation that is robust to drastic tempo changes.

16.5.2 Filtering and Elaborating

The second approach uses the detected onsets as a 'decision grid'. Each time an onset is detected the Jambot considers its potential actions. If the onset is tolerably close to a beat then it will make a stochastic decision regarding whether to take an action. If it does take an action, that action may be to play a note (which note depends on whether this beat is believed to be the downbeat or not), or to play a fill. A fill consists of playing a note followed by a series of notes that evenly subdivide the gap between the current beat and the next beat. If the onset is not tolerably close to the beat then no action is taken.

The musical understanding, which in this case consists of knowing where the upbeat and downbeat are, is thus incorporated by adjusting the weightings for choosing whether or not to play a note, for which note to play, and for the timing of the subdivisions of the fills. The inclusion of fills means the Jambot is not restricted to playing only when an onset is detected, however, anchoring the decision points to detected onsets provides a good deal of robustness.

Using this second approach, if no onsets are detected then the Jambot does not play. Although in some musical circumstances it would be desirable to have the Jambot playing in the absence of any other percussion (such as taking a solo), in practice limiting the Jambot to play only when other ensemble members are playing is frequently desirable. It means that the Jambot will not play before the piece starts or after it finishes, and allows for sharp stops; the most the Jambot will ever spill over into a pause is one beat's worth of fill. It also means that it is highly responsive to tempo variation, and can cope with sudden or extreme time signature changes – this is especially robust when used in combination with confidence thresholding described above.

16.5.3 Measured Deviation

The third approach is to make measured deviations from a baseline of imitative action according to a salient parametrisation of rhythm space. As discussed above, the Jambot performs a number of rhythmic analyses, which together form a salient representation of rhythm space. This means that any rhythm can be represented in terms of a collection of musically significant parameters. This type of representation contrasts with statistical/mathematical models (such as Markov chains and neural nets) commonly used in interactive music systems, whose internal parameters do not correspond directly to musically significant features.

Representing rhythm space via a salient parametrisation facilitates deviation from a baseline of imitative action in a musically appropriate fashion. For example, the Jambot's understanding of the musical context might suggest that a lower rhythmic density would be musically appropriate. It can then transform its imitative action along the dimension of density, whilst holding the other rhythmic properties constant.

In this way the generated rhythm still benefits from inheriting musicality from the human performer along some rhythmic dimensions, whilst having the flexibility to incorporate musical decisions along other dimensions.

16.6 Intelligent Improvisation

The Jambot is an improvisatory agent. Its goal is to improvise appropriate and complementary accompaniment in an ensemble setting. In order to codify a sense of musical appropriateness and complementarity I have drawn upon theories of music perception, discussions of improvisatory approaches by practicing musicians, and my own experience as an improvising musician.

The main insight I have utilised is that in improvisation one must strike a balance between novelty and coherence. The sections below elaborate on this idea, and introduce some theories of music perception relating to musical expectations and ambiguity. The gist of the argument is that multiple expectations give rise to ambiguities, and manipulation of the level of ambiguity present in the improvisation provides a mechanism for altering the balance between novelty and coherence.

16.6.1 Balancing Novelty and Coherence

In musical improvisation there is a constant tension between maintaining a coherent foundational structure and keeping the music interesting. Free jazz saxophonist David Borgo comments:

> When a listener (or performer) hears what they expect, there is a low complexity and what is called "coherence" ... and when they hear something unexpected, there is "incoherence" ... this creates a dilemma for improvisers, since they must constantly create new patterns, or patterns of patterns, in order to keep the energy going, while still maintaining the coherence of the piece. (Borgo and Goguen 2004)

Part of the art of improvisation (and composition) is to strike the right balance between coherence and novelty. For the listener to perceive coherent and interesting structure, there must be some element of surprise, but not so much that the listener loses their bearings entirely.

Fig. 16.2 Coherence meter

'good' music ... must cut a path midway between the expected and the unexpected ... If a works musical events are all completely unsurprising ... then the music will fulfill all of the listener's expectations, never be surprising – in a word, will be boring. On the other hand, if musical events are all surprising ... the musical work will be, in effect, unintelligible: chaotic. (Kivy 2002)

The Jambot attempts to strike a balance between coherence and novelty by maintaining an ongoing measure of the level of coherence in the improvisation. Figure 16.2 shows a whimsical portrayal of a 'coherence meter', displaying a real-time measure of coherence. A target level of coherence is set either by a human or by a higher order generative process. The Jambot then takes musical actions to alter the level of coherence to maintain this target.

In order to model the coherence level of the improvisation, I have utilised notions of ambiguity and expectation. Borgo and Kivy (above) both identify expectations regarding future musical events as a key contributor to the sense of coherence of the improvisation. By creating multiple expectations, a sense of ambiguity can be created, which in turn decreases the coherence level. Conversely by highlighting a single expectation, ambiguity is decreased and coherence increased. The next sections discuss some theories from music perception regarding musical expectations, and their relation to notions of musical ambiguity.

16.6.2 Expectation

The importance of taking account of the dynamic nature of musical expectations when considering musical experience has been acknowledged in the music theory literature for some time (Lerdahl and Jackendoff 1983; Meyer 1956; Narmour 1990; Bharucha 1991) but has only recently been translated into computational descriptions and rarely been the basis for algorithmic music systems. Meyer suggests that affect in music perception can be largely attributed to the formation and subsequent fulfillment or violation of expectations. His exposition is compelling but imprecise as to the exact nature of musical expectations and their mechanisms of formation.

A number of extensions to Meyer's theory have been proposed, which have in common the postulation of at least two separate types of expectations; structural expectations of the type considered by Meyer, and dynamic expectations. Narmour's (1990) theory of Implication and Realisation, an extension of Meyer's work, posits two cognitive modes; one of a schematic type, and one of a more innate expectancy type. Bharucha (1991) also discriminates between schematic expectations (expectations derived from exposure to a musical culture) and veridical expectations (expectations formed on the basis of knowledge of a particular piece).

Huron (2006) has recently published an extensive and detailed model of musical expectations that builds further on this work. He argues there are, in fact, a number of different types of expectations involved in music perception, and that indeed the interplay between these expectations is an important aspect of the affective power of the music. Huron extends Bharucha's categorisation of schematic and veridical expectations, and in particular makes the distinction between schematic and dynamic expectations.

Dynamic expectations are constantly learned from the local context. Several authors have suggested that these dynamic expectations may be represented as statistical inferences formed from the immediate past (Huron 2006; Pearce and Wiggins 2006). Like Bharucha, Huron argues that the interplay of these expectancies is an integral part of the musical experience.

16.6.3 Metre as an Expectational Framework

Musical metre is frequently described as the pattern of strong and weak beats in a musical stream. From the point of view of music psychology, metre is understood as a perceptual construct, in contrast to rhythm, which is a phenomenal pattern of accents in the musical surface.

Metre is inferred from the surface rhythms, and possesses a kind of perceptual inertia. In other words, once established in the mind, a metrical context tends to persist even when it conflicts with the rhythmic surface, until the conflicts become too great (Lerdahl and Jackendoff 1983:17).

Within the music perception field metre is generally considered as an expectational framework against which the phenomenal rhythms of the music are interpreted (London 2004; Huron 2006). Jones (1987), for example, argues that metre should be construed as a cognitive mechanism for predicting when salient musical events are expected to happen. This description of metre has been widely accepted within the music psychology community (Huron 2006; Large 1994; London 2004).

16.6.4 Ambiguity

Meyer (1956) identifies ambiguity as a mechanism by which expectations may be exploited for artistic effect. In this context ambiguity refers to musical surfaces that create several disparate expectations. The level of ambiguity in the music creates a cycle of tension and release, which forms an important part of the listening experience in Meyer's theory. An ambiguous situation creates tension – the resolution of which is part of the art of composition (or improvisation).

> Ambiguity is important because it gives rise to particularly strong tensions and powerful expectations. For the human mind, ever searching for the certainty and control which comes with the ability to envisage and predict, avoids and abhors such doubtful and confused states and expects subsequent clarification. (Meyer 1956:27)

Temperley notes that ambiguity can arise as the result of multiple plausible analyses of the musical surface:

> Some moments in music are clearly ambiguous, offering two or perhaps several analyses that all seem plausible and perceptually valid. These two aspects of music – diachronic processing and ambiguity – are essential to musical experience. (Temperley 2001:205)

I have been discussing ambiguity as inversely related to coherence. However, the notion of ambiguity has an extra nuance that is worth mentioning. Certainly, an unambiguous (musical) situation should be highly coherent. A high level of ambiguity, however, should not be confused with vagueness; where vagueness implies a lack of any strong suggestion, ambiguity implies a multiplicity of strong suggestions.

16.6.5 Multiple Parallel Analyses

The concept of systems of musical analysis that yield several plausible results has been posited by a number of authors as a model of human musical cognition. Notably, Jackendoff (1992:140) proposed the multiple parallel analysis model. This model, which was motivated by models of how humans parse speech, claims that at any one time a human listening to music will keep track of a number of plausible analyses in parallel.

In a similar vein, Huron describes the competing concurrent representation theory. He goes further to claim that, more than just a model of music cognition, "Competing concurrent representations may be the norm in mental functioning" (2006:108).

16.6.6 Ambiguity in Multiple Parallel Representations

An analysis system that affords multiple interpretations provides a natural mechanism for the generation of ambiguity. In discussing their Generative Theory of Tonal Music (GTTM), Lerdahl and Jackendoff observe that their "rules establish not inflexible decisions about structure, but relative preferences among a number of logically possible analyses" (1983:42), and that this gives rise to ambiguity. In saying this Lerdahl & Jackendoff are not explicitly referencing a cognitive model of multiple parallel analyses; the GTTM predates Jackendoff's construction of this model, and does not consider real-time cognition processes. Indeed it was considerations of the cognitive constraints involved in resolving the ambiguities of multiple interpretations that led Jackendoff to conclude that the mind must be processing multiple analyses in parallel (Jackendoff 1992).

Temperley has revisited the preference rule approach to musical analyses in a multiple parallel analyses model:

> The preference rule approach [is] well suited to the description of ambiguity. Informally speaking, an ambiguous situation is one in which, on balance, the preference rules do not express a strong preference for one analysis over another ... At any moment, the system has a set of "best-so-far" analyses, the analysis with the higher score being the preferred one. In some cases, there may be a single analysis whose score is far above all others; in other cases, one or more analyses may be roughly equal in score. The latter situation represents synchronic ambiguity. (2001:219)

In a similar spirit, Huron (2006:109) argues that multiple parallel analyses (or competing concurrent representations, as he calls them) must all be generating expectations, and consequently must give rise to the kind of expectational ambiguity that was argued above to play a central role in producing musical affect.

16.7 Utilising Metrical Ambiguity

The view of metre as an expectational framework suggests the possibility of manipulating the level of metric ambiguity as an improvisatory device. As discussed above the Jambot seeks to maintain a target level of ambiguity in the ensemble improvisation. The Jambot does this by simultaneously reinforcing a multiplicity of metrical possibilities when it believes the coherence level to be too high. The multiplicity of expectations creates ambiguity, which decreases the coherence.

Conversely if the coherence level is assessed to be too low (i.e. the improvisation has become too chaotic), then the Jambot will strongly reinforce the most plausible metric possibility to lower the ambiguity level.

The Jambot has three different modes for controlling the level of ambiguity:

1. **Disambiguation:** utilise only the most plausible metre.
2. **Ambiguation:** utilise all plausible metres with equal weight, regardless of their plausibility.
3. **Following:** utilise all plausible metres, with weight according to their plausibility.

A QuickTime video example of the Jambot using these three modes is provided for demonstration.[3] In this demonstration the Jambot is jamming to a short drum loop. The Jambot is also playing a drum-kit. It starts jamming in *Disambiguation* mode. The combined rhythm strongly reinforces the dominant metric interpretation. The Jambot then switches to *Ambiguation* mode, in which it seeks to highlight all plausible metric interpretations. The triplet feel of the kick drum gives rise to a secondary metric interpretation (of being in three) which the Jambot highlights. The combined rhythm has a more polyrhythmic feel. The Jambot then switches to *Following* mode. The combined rhythm still has a polyrhythmic feel, but is more suggestive of the dominant metre. Finally the Jambot switches back to *Disambiguation*, resulting in a fairly 'straight' rhythm.

16.8 Conclusion

Interactive music systems produce musical material in performance. For systems that are operating as independent musical agents in an ensemble, a key issue is how to improvise material that is musically appropriate, and complementary to the ensemble.

This chapter argued that, in order to produce appropriate and complementary accompaniment in a robust fashion, it is beneficial to *operate from a baseline of transformed imitation, using moments of confident understanding to deviate artfully from this baseline.*

Three approaches to combining imitative actions with intelligent actions (i.e. actions based on some abstract musical understanding) were described:

1. Mode Switching: Switching between imitative and intelligent actions based on confidence of understanding.
2. Filtering and Elaboration: Using aspects of musical understanding to filter, or interpolate between, imitative actions.
3. Measured Deviation: Deviating from a baseline of imitation according to a salient parametrisation of rhythm space.

[3] http://dr.offig.com/research/chapters/MusicInteraction/Ambiguity.mov

A brief description of the Jambot was given. The Jambot is a computational musical agent that listens to an audio stream, and produces real-time improvised percussive accompaniment. An audio example of the Jambot using Mode Switching was given.

In order to produce complementary accompaniment, the Jambot seeks to maintain a balance of novelty and coherence in the overall ensemble rhythm. It does this by targeting a level of the metric ambiguity for the ensemble rhythm. This in turn is achieved by selectively highlighting one, or several, plausible metric interpretations of the rhythm. An audio example of the Jambot using this technique was given.

By combining this approach with imitative actions the Jambot is able to produce musically appropriate improvised rhythms, which complement the ensemble. By operating from a baseline of transformed imitation, the Jambot's improvisation can operate robustly in a variety of styles, in the presence of tempo changes, or other unanticipated musical events.

References

Bharucha, J. (1991). Pitch, harmony and neural nets: A psychological perspective. In P. Todd & G. Loy (Eds.), *Music and connectionism*. Cambridge, MA: MIT Press.

Borgo, D., & Goguen, J. (2004). Sync or swarm: Group dynamics in musical free improvisation. In R. Parncutt, A. Kessler, & F. Zimmer (Eds.), *Conference of interdisciplinary musicology*, University of Graz.

Collins, N. (2006). *Towards autonomous agents for live computer music: Real-time machine listening and interactive music systems*. Dissertation, Cambridge University.

Davis, M. (1999). *The philosophy of poetry: On Aristotle's poetics*. South Bend: St. Augustine's Press.

Dean, R. (2003). *Hyperimprovisation: Computer-interactive sound improvisation*. Madison: A-R Editions.

Gifford, T., & Brown, A. R. (2008). Stochastic onset detection: An approach to detecting percussive onsets attacks in complex audio. In *Proceedings of the 2008 Australasian Computer Music Conference*, Sydney. Melbourne: Australian Computer Music Association.

Gifford, T., & Brown, A. R. (2009). Do androids dream of electric Chimaera? In *Proceedings of the 2009 Australasian Computer Music Conference*, Brisbane. Melbourne: Australian Computer Music Association.

Gifford, T., & Brown, A. R. (2010). Anticipatory timing in algorithmic rhythm generation. In *Proceedings of the 2010 Australasian Computer Music Conference*, Canberra. Melbourne: Australian Computer Music Association.

Huron, D. (2006). *Sweet anticipation*. Cambridge, MA: MIT Press.

Jackendoff, R. (1992). *Languages of the mind*. Cambridge, MA: MIT Press.

Jones, M. R. (1987). Dynamic pattern structure in music: Recent theory and research. *Perception and Psychophysics, 41*, 621–634.

Kivy, P. (2002). *Introduction to the philosophy of music*. Oxford: Oxford University Press.

Large, E. W. (1994). *Dynamic representation of musical structure*. Dissertation, Ohio State University.

Lerdahl, F., & Jackendoff, R. (1983). *A generative theory of tonal music*. Cambridge, MA: MIT Press.

London, J. (2004). *Hearing in time*. Oxford: Oxford University Press.

Machover, T., & Chung, J. (1989). Hyperinstruments: Musically intelligent and interactive performance and creativity systems. In *Proceedings of the 15th international computer music conference*, Columbus. San Francisco: International Computer Music Association.

Meyer, L. (1956). *Emotion and meaning in music*. Chicago: Chicago University Press.

Narmour, E. (1990). *The analysis and cognition of basic musical structures*. Chicago: University of Chicago Press.

Pachet, F. (2006). Enhancing individual creativity with interactive musical reflective systems. In G. Wiggins & I. Deliege (Eds.), *Musical creativity: Current research in theory and practice*. London: Psychology Press.

Pearce, M., & Wiggins, G. (2006). Expectation in melody: The influence of context and learning. *Music Perception, 23*(5), 377–405.

Persson, P., Laaksolahti, J., & Lonnqvist, P. (2001). Understanding socially intelligent agents: A multilayered phenomenon. *IEEE Transactions on Systems, Man, and Cybernetics, 42*(6), 349–360.

Rowe, R. (1993). *Interactive music systems*. Cambridge, MA: MIT Press.

Temperley, D. (2001). *The cognition of basic musical structures*. Cambridge, MA: MIT Press.

Index

S. Holland et al. (eds.), *Music and Human-Computer Interaction*, Springer Series on Cultural Computing, DOI 10.1007/978-1-4471-2990-5,

Printed in the United States
By Bookmasters